Readings in Learning and Memory

Roger M. Tarpy
Bucknell University

Richard E. Mayer
University of California at Santa Barbara

Scott, Foresman and Company   Glenview, Illinois
Dallas, Texas   Oakland, New Jersey   Palo Alto, California
Tucker, Georgia   London, England

Library of Congress Cataloging in Publication Data

Main entry under title:

Readings in learning and memory.

Includes bibliographies.
1. Conditioned response—Addresses, essays, lectures.
2. Memory—Addresses, essays, lectures. 3. Psychology, Comparative—Addresses, essays, lectures. I. Tarpy, Roger M., 1941 – II. Mayer, Richard E., 1947 –
BF319.R387   153.1'08   78–32015
ISBN 0–673–15110–7

12345678910–EBI–8584838281807978

Preface

The study of learning and memory research can be richly enhanced by an opportunity to read some of the actual papers that have shaped, and continue to influence, the field. *Readings in Learning and Memory*, a collection of original landmark papers, provides just this opportunity.

Although the format of this reader corresponds to our textbook, *Foundations in Learning and Memory* (Scott, Foresman and Company, 1978), it has been designed to function as a supplement to other texts as well. In certain research-oriented courses it may even stand alone as a comprehensive source of experimental techniques and outcomes in this field. The book is therefore appropriate for undergraduate and graduate courses in learning and/or memory, including both animal and human studies. It is also suitable for laboratory courses in these areas.

The readings themselves are conveniently organized into twelve chapters. The first seven of these are devoted to studies in animal learning; the last five deal with human learning and memory processes. Preceding each chapter is a carefully prepared introduction that points to the relations among the papers grouped within a specific area of research. We have also prepared an overview of each individual paper, in which the major points of interest are outlined and, in many cases, supplemented by outside references to further reading (see Bibliography, page 376).

Six major criteria were used in the important task of selecting the papers for this reader. Our first concern was that the papers should be landmark studies, still widely recognized as significant contributions to the literature of learning and memory. Second, the papers had to be readable— that is, elegantly simple in their explanation of the process by which theory is experimentally tested. Third, we selected the more current papers in learning and memory so that the student could see what progress has been made to date; but we have also included an occasional older paper if it is still actively discussed in the field. Fourth, we decided to concentrate on a representative set of fundamental issues, rather than attempting a less thorough coverage of the entire field. Fifth, we selected only those papers that present single studies in some detail so that the student can follow the details of an experiment toward the answer to an important theoretical question. In this way, the student may be helped to develop the discipline underlying research techniques in general. Finally, and most importantly perhaps, all of the papers reproduced here were chosen on the basis of their effectiveness in our classes.

We wish to thank the many authors and publishers who have given us permission to use their materials. In a few cases, papers were edited to eliminate lengthy literature reviews or long sets of replicatory experiments; we have endeavored to retain the author's major thrust in every instance. In addition, thanks are due the editors at Scott, Foresman and Company, including James Romig, Isobel Hoffman, and Christine Arden. Last, we would like to thank the students who have indicated in our classes which papers they felt were interesting and readable, our colleagues whose suggestions contributed immeasurably to our final selection of readings, and our families who supported our efforts in many ways.

Roger M. Tarpy
Richard E. Mayer

Table of Contents

1/Classical Conditioning

2/Instrumental Conditioning

3/Aversive Control

4/**Extinction**

5/**Generalization and Discrimination**

6/**Biological Perspectives in Animal Learning**

7/**Cognitive Perspectives in Animal Learning**

8/**Verbal Learning**

9/**Human Information Processing**

10/**Memory for Meaning:**
Abstraction of Meaning from Text

11/**Memory Processes:**
Stage Analysis of Intellectual Tasks

12/**Concept Learning**

Bibliography

1/ Classical Conditioning

Classical conditioning has been defined as any situation where two stimuli, usually an innocuous conditioned stimulus (CS) and a more biologically potent unconditioned stimulus (US), are contiguously presented independent of the subject's behavior. Initially, the CS is "weak" in that it does not elicit a very noticeable reaction. In contrast, the US invariably provokes a strong unconditioned response. The result of pairing the CS and US is an association between the two stimuli: the CS itself gradually comes to elicit a conditioned response, that is, a behavior that closely resembles the original unconditioned response.

One can actually identify several levels of conditioning that occur in the classical conditioning paradigm. First, of course, is the overt behavioral CR. The reaction may range from salivation, as in Pavlov's original work, to eyeblink, to heart rate or other physiological behaviors, depending on the nature of the US. Second, conditioning may involve emotional reactions. If, for example, the US were a painful shock, the CS would induce fear in the subject because of the CS–US association. Finally, Pavlovian conditioning can be considered to involve cognitive learning. That is, subjects come to expect certain outcomes following a signal (the CS); the greater the correlation between a signal and a particular outcome, the greater the expectation of that outcome by the subject.

This concept of CS-outcome correlation is paramount in associative conditioning. It suggests not only that a subject will come to expect the US when the CS–US correlation is strong and positive, but also that a subject may come to anticipate no US when the CS is reliably followed by the absence of the US. This latter form of conditioning, leading to an inhibitory CR, confirms the complexity and richness of the Pavlovian conditioning paradigm as one that involves both emotional and cognitive states in addition to the usual overt behavioral reactions.

Space limitations prevent us from illustrating more than a few of the phenomena relevant to this vast topic (but see related papers in Chapter 7). The idea that the CS-outcome correlation is the fundamental mechanism for associative learning is addressed in Rescorla's paper. Rescorla (1968) confirms that a CS derives meaning or strength only when it reliably predicts the US occurrence. The second topic covered here, by Gamzu and Williams (1971), deals with the concept of autoshaping: a skeletal response, such as pecking by birds, also complies to the principles of Pavlovian conditioning (that is, the concept of CS-outcome correlation) despite the fact that until recently, many psychologists believed that pecking was an operant response controlled through instrumental reward procedures.

PROBABILITY OF SHOCK IN THE PRESENCE AND ABSENCE OF CS IN FEAR CONDITIONING

Robert A. Rescorla

This paper, by Robert A. Rescorla (1968) of Yale University, contributed significantly to our understanding of Pavlovian conditioning because it was the first to investigate, thoroughly and directly, the importance of the CS-outcome correlation relative to CS–US pairings in conditioning. Only a year earlier in 1967, Rescorla had published what was essentially an important new theory of conditioning: the correlation between a CS and its outcome was the factor that determined CS strength, not simply the number of CS–US pairings as was traditionally thought. Here we see a direct test of this new theory.

Rescorla used the popular CER (conditioned emotional response) technique to assess CS strength. In Experiment 1, rats were taught to press a lever for food pellets until they achieved a stable rate; then Pavlovian conditioning was given. For the R-1 and R-2 subjects, the CS (a 2-minute tone) and the US (a brief shock) presentations were entirely random; for Group G subjects, however, the shock US always occurred in the presence of the tone CS. That is, the CS–US correlation was high. After this Pavlovian conditioning phase, the CS was presented while the subjects were lever pressing and suppression of responding was observed. The stronger the conditioning had been to the CS, the greater the disruption of lever pressing. The results revealed that Group G subjects were far more suppressed than the other subjects. In fact, the CS appeared to have no strength whatsoever in the two R groups.

Experiment 2 was an extension of the first study. The method was the same, but various intermediate levels of CS–US correlations were investigated as well. Specifically, the ten groups of rats differed according to the probability that the shock US would be given during the tone CS rather than without it. When it was equally likely that the US would occur during the CS as in its absence, little conditioning occurred; the CS did not predict the US occurrence very adequately. However, as the probability increased that the US *would* occur during the CS relative to its absence, conditioning strength increased accordingly. This was true even though some groups were equated in terms of the number of CS–US pairings (for example, Groups .4– .4 and .4 – .1 had the same *number* of CS–US pairings, but they differed in terms of the CS–US correlation and, thus, strength of conditioning). In conclusion, Rescorla provided strong support for his theory of classical conditioning: The essential basis for Pavlovian conditioning is the predictability of the CS, that is, the magnitude of the CS-outcome correlation.

Two conceptions of Pavlovian conditioning have been distinguished by Rescorla (1967). The first, and more traditional, notion emphasizes the role of the number of pairings of CS and US in the formation of a CR. The second notion suggests that it is the contingency between CS and US which is important. The notion of contingency differs from that of pairing in that it includes not only what events are paired but also what events are not paired. As used here, contingency refers to the relative probability of occurrence of US in the presence of CS as contrasted with its probability in the absence of CS. The contingency notion suggests that, in fact, conditioning only occurs when these probabilities differ; when the probability of US is higher during CS than at other times, excitatory conditioning occurs; when the probability is lower, inhibitory conditioning results. Notice that the probability of a US can be the same in the absence and presence of CS and yet there can be a fair number of CS –US pairings. It is this that makes it possible to assess the relative importance of pairing and contingency in the development of a CR.

Several experiments have pointed to the usefulness of the contingency notion. Rescorla (1966) reported a Pavlovian fear conditioning experiment with dogs, using CS-induced changes in avoidance rate as an index of fear. Three groups were run: (a) a random group in which the probability of US was the same in the presence and absence of CS; (b) an excitatory conditioning group in which the probability of US during CS was the same as in the random group but for which US never occurred in the absence of CS; and (c) an inhibitory group in which the probability of US in the absence of CS was the same as in the random group but for which US never occurred during CS. Later presentation of these stimuli in the course of free-operant avoidance behavior indicated that the second group showed fear conditioning to CS, the third group showed inhibition of fear, and the first group showed no evidence of any conditioning. This result occurred despite the fact that the first and second groups had the same number of CS –US pairings and differed only in the degree to which the US was uniquely paired with the CS. The experiments reported here extend this result.

Experiment 1

In Experiment 1, the Rescorla (1966) finding is essentially replicated with a different organism and a further control procedure is run.

METHOD

Subjects. Twenty-four male Sprague-Dawley rats, about 150 days old at the start of the experiment, were maintained in individual cages at 80% of their normal body weight.

Apparatus. Each of four identical 9 × 8 × 8-in. Skinner boxes had a recessed food magazine in the center of the end wall and a retractable lever to the left of the magazine. During Pavlovian conditioning sessions, aluminum blanks covered the magazine and bar apertures. The floor of the chamber was composed of 3/16-in. stainless-steel rods spaced ¾ in. apart and could be electrified through a relay-sequence scrambler (Hoffman & Fleshler, 1962) from a high-voltage high-resistance shock source. The two end walls of the chambers were aluminum; the side walls and top were clear Plexiglas. Mounted on the ceiling of the sound and light resistant ice chest, which enclosed each Skinner box, were a 6½-w. bulb and two speakers, permitting the presentation of a constant white masking noise and of a 720-cps tone CS. Experimental events were controlled and recorded automatically by relay equipment located in an adjoining room.

Procedure. Each S was maintained at 80% body weight for 1 wk. prior to the first experimental session during which S was magazine trained automatically with food pellets delivered on a 1-min. VI schedule. In addition, each bar press yielded a food pellet. This session continued until S had emitted about 60 bar presses; shaping was used if necessary. Starting with the second experimental day, all sessions were 2 hr. long and S was placed on a VI schedule of reinforcement. For the first 30 min. of this session the schedule was 1-min. VI; thereafter it was 2-min. VI. After 5 days of VI training, the bars were removed from the Skinner boxes and five daily sessions of Pavlovian fear conditioning were administered. For eight Ss in Group R-1 (random), 12 2-min. tone CSs were given in each session with a mean intertone interval of 8 min. with 12 .5-sec. .9-ma. electric shocks programmed randomly throughout the session; shocks were programmed independently of the tones in such a way that shock was equiprobable at any time within the session. The eight Ss in Group G (gated) received a treatment identical to that of Group R-1 except that all shocks which would have occurred in the absence of the tone CS were simply omitted. This means that on the average Ss in Group G received the same number of shocks during CS as Ss in Group R-1, but Ss in Group G received no shocks in the absence of CS and therefore fewer total shocks. The eight Ss in Group R-2 received a treatment identical to those of Group R-1 except that the average number of shocks they received (2.4 per session) was the same as that for Group G. These shocks were programmed randomly throughout the session, independently of the tones.

Following Pavlovian conditioning, two 2-hr. VI sessions were given to assure a stable bar-pressing rate, followed by ten test sessions. During each 2-hr. test session 2-min. VI reinforcement remained in effect for bar pressing; superimposed upon this performance were four 2-min. presentations of the tone CS, with a mean intertrial interval of 30 min. No shocks were administered during any of these sessions.

In order to attenuate the effects of individual differences in general rate of responding, results are plotted in terms of a suppression ratio of the form $A/(A + B)$ where A is the rate of responding in CS and B is the rate of responding in a comparable period prior to CS onset. Thus a suppression ratio of 0 indicates no responding during CS while one of .5 indicates similar rates of responding during CS and the pre-CS period. Rates of responding in the pre-CS period were not reliably different for the three groups.

Results

It is clear from Figure 1 that the presentation of CS had little effect upon Groups R-1 and R-2. Throughout testing they responded similarly in the pre-CS and CS periods. In contrast, however, the CS produced a sharp reduction in response rate in Group G. With repeated presentation of CS in the absence of all shocks, the suppression in Group G extinguished almost to the level of the two random groups. An analysis of variance performed on the suppression scores for the three groups over the ten extinction sessions showed a significant difference among groups (F = 15.38, df = 2/21, $p < .01$) and an effect of extinction days (F = 8.80, df = 18/189, $p < .01$). Individual comparisons indicated that these effects were due to the difference between Group G and the other two groups.

Response suppression was not uniform throughout CS for Group G; suppression was maximum at CS onset and became attenuated as CS continued. Figure 2 shows the distribution of suppression in four 30-sec. segments of CS over the first 5 extinction days. A two-way analysis of variance confirmed the observation that suppression was greatest at CS onset (F = 4.69, df = 4/28, $p < .01$) as well as the obvious extinction of suppression over days. In addition, the Extinction Days × Periods during CS interaction was reliable (F = 2.16, df = 12/84, $p < .05$), indicating that extinction of suppression occurred first for the later periods during CS.

Discussion

The results of this experiment confirm the earlier findings of Rescorla (1966). Only when the probability of shock was higher during CS than at other times did conditioning occur. Groups with either the same number of CS–US pairings or the same number of USs, but lacking an increased probability of US during CS, failed to condition. These results add considerable weight to the contention that in Pavlovian fear conditioning the contingency of US upon CS is of primary importance.

FIGURE 1

Median suppression ratio for each group over the ten test sessions of Experiment 1.

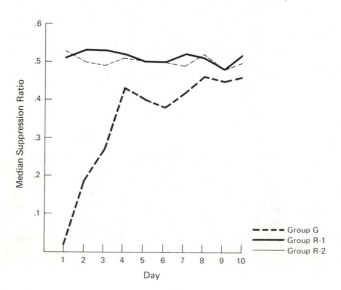

FIGURE 2

Distribution of suppression during CS for Group G on each of the first 5 test days.

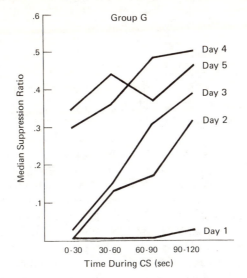

Experiment 2

Previous experiments have compared only a few levels of the contingency of US upon CS. In Experiment 1, a high degree of dependence (in Group G) was compared with complete independence (Groups R-1 and R-2). The present experiment explores intermediate contingency relations in an attempt to assess the contingency notion over a wider range of experimental conditions.

METHOD

Subjects. Eighty male Sprague-Dawley rats, about 100 days old at the start of the experiment, were maintained in individual cages at 80% of their normal body weight.

Apparatus. The apparatus was that of Experiment 1, except that different chambers were used during the conditioning phase. These chambers were identical to the Skinner boxes used in VI training, except that both end walls were plain aluminum.

Procedure. The Ss were bar-press trained in the manner described in Experiment 1. After five 2-hr. sessions of VI bar pressing, five daily 2-hr. Pavlovian conditioning sessions were administered. The Ss were divided into ten groups, each receiving a different probability of shock during the presence and absence of CS. For all groups, 12 2-min. 720-cps tones were administered with a mean intertone interval of 8 min. The different probabilities of shock per 2-min. interval were .4−.4, .2−.2, .1−.1, 0−0, .4−.2, .4−.1, .4 −0, .2−.1, .2−0, .1−0, where the first number designates the probability of shock in CS and the second the probability of shock in the absence of CS. Shocks of .5-sec. duration at .9 ma. were randomly distributed throughout the session in such a way that they had a fixed probability in each second of the session; the occurrence of CS changed that probability value appropriately. Only the expected probability of USs were explicitly programmed; the actual sequence of USs was generated separately for each S during each conditioning session.

After five conditioning sessions, two 2-hr. VI sessions were given to assure a stable bar-pressing rate during the subsequent 6 days of test sessions; during each test session VI-2 reinforcement remained in effect and four 2-min. CSs were presented with a 30-min. mean intertone interval. No shocks were administered during any of these sessions.

Results

Despite the fact that different groups received different total numbers of shocks, there were no reliable differences among groups in responding in the absence of CS on either VI training or tests days that followed conditioning.

Figure 3 shows the suppression ratios during the six extinction test sessions. It is clear that within each panel, the groups order themselves according to the probability of shock in the absence of CS, with the lowest probability producing the most suppression. When the probability of shock in the presence and absence of CS is the same there is little or no suppression. Comparing panels, it is also clear that with a fixed probability of shock in the absence of CS, increasing the probability of shock in its presence produced increasing suppression. An overall analysis of variance indicated that these observations were reliable. There was a significant effect of groups ($F = 11.69$, $df = 9/70$, $p < .01$), of extinction days ($F = 79.84$, df 5/320, $p < .01$), and a Groups × Extinction Days interaction ($F = 10.58$, $df = 45/320$, $p < .01$). Individual comparisons on the first test day, using Duncan's multiple range test, indicated that within each panel all pairwise differences were reliable. Across panels, the four groups with equal probability of shock during and in the absence of CS did not differ from each other.

As in Experiment 1, suppression was not uniform through CS. For those groups showing response decrement during CS, the decrement was maximal at CS onset and became less as CS continued. Groups which failed to show overall suppression responded relatively uniformly throughout CS.

Discussion

The results of this experiment can be succinctly described by three statements. (a) Independent of the overall probability of shock, there was little or no suppression if shock came with equal probability in the presence and absence of CS. (b) With a fixed probability of shock during CS, increasing the probability in the absence of CS attenuated suppression. (c) With a fixed probability of shock in the absence of CS, increasing the probability of shock in the presence of CS enhanced suppression.

Statement (c) agrees with the traditional notion that it is the number of simultaneous occurrences of CS and US that is important in conditioning. However, the amount of suppression obtained cannot be entirely accounted for in terms of either the total number of US events or the number

FIGURE 3

Median suppression ratio for each group over the six test sessions of Experiment 2. (Within each panel, all groups have the same probability of US during CS: the parameter in each panel is the probability of US in the absence of CS.)

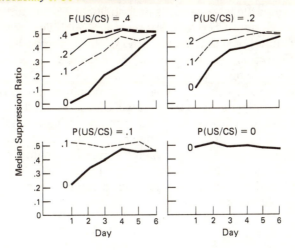

of USs during CS. For instance, Group .1–0 received far fewer shocks during CS than did Group .4–.4, yet showed considerably greater suppression.

Any account of the present data must include the disruptive effects upon conditioning of shocks occurring in the absence of CS. One way of viewing this effect has been suggested by Rescorla and LoLordo (1965). They found that presenting USs exclusively in the absence of CS led to the establishment of that CS as a conditioned inhibitor of the CR. They suggested that such a conditioning procedure, presenting USs in the absence of CS, leads to the development of Pavlovian inhibition in response to CS. One can, then, view the present results as the product of two separate acquisition processes: (a) the development of Pavlovian conditioned excitation as a result of CSs and USs occurring together, and (b) the development of Pavlovian conditioned inhibition as a result of USs occurring in the absence of CS. It is perhaps fortuitous that these two processes are balanced when there is equal probability of US in the presence and absence of CS.

Alternatively, one might view these results in terms of attention to CS. It might be argued that conditioning occurs, as has traditionally been thought, whenever CS and US occur together; however, presentation of US at other times leads the organism to attend to a variety of stimuli other than CS. Thus the disruption of suppression as a result of USs occurring in the absence of CS represents not a failure of Pavlovian conditioning but a failure of S to attend to the CS during testing. Our task then becomes one of specifying the variables controlling this attention. Although such an account is plausible for the present data, it fails to explain the active inhi bition of fear found by Rescorla and LoLordo (1965), Rescorla (1966), and Hammond (1967).

One unexpected finding of these experiments was that suppression was not uniform during CS. This seems surprising on the contingency view which emphasizes the instantaneous probability of US, for that probability is constant throughout CS. There are several possibilities for understanding this distribution of suppression during CS in terms consistent with the contingency viewpoint. One possibility is that the reduced suppression later in the CS is an artifact of the measuring technique. A VI schedule of reinforcement is such that the longer S has refrained from pressing, the higher the probability that its next press will be reinforced. Thus the longer S suppresses, the more "pressure" the base-line operant schedule places on it to respond. Fear conditioning may be constant throughout; only the tendency to press, which fear counteracts, may be changing. A second possibility is simply that the onset of CS is a more discriminable stimulus than its continued presence and thus shows superior conditioning even with equal probabilities of US.

References

Hammond, L. O. A traditional demonstration of the active properties of Pavlovian inhibition using differential CER. *Psychon. Sci.*, 1967, **9**, 65–66.

Hoffman, H. S., & Fleshler, M. A relay sequencing device for scrambling grid shock. *J. Exp. Anal. Behav.*, 1962, **5**, 329–330.

Rescorla, R. A. Predictability and number of pairings in Pavlovian fear conditioning. *Psychon. Sci.*, 1966, **4**, 383–384.

Rescorla, R. A. Pavlovian conditioning and its proper control procedures. *Psychol. Rev.*, 1967, **74**, 71–80.

Rescorla, R. A. & LoLordo, V. M. Inhibition of avoidance behavior. *J. comp. physiol. Psychol.*, 1965, **59**, 406–412.

CLASSICAL CONDITIONING OF A COMPLEX SKELETAL RESPONSE

Elkan Gamzu and David R. Williams

This experiment addresses a very important topic in contemporary learning research — the study of autoshaping. For many years, it was believed that key pecking in birds was an arbitrary, operant response that could be strengthened only through instrumental reward procedures. However, the discovery by Brown and Jenkins in 1968 that key pecking could be established, even though the food reward was *not* contingent on the pecking responses, required psychologists to reconsider the nature of this fundamental research paradigm. Many findings have surfaced in the decade following the discovery of autoshaping, and several of the more important ones have been contributed by Elkan Gamzu and David R. Williams (1971). This particular study shows that pecking an illuminated key by pigeons is fundamentally a Pavlovian phenomenon. It is interesting to note that the method used is quite similar to the one introduced by Rescorla in the previous paper.

Hungry pigeons were placed in a box containing a food trough and a plastic disk which could be illuminated from behind. During each training session, fifty 8-second presentations of the lighted key were given to the subjects. In addition, food was provided during thirteen of these CS presentations on the average (although during the first phase of the study, food was never given in the absence of the CS). Illumination of the disk thus signaled an increase in the probability of food presentation: the probability of receiving food during the CS was about .26, whereas the probability of receiving food during its absence was zero. Gamzu and Williams called this the "differential" procedure. The results of this phase were unambiguous: all subjects showed considerable pecking behavior during the CS even though food presentation was unrelated to pecking.

In the second phase of the study, using the "nondifferential" procedure, food was presented in the absence of the CS as many times as it was given during the CS. Under these conditions, where the CS did not signal an increase in the probability of food, subjects did not peck the disk. That pecking occurs under the "differential" but not under the "nondifferential" conditions was confirmed further with other subjects who received the treatments in the reverse order.

These results indicate that a specific CS—US relationship is not necessary for autoshaping: pigeons peck the disk when the probability is greater that the US will occur during the CS rather than in the absence of the CS. This finding is precisely the one advanced by Rescorla (see the previous paper), although Rescorla was referring to a fear reaction, whereas here, Gamzu and Williams are dealing with a skeletal CR. Either way, the conditioned response strength in both studies is based on the degree to which the Pavlovian CS predicts the US.

Brown and Jenkins (1968) recently reported that hungry pigeons would spontaneously begin pecking a disk mounted on the wall of an experimental chamber if illumination of the disk signaled the forthcoming presentation of grain. The procedure closely resembled Pavlovian delay conditioning, and its effectiveness with pecking—a complex skeletal act directed outward at the environment—potentially represents a significant extension of the domain of classical conditioning. The delay conditioning procedure exerts such powerful control that birds frequently peck the disk even when conditions are changed so that pecking the disk presents the opportunity to eat (Williams and Williams, 1969). Under these artificial laboratory conditions, such behavior appears maladaptive and is difficult to encompass in a biological approach to learning based on the reward value of external events.

In the experiments reported here, we explored the limits of applicability of the classical conditioning paradigm by using a procedure that avoids the specific "pairing" relationship between response key and food, which was characteristic of the earlier procedures. Pairing the response key with food according to the Pavlovian delay paradigm involves the precise signaling of the time of presentation of the unconditioned stimulus (for example, food). By circumventing this intimate signaling relationship, we hoped to determine whether the remarkable stimulus control over the act of pecking was attributable to a peculiarity of the Pavlovian procedures used earlier or whether it represents a more general manifestation of associative learning through classical conditioning.

The new procedure that we used was a variant of one introduced by Rescorla (Rescorla, 1967). Throughout the course of these experiments, a pecking disk was illuminated for 8.6-second periods, which were distributed randomly throughout each experimental session with a mean interstimulus interval of 30 seconds. In the presence of the illuminated disk, 4-second periods of access to a grain hopper were provided on a random basis; the probability of initiating such a period of access was .03 at the start of each second of key illumination. We compared pecking to the key under two conditions: a "differential condition," where the probability of access to grain when the disk was not illuminated was zero; and a "non-differential" procedure, where the probability of grain presentation was the same in the presence and the absence of illumination of the disk. At no point in the experiment did the disk signal the actual time of presentation of reinforcement; it merely accompanied a condition where 4-second access to grain was provided on the average of once every 33 seconds.

Naive adult male Silver King pigeons maintained at 80 percent of their free feeding weight were tested in a standard pigeon chamber measuring 28 by 28 by 26 cm. One wall of the chamber housed a standard pecking disk, which could be transilluminated with white light. The disk was 19 cm above the floor of the compartment, and the grain hopper was centered 11 cm below the pecking disk. At the beginning of the first session, birds were trained to approach rapidly and to eat from the hopper whenever it was presented; they were then immediately exposed to the experimental procedure. A daily session comprised 50 trials of disk illumination, distributed geometrically with a range of 10 to 120 seconds between trials. In the presence of the key, an average of 13 reinforcements were typically presented during 50 daily trials. Grain presentation was always independent of the pigeons' behavior and could be initiated immediately at the onset of a trial or at the start of any other 1-second interval during the trial. Pecking had absolutely no effect on the experimental procedure.

Figure 1 traces the course of development of pecking for each of four birds studied under the differential procedure. Despite marked differences in rate of acquisition, all birds learned to peck the disk at rates substantially above one per second. Because illumination of the disk accompanied a change in the frequency of reinforcement but did not signal particular occurrences of reinforcement, it is clear that disk illumination need have no

FIGURES 1 AND 2

Fig. 1 (left). Individual acquisition curves indicate rate of responding within each session from the outset of the experiment. Fig. 2 (right). Individual rates per session in sessions that immediately followed the sessions of Fig. 1. The rate declined under the nondifferential condition and recovered after reinstatement of the original procedure.

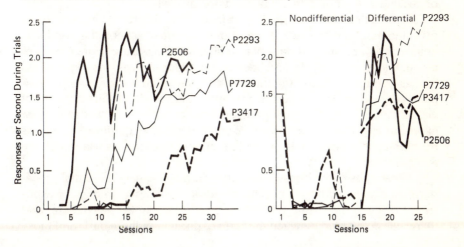

precise relationship to specific instances of food presentation. This property of the Pavlovian delay procedure, as such, is not necessary for the development of pecking.

To explore whether the pecking engendered by this procedure was dependent primarily on occasions of feeding in the presence of the disk or whether the differential association was a necessary aspect of the procedure, we began presenting grain in the absence of the illuminated disk at the same frequency as we had previously been presenting it in the presence of the illuminated disk, in sessions that immediately followed those illustrated in Figure 1. Thus, we changed conditions only during the "intertrial interval" and not during the "trial interval" itself. Results from this nondifferential condition are shown in Figure 2. Levels of responding to the disk during its periods of illumination fell rapidly to zero. Although a modest "recovery" of rate was observed in one bird over a 4-day period, and in another for a single day, these elevated levels of performance were not sustained. Two other birds showed no tendency to resume responding during the 14-day period. In addition, no bird developed sustained pecking during the interval between trials, when grain was presented but the disk was dark. It is apparent, then, that the presentation of grain in the presence of the illuminated disk is not a sufficient condition to engender pecking: the disk must at least accompany a change in the frequency of grain presentations. Figure 2 also shows that, when the differential condition was reinstated, pecking quickly regained its previous levels. These findings are similar to those of Rescorla, who used a classically conditioned fear response in dogs and rats (Rescorla, 1968).

The failure of the nondifferential condition to sustain pecking indicates that adventitious reward of pecking probably does not play a major role in this phenomenon. The rapid decline of pecking during periods of key illumination took place even though there was no change in response-reinforcer correlations (spurious or otherwise) in the presence of the illuminated disk. If adventitious reward were effective during the differential condition, surely it would continue to be effective in sustaining a high rate of pecking in the nondifferential condition as well.

As a further check on the importance of the differential association of disk illumination with feeding, we studied five new birds on the nondifferential condition. After 14 days of nondifferential exposure to grain presentation, a total of ten pecks had been recorded for all five birds together. All of these occurred during the intertrial interval when the key was not illuminated. Apparently, the decline in responding seen in the first experiment was not an artifact of changing the procedures, nor was it related to prior exposure to a difference in reinforcement density. Acquisition, as well as maintenance of pecking, is dependent on a differential association of key and reinforcer.

When these new birds were shifted to the original differential procedure, all eventually began pecking the disk. Even after 35 days of exposure, however, the mean rate of response was only 20 per minute, and there was no overlap between the rates of pecking of these birds and those of the first group, whose mean terminal rate was 101 responses per minute. Thus, there was a residual effect of nondifferential reinforcement, even after successful acquisition had taken place.

These results demonstrate three important aspects of the autoshaping phenomenon, all of which are consistent with the assumption that classical conditioning is a fundamental factor in the phenomenon. First, we have shown that a specific signaling relationship is not important for acquisition or sustained maintenance of behavior. Second, the necessity for differential pairing in maintenance, as well as acquisition, indicates that informational properties of the stimulus, rather than its mere association with feeding, are responsible for the phenomenon. Third, the phenomenon, although obviously susceptible to analysis by principles of classical conditioning, offers little basis for an account in terms of adventitious reinforcement.

The pecking engendered by autoshaping is directed to a significant part of the environment—that is, a part correlated with the opportunity to eat. The strong and direct control over behavior exerted by this part of the environment indicates the operation of a mechanism in pigeons by which skeletal acts are controlled without the involvement of reward and punishment. The findings of the Brelands (1961) in a number of nonavian species suggest that such mechanisms are not peculiar to pigeons. Although study of the way in which complex activities are developed and learned has largely excluded effects other than those of reward and punishment, it now seems necessary to include some other factors as well, if the principles of adaptive learning are to provide an adequate account of the development and maintenance of effective but often nonarbitrary behavior. It is apparent that animals do not select behaviors randomly from their repertoire in new situations. The manifestation of associative learning that we have explored in this report may reflect a process by which organisms tailor their behavior nonrandomly to new environments, prior to any "shaping" effect by rewards and punishments.

References

Breland, K. & Breland, M. *American Psychologist*, 1961, **16**, 681.
Brown, P. L. & Jenkins, H. M. *J. Exp. Anal. Behav.*, 1968, **11**, 1.
Rescorla, R. A. *Psychological Review*, 1967, **74**, 71.
Williams, D. R. & Williams, H. *J. Exp. Anal. Behav.*, 1969, **12**, 511.

2/ Instrumental Conditioning

In instrumental conditioning, unlike classical conditioning, the behavior of the subject must occur before the US (or reinforcement) is delivered; that is, the presentation of stimuli by the experimenter is entirely contingent on the prior execution of the appropriate CR by the subject. There are four major categories of instrumental learning. In reward conditioning, by far the most commonly studied form, the subject's behavior is reinforced by the presentation of a positive US such as food. By contrast, in omission training, the reward is omitted if the subject makes the designated response. Here, the result is a suppression of behavior. The last two forms of instrumental conditioning are escape/avoidance learning and punishment. Performance increases when the subject can respond to terminate or avoid an unpleasant US; conversely, performance declines when the execution of the CR is followed by an aversive stimulus.

There are a vast number of phenomena relevant to instrumental conditioning, some of which are influenced by the characteristics (such as size or immediacy) of the reward, the schedules of reward presentation, or the types of behaviors that are susceptible to instrumental training procedures. We have chosen three papers that represent important areas of research and/or important points of view in the field. The first, by Premack (1961), shows that a behavior will function as a reinforcer if its preferability is higher than the activity on which it is contingent. Using Premack's system, therefore, one can determine a priori which activity will serve as a reinforcer.

The last two papers show how instrumental training procedures have been applied to important "real-world" situations. For example, Schwartz (1975) reports that specific biological patterns, involving blood pressure and heart rate may be altered by instrumental reward;

this area of biofeedback research holds great promise for the future treatment of harmful medical conditions such as hypertension. The third paper by Ayllon and Haughton (1964) demonstrates that socially appropriate verbal behaviors may be conditioned in patients who have previously lacked such behaviors. This paper illustrates one facet of the broader approach to the treatment of mental disorders termed "behavior therapy."

REVERSIBILITY OF THE REINFORCEMENT RELATION

David Premack

The first paper in this chapter on instrumental conditioning is by David Premack (1961), whose work in the early 1960s focused on his *prepotent theory of reinforcement*. According to Premack, the concept of reinforcement can be approached from an empirical point of view. Specifically, one activity would reinforce another activity if the former were more probable (or prepotent) and if access to it were made contingent on the latter; the result would be an increase in the performance of the contingent activity. Premack's theory is an important contribution to the study of learning because it allows one to predict a priori, on the basis of the initial response preferences, which activities will serve as reinforcers for which other activities.

One implication of Premack's theory is that behaviors are not inherently reinforcing. Rather, their reinforcing potency depends entirely on their preferability relative to the preferability of the to-be-reinforced behavior. For example, drinking is usually a potent reinforcer, not because it is inherently reinforcing, but because it is invariably contingent on a less preferable behavior such as running. However according to Premack's theory, one should be able to show that such a typical reinforcement relationship could be reversed: running, if more probable than drinking and if made contingent on drinking, should therefore reinforce drinking. This prediction is, in fact, confirmed in this paper. Preferability of these two activities was varied by restricting access to water (making drinking more preferable than running) or to an activity wheel (making running more preferable than drinking). The results indicate that when the preferability of *either* response was high relative to the other, that response could serve as a reinforcer.

Food or water are used customarily to reinforce the bar press or running, but it is not asked, Can this relation be reversed? Will the bar press or running reinforce eating or drinking? The traditional account of reinforcement does not generate this question, for it assumes categorical reinfor-

From "Reversibility of the Reinforcement Relation" by David Premack in *Science*, Volume 136, April 20, 1962. Copyright 1962 by the American Association for the Advancement of Science. Reprinted by permission.

cers, food and water being prime examples (Hull, 1943; Skinner, 1938). Furthermore, the traditional account was not changed basically even by the finding that light and sound also reinforce (Barnes and Kish, 1961; Butler, 1953; Kish, 1955; Marx et al., 1955). To incorporate these "new" reinforcers the reward category was simply enlarged, admitting unforeseen kinds of stimulation, and inferring additional drives and needs. The logic of the traditional account remains one that distinguishes between categories of positive and neutral events; only the events to which this logic is applied have changed.

We have proposed a model of positive reinforcement (Premack, 1959 and 1961) whose major assumption is simply that, for any pair of responses, the independently more probable one will reinforce the less probable one. In this model the traditional vocabulary of drive, reward, and goal becomes either meaningless or misleading, for the model leads to the predictions that (i) the eating or drinking response is itself reinforcible[1] and, more important, (ii) the reinforcement relation is reversible.

Are there intervals of time in which eating or drinking are less probable than certain other responses, as well as other intervals in which the probabilities are reversed? Although the present model cannot make such predictions, but predicts only after the response probabilities are given, parameters were recently found in the rat that satisfy both conditions.

With free access to both food and an activity wheel, but access to water for only 1 hour per day, mean total drinking time for a group of six female rats was about 4 minutes, and mean total running time in the same period was only about 0.9 minute. With free access to both food and water, but access to the wheel for only 1 hour per day, mean total drinking time per hour was only about 28 seconds, and mean total running time in the same period was about 329 seconds. Thus it should be possible, according to the present model, not only to reinforce drinking with running but also to reverse the reinforcement relation in the same subject merely by changing from one set of parameters to the other.

Apparatus used to test these predictions was a modified Wahmann activity wheel equipped with a brake and a retractable drinkometer. Joint access to the wheel and water was provided by releasing the brake on the wheel and moving the drinkometer up to a hole on a stationary plate enclosing the open face of the wheel. Drinking contingent upon running was arranged by retracting the drinkometer, freeing the wheel, and making availability of the drinkometer contingent upon running. Conversely, running contingent upon drinking was arranged by locking the wheel, moving in the drinkometer, and making release of the wheel contingent upon drinking.

Because the outcome for the conventional experiment was not in doubt, the case of running contingent upon drinking was tested first. Four

---

[1] D. R. Williams and P. Teitlebaum [*Science* 124, 1294 (1956)] have reported the negative reinforcement of drinking—drinking turning off electric shock—but I can find no report of the positive reinforcement of eating and drinking responses

female albino rats, about 200 days old, Sprague-Dawley strain, were given daily 1-hour conditioning sessions, followed by daily 1-hour extinction and reconditioning sessions. A fixed ratio schedule was used in which each five licks freed the wheel for 10 seconds. Throughout this training, food and water were continuously available in the home cage; after the last reconditioning session, water was removed from the home cage, and on the next day training was begun with the reverse contingency—drinking contingent upon running.

With running contingent upon drinking, total drinking time was increased in all subjects by a factor of from three to five. For operant-level

FIGURE 1

Esterline Angus samples of all phases of training. Top three records show the reinforcement of drinking by running ($L \supset R$) and subsequent extinction of drinking. Middle records compare the lick pattern for conditioning and reconditioning. Bottom records show the reinforcement of running by drinking ($R \supset L$). R designates running, where each 90 degrees of turn deflected the needle, and L represents drinking, where each lick deflected the needle. Records read from right to left.

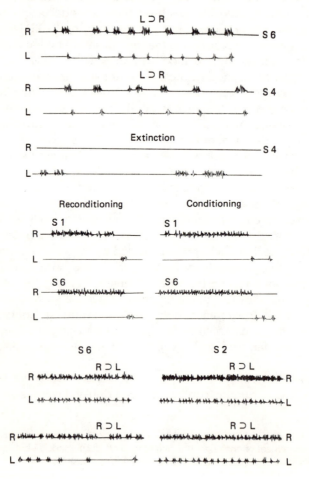

drinking, with only the tube present, mean total drinking time was about 28 sec/hr; with both tube and wheel present, it was 23 sec/hr; and with running contingent upon drinking, 98 sec/hr. Moreover, the first extinction session further increased mean total drinking time to about 175 sec/hr.

Samples of all phases of training are shown in the Esterline Angus records of Figure 1. The top records show the reinforcement of drinking by running in rats S-4 and S-6, characterized by alternating bursts of licking and running. A representative example of extinction—drinking no longer producing the opportunity to run—is provided by the record for rat S-4; both the atypical periodicity and brevity of the lick bursts have largely disappeared. Of interest in the middle records, which show fine-grain examples of conditioning and reconditioning, is the recovery of the noninstrumental lick pattern that followed extinction. Throughout the original conditioning, the five licks or more that were required for running tended to be dispersed, whereas during reconditioning, licking occurred in bursts typical of routine drinking. The picture is completed by the two bottom records; these provide examples of the evident increase in running subsequently produced by the conventional case, where 450 degrees of wheel turn were required for first, 10 seconds, and later, 5 seconds of tube-time. Hence parameters were demonstrated which made running more probable than drinking, and vice versa, and subsequently, that it was possible not only to reinforce drinking with running, but also to reverse the reinforcement relation in the same subjects merely by changing from one set of parameters to the other.

References

Barnes, G.W. & Kish, G.W. *Experimental Psychology*, 1961, **62**, 164.

Butler, R.A. *J. Comp. and Physiol. Psychol.*, 1953, **46**, 95.

Hull, C.L. *Principles of Behavior*, New York: Appleton-Century, 1943, pp. 68–83.

Kish, G.W. *J. Exp. Psychol.*, 1955, **48**, 261.

Marx, M.X., Henderson, R.L., & Roberts, C.L. *J. Exp. Psychol.*, 1955, **48**, 73.

Premack, D. *Psychological Review*, 1959, **66**, 219.

———. *Experimental Psychology*, 1961, **61**, 162.

Skinner, B.F. *The Behavior of Organisms*, New York: Appleton-Century, 1938, pp. 61–115.

BIOFEEDBACK, SELF-REGULATION, AND
THE PATTERNING OF PHYSIOLOGICAL PROCESSES

Gary E. Schwartz

The second paper in this chapter is a review of research on biofeedback by Gary E. Schwartz (1975). Biofeedback is a general term referring to instrumental conditioning procedures that provide the subject with information (or feedback) about internal biological responses, such as heart rate or blood pressure, and, usually, some sort of reward for changing those responses. When these two conditions are met, it is observed that subjects are able to "control" or modify their internal states.

This important area of study has received a great deal of attention in recent years for two major reasons. First, the notion that internal, physiological reactions can be conditioned with instrumental conditioning procedures is of great theoretical interest. It has long been believed that biological reactions could be conditioned only by using Pavlovian procedures, where the strong, biologically relevant USs reflexively induce physiological changes. In contrast, instrumental procedures do not involve strong eliciting stimuli prior to the response; the behaviors are supposedly "voluntary," not "reflexive" like internal biological reactions. Nevertheless, as Schwartz' paper clearly demonstrates, instrumental procedures are indeed quite powerful in producing learned changes in physiological states. In fact, Schwartz' own research has demonstrated that instrumental conditioning procedures are capable of modifying remarkably complex and subtle physiological patterns.

A second reason for interest in biofeedback research is the possibility that effective therapies will be established for the treatment of certain physiological disorders. For example, if a person with severe hypertension could learn to control blood pressure levels with simple instrumental conditioning techniques, then the need for drugs or more complicated procedures would be eliminated. As noted by Schwartz, some of the results obtained thus far appear to be promising in this regard.

Although we do not usually think about it, we are constantly regulating complex patterns of neural and visceral processes in our dynamic interchange with our environment. How often do we ponder the multiplicity of biological processes we must voluntarily orchestrate in order to perform an everyday act like writing a sentence? Not very often; for we usually direct our attention to the goal of our actions rather than reflecting upon the pattern of interacting processes we generate to produce the desired behavior. But if a skill is unique or unexpected—like the feats of bodily or cognitive self-regulation long claimed by certain yogis and meditators, and more recently demonstrated with biofeedback, our fascination with the nature of the processes involved is rekindled.

It has been found that, if humans and lower animals are provided with (1) new information in the form of biofeedback for internal responses such as heart rate, blood pressure, and electrical activity of the brain, and (2) incentives or rewards for changing or controlling the feedback, they can learn to control voluntarily the physiological responses associated with the feedback. Biofeedback research has raised the question whether responses once considered to be involuntary may be controlled consciously (Miller 1969). It has also stimulated interest in the use of self-regulation techniques in both clinical treatment and in research which seeks to determine the limits of self-control.

Despite the abundance of research in this area (see Barber et al. 1971; Kamiya et al. 1971; Stoyva et al. 1972; Shapiro et al. 1973; Miller et al. 1974), there has been little effort to explain exactly how self-regulation develops or what are the underlying psychobiological mechanisms and constraints (Miller 1974). Most research treats only single responses or response systems and fails to address the more normal but complex phenomenon of the voluntary coordination of multiple physiological processes. Drawing upon research conducted by my colleagues and students over the past six years, I will describe in this paper experiments using biofeedback procedures to teach voluntary control of combinations of responses, and then relate our findings to the broader question of the biocognitive mechanisms involved. This includes our research on the regulation of imagery and emotion and its clinical application to elucidating the mechanisms underlying relaxation, meditation, and other self-regulation therapies. Biofeedback and related cognitive procedures provide a unique and powerful research tool for investigating both the interrelationships among physiological systems and their constraints in the intact human and the role of patterns of physiological responses in the generation of subjective experience (Schwartz 1974).

I hope that this paper will also help to dispel some of the prevailing popular notions about biofeedback. Unfortunately, research on biofeedback and on related cognitive self-regulation procedures such as meditation is tainted by simplistic and at times wild speculation by scientists and journalists alike. It is understandable how research that challenges our basic conception of man's biological structure and psychological capabilities can stimulate novel ideas about basic research and clinical issues, but such theorizing has alienated an important segment of the scientific community. One area of controversy involves the application of visceral self-regulation to psychosomatic disorders; another is the application of brain wave biofeedback to bring about altered states of consciousness. At one extreme are those who argue that biofeedback can enable us to control literally any aspect of our biology at will; at the other extreme are a growing number who dismiss biofeedback as a useless gimmick. I suggest that neither of these extremes is appropriate and that current research on biofeedback from a pattern perspective not only expands our understanding of human self-regulation but helps us to recognize its limitations.

Specificity and the brain

The capacity of the human brain to regulate various dynamic patterns of neural, skeletal, and visceral responses grows out of its extraordinary capacity for response specificity. In this respect the brain is a highly efficient organ, for under most circumstances it is capable of recruiting and coordinating only those sensory, visceral, and motor processes needed to perform a given task. Biofeedback procedures have been applied to the voluntary control of individual skeletal muscles, and Basmajian (1972) has shown that subjects can learn to control individual motor units within a specific muscle when given feedback and reward for activity of the designated unit. He finds that, early in training, adjacent motor units in the muscle are also activated, but as the subject practices controlling the feedback, the irrelevant units drop out. At a more general level, Germana (1968) illustrates how, as subjects learn a variety of cognitive and motor tasks, initial learning is accompanied by increases in multiple responses including heart rate, sweat gland activity, and muscle tension over much of the body. However, as the subject masters the specific task, activation peaking occurs, and the various physiological responses return to levels adjusted to maintaining effective performance. In both of these examples, learned specificity grows out of more general physiological arousal.

The motor system is a good model for conceptualizing the self-regulation of autonomic and electrocortical responses, because it highlights the principle that learning typically progresses from more general arousal to greater response specificity with training. Cardiovascular biofeedback researchers such as Lang (1974) and Brener (1974) have recently begun to emphasize specificity of motor skill learning and its interaction with biofeedback. In my laboratory we have applied to heart rate control Fleishman's (1966) model for understanding the acquisition of autonomic skills. Fleishman describes five basic components of complex motor skills: strength, endurance, steadiness, control precision, and reaction time. With few exceptions, biofeedback research has used a combination of the strength and endurance paradigms—the subject's task being to increase or decrease the frequency or amplitude of the response as much as possible and sustain the effect for some period of time (e.g. a minute). Schwartz, Vogler, and Young have developed a different autonomic skill—a cardiac reaction-time paradigm—in which the subject's primary task is to raise (or lower) his heart rate as quickly as possible at the onset of the trial, briefly holding control for 3 consecutive seconds. On the basis of the motor skills literature, we predicted that specificity of cardiac skill learning would show little transfer of training between the strength-endurance and the reaction-time skills. Our experiment bore out the prediction.

This finding of specificity of skill learning *within a single autonomic response* underscores the power of biofeedback procedures to tap specific capabilities for learned self-regulation normally not exercised by human beings. The study may be taken as one model for studying the similarities and differences between specific motor and visceral self-regulatory processes. However, the specific-skills approach to biofeedback leads us away from rather than toward the major concern of this paper—the nature of self-regulation of combinations of responses. We did not recognize the full importance of learned specificity with biofeedback until we were confronted with selective voluntary control of systolic blood pressure versus heart rate; this discovery prompted the development of pattern biofeedback procedures.

Systolic pressure and heart rate control

One of the most convincing, but initially surprising, illustrations of the specificity of human self-regulation in the autonomic nervous system emerged in our early studies on the self-regulation of systolic blood pressure and heart rate (Shapiro et al. 1969; Shapiro, Tursky, and Schwartz 1970a, 1970b). In the first two experiments, subjects were given binary (on/off) feedback (a light and tone) at each heart beat when systolic blood pressure was either higher or lower than the median blood pressure for a 50-beat trial (Tursky, Shapiro, and Schwartz 1972). Subjects were instructed to make the feedback light and tone occur as often as possible; however, they were not told the nature of the response or the direction in which it was to change. As an added incentive, subjects were shown bonus slides after every 20 feedback stimuli (in the early studies, the all-male subjects were shown pictures of nude females; later, a variety of rewards including travel slides and monetary bonuses were added). The results of both experiments showed that, in a single experimental session, subjects could exert relative self-control over their blood pressure and that these changes were independent of heart rate.

In the third experiment, the procedure was reversed; subjects were given feedback and reward for raising and lowering heart rate while systolic blood pressure was monitored; here subjects showed relative self-control of heart rate independent of blood pressure. As we discovered from postexperimental questionnaires, the essentially *uninstructed* subjects did not report using consistent cognitive or somatic strategies; for example, those who decreased their blood pressure or heart rate did not use relaxing imagery more frequently than those who increased these responses.

Given the complex physiological constraints between these two responses (heart rate, in addition to stroke volume and peripheral resistance, can act as a physical determinant of blood pressure), the ease and speed with which specificity was learned was surprising. The biofeedback results seemed to be pointing to something specific about the behavioral relationship (presumed but not explicitly measured) between the two responses (Schwartz 1972).

If systolic blood pressure and heart rate were so related over time that increases in one were always associated with increases in the other, then when an experimenter gave feedback and reward for one, he would unwittingly provide it for the other as well. Therefore, we would expect that both functions should be learned simultaneously and in the same direction. But if these two functions were so related that when one increased, the other simultaneously decreased, then if feedback and reward were given for one, the other would simultaneously receive the opposite inducement. Both functions should again be learned, only now in opposite directions. However, since neither of these findings was empirically obtained in our prior research, it would follow that systolic blood pressure and heart rate must be so related that binary feedback for one causes simultaneous *random* feedback for the other.

If this were so, how could a subject be taught to control both processes? One approach might be to give the feedback and reward only when the desired *pattern* of responses occurs. In theory, it should be possible to teach a person to integrate his systolic blood pressure and heart rate voluntarily (make both functions increase or decrease together) or differentiate them (make them go in opposite directions) by providing feedback and reward for the desired pattern. The required procedure for tracking, in real time, patterns of phasic and tonic changes in both systems was developed based on the binary feedback model that detected at each heart beat whether blood pressure and heart rate were in one of the 4 possible states: $BP^{up}HR^{up}$, $BP^{up}HR_{down}$, $BP_{down}HR^{up}$, or $BP_{down}HR_{down}$ (Schwartz, Shapiro, and Tursky 1971).

If behavior operated without physiological constraints, a straight behavioral analysis of the feedback-response relationship could alone predict learned patterning. But these predictions would fail to the extent that bio-

FIGURE 1

A strong blood pressure-heart rate (BP–HR) integration constraint emerges with pattern biofeedback. In one experiment, each of 4 groups of subjects received biofeedback for one of the 4 possible BP or HR patterns. Simultaneous control of systolic blood pressure (light line) and heart rate (bold line) was achieved rapidly when subjects were required to integrate these functions (raising or lowering them together) (*left*). When subjects were required to differentiate the two—to make blood pressure change in the opposite direction from heart rate—only moderate control was attained (*right*). Curves represent the mean of 10 subjects, 5 trials each, set to zero by the pre-experimental baseline values; beats per minute and millimeters of mercury are therefore on the same axis. (From Schwartz 1972.)

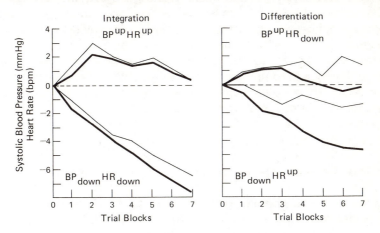

logical constraints are operative. This realization led to the hypothesis that, by determining the ease with which subjects could learn both to integrate and to differentiate various combinations of physiological responses, it would be possible to uncover and assess natural biological relationships in the intact human (Schwartz 1972). Quite unexpectedly, the pattern bio-feedback procedure was found to be a far more sensitive indicator of underlying constraints than the single-system biofeedback procedure.

We next performed an experiment using binary feedback and instructions like those of the initial studies, but with four groups of subjects, each of which received biofeedback for one of the four possible BP–HR patterns (Schwartz 1972). Analysis of the resting frequency of the BP–HR patterns indicated that each occurred spontaneously about 25% of the time; this supported the initial prediction that systolic BP and HR are phasically unrelated, at least from the point of view of a simple binary feedback system. However, as can be seen in Figure 1, pattern feedback uncovers strong constraints between the systems that were not exposed with single-system training.

When subjects were required to produce an integration pattern (BP^{up}HR^{up} or BP$_{down}$HR$_{down}$) they showed simultaneous control of both blood pressure and heart rate in the same direction. This is in contrast to the previous findings, which showed specific control of one response without simultaneous changes in the other. More important, however, is that feedback for the integration patterns produces more rapid learning and somewhat larger changes than biofeedback for the single systems alone! The findings for the differentiation conditions bore out this conclusion. Although the curves suggest that some $BP_{down}HR^{up}$ and $BP^{up}HR_{down}$ control was achieved, the magnitude of control was substantially less than that obtained for integration control.

An additional finding of particular importance to the pattern concept was that when subjects were taught to lower *both* functions simultaneously (as opposed to lowering either function alone), they began spontaneously and consistently to report feelings of relaxation and calmness, a subjective state we would expect to be associated with more diffuse physiological relaxation. If we recall that these subjects were told nothing about the precise meaning of the feedback, this finding becomes even more significant. In the attempt to understand and extend biofeedback techniques to patterns of responses, the research uncovers new information about the nature of the physiological systems and constraints and their relation to subjective experience.

EEG and heart rate control

If pattern biofeedback training can be used effectively to study relationships *within* the autonomic nervous system, then perhaps the pattern approach may have more general use in investigating integrations and constraints across sensory, visceral, and motor systems (Schwartz 1974; Black 1974). My laboratory has recently been using the pattern biofeedback approach to examine the role of cortical processes in the self-regulation of autonomic activity. At the outset, it became clear that it would be desirable to teach an individual rapidly to regulate, on command, a host of different patterns of EEG and autonomic activity, so as to reduce problems of intersubject variability and to enable us to assess the stability of constraints over time.

Learning to perform a dual task—for example, rubbing the stomach with one hand and patting the head with the other—can be difficult. One way to achieve a patterned skill is to practice each response alone and then coordinate the two. This training strategy is valuable for a number of reasons. Unlike the direct pattern feedback approach, which requires digital logic or computer facilities to quantify complex patterns on-line to provide feedback (we currently use a PDP11 system for measuring multiple responses on-line), the coordination approach requires simple biofeedback equipment. Separate portable devices for different responses can be used to train combinations of responses outside the laboratory. In addition, this procedure stimulates the subject to develop self-control naturally. He is allowed to experiment at his own pace in learning what strategies are effective for increasing and decreasing the feedback (Engel 1972), and the "free play" periods interspersed with test trials make the task both more challenging and more rewarding.

Previous single-system studies have suggested that, while heart rate control has no appreciable effect on EEG from the occipital region (Schwartz, Shaw, and Shapiro 1972), self-regulation of occipital alpha may have a small effect on heart rate (Beatty and Kornfeld 1973). Occipital alpha is an EEG wave of 8–13 hz recorded from the back of the head. It is most prevalent in the typical subject when he is relaxed, with eyes closed.

In a series of studies, we have examined both single-system and pattern training for occipital alpha and heart rate using the coordination training procedure (Hassett and Schwartz, in press). In one experiment, 12 subjects were studied over two sessions, receiving single-system training for EEG alpha from the right occipital region and heart rate in Session 1, and coordination training with simultaneous biofeedback for the two systems in Session 2. The results showed that subjects were able to produce on command, within specific limits, all eight patterns of occipital alpha and heart rate.

More interesting, however, was the consistency of the alpha-heart rate constraints. The results showed that occipital alpha regulation influenced heart rate, while the opposite was not the case. This effect was especially evident in the pattern conditions, where heart rate control was actually enhanced when alpha was simultaneously self-regulated in an arousal pattern (e.g., $HR^{up}alpha^{off}$). Conversely, differentiation of heart rate and alpha led to an impairment of heart rate regulation, compared to single-system heart rate control. These results were maintained even when subjects were tested after training without feedback.

Three subjects have been run for 8 training sessions, and the results, especially for the pattern conditions, are quite consistent from day to day. A particularly good self-regulation subject, showing exceptional specificity during single-system control in both responses over the 8 days, is shown in Figure 2. Whereas during integration he produced substantial regulation of both responses, during differentiation he showed reduced heart rate control and slightly enlarged alpha control (but in the opposite direction, as expected). The consistency of this pattern effect with repeated training and testing makes the concept of a one-way occipital alpha–heart rate constraint more compelling. When two of the subjects were posttested, in a ninth session 7 months after the training sessions, self-regulation of the patterns was retained, as was the alpha–heart rate constraint.

Cognitive mechanisms in pattern control

Given that subjects can learn with the aid of pattern biofeedback training to regulate combinations of autonomic and brain wave activity, the next question is, How do they do it? We might begin by asking them—and this leads us to the question of the relationship between cognitive strategies and the control of particular patterns of physiological activity. Can cognitive processes elicit or "mediate" patterned physiological changes?

The idea that cognition was an epiphenomenon, either unimportant or downright interfering, was long held by strict behaviorists and is still in vogue in some quarters. Katkin and Murray (1968) went so far as to conclude that, in order to demonstrate true instrumental conditioning of an autonomic response in humans, it would be necessary for the subjects to be paralyzed by curare (to remove overt skeletal mediators) and to be rendered unconscious (to eliminate cognitive mediators)! In reply to this article, Crider, Schwartz, and Shnidman (1969) pointed out that there was surprisingly little experimental data from which to argue that cognitive events could influence discrete physiological responses in the first place. More recently, Kimmel (1974) in an evaluation of the blood pressure-heart rate pattern findings, stated that "mediationists may also have to become cognitive contortionists to deal with data such as these." However, data and theory have made substantial progress over the past six years, and Kimmel's conclusion needs to be qualified.

Carefully controlled studies have demonstrated that cognitive activity *can* elicit physiological responses (McGuigan and Schoonover 1973). Self-induced affective thoughts can themselves elicit increases in heart rate (Schwartz 1971). In another experiment (Schwartz and Higgins 1971), generating a verbal image (silently thinking the word "stop") at the end of a 5-second light elicited anticipatory time-locked changes in heart rate comparable to those observed when subjects performed a simple task

FIGURE 2

Studies of relationships between cortical processes and autonomic activity reveal an apparent one-way constraint of occipital alpha (an EEG wave of 8 –13 hz [light line] and heart rate [bold line]). The results for one subject in a series of 8-day tests are shown here. The subject achieved very specific control in the single-system response tests, and when instructed to integrate the two responses, he was able to do so fairly successfully. But instructions to differentiate them resulted in reduced heart rate control with slightly enhanced alpha control. The consistency with which this constraint is found during pattern regulation suggests that occipital alpha may influence heart rate, but not vice versa. (From Hassett and Schwartz, in press.)

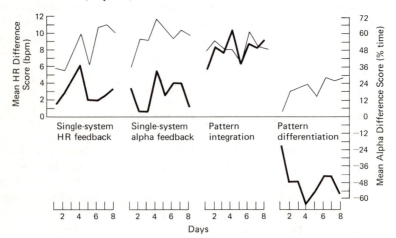

FIGURE 3

Studies have shown that cognitive activity can elicit physiological responses. In one study, silently thinking the word "stop" at the end of a 5-second warning light produced (*right*) changes in heart rate comparable to those elicited when subjects responded overtly to the signal by pushing a button (*left*). In both cases, fast responses to the signal (light line) are preceded by a slowing down of heart beat that reaches its trough sooner than if the same task is performed slowly (bold line). Curves represent mean heart rate values at critical points in the trial for 20 subjects. (From Schwartz and Higgins 1971.)

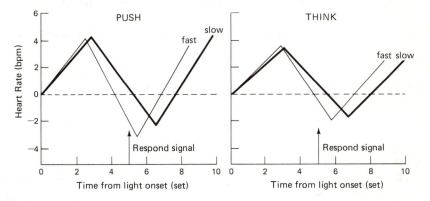

(pushing a button). As shown in Figure 3, fast button-presses are *preceded* by a cardiac deceleration that reaches its trough sooner than if button-presses are made deliberately slow; the identical, although slightly attenuated, anticipatory heart rate curves are generated when the same paced task is performed cognitively with no obvious overt response. In other words, thoughts can act as both "stimuli" and "responses" with predictable physiological consequences.

Patterns of hemispheric asymmetry

Another important illustration of how self-regulated cognitive processes can be associated with discrete patterns of physiological activity has emerged recently from studies of hemispheric asymmetry and human behavior. By means of a variety of EEG and behavioral indices, it has been found that cognitive tasks requiring verbal or sequential processes are associated with activity in the left hemisphere of the brain (in the normal right-handed subject), while tasks requiring spatial, musical, or simultaneous processes tend to be associated with activation of the right hemisphere (Galin and Ornstein 1972; Kinsbourne 1972; Kimura 1973).

If the pattern perspective on self-regulated physiological activity can be generalized, then, on the basis of the analogy with tasks requiring dual motor skills, self-regulated patterns of cognitive and affective processes may be considered complex neuropsychological skills with associated physiological response patterns. For example, Schwartz, Davidson, Maer, and Bromfeld (1974) have observed that speaking the lyrics to a familiar song in a monotone produces relative activation of the EEG (alpha[off]) over the left hemisphere, while whistling the song produces relative activation of the EEG over the right hemisphere. We would hypothesize that singing, a dual skill pattern, is a complex task involving, at least initially, activation and coordination of both hemispheres. The EEG data bear this out.

Similarly, we have found that the nonverbal component of emotion (like music, which long has been used as a stimulus for influencing mood) involves the right hemisphere. Questions involving both verbal (left hemisphere) and emotional (right hemisphere) processes (e.g., What is the primary difference in the meaning of the words "anger" and "hate"?) accordingly elicit evidence of dual hemispheric activation. Questions that involve both spatial (right hemisphere) and emotional (right hemisphere) processes (e.g., Picture your father's face—what emotion first strikes you?) elicit evidence of accentuated right hemispheric activation.

The hemispheric asymmetry data are important because they lead us to dissect complex self-regulated cognitive tasks or "states" into components that make neuropsychological sense. Once the basic processes have been isolated, we can investigate how the components can be voluntarily combined into more complex gestalts with their associated physiological pattern correlates. Subjects may then be trained with biofeedback to regulate specific patterns of EEG activity across the hemispheres and to relate these physiological states to specific underlying cognitive and affective experiences.

The question remains whether there is any evidence that classes of cognitive events can elicit specific *patterns* of physiological responses corresponding to those regulated through biofeedback. And if so, are we therefore justified in concluding that the strategies reflect underlying neural mechanisms involved in regulating the physiological changes? In the clinical area, in a series of classic studies in the 1950s (reviewed by Graham 1972), Graham and his associates demonstrated that various psychosomatic disorders were associated with definable attitudes in patients. For example, hypertensive patients reported feeling threatened with harm and having to be ready for anything. Further, when such attitudes were suggested to normal subjects under hypnosis, the suggestion elicited measurable changes that mimicked the patterns originally observed in the patients. It is unfortunate that these early studies have not been followed up, for current advances in psychophysiology and neuropsychology provide a framework in which such findings can be understood.

Patterns of facial muscle activity

Drawing on Darwin's early observations of emotion in lower animals and man (1872), Ekman, Friesen, and Ellsworth (1972) and Izard (1971) have provided experimental data indicating that specific facial expressions reflect distinct emotions which are innate and universal, although their overt

FIGURE 4

Emotional states are associated with identifiable covert facial expressions that may not be readily discernible to either the casual observer or the subject himself. The expressions may be monitored by recording and quantifying electromyographic (EMG) activity by means of electrodes placed over specific muscles. The muscles involved and the positioning of the electrodes are shown here. (From Schwartz et al. 1974b.)

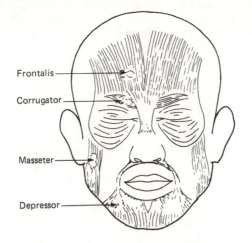

manifestation can be regulated to some extent. Of particular importance for the self-regulation pattern concept is Izard's neurophysiological theory of emotion, which postulates that discrete patterns of facial and postural muscle activity are processed in parallel and integrated by the brain and, in fact, make up a significant component of the conscious experience of emotion.

We have recently extended this concept to self-regulated imagery, demonstrating that small but discrete patterns of facial muscle activity are reliably generated when a person simply thinks about prior emotional experiences (Schwartz et al. 1974). Electrodes are placed over carefully selected muscles, and low levels of electromyographic (EMG) activity are recorded and quantified (Figure 4).

In one experiment 12 normal subjects were requested to generate happy, sad, or angry imagery while EMG from the corrugator, frontalis, depressor, and masseter muscle regions was continuously monitored (Schwartz et al. 1974b). The results showed that the self-induced emotional states were associated with identifiable "covert" facial expressions not typically noticeable by either the casual observer or the subject himself. As seen in Figure 5, "happy" imagery in normal subjects is associated with decreases in corrugator EMG below resting levels, while "sad" imagery produces increases in corrugator EMG. On the other hand, "angry" (more than "sad") imagery elicits reliable activity over the depressor region of the mouth.

It is interesting to note the similarity in the normal subjects' "happy" and "typical day" graphs in Figure 5. Asked to think about a "typical day,"

FIGURE 5

Changes in facial muscle tension (EMG) were monitored for 12 normal subjects and 12 depressed subjects who were instructed to generate imagery for happiness, sadness, anger, and a "typical day." The muscle regions monitored, the frontalis (F), corrugator (C), masseter (M), and depressor (D), are shown in Figure 4. For the normal subjects, the 3 classes of affective imagery elicit different EMG patterns, while the "typical day" imagery produces a miniature "happy" pattern. The depressed subjects show strong EMG patterns for sad and angry imagery, but they are less able to generate a "happy" image pattern; for them the "typical day" EMG pattern is one of sadness. The data represent integrated EMG, with 1 mm = 45 microvolts/30 sec. (From Schwartz et al. 1974b.)

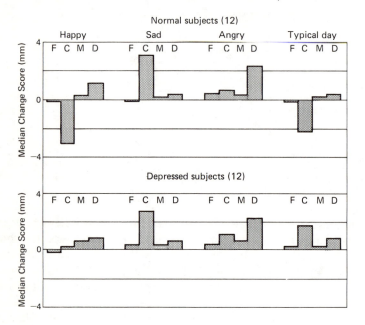

normal subjects generated an EMG pattern very like the happiness pattern. Another comparison of interest is between the normal results and those obtained from 12 subjects who were clinically depressed. In the depressed state people characteristically feel sad, blue, and often angry. At the same time, they feel incapable of making themselves feel happy—that is, of regulating a happy state. The EMG patterns for the four imagery conditions provide objective support for this generalization. While depressed subjects produce EMG patterns comparable to those of normal subjects for sadness and anger, they show attenuated EMG patterns for the self-induced happy condition. And when depressed subjects are asked to think about a typical day, the resulting EMG pattern is one of sadness.

    The ability of affective imagery to produce discrete muscular patterns supports the view that specific self-induced cognitive states can generate discrete bodily patterns, and that these heretofore unnoticed somatic patterns may serve as a major physiological mechanism allowing imagery to elicit the subjective feelings associated with different emotions. In other words, a self-regulated internal feedback loop may be created, when the particular "thought" triggers a specific *pattern* of peripheral physiological activity which is then itself reprocessed by the brain, contributing to the unique "feeling" state associated with the image. The EMG findings for depressed subjects indicate that a person's ability to regulate patterns of physiological activity by means of imagery depends in part on his emotional state.

Cognitive and somatic patterning

As compelling as these data are, are we justified in concluding that *all* physiological self-regulation has a discrete or identifiable cognitive referent? Clearly, regulation of specific muscles or patterns of motor behavior is not necessarily associated with specific cognitive referents (if asked How do you move your arm? most people cannot tell you). Similarly, control of individual physiological responses may not typically have identifiable subjective states. But we can hypothesize that certain self-regulated *patterns* of sensory-autonomic-motor activity do have strong subjective referents, and when a person generates those subjective experiences, he is also regulating their associated physiological patterns.

Humans, unfortunately, are not very good at observing and categorizing internal sensations. Therefore we must avoid taking subjects' reports at face value and must place such reports in a neuropsychological framework if we are to understand them. When subjects are simply *instructed*, without feedback, to "control and raise your heart rate" when one light comes on and to "control and lower your heart rate" when another light comes on, the typical subject almost immediately produces up-minus-down differences in heart rate on the order of 8 beats per minute (Bell and Schwartz).

When these instructed subjects are asked later to list what kinds of thoughts they used, they report generating angry, aggressive, tense, or sexual fantasies while raising heart rate, and quiet, relaxing fantasies while lowering it. This consistency in subjective strategy is very different from that observed in the previous single-system studies, where subjects were not so instructed. Instructions lead subjects to draw immediately on previously learned cognitive strategies; the few data on this suggest that such instructions actually elicit patterns of autonomic arousal out of which specificity can grow with biofeedback training (Klinge 1972; Brener 1974).

But to what extent are these cognitive images the sole mechanism eliciting the observed heart rate changes? If subjects were directly instructed to "make yourselves aroused by thinking arousing thoughts," this should presumably elicit large heart rate changes, comparable to those observed with "control and raise" instructions. But this hypothesis does not take into account that one of the major physiological determinants of heart rate is somatic activity and associated metabolic demands (Obrist et al. 1974). Obrist and his colleagues have shown that, as subjects are given, via instructions, more and more freedom to move around and use their muscles in the heart rate biofeedback situation, larger and larger heart rate increases are observed.

In light of these findings, Bell and Schwartz (1973) predicted that simple instructions to "think arousing thoughts," without mentioning control of heart rate, would not generate large heart rate increases in comparison to "control and raise" instructions. We hypothesized that the "think" instructions would lead subjects to direct so much of their attention to the generation of imagery per se that this would produce a relative inhibition of general body movement; on the other hand, the "control" instructions would lead the subjects actively to generate subtle movement commands in concert with the imagery, even though they might not be aware of it. When this experiment was performed, our prediction was confirmed. Apparently there is a major difference between *having* a fantasy and *acting* upon it.

We are only beginning to accumulate data on combinations of cognitive and somatic mechanisms in biofeedback, and many questions remain. Recording discrete patterns of physiological activity selected because of their neuropsychological association with the processes under study is a fruitful direction in which to move. One strategy is to look at patterns of cortical activity generated when subjects are instructed to use various strategies to regulate a given response (or pattern of responses) with biofeedback. Neyers and Schwartz (MS in preparation) have recently found that when subjects are instructed to use muscle tension and relaxation as the main strategy to regulate their heart rate with biofeedback, associated EEG activation (alpha^{off}) can be found over the left sensory motor area (Sterman 1973) but not over the left occipital area, which is involved with visual processes (Mulholland 1973). But when subjects are instructed to regulate their heart rate by "thinking arousing thoughts," the sensory motor EEG differences over the left hemisphere are attenuated or disappear.

In our laboratory we are currently using pattern biofeedback training to assess the degree of self-regulated integration and differentiation that can be achieved between heart rate and these two different cortical EEG sites. If heart rate-sensory motor EEG pattern regulation shows enhanced integration and restricted differentiation compared to heart rate-occipital alpha EEG, this finding will provide further evidence of a cardiosomatic constraint at the level of the brain (Obrist et al. 1974). We are also investigating the possibility that the "thinking arousing thoughts" strategy, in light of our previous hemispheric asymmetry data, may involve right rather than left hemispheric sensory-motor sites.

Researchers interested in the mechanisms by which people learn to control specific functions or patterns of functions have an obvious interest in assessing cognitive correlates. However, this requires the use of sophisticated cognitive paradigms and neuropsychological strategies on a par with the methodology already developed for physiological recording and feedback displays. Such cognitive approaches are available (e.g., Luria 1973) and may be combined with the biofeedback paradigm. In addition, biofeedback may be used as the independent variable in investigating the physiology of subjective experience. By training uninstructed subjects to control patterns of physiological activity, it is possible to study how patterns of physiological responses combine to elicit unique subjective states. Here, pattern biofeedback is used as an objective research tool for investigating the psychobiology of human consciousness.

Meditation and patterns of relaxation

One aspect of our self-regulation pattern approach with direct clinical applications involves physiological states produced by meditation and other relaxation procedures. Wallace and Benson (1972) have described a "hypometabolic" state produced by transcendental meditation—a simple, passive procedure in which the subject silently repeats to himself a Sanskrit word, or mantra. During meditation, decreases occur in many responses, including heart rate, blood pressure, sweat gland activity, respiration rate, EEG frequencies (to alpha/theta ranges), level of lactate acid in the blood, and measures of body metabolism. Although the EEG patterns superficially represent a drowsy or Stage 1 sleep pattern, and the decreases in metabolism appear equal to, if not greater than, those occurring during sleep, the meditator claims to feel awake and alert.

Recently, Benson and his colleagues have described this pattern as reflecting a more centrally integrated "relaxation response" (Benson, Beary, and Carol 1974), opposite to the fight-or-flight response originally described by Cannon (1936). Claiming that it is an innate, integrated neurophysiological pattern, they show that when subjects regulate a simple pattern of attention and cognition, attending passively to their breathing and saying the word "one" after each breath—an American analogue of certain Zen procedures—marked decreases in metabolism are obtained (Beary and Benson 1974).

Stimulated by such findings, many biofeedback researchers formulated the following hypothesis: since low-frequency EEG occurs in passive meditation, and subjects can learn with biofeedback to regulate such EEG patterns, then biofeedback for these changes will lead to deep relaxation—an "instant, electronic yoga." The major fallacy in this logic is that single-system biofeedback training is prone to emphasize specificity, not patterns. As mentioned earlier, consistent reports of subjective relaxation emerged when uninstructed subjects were lowering a *pattern* of low blood pressure and low heart rate ($BP_{down}HR_{down}$); decreases in either one alone did not produce this result (Schwartz 1972). Similarly, when subjects regulate patterns of occipital alpha and heart rate (Hassett and Schwartz, in press), they report that $HR_{down}alpha_{on}$ is quite relaxing. In fact, one of the subjects run for 8 sessions found this particular pattern so rewarding that she continued to practice it outside the laboratory as a means of producing relaxation. Deep physiological relaxation is not simply low frontalis muscle activity, or low heart rate, or occipital alpha, or slow breathing, but rather the combination of such changes.

Individuals differ in their patterns of response to stress (Lacey 1967), and the systems or combinations of systems associated with deep relaxation also depend on the individual. If subjects are trained with biofeedback to decrease their heart rate voluntarily in anticipation of receiving a noxious stimulus, the pain is experienced as less intense. However, this effect occurs primarily in subjects who report experiencing cardiac symptoms in normal stress situations (Sirota, Schwartz, and Shapiro 1974).

Patterns in meditation are likely to be even more complex than currently acknowledged. In *Psychophysiology of Zen*, Hirai (1974) provides physiological data from Japanese subjects and argues for the concept of a state of "relaxed awareness." Similarly, in the U. S., Goleman and Schwartz (MS) have found evidence that a major effect of transcendental meditation is the generation of a unique and somewhat paradoxical pattern of cortical and limbic arousal, roughly equivalent to the differential subjective experiences of perception versus emotion. We hypothesize that passive meditation practices can lead to *heightened cortical arousibility* plus *decreased limbic arousibility at the same time*, experienced as heightened perceptual awareness and simultaneously reduced emotional arousal and stress.

If this conclusion is generally correct, several important issues arise: Is it possible, using biofeedback techniques, to mimic this psychophysiological state? What combination of responses and biofeedback training procedures would be necessary to match the pattern of physiological changes that occur naturally during meditation? And if it is possible, is it worth the effort?

My own response is divided according to the needs of basic research versus clinical applications. The pattern biofeedback approach provides a new research procedure for investigating how patterns of physiological systems combine to produce unique subjective gestalts and behavioral correlates; at this level, the approach promises to be quite fruitful. However, if the physiological patterns produced by meditation or other relaxation techniques are of therapeutic value (e.g., for reducing overall limbic stress and its many expressions in diseases; Selye 1973), then they should be induced and practiced using the nonelectronic, easily portable, and generalizable machinery of our own biocognitive system.

When we consider the phenomenon of relaxation still more broadly, it becomes clear that various patterns of cognitive, attentional, and somatic strategies can be brought into play, and that different relaxation procedures emphasize the regulation of *different combinations* of processes. Davidson and Schwartz have outlined how relaxation paradigms utilize different combinations of strategies, which will be reflected in different patterns of physiological responses. Similarly, it is possible to classify various kinds of anxiety, involving combinations of cognitive, visceral, and somatic components. The most effective relaxation procedure may depend on the type of anxiety the person is experiencing at the time.

Take for example a case of high cognitive –low somatic anxiety, in which a person, although physically exhausted, is unable to fall asleep because his mind is racing with disturbing images and thoughts. The age-old treatment for this pattern of anxiety is to visualize sheep and count them—a cognitive self-regulation procedure that may be effective because it blocks both unwanted visual (right hemisphere) and verbal (left hemisphere) images at the same time.

Another pattern is exemplified by the person who feels somatically tense and jittery, but can point to no particular cause for his anxiety (no specific images come to mind). For such cases of low cognitive—high somatic anxiety, effective "relaxation" strategies include jogging, gardening, or other self-generated somatic activities that serve to block the undesirable somatic state and use up some of the unwanted metabolism at the same time, thereby producing fatigue.

The pattern orientation to anxiety assessment and relaxation treatment is not unlike Lazarus's (1973) concept of multimodality therapy, which seeks to classify for the individual the patterns of responses that need to be modified and treat them either singly or in combination, recognizing that the selected treatment for one component will not necessarily lead to reductions in others. Similar applications of the pattern approach to biofeedback therapy are described elsewhere (Schwartz, 1974).

Pattern biofeedback and emergent property

One major thesis that has slowly emerged from biofeedback research is that patterns of physiological processes can be both generated and processed by the brain, producing unique cross-system interactions and perceptual gestalts that make up a significant component of human behavior and subjective experience. The concept of pattern refers not simply to viewing, in isolation, combinations of physiological responses, but rather goes beyond the individual responses making up the pattern to recognize the novel, interactive, or emergent property that patterns can acquire. Simply stated, the whole can be qualitatively different from the sum of its parts, and yet be dependent upon the organization of its parts for its unique properties. This phenomenon is seen at all levels of physics and chemistry and extends through biology and neuropsychology (Weiss 1969).

The concept of emergent property is what I wish to emphasize in patterning. Although it is not new, with few exceptions it is still ignored. Neuropsychologists concerned with the biology of consciousness employ the same idea when they speak of cell assemblies (Hebb 1974), neural engrams (John 1972), holograms (Pribram 1971), dynamic neural patterns (Sperry 1969), or functional systems (Luria 1973). Emotion was described by William James (1890) as the perception of patterns of autonomic consequences of action. More recent researchers, such as Schachter and Singer (1962), have added cognitive processes to autonomic arousal as an integral part of this pattern. Today, theorists like Izard (1971) stress the interaction of combinations of neurophysiological systems, including discrete patterns of postural and facial muscle activity, as the mechanism underlying the emergent experience of emotion.

Research on biofeedback and the regulation of combinations of responses extends this basic concept of patterning by providing a new paradigm for investigating physiological relationships in the intact human. Self-regulation as a general research strategy is useful because it enables researchers to isolate component parts of systems and then examine how they combine to produce unique physiological and associated subjective states. Our laboratory has shown that the regulation of patterns of responses can produce effects that are different from those observed when single functions are regulated. As I have illustrated, this simple principle proves to have important basic as well as clinical ramifications.

It is not inconceivable, however, that the act of regulating a pattern of responses will have consequences somewhat different from those found when a similar pattern is elicited by other means. If future research proves this to be true, it would limit the general applicability of the approach. On the other hand, such a finding could provide a further key to the nature of the self-regulation process itself.

References

Barber, T. X., L. V. DiCara, J. Kamiya, N. E. Miller, D. Shapiro & J. Stoyva, eds. *Biofeedback and Self-Control (1970): An Aldine Annual on the Regulation of Bodily Processes and Consciousness.* Chicago: Aldine-Atherton, 1971.

Basmajian, J. V. Electromyography comes of age. *Science*, 1972, **176**, 603–9.

Beary, J. F. & H. Benson, with H. P. Klemchuk. A simple psychophysiologic technique which elicits the hypometabolic changes of the relaxation response. *Psychosomatic Med.*, 1974, **36**, 115–20.

Beatty, J. & C. Kornfeld. Relative independence of conditioned EEG changes from cardiac and respiratory activity. *Physiology and Behavior*, 1973, **9**, 773–36.

Bell, I. & G. E. Schwartz. Cognitive and somatic mechanisms in the voluntary control of human heart rate, 1973. In Shapiro et al., eds., *Biofeedback and Self-Control, 1972.*

Bell, I. R. & G. E. Schwartz. Voluntary control and reactivity of human heart rate. *Psychophysiology*, in press.

Benson, H., J. F. Beary & M. P. Carol. The relaxation response. *Psychiatry*, 1974, **37**, 37–46.

Black, A. H. Operant autonomic conditioning: The analysis of response mechanisms. In P. A. Obrist, A. H. Black, J. Brener and L. V. DiCara, eds., *Cardiovascular Psychophysiology.* Chicago: Aldine, 1974.

Brener, J. A general model of voluntary control applied to the phenomena of learned cardiovascular change. In Obrist et al., eds., *Cardiovascular Psychophysiology*, 1974.

Cannon, W. B. *Bodily Changes in Pain, Hunger, Fear, and Rage.* N.Y.: Appleton-Century, 1936.

Darwin, C. *The Expression of the Emotions in Man and Animals*. London: John Murray, 1872.

Davidson, R. J. & G. E. Schwartz. Psychobiology of relaxation and related states: A multi-process theory. In D. Mostofsky, ed., *Behavior Control and Modification of Physiological Activity*. Englewood Cliffs: Prentice-Hall, in press.

Ekman, P., W. V. Friesen & P. Ellsworth. *Emotion in the Human Face*. N.Y.: Pergamon, 1972.

Engel, B. T. Operant conditioning of cardiac function: A status report. *Psychophysiology*, 1972, **9**, 161–77.

Fleishman, E. A. Human abilities and the acquisition of skill. In E. A. Bilodeau, ed., *Acquisition of Skill*. N.Y.: Academic Press, 1966.

Galin, D. & R. Ornstein. Lateral specialization of cognitive mode: An EEG study. *Psychophysiology*, 1972, **9**, 412–18.

Germana, J. The psychophysiological correlates of conditioned response formation. *Psychological Bull.*, 1968, **70**, 105–14.

Goleman, D. J. & G. E. Schwartz. Fractionation of skin conductance level and responses in meditators and controls: A dual component theory, MS.

Graham, D. T. Psychosomatic medicine. In N. S. Greenfield & R. A. Sternbach, eds., *Handbook of Psychophysiology*. N.Y.: Holt, Rinehart and Winston, 1972.

Hassett, J. & G. E. Schwartz. Relationships between heart rate and occipital alpha: A biofeedback approach. *Psychophysiology* (abstract), in press.

Hebb, D. O. What psychology is about. *Am. Psychologist*, 1974, **29**, 71–79.

Hirai, T. *Psychophysiology of Zen*. Tokyo: Igaku Shoin, 1974.

Izard, C. E. *The Face of Emotion*. N.Y.: Appleton-Century-Crofts, 1971.

James, W. *Principles of Psychology*. N.Y.: Holt, 1890.

John, E. R. Switchboard versus statistical theories of learning and memory. *Science*, 1972, **177**, 850–64.

Kamiya, J., L. V. DiCara, T. X. Barber, N. E. Miller, D. Shapiro & J. Stoyva, eds. *Biofeedback and Self-Control: An Aldine Reader on the Regulation of Bodily Processes and Consciousness*. Chicago: Aldine-Atherton, 1971.

Katkin, E. S. & E. N. Murray. Instrumental conditioning of automatically mediated behavior: Theoretical and methodological issues. *Psychological Bull.*, 1968, **70**, 52–68.

Kimmel, H. D. Instrumental conditioning of autonomically mediated responses in human beings. *Am. Psychologist*, 1974, **29**, 325–35.

Kimura, D. The asymmetry of the human brain. *Sci. Am.*, 1973, **228**(3), 70–80.

Kinsbourne, M. Eye and head turning indicates cerebral lateralization. *Science*, 1972, **176**, 539–41.

Klinge, V. Effects of exteroceptive feedback and instructions on control of spontaneous galvanic skin response. *Psychophysiology*, 1972, **9**, 305–17.

Lacey, J. Somatic response patterning and stress: Some revisions of activation theory. In M. Appley and R. Trumbull, eds., *Psychological Stress*. N.Y.: Appleton-Century-Crofts, 1967.

Lang, P. J. Learned control of human heart rate in a computer-directed environment. In Obrist et al., eds., *Cardiovascular Psychophysiology*, 1974.

Lazarus, A. A. Multimodal behavior therapy: Treating the "Basic Id." *J. Nervous and Mental Disease*, 1973, **156**, 404–11.

Luria, A. R. *The Working Brain: An Introduction to Neuropsychology*. N.Y.: Basic Books, 1973.

McGuigan, F. J. & R. A. Schoonover, eds. *The Psychophysiology of Thinking*. N.Y.: Academic Press, 1973.

Miller, N.E. Learning of visceral and glandular responses. *Science*, 1969, **163**, 434–45.

———. Introduction: Current issues and key problems. In Miller et al., eds., *Biofeedback and Self-Control 1973*, 1974.

————, T. X. Barber, L. V. DiCara, J. Kamiya, D. Shapiro & J. Stoyva, eds. *Biofeedback and Self-Control (1973): An Aldine Annual on the Regulation of Bodily Processes and Consciousness.* Chicago: Aldine, 1974.

Mulholland, T. Objective EEG methods for studying covert shifts of visual attention. In McGuigan and Schoonover, eds., *The Psychophysiology of Thinking,* 1973.

Neyers, M. A. & G. E. Schwartz. Patterning of sensory-motor and occipital alpha in the self-regulation of heart rate, in prep.

Obrist, P. A., J. L. Howard, J. E. Lawler, R. A. Galosy, K. A. Meyers & C. J. Gaebelein. The cardiac-somatic interaction. In Obrist et al., eds., *Cardiovascular Psychophysiology,* 1974.

Pribram, K. H. *Languages of the Brain: Experimental Paradoxes and Principles in Neuropsychology.* Englewood Cliffs: Prentice-Hall, 1971.

Schachter, S. & J. E. Singer. Cognitive, social and physiological determinants of emotional state. *Psychological Rev.,* 1962, **69**, 379–99.

Schwartz, G. E. Cardiac responses to self-induced thoughts. *Psychophysiology,* 1971, **8**, 462–67.

————. Voluntary control of human cardiovascular integration and differentiation through feedback and reward. *Science,* 1972, **175**, 90–93.

————. Biofeedback as therapy: Some theoretical and practical issues. *Am. Psychologist,* 1973, 666–73.

————. Toward a theory of voluntary control of response patterns in the cardiovascular system. In Obrist et al., eds., *Cardiovascular Psychophysiology,* 1974.

————. Self-regulation response patterning: Implications for psychophysiological research and therapy. *Biofeedback and Self-Regulation,* in press.

————, R. Davidson, F. Maer & E. Bromfield. Patterns of hemispheric dominance during musical, emotional, verbal, and spatial tasks. *Psychophysiology,* 1974, **11**, 227 (abstract).

————, P. L. Fair, P. S. Greenberg, M. Freedman & J. L. Klerman. Facial electromyography in assessment of emotion. *Psychophysiology,* 1974a, **11**, 237 (abstract).

————, P. L. Fair, P. S. Greenberg, M. R. Mandel & J. L. Klerman. Facial expression and depression: An electromyographic study. *Psychosomatic Med.,* 1974b, **36**, 458 (abstract).

————, P. L. Fair, P. S. Greenberg, J. M. Foran & G. L. Klerman. Self-generated affective imagery elicits discrete patterns of facial muscle activity. *Psychophysiology* (abstract), in press.

————, P. L. Fair, P. S. Greenberg, M. R. Mandel & G. L. Klerman. Facial expression and depression II: An electromyographic study. *Psychosomatic Med.* (abstract), in press.

———— & J. D. Higgins. Cardiac activity preparatory to overt and covert behavior. *Science,* 1971, **173**, 1144–46.

————, D. Shapiro & B. Tursky. Learned control of cardiovascular integration in man through operant conditioning. *Psychosomatic Med.,* 1971, **33**, 57–62.

————, G. Shaw & D. Shapiro. Specificity of alpha and heart rate control through feedback. *Psychophysiology,* 1972, **9**, 269 (abstract).

————, J. Vogler & L. Young. Heart rate self-regulation as skill learning: Strength endurance versus cardiac reaction time. *Psychophysiology* (abstract), in press.

Selye, H. The evolution of the stress concept. *Am. Sci.,* 1973, **61**, 692–99.

Shapiro, D., T. X. Barber, L. V. DiCara, J. Kamiya, N. E. Miller & J. Stoyva, eds. *Biofeedback and Self-Control (1972): An Aldine Annual on the Regulation of Bodily Processes and Consciousness.* Chicago: Aldine, 1973.

————, B. Tursky, E. Gershon & M. Stern. Effects of feedback and reinforcement on the control of human systolic blood pressure. *Science,* 1969, **163**, 588–89.

————, B. Tursky & G. E. Schwartz. Control of blood pressure in man by operant conditioning. *Circ. Res.*, 1970a, **26**, supp. 1; **127**, I-27–I-32.

————, B. Tursky & G. E. Schwartz. Differentiation of heart rate and blood pressure in man by operant conditioning. *Psychosomatic Med.*, 1970b, **32**, 417–23.

Sirota, A. D., G. E. Schwartz & D. Shapiro. Voluntary control of human heart rate: Effects on reactions to aversive stimuli. *J. Abnormal Psychology*, 1974, **83**, 261–67.

Sperry, R. W. A modified concept of consciousness. *Psychological Rev.*, 1969, **76**, 532–36.

Sterman, M. B. Neurophysiologic and clinical studies of sensorimotor EEG biofeedback training: Some effects on epilepsy. *Seminars in Psychiatry*, 1973, **5**, 507–24.

Stoyva, J., T. X. Barber, L. V. DiCara, J. Kamiya, N. E. Miller & D. Shapiro, eds. *Biofeedback and Self-Control (1971): An Aldine Annual on the Regulation of Bodily Processes and Consciousness*. Chicago: Aldine-Atherton, 1972.

Tursky, B., D. Shapiro & G. E. Schwartz. Automated constant cuff pressure system to measure average systolic and diastolic blood pressure in man. *IEEE Transactions on Biomedical Engineering*, 1972, **19**, 271–75.

Wallace, R. K. & H. Benson. The physiology of meditation. *Sci. Am.*, 1972, **226**(2), 84–91.

Weiss, P. A. The living system: Determinism stratified. In A. Koestler and J. R. Smythies, eds., *Beyond Reductionism: New Perspectives in the Life Sciences*. Boston: Beacon Press, 1969.

MODIFICATION OF SYMPTOMATIC VERBAL BEHAVIOUR OF MENTAL PATIENTS

T. Ayllon and E. Haughton

The final paper in this chapter, by T. Ayllon and E. Haughton (1964), was chosen for several reasons. First, it illustrates many of the salient principles of instrumental conditioning—among them, for example, the exceedingly important concept of reinforcement contingency. Second, the studies reflect many of the methodological techniques that are common in research on instrumental learning—accurate recording of baseline behaviors, reward or extinction procedures, identification of adequate reinforcers, time sampling, and so on. Finally, and most importantly, this paper is a very good example of the many hundreds of studies in which the basic concepts and methods of instrumental learning have been applied to complex human behaviors of great social import. Such use of laboratory techniques in a clinical setting has proven to be an effective tool in the treatment of psychological disorders. In fact, behavior therapy has become a major industry in the field of mental health care and its success has depended, in part, on the theoretical and methodological achievements in laboratory research programs.

In this particular paper, the verbal behavior of three hospitalized patients was studied and manipulated through conditioning procedures (Ayllon and Haughton properly note that therapy and other forms of social contact rely on appropriate verbal communication). More specifically, Experiment 1 demonstrated that the bizarre utterances by a psychotic patient could be increased through the application of rewards or decreased through extinction procedures. In Experiment 2, psychosomatic verbal behaviors were similarly changed by means of the treatment conditions. That is, "paying attention to" (reinforcing) verbal complaints increased their frequency while "ignoring" (extinguishing) them reduced their frequency. Ayllon and Haughton's results demonstrate that maladaptive verbal behaviors may be modified by instrumental conditioning procedures. Their results also support the hypothesis that various psychotic utterances may, unwittingly, stem from or be maintained by the social interactions of the patients.

In the past few years there has been a great deal of experimental work in the area of verbal conditioning. In most of this work, the verbal response has been regarded as an operant which can be made to increase or decrease in frequency by the appropriate use of social consequences (Krasner, 1958; Salzinger, 1959).

Few studies have attempted to manipulate the actual content of verbal behaviour primarily because of the difficulties in identifying the response and classifying the content of speech (Salzinger and Pisoni, 1960; Verplanck, 1955; Azrin et al., 1961). Yet, the feasibility of a functional analysis of verbal behaviour is no longer in question. Indeed, Lindsley (1956, 1959) and others (Lane, 1960) have shown that vocal behaviour can be effectively manipulated by controlling its consequences.

These findings have implications for research in clinical problems since diagnosis and psychotherapy are primarily dependent upon a person's verbalizations. For example, a patient who talks about the effects of "television radiation", and reports that certain mysterious other-worldly figures "are out to get him" will be classed as a paranoid schizophrenic.

Although the bizarre quality of the patient's statements is usually the most dramatic aspect of abnormality, sometimes abnormality is reflected solely in the rate of verbal behaviour. For example, rate of verbal behaviour in its two extreme instances would include the case of the person who talks incessantly and that of the person who seldom talks.

Current therapies attempt to alter behaviour indirectly through the manipulation of the verbal interaction between patient and therapist. Typically, the content, as well as the rate of verbal behaviour, constitute the objective of therapeutic modification in the interview situation. Irrespective of the form of therapy to be used, the primary purpose of talking to the patient is to encourage him to verbalize about things which would rarely be said to most people. For example, when the therapist is concerned with the sexual content of the patient's verbalizations the patient is encouraged to talk about it in preference to other topics. Sometimes, the patient may talk on a given subject but do so only rarely. When this is the case, the therapist may well encourage a greater frequency of this verbal response. It may be said that, in general, both the content and the rate of verbal behaviour are of much interest to the therapist in his attempt to modify other behaviour in the patient.

Although it is clear that psychotherapy relies heavily on the verbal output of the patient, the actual techniques employed to manipulate the verbal interaction between patient and therapist are couched in the kind of terminology that makes it sometimes very difficult to assess or evaluate the effects of each procedure. Recently, an alternative approach to the study of verbal behaviour has been advanced by Skinner (1957). He defines verbal behaviour as "behaviour reinforced through the mediation of other persons", and in so doing, identifies the environmental agency through which verbal behaviour is maintained. The findings in the experimental analysis of behaviour indicate that the behavioural consequence following a response is responsible for the development and maintenance of that response. In extrapolating this finding to verbal behaviour, it means that the social reaction following a specific verbalization constitutes the behavioural consequence which may develop and maintain this verbalization. Therefore, control of the social environment in which certain kinds of statements and verbalizations are to be encouraged or eliminated has implications for research in psychotherapy that may lead to something resembling "programmed" therapy. The present report illustrates just such a possibility.

METHOD

The experimental ward

The two experiments reported here were conducted in a psychiatric hospital. A self-contained ward was set aside for the experimental investigation of operant techniques and their application to psychiatric problems.

The ward staff was composed of trained psychiatric nurses and aides who volunteered to work on the research ward. In addition a physician was consultant to the ward regarding medical problems. The administrative control of the ward was exercised by the authors.

Procedure

Three female patients were selected for this investigation. All three subjects showed very stereotyped symptomatic verbalizations. The characteristics of each patient's verbal behaviour were determined by a preliminary period during which the nurses wrote down a verbatim report of their verbal interaction with each of these subjects. This preliminary information made it possible to identify at least two general classes of verbal behaviour that were independent of each other. That is to say, the response classes were not dichotomous; therefore, increases in one class would not automatically result in a decrease in the other class. Specific classes of verbal responses were defined for each subject and the social reaction of the nurses involved the use of reinforcement and extinction procedures.

Recording the response

Nurses were specifically trained to record each verbal interaction with any of the three patients until they achieved adequate skills. The nurses were given specially prepared slips on which to record the classes of verbal behaviour. To avoid unsystematic nurse–patient interactions, the nurses were instructed to (1) avoid unnecessary contact with the patient and (2) limit each contact with the patient to a maximum of 3 min. When a patient approached a nurse, the nurse herself was to maintain the conversation within the maximum time limit, to follow whatever specific procedure was in effect at the time, and to record the interaction. Slips were submitted by the nurses at the end of each shift. The data was then analysed by the authors.

Auxiliary behavioural records were taken throughout this investigation. Using a time sample technique, the behaviours of these three patients were observed. This technique, which was utilized in earlier work (Ayllon and Michael, 1959), produced quantitative records on the amount of time a patient engaged in gross motor behaviour. Among the behaviours classified in following this technique were lying, sitting, and walking. The period during which these observations were taken was from 7 a.m. to 11 p.m. They were made every 30 min and they consisted of behavioural descriptions of a patient's activities.

Behavioural consequences

The behavioural consequences to be applied to specific classes of verbal behaviour involved reinforcement and extinction procedures. These were especially adapted to be used by relatively untrained personnel.

Reinforcement. Reinforcement consisted of listening to or taking interest in the patient's verbalization. In some instances this attention involved the offer of a cigarette or a piece of candy to the patient. Sometimes the nurse simply paid attention to the patient by lighting a cigarette herself and joining the patient. In general, the patient–nurse interaction followed a casual, social, form the primary object of which was to demonstrate interest in the patient.

Extinction. Extinction consisted of withholding social attention and the other tangible reinforcers already described. The attendants became, with some practice, quite skilful in appearing distracted or bored. Generally, the nurse was instructed to "look away" and "act busy". This was easily accomplished by teaching the nurses to shift their attention to some other event taking place on the ward.

Considerations regarding the validity of the recording and behavioural manipulation

Because the methodology in this investigation was implemented through relatively untrained personnel, several considerations had to be observed in an attempt to avoid observer bias.

First of all the behaviour studied was measured continuously and for long periods of time. This is quite in contrast to current verbal conditioning studies where the total time spent studying the behaviour is typically less than two hours. In this investigation each subject was observed and her verbal behaviour recorded for 15–20 days preceding manipulation of the social (verbal) audience. In each case this baseline period of observation represented a measure of the patient's relatively stable classes of verbal behaviour. One of the three subjects (experiment I) was intensively studied for approximately 180 days. The other two subjects (experiment II) were studied each for approximately 500 continuous days.

Secondly, nurses who recorded and applied the consequences to the patient's verbal behaviour were not sophisticated in theories of conditioning. The staff's lack of knowledge regarding conditioning seemed to facilitate their following instructions. Because the ward had been organized as a research ward, the procedures introduced there were not regarded as "mental treatment" or psychological solutions. Rather, the procedures followed on the research ward were regarded as necessary means for the collection of information concerning patients' behaviour. Moreover, the research character of the investigations was emphasized by including the performance of seemingly contradictory approaches to the same behaviour. Thus, a patient's complaints were at one time listened to and at another "ignored".

Thirdly, the actual procedures performed daily by nurses required that different nurses participate in the investigation daily. This was accomplished by having a daily rotation of each nurse assigned to the patient to be observed and, in addition, by having all nurses on the ward rotated every four weeks from night shift to morning shift, or to evening shift. The net result of this rotation was that each nurse participated in each experiment but at different stages. A total of 21 nurses were involved in this investigation.

Fourthly, the class of verbal behaviour manipulated was both reinforced and extinguished at different stages of each experiment. Each patient was essentially her own control. In this manner, the possibility of a behaviour change occurring due to the passage of time or to some systematic bias was ruled out. Thus, the magnitude of each behaviour change cannot easily be regarded as fortuitous or attributed to some systematic error or bias.

Experiment I illustrates the class of verbal behaviour associated with severe "depersonalization" and psychosis. Experiment II illustrates the class of verbal behaviour regarded as "psychosomatic" and involves two patients.

Experiment I

Modification of psychotic verbal behaviour

Subject. Kathy was a 47-year-old female patient diagnosed as chronic schizophrenic. She had been in the hospital for 16 years. The patient's verbal behaviour centered around so-called "delusions". The content of her verbal behaviour was characterized by frequent references to "Queen Elizabeth", "King George", and the "Royal Family". A sample of her talk is as follows: "I'm the Queen. Why don't you give things to the Queen? The Queen wants to smoke . . . . how's King George, have you seen him?" These self-references were traced through hospital records and had been reported over the preceding 14 years. The staff stated that references to herself as "the Queen" had been virtually her only topic of conversation for the eight years immediately prior to this investigation. The patient had undergone a bilateral prefrontal lobotomy without apparent change in her verbal behaviour. As she was on a maintenance dosage of barbiturates when this investigation was initiated, this medication was maintained throughout.

Procedure

Two classes of verbal responses were selected for recording. One class of verbal responses was defined as "psychotic" when it included references to "the Queen", "King", and "the Royal Family". A class of "neutral" verbal responses included all verbal responses excluding psychotic responses. For example, such remarks as "it's nice today", "what time is it?", "I'd like some soap" and similar ones were classified as non-psychotic or "neutral".

The experimental procedure included a baseline period during which the staff kept a continuous record of the patient's verbal behaviour. During this period no reinforcement contingencies were altered. The staff responded to the patient as they usually had and simply recorded every verbal interaction they had with the patient and its content. The verbal interaction between patient and staff required that the staff remain with the patient for a period of approximately 3 min. During this time the patient's verbal behaviour could take two different forms; it could be pure (psychotic or neutral alone) or it could be mixed, psychotic and neutral verbalizations alternating. A verbal interaction was classified as psychotic when a psychotic verbal response occurred in pure or mixed form.

To explore the possibilities of control of distinct classes of verbal behaviour for the first period of 75 days, the class of "psychotic" verbal responses was reinforced while the "neutral" class of responses was under extinction. The reinforcement procedure required that the staff offer the patient one cigarette and remain conversing with her for about 3 minutes when her verbal behaviour included a psychotic response. Extinction of the neutral class of verbal responses involved the withdrawal of cigarettes and social attention. The extinction procedures required that the staff withdraw its attention, look away from the patient and act interested or busy in something else. When the verbal interaction alternated between psychotic and neutral (mixed form), the staff was trained to alternate their reaction accordingly.

During the second period of 90 days, this procedure was reversed and neutral verbal responses were reinforced with cigarettes and social attention, while psychotic verbal responses were extinguished.

Results

The frequency of psychotic verbal behaviour can be increased or decreased as a function of the reinforcement provided by the verbal audience. Figure 1 shows that upon reinforcing psychotic verbal responses they gradually increased to twice their baseline frequency. Upon withdrawal of reinforcement for psychotic verbal behaviour a rapid decrease in its frequency is observed. Again, when neutral verbal behaviour is under extinction, there is a marked drop in its frequency. Upon reinforcement of neutral verbal behaviour its frequency shows an increase once again.

Discussion

It is well to note that both classes of verbal responses, neutral and psychotic, were of equal strength during the baseline (each accounting for 50 per cent of responses) of this experiment. Through the manipulation of reinforcement, each class of responses was independently strengthened

FIGURE 1

This figure shows that the baseline (first period) included both psychotic and neutral verbal behaviour in equal strength. The second period shows that reinforcement increased psychotic verbal behaviour while extinction decreased the neutral one. The third period shows that in reversing this procedure the neutral verbal behaviour increased while the psychotic verbal behaviour decreased.

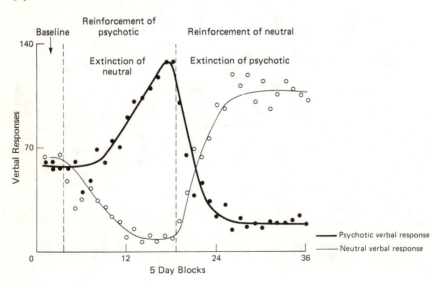

and weakened. The rapid manner in which the patient's verbalizations switched from neutral to psychotic (and vice versa) suggests that by allowing an alternative class of responses to be reinforced, the process of discrimination was hastened. These results cannot be interpreted as simply the substitution of one response for the other since, it must be remembered, each class of verbal responses was independent of the other.

In this experiment, we have a clearer picture of the degree of behavioural modification that is possible by differentially reinforcing selected classes of verbal behaviour. Despite the patient's severe psychosis the verbal modification obtained represents a very encouraging step toward a more parsimonious view of the development of peculiar verbal behaviour in schizophrenic patients. These data suggest that unusual verbal repertoires can be shaped by the social environment. Therefore, the notion of aberrant verbal behaviour as indicative of inner processes that are malfunctioning may be unnecessary. At least to the extent that the community appears to exercise considerable control over this behaviour, we may understand the frequency of different classes of verbal behaviour as being dependent upon reinforcement contingencies found in the social environment.

Experiment II

Modification of psychosomatic verbal behaviour

Subjects. The subjects in this experiment were two female patients, hereafter, referred to as Suzy and Wilma.

Suzy was a 65-year-old female patient who had been admitted to psychiatric hospitals several times during the past 20 years. She was diagnosed as chronic schizophrenic.

For the three years preceding her transfer to the experimental ward, Suzy was described as continually "complaining, tearful, depressed, whining, and crying. . . ." The medical reports described frequent inflammation of her eyes due to her crying. The following is a sample of her complaints: ". . . my nerves are shot. I can't hear anymore . . . for weeks I don't have any sleep and I'm scared to go to bed at night". While crying unconsolably, she begged the nurses to ". . . please call my daughter, I can't stand it anymore. I feel I'm going to die. Will you call the priest for me, please?" She was reported to have difficulty eating and sleeping; as a result, she was intermittently taken to the dining room and spoonfed. The patient had been given a variety of tranquilizers and medications during her hospitalization, but her complaints persisted in spite of these treatments.

Wilma was 57 years old and was diagnosed as suffering from involutional depression. In the three years preceding admission to the hospital, the patient complained of difficulty in sleeping and reported various pains centering in her back, chest, head and shoulders. Regular visits to general hospitals had failed to bring relief of her pains. She reported so many symptoms in the absence of any organic dysfunction that she was finally admitted to the mental hospital. During the two years of her hospitalization she intermittently underwent electroconvulsive therapy. Her somatic complaints, however, remained unaltered. According to the psychiatrist and nursing staff in charge of her treatment, the patient would "recite an interminable list of minor aches and pains and itchings."

Procedure

Because of their common behaviour characteristics the same technique for behavioural recording and modification was used for both patients. The experimental procedure included a baseline period during which the staff kept a continuous record of each patient's verbal approaches to the staff. During this period no reinforcement contingencies were altered.

To avoid unsystematic long conversations with a patient, all nurse—patient verbal interactions were limited to a maximum of approximately 3 min. A patient's verbal behaviour was recorded as "somatic" when it involved any references to her physical or bodily state. Typical examples of such statements were the following: "My shoulder is bothering me", "I got gas in my stomach", "I can't seem to walk", "I feel dizzy", "My nerves are shot", "I can't hear", "I feel I'm going to die", and other statements of related content. Typical examples of "neutral" verbal behaviour were: "What time is it?", "I'd like to have some paper", and "Have I got any mail?" During the patient—nurse verbal interaction, the patients' verbal behaviour could take two different forms; it could be pure (somatic or neutral alone) or it could be mixed, somatic and neutral verbalizations alternating. A verbal interaction was classified as somatic when a somatic verbal response occurred in pure or mixed form.

The baseline was followed by three experimental periods during which the nurses' reaction to the patients' somatic statements were manipulated. The first period involved extinction for somatic statements. The traditional methods for verbal interaction with the patients were discontinued. The patients were no longer consoled, given verbal encouragement, sympathy, or attention for their somatic verbalizations. The second period involved the reinforcement of somatic verbalizations. The patients were given attention and verbal encouragement for their somatic statements. The third period was a return to the extinction procedure for somatic verbalizations. Neutral statements were reinforced throughout the experiment. When the verbal interaction alternated between somatic and neutral (mixed form), the staff was trained to alternate their reaction accordingly.

Results

Listening, paying attention to and showing interest in somatic verbal responses increase the responses whereas not listening to, "ignoring" them, result in their virtual elimination. As shown in Fig. 2 and Fig. 3, the period of extinction following the baseline markedly reduced the frequency of somatic responses. These same somatic responses increased when they were followed by social reinforcement. The degree of behavioural control is clearly seen when extinction is again in force and a rapid decrease of somatic responses is observed. In both cases, extinction reduced the so-

FIGURE 2

This figure shows the original frequency of somatic verbal responses in the baseline (first period). The second period shows that extinction resulted in a drastic drop in frequency of somatic verbal responses. The third period shows that in reversing this procedure the frequency of somatic verbal responses increased although not to their original level. During the fourth period extinction was again in force and the frequency of somatic verbal responses was once again virtually eliminated. The arrow on the fourth period indicates the time when Suzy had visitors. The effects from this event seem to linger for about 4 weeks.

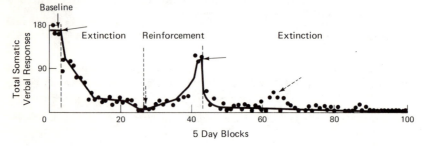

FIGURE 3

This figure shows the original frequency of somatic verbal responses in the baseline (first period). The second period shows that extinction resulted in a drastic drop in frequency of somatic verbal responses. The third period shows that in reversing this procedure the frequency of somatic verbal responses increased although not to their original level. During the fourth period extinction was again in force and the frequency of somatic verbal responses was once again virtually eliminated.

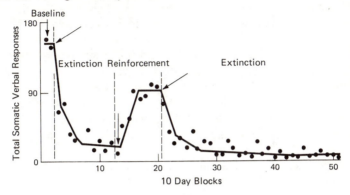

matic responses and reinforcement increased them. The broken arrow in Fig. 2 shows one instance where an extraneous event temporarily influenced the frequency of somatic responses. This occurred when a relative visited Suzy at the hospital and informed her that she had to sign some property over to her. Two days later she was interviewed by a legal adviser regarding her property. During this period the patient was particularly distressed because she regarded her relative's insistence on having the patient's property signed over to her as evidence that her family planned to leave her in the hospital.

Discussion

This experiment demonstrates that the frequency of a specific class of verbal responses can be strengthened or weakened by making social reinforcement contingent upon the presence or absence of a response. Because neutral responses were reinforced throughout this experiment, there was a time when somatic and neutral responses were reinforced concurrently. This may account for the fact that the patients' somatic verbal responses did not increase to their previous level despite over 60 days of continuous reinforcement.

During the reinforcement of somatic responses, a distinctive emotional component was observed in the patients' verbal responses. Because crying, sobbing, and sniffling occurred occasionally in association with the somatic verbal responses, the emotional component was reinforced adventitiously. During the second period of extinction the emotional behaviour decreased and the somatic responses occurred in an almost "affectless" manner, i.e., without crying or sniffling. These two patients talked to each other a great deal, and therefore, the possibility existed for them to reinforce each other's somatic responses. This potential source of reinforcement did not appear to affect the frequency of complaints as recorded by the staff. In fact, at different points in this investigation, each patient confided to our staff that the other was not "really sick". Wilma once told a staff member that she was tired of listening to Suzy complain of her aches and pains and wanted to know what she should do about it.

During the initial period of extinction for somatic responses, these patients complained that they had not eaten while in actual fact they had. Other times they complained they had been up all night unable to sleep while in fact the record showed that they not only slept but even snored! The point to be made here is that auxiliary observation involving most ward activities enabled the staff to follow accurately the patient's treatment progress.

Anyone interested in influencing the frequency of somatic verbal responses must be certain, of course, that no organic basis accounts for the patient's physical complaints. In this investigation the two patients who presented physical complaints were examined by the ward nurse on a routine basis.

What would happen when there is some basis for physical complaints is illustrated in the case of Wilma. At one point (Fig. 3, block 26) there was a substantial increase in Wilma's somatic complaints. Verbatim reports from the attendants indicated that, rather than making general somatic references, her complaints centred on a toothache. Auxiliary records revealed other behaviour changes. For example, the time sample data indicated that the patient was lying on her bed much more than usual. Further, the ward records indicated that Wilma had begun to miss meals, and also failed to participate in ward activities or to go on walks as was her custom. All of these behavioural changes suggested strongly that the patient required medical attention. Therefore, she was sent to the medical ward. There it was found that she had an abscessed tooth, and the tooth was extracted. This event points out the necessity and sensitivity of the various behavioural measures that were collected concurrently. Her overall behaviour pattern was a sensitive index of her physical well-being. Even when it had been determined that the patient was suffering some discomfort, there was no need to reinforce unduly physical complaints. In this case, the patient's physical health was attended to, and she returned to the ward where she was reinforced for her usual neutral verbalizations but not for her complaints.

At the end of this experiment, Wilma was visited by her relatives who requested that she be released from the hospital. She was discharged and has remained in the community for over three years at the time of this writing. Suzy's relatives refused to take her back to the community, but made arrangements for Suzy to visit with them from time to time.

Conclusions

The verbal interaction between attendants and patients has a controlling effect on the behaviour of psychiatric patients. These findings are in line with other data collected in clinical settings (Ayllon and Michael, 1959; Isaacs, Thomas and Goldiamond, 1960; Ayllon and Haughton, 1962; Wolf, Mees and Risley, 1963; Ayllon, 1963). The data show that social attention can be arranged so as to reinforce either normal or aberrant verbalizations.

A recurring theme found in the verbal behaviour of many mental patients concerns their physical condition. For example, some patients spend much of their time drawing the doctor's and staff's attention to headaches, dizzy spells, rashes, toothaches and sundry aches. When these somatic complaints have no organic basis, the unceasing character of the patients' complaints is not only difficult for the staff to handle but their handling may not be beneficial to the patient. What to do with a patient who complains incessantly in the absence of any organic basis still remains a practical and urgent problem in the face of the most sophisticated psychological diagnosis and therapy.

Typically, there are two ways in which the hospital staff attempts to treat or handle the patient when the patient presents obvious somatic complaints. First, the patient is given emotional support or reassurance primarily in the form of private interviews with the doctor or psychologist, or casual talks with the nurses and attendants. As the patient wears down the staff's patience, they resort to humouring the patient or "going along" with her complaints. For example, they may say, "now it isn't that bad, is it" or "why don't you rest for awhile until you feel better".

The second way of treating the patient consists of explaining to the patient the actual facts of her illness. For example, the patient may be told that there is really nothing physically wrong with her. Hospital staff frequently use a mixture of both ways of treating the patients' excessive complaints. A somewhat similar approach is followed when the patient talks in a blatantly psychotic fashion. For example, the staff may sometimes humour the patient when she claims to be "Queen Victoria", and at other times the staff may be bent on showing the patient the errors of her claims.

The effectiveness of these methods of handling undesirable verbal behaviour is highly questionable. Indeed, our findings suggest strongly that much of what passes as psychotic talk and psychosomatic complaints is strengthened, unwittingly to be sure, by the very social reaction of the staff. Further, in using an unsystematic or mixed approach to the patient's behaviour the staff may only make such verbalizations much more resistant to elimination. One of the well established findings in the behavioural laboratory is that concerning the development of extinction when the organism has had a history of continuous versus intermittent reinforcement. A daily observation in the laboratory is that extinction occurs much quicker and more completely when the organism has had a history of continuous reinforcement for the response that is to be eliminated. When the organism has had a history of intermittent reinforcement, however, the behaviour to be eliminated is highly resistant to extinction.

In the clinical situation it means that unless the psychotherapist and ward staff are intent on reinforcing and extinguishing the same classes of verbal behaviour, their inconsistent mixed approach will have the net effect of maintaining the maladaptive verbal behaviour they are expected to eliminate.

Just as it is possible to eliminate the patient's maladaptive behaviours, it is also possible to bring them back and maintain them. The powerful effectiveness of the environment in molding behaviour must not be underestimated. Hence, the hospital environment in which the patient lives must become a therapeutic environment, no longer in abstract and empty words, but in deed. The future of such an attempt lies, therefore, in a concerted effort toward "programmed therapy". Therapy must be couched in a set of objective techniques which can be easily taught and implemented by relatively untrained personnel. Whereas therapy is presently discussed at hospital staff meetings, ward meetings, and sundry meetings, the actual step-by-step method of influencing the patient's behaviour is left to the imagination of nurses and attendants.

All the sophisticated professional staff composed of psychiatrists, social workers, psychologists, counsellors, recreational therapists, etc., will not suffice if the dynamics of therapy are not translated into a practical down-to-earth form to be used by the very personnel entrusted to care for the patients. This personnel is at present made up of attendants and nurses whose day-to-day treatment of the patient is primarily based on common sense and sometimes outright superstition. The techniques illustrated in this investigation constitute an objective therapeutic tool which can be used effectively by relatively untrained hospital personnel. Hence, irrespective of theoretical persuasion and clinical conviction this tool represents a powerful instrument in the development of normal behaviour and the elimination of maladaptive behaviour in schizophrenic patients.

References

Ayllon T. and Michael J. The psychiatric nurse as a behavioral engineer. *J. exp. Anal. Behav.*, 1959, **2**, 323–334.

Ayllon T. and Haughton E. The control of behavior of schizophrenic patients by food. *J. exp. Anal. Behav.*, 1962, **5**, 343–352.

Ayllon T. Intensive treatment of psychotic behavior by stimulus satiation and food reinforcement. *Behav. Res. Ther.*, 1963, **1**, 53–61.

Azrin N. H., Holz W. C., Ulrich R. E. and Goldiamond I. The control of the content of conversation through reinforcement. *J. exp. Anal. Behav.*, 1961, **4**, 25–30.

Isaacs W., Thomas J. and Goldiamond I. Application of operant conditioning to reinstate verbal behavior in psychotics. *J. Speech Hear. Dis.*, 1960, **25**, 8–12.

Krasner L. Studies of the operant conditioning of verbal behavior. *Psychol. Bull.*, 1958, **55**, 148–170.

Lane H. Temporal and intensive properties of human vocal responding under a schedule of reinforcement. *J. exp. Anal. Behav.*, 1960, **3**, 183–192.

Lindsley O. Operant conditioning methods applied to research in chronic schizophrenia. *Psychiat. Res. Rep.*, 1956, **5**, 118–139.

Lindsley O. Reduction in rate of vocal psychotic symptoms by differential positive reinforcement. *J. exp. Anal. Behav.*, 1959, **2**, 269.

Salzinger K. and Pisoni S. Reinforcement of affect responses of schizophrenics during the clinical interview. *J. abnorm. (soc.) Psychol.*, 1958, **57**, 89–90.

Salzinger K. Experimental manipulation of verbal behavior: a review. *J. genet. Psychol.*, 1959, **61**, 65–95.

Skinner B. F. *Verbal Behavior*. Appleton-Century-Crofts, New York.

Verplanck W. S. The control of the content of conversation: reinforcement of statements of opinion. *J. abnorm. (soc.) Psychol.*, 1955, **51**, 668–676.

Wolf M. Mees H. and Risley T. Application of operant conditioning procedures to the behavior problems of an autistic child. *Behav. Res. Ther.*, 1963, **1**, 305–312.

3/ Aversive Control

Aversive control normally refers to any instrumental conditioning procedure in which the experimenter controls behavior by presenting or withholding an aversive US. In escape and avoidance conditioning, for example, the designated response increases in probability (speed, frequency, and so on) over trials when termination (in the case of escape) or nonoccurrence (in the case of avoidance) of the painful US is contingent on the CR. In contrast, behavior is suppressed during punishment because shock or some other aversive US is delivered following the response.

The study of aversive control has been uniquely important in learning research for a variety of reasons. First, it has provided the testing ground for a number of theories (for example, Mowrer's two-factor theory) that have implications ranging far beyond the paradigm in which they are studied. Second, the study of aversive control has helped psychologists to better understand the mechanisms by which punishment or threat of punishment affects us and, in particular, the relationship between punishment procedures and mental disorders. Finally, the study of avoidance and punishment has provided a useful perspective to our overall understanding of the learning process. Because many of the stimuli in our environment that foster learning are highly aversive, it is important not to ignore the study of aversive control.

Two papers have been selected to represent current work in this area. The first, by Bolles, Stokes, and Younger (1966), deals with the two-factor theory. It shows that although immediate offset of the CS during avoidance training does facilitate performance (a prediction that is crucial for Mowrer's theory), the offset does not serve as the reinforcer per se. The second paper, by Church, Wooten, and Matthews (1970), shows that an aversive US presentation leads to two separate outcomes: fear of the stimulus that preceded the punisher and suppression of the particular response on which the punisher was contingent. Papers such as these have deepened our understanding of aversive control as it operates both in the laboratory and in our society.

DOES CS TERMINATION REINFORCE AVOIDANCE BEHAVIOR?

Robert C. Bolles, Louis W. Stokes, and Mary Sue Younger

This paper by Robert C. Bolles, Louis W. Stokes, and Mary Sue Younger (1966) deals with the following important question: "What is the reinforcer for avoidance learning?" According to traditional theory, the CS plays a significant role in avoidance. For example, the CS was thought to create fear in the subjects (of the pending aversive US) and its offset was claimed to be the reward. In other words, the onset of the CS was fear-*inducing* (it motivated the subject to perform) while the offset of the CS was fear-*reducing* (it reinforced the behavior that preceded the offset). It is this latter notion, that the CS offset is the reinforcing event for avoidance behavior, that is addressed in this important paper.

The first two experiments are the most significant. All the subjects were given a noise CS followed 10 seconds later by a shock US; the measure of avoidance learning was the number of responses (running from one compartment to the other) made to the CS alone. The groups differed in terms of what effect their response had on the CS and US. For some rats, a response during the CS avoided shock (A condition); for others, a running response terminated the shock (the E condition); and for still other rats, a response during the CS immediately terminated the noise (the T condition). This latter condition, of course, should be the most important factor leading to avoidance learning if, indeed, the traditional theory were correct.

The results disconfirmed traditional theory: CS-offset was not the most critical aspect for avoidance learning (although having the ability to terminate the noise CS did lead to more efficient performance). What appeared to be the most important factor was the actual ability to avoid the shock.

Experiments 3 through 5 were essentially control studies designed to discount alternative explanations. In the first of these, the US duration was varied. The results, like those in Experiment 1, confirmed that the avoidance behavior had not been learned "superstitiously" as a result of shock termination. In Experiments 4 and 5, a trace conditioning procedure was employed: the brief CS was terminated well before the shock presentation, thus discounting CS-offset as a potential reinforcer for avoidance. Again, in both of these last experiments, the ability to avoid the shock proved to be most important for avoidance learning.

Many theorists rely almost exclusively upon the idea that discriminated avoidance behavior is reinforced by CS termination. Either it is assumed that the CS itself acquires aversive properties so that escaping it is reinforcing (Schoenfeld, 1950), or it is assumed that CS termination reduces the acquired fear drive (Miller, 1951). But there is a growing body of evidence which makes it increasingly difficult to attribute the maintenance of avoidance behavior solely to CS termination. For example, Kamin, Brimer, and Black (1963), using a CER procedure to monitor fear of the CS, tested different Ss at different stages of avoidance training and found that fear diminished as avoidance became stronger. They concluded that avoidance behavior was maintained by variables other than fear of the CS.

Sidman (1955) and Sidman and Boren (1957) employed an experimental design in which Ss could avoid or postpone the US by responding during the CS and could also postpone the CS by responding prior to its onset. Contrary to what would be expected if the CS were aversive, the discrimination procedure resulted in a concentration of responses in the presence of the CS and little indication that Ss would postpone its occurrence. Keehn (1959) reported a similar finding in a wheel-running situation. The CS in these cases appears to serve a discriminative rather than aversive role. Further evidence for a nonaversive property of the CS was found by Lockard (1963), who gave Ss unavoidable shocks, but gave them a choice of having shock preceded by a CS or not preceded by a CS; Ss preferred having the CS.

We will not consider here the difficult problem of accounting for the acquisition of avoidance when there is no explicit CS (Sidman, 1953); there is trouble enough with the CS-termination hypothesis even in those situations which are arranged to favor it.

Experiment 1

Kamin (1956) attempted to separate CS termination and US avoidance as potential sources of reinforcement for avoidance behavior in a shuttle box. The Ss run under "normal" conditions could both terminate the CS and avoid the US by making a response during the CS-US interval. Such Ss achieved a level of performance of 78%, while control Ss who could neither terminate the CS nor avoid the US performed at only the 22% level. The Ss who could avoid the US but not terminate the CS responded at 47%, while those who could not avoid the US but could terminate the CS responded at 43%. Kamin argued that CS termination was the important factor in reinforcement, and that those Ss who appeared to be reinforced by avoidance of shock were in fact reinforced by the delayed termination of the CS. The reason given why Ss who could only terminate the CS did not do better than they did was that for them the response was invariably followed by shock.

From "Does CS Termination Reinforce Avoidance Behavior?" by Robert C. Bolles, Louis W. Stokes and Mary Sue Younger in *Journal of Comparative and Physiological Psychology*, Volume 62, Number 2, 1966. Copyright 1966 by the American Psychological Association. Reprinted by permission.

However, there is another source of response strength in Kamin's situation, namely, the shock-escape contingency. All of Kamin's Ss had to terminate shock by making this same response. It will be argued here that escape from shock is the principal source of response strength under all of the conditions Kamin used and that CS termination is at best a minor factor in avoidance. In Experiment 1, four groups of Ss were run in a replication of Kamin's study, and four additional groups were run under conditions in which the US was of very short duration, too short for S to escape.

METHOD

Subjects and apparatus. The Ss were 80 female Sprague-Dawley rats, about 90 days old. The apparatus was a black shuttle box 6 × 25 × 21 in. The door between the two compartments was always open. The box was enclosed in a soundproof cabinet with a one-way window. Throughout these experiments the shock was 1.1 ma. dc from a constant current source fed through a Lehigh Valley scrambler to the grid floor, and the CS was white noise of about 80 db. Automatic timing and other programming apparatus were located in a separate room. The *E* pressed one button to register the occurrence of a criterion response, and another to present the short shock.

Procedure. The CS came on 10 sec. before a scheduled shock and, unless it was terminated by S's response, lasted just 10 sec., i.e., CS and US never overlapped. For the four shock-escape groups (designated E) shock remained on until S escaped it by running to the other side, but for the four short-shock groups the shock had an approximately constant duration of .3 sec. The criterion response (CR) for all groups was defined as moving from one side of the box to the other in the presence of the CS. For the avoid-only Ss (Groups AE and A) a CR would prevent shock onset but would not terminate the CS. For the terminate CS-only Ss (Groups TE and T) a CR would terminate the CS but would not prevent onset of the US. For the "normal" Ss (Groups TAE and TA) a CR effected both shock avoidance and CS termination, while for the "control" *Ss* (Groups E and —) a CR neither avoided the US nor terminated the CS.

Preliminary investigation had shown that *Ss* run under the short-shock conditions responded on only about 15% of the trials; hence in the present study *Ss* in the short-shock groups received the advantage of additional reinforcements in the attempt to shape up their behavior to successive approximations of the desired CR. Since the predominant initial behavior was freezing, the potential reinforcing events (termination of the CS or avoidance of the shock) were initially made contingent upon the occurrence of any bodily movement. Subsequently, an orientation toward the door was required; ultimately the full running response was required. The full CR was always reinforced when it occurred, however. The inter-trial interval was 30 sec., and all *Ss* were run for a single session of 100 trials.

Results

Since all of the analyses of response strength yielded the same pattern, only the data from the number of CRs per session will be presented. The median number of CRs for each group is shown in Table 1. An analysis of variance of the number of CRs per *S* showed that all three main effects were highly significant. The most impressive source of variation, accounting for over one-quarter of the total, was that attributable to whether or not shock could be avoided ($F = 34.5$, $df = 1/72$, $p < .0001$). The difference between the escapable and inescapable shock Ss was highly significant ($F = 18.1$); the CS-termination variable was significant ($F = 8.6$), as

TABLE 1

Median CRs in 100 Training Trials as a Function of Whether the CR Terminates the CS (T), Avoids the US (A), or Escapes the US (E)

		Experimental condition	Median CRs
	A	E	70
		—	37
T			
		E	31
	—	—	10
		E	40
	A	—	15
—			
		E	9
	—	—	14

were the T × E interaction ($F = 4.7$) and the A × T × E interaction ($F = 11.7$). These interactions took the form of the CS-termination contingency having little efficacy unless S had the shock-escape or shock-avoidance contingency as well.

It is not simply the case that the operant rate of the CR was too low for the reinforcement contingencies to be applied. The complete CR occurred on about 15% of the trials, even for the poorest groups, and occurred in partial or incomplete form on approximately another 20% of the trials in which the US-avoidance or CS-termination contingencies were applied in an attempt to shape up the CR. The poor performance of the T and A groups therefore indicates that neither withholding the US alone nor terminating the CS alone was effective in maintaining avoidance behavior. And, indeed, it would appear from these results that no one of the three potential reinforcement contingencies acting by itself was able to maintain avoidance behavior.

Experiment 2

The question here is what would happen if the criterion response were one which had a much higher initial rate in the avoidance situation than running has in the shuttle box. Specifically, what would happen if the CR were of considerable strength because of the peculiar nature of S, or of the test situation, rather than because it had acquired strength through shock-escape training?

METHOD

Of 55 female Sprague-Dawley rats, 2 Ss were discarded for exceeding an arbitrary upper limit of spontaneous intertrial responses during training, while 5 other Ss were discarded for failure to respond.

A running wheel was constructed with Plexiglas sides, an inside width of 4½ in., and a diameter of 14 in. The grid floor was ⅜-in. stainless steel bars 1 in. center to center. Current was brought to the grid floor by a slip ring commutator. An inner ceiling of Plexiglas prevented S from jumping onto the axle. The wheel was quite heavy, requiring a force of approximately 120 gm. applied tangentially to start it moving.

To allow for spontaneous running immediately prior to onset of the CS, such running was not considered a CR. To be credited with a CR, S had to stop and initiate a new run during the remaining part of the CS-US interval; failure to do so led to shock. The CR was defined as a quarter turn of the wheel in either direction. The experimental design, involving termination of the CS, avoidance of the US, and escape from the US, and the procedure were the same as in Experiment 1.

Results

Figure 1 gives the mean number of CRs for each group by blocks of 20 trials. An analysis of variance of the number of CRs for each S indicated that there was a huge effect attributable to the avoidance-no avoidance variable ($F = 32.1, df = 1/40, p < .0001$), and a smaller but still significant effect of the CS-termination variable ($F = 5.7$). Neither the US-escape variable nor any of the interactions was significant. Other measures of CR strength, such as trials to a criterion, number of consecutive CRs, and latency of the CR, showed the same pattern.

It should be noted that the number of intertrial responses (ITRs) was considerably higher in the running wheel than it was in the shuttle box. Moreover the number of ITRs was highly correlated across conditions with avoidance performance. However, the good avoidance performance of

FIGURE 1

The acquisition of the CR in a running wheel as a function of whether CS could be terminated (T), US could be avoided (A), or US could be escaped (E).

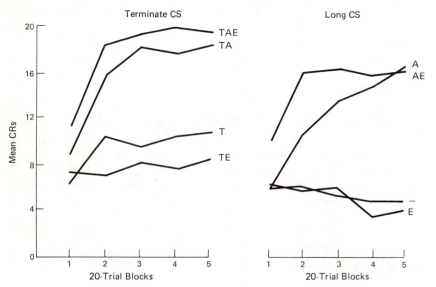

the avoidance *S*s cannot be explained just on the basis of their high level of wheel running. Most ITRs occurred shortly after the occurrence of a CR and the rate dropped over the intertrial interval. Considering the four avoidance groups, there were no ITRs on over one-third of the trials, and on nearly two-thirds of the trials there were no ITRs during the 10 sec. immediately preceding CS onset. By contrast, the median latency of the CR over all trials for the avoidance *S*s was 4 sec. Thus the probability of responding to the CS was much higher than would be expected from the rate of ITRs, and therefore, although the avoidance performance of these *S*s was highly correlated with their ITR rate, both factors must be attributed to some aspects of the experimental situation other than, or in addition to, the high operant rate of running in the wheel.

It is suggested that running occurred in the wheel primarily because such a response is compatible with the rat's "natural" defense reactions in fear-eliciting situations, and that running occurred in the shuttle box primarily because the shock-escape response generalized forward in time. Then in both cases the response can be assumed to continue at strength as long as fear is maintained (see Experiment 5), and as long as the CR avoids shock, i.e., provided it is not followed by shock.

Experiment 3

It is possible that as short as the US was in the previous experiments, it was long enough to provide some superstitious reinforcement by US termination. Or perhaps the CR was reinforced even if *S* started to respond at the time the US went off. Experiment 3 tested this possibility by systematically varying US duration from a value shorter than *S*'s reaction time to a value longer than that used in the previous experiments.

METHOD

Four groups of 10 *S*s each were run under the same conditions and with the same apparatus as the short-shock *S*s of Experiment 2, except that for different groups shock was presented for .1, .2, .3, or .4 sec. A Foringer grid scrambler was used because it administered shock to *S* sooner, on the average, when shock was nominally presented.

Results

The duration of short shocks was not a critical variable in the acquisition of avoidance under these circumstances. The median percentage of CRs over the session for each group was: .1 sec., 86%; .2 sec., 91%; .3 sec., 88%; and .4 sec., 88%. At .1 sec., a duration so short that *S* frequently failed to react visibly to it, *S* still showed very good avoidance learning. There were no systematic differences in the rate of CR acquisition or in the latency of the CR as a function of US duration.

The finding that the acquisition of avoidance is relatively independent of the duration of the US suggests that (*a*) the previous experiments were not seriously limited by the human element in US presentation, and (b) avoidance behavior was not being superstitiously maintained in this situation by being coincident with US termination.

Experiment 4

The following experiment elaborated Experiment 2 by using a trace conditioning procedure to eliminate the possibility of delayed reinforcement from the delayed termination of the CS for the avoid-only Ss. It is, of course, somewhat embarrassing for the CS-termination hypothesis that avoidance can be acquired at all with a trace procedure (Kamin, 1954).

METHOD

Thirty-two naive female Sprague-Dawley rats approximately 90 days old were run in the running wheel described above.

The CS was presented for .5 sec., its onset preceding shock onset by 10 sec., as in Experiment 2. Four groups were run, two which could avoid the US and two which could not. For each pair of groups the US was escapable for one group and of fixed .5-sec. duration for the other. Other procedures were the same as in Experiment 2.

Results

Figure 2 gives the mean number of CRs for each group by blocks of 20 trials. An analysis of variance of the number of CRs for each S showed that the avoidance variable was highly significant ($F = 19.0$, $df = 1/28$, $p < .001$), and the escape contingency was just significant ($F = 4.41$). The

FIGURE 2

The acquisition of the CR in a running wheel as a function of whether US could be avoided (A), or US could be escaped (E).

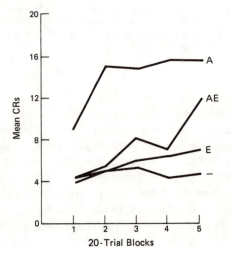

significant interaction ($F = 7.71$) indicates that the shock-escape contingency led to poorer performance in Ss that could avoid the US. Evidently the escape contingency can lead to interference in the acquisition of the avoidance response, even though ostensibly the same response is required in the two situations. Although comparisons across studies must be made with some reservation, it appears that all groups showed some decrement in performance compared with the respective groups in Experiment 2, and that the AE group showed a marked decrement.

The number of ITRs was approximately the same for comparable groups between Experiments 2 and 4 also, except for Group A, which had a disproportionately high number of ITRs. Indeed, the amount of ITR behavior was so high among Group A Ss as to raise the suspicion that they might not be responding differently to the CS. This suspicion was confirmed by running several supplementary Ss under the avoidance-only condition for 30 trials, at which point the percentage CRs was over 80%, and by then simply omitting the CS for the last 70 trials. The mean percentage of CRs, i.e., avoidance responses during the 10 sec. preceding shock, was 86%. These Ss were avoiding shock by responding on what amounts to a Sidman schedule, i.e., in the absence of any specific CS. It seems most likely that Ss in Group A reported in Figure 2 were also avoiding without responding to the CS.

This conclusion gives further support to the hypothesis that in the running wheel the avoidance response quickly comes to predominate in S's behavior because it is a natural defense reaction elicited by fear in the situation. It is no less an avoidance response on that account. We propose that the avoidance response fails to become conditioned specifically to the CS, not because it no longer terminates the CS, but more simply because the CS is no longer present when the response occurs. With the trace procedure S is deprived not only of the opportunity to terminate the CS, but also of the CS itself. The poorer performance of the short-CS groups relative to the long-CS groups of Experiment 2 can then be attributed to the reduced stimulus support provided for the avoidance response. The poorer performance of both sets of groups relative to the T groups in Experiment 2 can be attributed to the reduction in immediate sensory feedback following the CR, a factor which Bolles and Popp (1964) have reported to be of some importance in the acquisition of Sidman avoidance. So rather than CS termination being considered reinforcing because the CS is aversive, we propose that when CS termination is found to facilitate the acquisition of avoidance, it is because it provides immediate sensory feedback.

Experiment 5

The purpose of this experiment was to examine the effectiveness of a trace conditioning procedure in maintaining avoidance behavior that had been partially learned under different conditions. It was hypothesized that once the correct response has acquired some strength, it will continue to gain in strength without the CS-termination contingency.

METHOD

Twenty-three naive female Sprague-Dawley rats approximately 90 days old were trained in the running wheel. All Ss were randomly assigned to running orders; if an S failed to reach the initial learning criterion of three consecutive CRs within the first 25 trials, it was discarded and replaced by the next S on the running list. Five Ss were discarded by this criterion.

Phase 1 of the experiment was identical for all groups. The Ss were given the usual training with a 10-sec. CS during which a CR would both terminate the CS and avoid the US; the US was escapable throughout. As soon as S made three consecutive avoidances it went immediately to Phase 2 of the experiment, in which a trace conditioning procedure was used. A .5-sec. CS began 10 sec. prior to US onset. The Ss in the AE group could avoid the US by responding during the 9.5-sec. period between CS offset and shock onset. The Ss in the E (no-avoid) group could not avoid the US but could escape the US. The Ss in Group C (control) received no shock during Phase 2 of the experiment whether or not they responded to the CS; but the brief CS came on as for the other Ss and any response during the following 9.5 sec. was counted as a CR. All Ss were run for 100 trials in Phase 2.

Results

Mann-Whitney U tests indicated no significant differences among groups in the first phase of training on trials to the first CR, latency of the first CR, trials to criterion, or number of CS-US pairing. Thus, there appears to have been satisfactory randomization of the groups.

Figure 3 gives the mean number of CRs for each group by blocks of 20 trials. The AE group was significantly superior to the other two groups ($F = 9.39$, $df = 2/15$, $p < .01$) in terms of number of CRs per session. So again the wheel-turning avoidance response was readily acquired without a CS-termination contingency provided that S was permitted to avoid the US.

The behavioral collapse of Group C, which received no US in Phase 2, demonstrated that the behavior of Group AE was not maintained merely because it was not punished. If such were the case, then the AE Ss should perform no better than the C Ss because both groups started Phase 2 with the response at the same strength and for both groups the response was free from punishment.[1] Actually, the C Ss showed marked immobility, and, later in the session, considerable grooming; one S went to sleep. Evidently the few shocks received by the AE Ss in Phase 2 were essential for the maintenance of suitable strengths of the running response and, presumably, fear. Running in the wheel, we propose, was governed primarily by fear.

These five experiments suggest that although CS termination may have some small effect on the strength of the CR (perhaps merely because

[1] The superiority of the AE Ss cannot be attributed to the E contingency since supplementary Ss run with just the A contingency, i.e., with short inescapable shock, also performed quite well.

FIGURE 3

The acquisition of the CR in a running wheel as a function of the avoidability and the presence of the US.

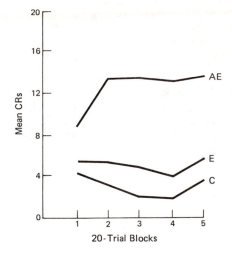

it is a distinctive stimulus), there is reason to doubt whether CS termination serves as the principal source of reinforcement for the CR. The major factor in avoidance learning appears to be the avoidance or the nonoccurrence of shock. It appears also that some factor other than avoidance can be important in the initial trials to insure that the response is of sufficient strength for avoidance to occur. Thus, if the response is initially very high in the animal's repertoire, i.e., one of the animal's species-specific defense reactions, then the avoidance response may be acquired just because it does avoid shock. Running in the wheel appears to meet these requirements. But in the shuttle box situation, where the rate of the required response is initially quite low, the strength that the response gains by termination of shock appears to be an important factor in raising it to the point where it is likely to occur prior to shock. However, we have seen that such shock-escape running in the wheel may interfere with the running controlled by fear or by the CS.

References

Bolles, R. C., & Popp, R. J. Parameters affecting the acquisition of Sidman avoidance. *J. exp. Anal. Behav.*, 1964, **7**, 315–321.

Kamin, L. J. Traumatic avoidance learning: The effects of CS-US interval with a trace-conditioning procedure, *J. comp. physiol. Psychol.*, 1954, **47**, 65–72.

Kamin, L. J. The effects of termination of the CS and avoidance of the US on avoidance learning. *J. comp. physiol. Psychol.*, 1956, **49**, 420–424.

Kamin, L. J., Brimer, C. J., & Black, A. II. Conditioned suppression as a monitor of fear of the CS in the course of avoidance training. *J. comp. physiol. Psychol.*, 1963, **56,** 497–501.

Keehn, J. D. The effect of a warning signal on unrestricted avoidance behavior. *Brit. J. Psychol.*, 1959, **50,** 125–135.

Lockard, J. S. Choice of a warning signal or no warning signal in an unavoidable shock situation. *J. comp. physiol. Psychol.*, 1963, **56,** 526–530.

Miller, N. E. Learnable drives and rewards. In S. S. Stevens (Ed.), *Handbook of experimental psychology.* New York: Wiley, 1951. Pp. 435–472.

Schoenfeld, W. N. An experimental approach to anxiety, escape, and avoidance behavior. In P. H. Hoch & J. Zubin (Eds.), *Anxiety.* New York: Grune & Stratton, 1950. Pp. 70–99.

Sidman, M. Two temporal parameters of the maintenance of avoidance behavior in the white rat. *J. comp. physiol. Psychol.*, 1953, **46,** 253–261.

Sidman, M. Some properties of the warning stimulus in avoidance situation. *J. comp. physiol. Psychol.*, 1955, **48,** 444–450.

Sidman, M., & Boren, J. J. A comparison of two types of warning stimulus in an avoidance situation. *J. comp. physiol. Psychol.*, 1957, **50,** 282–287.

DISCRIMINATIVE PUNISHMENT AND
THE CONDITIONED EMOTIONAL RESPONSE

Russel M. Church, Carol L. Wooten, and
T. James Matthews

This paper by Russell M. Church, Carol L. Wooten, and T. James Matthews (1970) represents an important contribution to our understanding of aversive control. Here, the authors have made an attempt to understand why the presentation of aversive stimuli suppresses behavior. Their studies specifically compare and contrast two sources of response suppression—one based on the stimulus/shock relationship, and the other on the response/shock relationship.

In Experiment 1, rats were first trained to press a lever to obtain food. Then, response suppression due to a CER (conditioned emotional response) procedure was compared with suppression due to a discriminated punishment procedure. The former case involves the presentation of a signal and shock (administered independent of lever pressing) whereas the latter procedure involves a response/shock contingency in addition to the signal/shock relationship. The results of this study clearly showed that suppression for the punishment group was much greater than for the CER group.

In a second experiment, the authors reasoned that suppression would not be as severe in the punished group once the type of response were changed; after all, much of the suppression was presumably due to the specific response/shock contingency which would be absent if the response were changed. However, a change from one type of response to another should not produce a change in suppression for the CER subjects; for them, the cause of suppression is merely the fear signal, not the specific behavior. Using two responses, lever pressing and chain pulling, but otherwise the same general methodology as in the first study, the authors confirmed their hypothesis.

The final study was an extension of Experiment 2. Here the authors were interested in showing that when all animals were required to make both responses, the punished response would become more suppressed than the response not directly followed by shock. Again, the results confirmed that the CER procedure involves only a single source of suppression (the signal/shock relationship) whereas the discriminated punishment method has an additional source (the specific response/shock contingency).

In a *discriminative punishment* situation an aversive event is contingent upon both a signal and a response. For example, a brief electric shock may occur only following the lever response of a rat in the presence of a white noise signal. Since the aversive event never occurs following any response other than a lever response, and since it never occurs in the absence of the white noise, the aversive event is contingent upon both a signal and a response. In a *conditioned emotional response* (CER) situation an aversive event is contingent upon a signal,[1] but independent of any response. For example, a brief electric shock may occur only in the presence of a white noise signal, regardless of the behavior of the animal.

The discriminative punishment procedure is related to the CER procedure since there is a contingency between signal and aversive event in both cases. This has led some psychologists to attempt to account for the results of punishment experiments in terms of a conditioned emotional response (the CER theory of punishment). Meanwhile, psychologists interested in the CER have noted that the aversive event in such procedures

[1] The experimenter-controlled stimulus in a classical conditioning procedure, such as CER, is usually identified as a conditioned stimulus (CS); the same stimulus in a situation involving instrumental training, such as the discriminative punishment procedure, is usually identified as a discriminative stimulus (SD). The word "signal" was chosen to refer to the experimenter-controlled stimulus in either classical conditioning or instrumental training procedures

often occurs shortly after an instrumental response. This has led to a punishment theory of CER. Neither of these attempts to unify discriminative punishment and the CER has been satisfactory.

The CER Theory of Punishment

A punishment procedure is one in which an aversive event is contingent upon a response, but a CER theory of punishment would attempt to explain the consequences of this procedure without reference to the response. The general notion is that response suppression occurs because of an association between signals and aversive events, not because of an association between responses and aversive events. Although response-contingent shock (punishment) may produce response suppression, a brief electric shock that is independent of any response may also disrupt the performance of an appetitive response. In both cases the magnitude of suppression is positively related to the severity of the aversive event (see, for example, Church, 1969). Presumably, the association of the electric shock with the contextual cues of the apparatus is sufficient to lead to a generalized suppression of active responses.

Estes (1944) made a direct comparison of the effects of response-contingent shock with noncontingent shock, and since the behavior of the subjects in these two groups of that experiment were indistinguishable, he concluded, "The important correlation appears to be that between the shock and the stimuli which normally act as the occasion for the occurrence of the response rather than between the shock and the response per se." In some cases, e.g., Estes (1944, Experiment L), the contingency between response and aversive event was a factor in the magnitude of suppression, and Estes concluded that "part of the effect of punishment is quite specific to the punished response."

For some time it has been clear that the magnitude of response suppression is greater when the aversive event is contingent upon a response than when it is independent of the response (Church, 1963), and recent research evidence continues to support this principle. If an aversive event becomes available at random intervals of time, the magnitude of response suppression is greater when the aversive event is presented immediately after the next response than when it is presented as soon as it is available. Furthermore, there is greater suppression if a response-contingent shock occurs as soon as it is earned rather than a long delay after it is earned (Camp, Raymond, & Church, 1967). The recent data from replications of Estes' procedures are also consistent with the principle that the magnitude of response suppression is greater if the aversive events are contingent upon a response than if they are independent of responding (Boe & Church, 1967). Since the magnitude of suppression is greater for punishment than for noncontingent shock, the CER is not a sufficient explanation of the suppression produced by punishment.

The comparisons that have just been discussed were between punishment and noncontingent shock, and they did not involve the presentation of an experimenter-controlled signal. Normally, the CER procedure involves an experimenter-controlled signal, and the effectiveness of the treatment is measured by the response rate during the signal relative to the response rate prior to the signal. Such comparisons between CER and discriminative punishment show that the magnitude of suppression during a signal is greater if the shock that occurs during signal is contingent upon a response rather than independent of a response (Azrin, 1956). This difference in the magnitude of suppression discredits the CER theory of punishment. Punishment may involve the CER, but it must also involve something additional. The correlation between the response and the aversive event is not inconsequential.

The Punishment Theory of CER

In most experimental studies of the conditioned emotional response a subject is first trained to make a response, and then it is exposed to a signal several times so that the mere occurrence of the signal will not reduce the response rate. These procedures virtually guarantee that the aversive event, delivered at the end of the signal of several minutes' duration, will occur only shortly after a response. Thus, a CER procedure may be characterized as involving a short, variable delay between response and aversive event (in the presence of a signal); a discriminative punishment procedure normally involves no delay between response and aversive event. The fact that discriminative punishment leads to greater suppression than CER is no embarrassment to the punishment theory of CER since greater suppression would be expected with an immediate than a delayed aversive event. Azrin (1956) noted that the reduction of response rate during the signal in the CER procedure "may very well be due to adventitious coincidences of the 'uncorrelated' shocks with the responses," and this is the punishment theory of CER.

The punishment theory of CER is untenable, however, for at least three reasons: (1) A signal will produce response suppression when the contingency between signal and aversive event was established in a different apparatus. Of course, one might argue that the signal, a secondary punisher, will often occur only shortly after a response, but this kind of argument regarding adventitious reinforcement or punishment is unconvincing. Only after the behavior of the animal has been described is it possible to invoke the principle of superstition to predict what the animal will do in the future and to explain why the animal is performing that response and not some other. (2) The critical fact is that the aversive event is not contingent upon a response, i.e., the probability of an aversive event given one or more responses in any interval of time is equal to the probability of an aversive event given no response in that interval of time. If an aversive event occurs shortly after a response, a subject may respond more slowly (punishment), but then the next aversive event is likely to occur when the subject is responding slowly so that it should increase its speed (Sidman avoidance). Aversive events occurring randomly in time affect behavior in various ways: they may retard the development of the learning of subsequent contingencies (Overmier & Seligman, 1967), they may lead to overall changes in response rate, and they may elicit various responses. The principle of adventitious punishment could account for an increase or a decrease in response rate with equal plausibility. It has been used post hoc to explain why behavior that emerged must have emerged, but it is a principle seldom invoked in the prediction of behavior. (3) The punishment theory of CER implies that differences between punishment and CER are only quantitative, but observers have reported gross differences in the behavior of subjects under the two procedures. Hunt and Brady (1955) described the CER subject as generally frightened (defecation, and immobility) and the discriminative punishment subjects as passive avoiders of a specific instrumental response (abortive lesser presses). The present study extends the examination of the qualitative differences in the suppression produced by CER and discriminative punishment.

Contingency of an Aversive Event upon Signal and Response

The present experiments were designed to evaluate the effect of the addition of a response contingency to signal contingency, i.e., to compare discriminative punishment with the conditioned emotional response procedure. The addition of the response contingency to the signal contingency was expected to increase the magnitude of the response suppression and to change its nature. The working assumption was that the suppression produced by the CER procedure would be independent of any particular response, but that the suppression produced by discriminative punishment would involve response specificity. Thus subjects in both situations would be afraid in the presence of the signal, but only subjects in the discriminative punishment procedure would be afraid of making any particular response.

METHOD

Subjects

The subjects were 108 naive, male, albino, Norway rats from hysterectomy-derived, barrier-sustained stock (Charles River CD) that arrived from the breeding laboratories at 49 days of age.

Apparatus

The apparatus consisted of six Skinner boxes with inside dimensions of 9⅛×8×8⅝ in. The front and back were aluminum, the two sides were transparent acrylic, and the floor was composed of 16 stainless steel bars, 5/32 in. in diameter and spaced 9/16 in. apart. The box was enclosed in an ice chest which also contained a pellet dispenser, a 7½-W bulb directly over the lever box, and a blower. The ice chest had an acrylic window to permit the experimenter to observe the rat during the experiment.

A lever and a bead chain could be inserted into the boxes. The stainless steel lever (½ × 2 in., and 2 in. above the floor) projected about ⅞ in. into the box, and it required a force of about 25 gm to activate a microswitch. The bead chain (7 in. long) hung into the chamber approximately 1 in. above the floor on the approximate location of the lever, and it was attached to a microswitch mounted on the top of the chamber.

Positive reinforcement was provided by 45-mg Noyes rat food tablets. The aversive event was an electric shock delivered from a matched impedance shock source (150-Kohms series resistance) to the bars of the floor, the aluminum walls, and the lever. The signal stimulus was white noise of approximately 70 db re .0002 dyne/cm² from a Grason-Stadler noise generator (Model 901A) into speakers located in each box. The control and recording apparatus was located in a separate room.

Pretraining Procedure

The rats were caged individually and water was accessible at all times in the home cages. They were fed a daily ration of 14 gm ground Purina Chow mixed with 25 cc of water, and during the week preceding the first pretraining session, each rat was removed from its cage, stroked for about 15 sec, and then returned to its home cage. In a single session of magazine training, the subject was placed in the Skinner box without either a lever or a chain, and one pellet was delivered each minute for 30 min. In the next pretraining session the lever was inserted in the box, and the subject was permitted to press the lever 30 times. Each of these responses was reinforced. Those subjects that had not made 30 responses in 30 min were trained with a shaping procedure. Except for these pretraining periods, all sessions were 30 min in length and each subject was given its session at approximately the same time each day, 5 days per week.

Measures

The two measures were the response rate and the suppression ratio.[2] The response rate was recorded separately during the signal and in the absence of the signal. The suppression ratio was $B/(A + B)$, where B was the response rate during the two 3-min signals of a session and A was the response rate during the 3-min periods prior to the signals.

Experiment 1

Magnitude of Suppression

The conditioned emotional response procedure involves a contingency between a signal and an aversive event, and it leads to response suppression. The discriminative punishment procedure involves a contingency between a response and an aversive event as well as a contingency between a signal and an aversive event. Because of the additional contingency, the discriminative punishment procedure may lead to greater response suppression than the conditioned emotional response procedure (Azrin, 1956).

Procedure

Reinforcement training (*Sessions 1–8*). Lever responses were reinforced on a 1-min variable-interval schedule, i.e., on the average of once a minute, a reinforcement was primed so that the next lever response was reinforced. In addition, during Sessions 6–8 a white noise signal was presented during Minutes 6–8 and 21–23 of the 30-min session. This was designed to produce habituation to the signal.

[2] The suppression ratio has been found to be more sensitive to treatment effects than several other measures of the magnitude of response suppression (Church, 1969). In the absence of any treatment effect, the expected value of the mean of a number of suppression ratios is .500. The ratio, B/A, although it is as sensitive as the suppression ratio, does not have this feature—in the absence of any treatment effect the expected value of the mean of a number of ratios is somewhat above 1.0.

Treatment (Sessions 9–13). Thirty subjects were randomly partitioned into two groups of 15 rats each. Both groups continued to receive the same schedule of reinforcement and the same signals as during Sessions 6–8. In addition, one group received a discriminative punishment treatment, and the other group received a conditioned emotional response treatment. During the two 3-min periods of signal, a shock was primed on a 1-min random-interval schedule (i.e., the probability of a shock in each 2-sec interval was 1/30, irrespective of the occurrence of any previous shocks).[3] The same random schedule was used for all subjects in a particular session, but a different schedule was used for each session. The shock was 210 V in intensity for a duration of 0.2 sec. These shocks were delivered either as soon as they were primed (CER) or immediately following the first response after they were primed (discriminative punishment).

Results

In the absence of the signal the mean response rate of the subjects in the discriminative punishment group and the CER group were similar (17.8 and 15.7 responses per minute, respectively; $F_{1,28} = 0.4, p > .05$). The mean suppression ratios during the five days of treatment are shown in Figure 1. Subjects in the discriminative punishment group were significantly more suppressed than subjects in the CER group ($F_{1,27} = 13.8, p < .001$). The treatment accounted for about 31% of the variance.[4]

Experiment 2

Response Specificity: The Response-Shift Procedure

The conditioned emotional response procedure does not involve a contingency between an aversive event and any particular response. The signal produces a general suppression of all active responses. Thus, if the CER were established while the animal was pressing a lever, the signal should lead to suppression of lever pressing, but it should also lead to suppression of chain pulling, panel pushing, or any other active response. The magnitude of the suppression of the lever response may be slightly greater than that of the other responses because of generalization decrement, but it should be roughly equivalent. In anthropomorphic terms one may say that the rat is afraid when the signal occurs, but it is not afraid of making any particular response.

The discriminative punishment procedure does involve a contingency between an aversive event and a particular response. If, during the occur-

---

[3] In most studies of the CER a single aversive event is presented at the end of the signal. With extended training temporal conditioning can occur, i.e., the magnitude of suppression may increase as the time for the aversive event approaches (Azrin, 1956). The use of a random schedule of shock presentation precludes temporal conditioning, i.e., the probability of a shock is not a function of the length of time that the stimulus has been on, and it is not a function of the time since the last shock.

[4] The proportion of variance dependent variable (Y) accounted for by an independent variable (X) is given by the index $\omega^2 = \dfrac{\sigma_Y^2 - \sigma^2_{Y/X}}{\sigma_Y^2}$. Estimates of ω^2 were made by methods described by Hays (1963).

FIGURE 1

Mean suppression ratio as a function of sessions of discriminative punishment (PUN) and conditioned emotional response (CER) treatment.

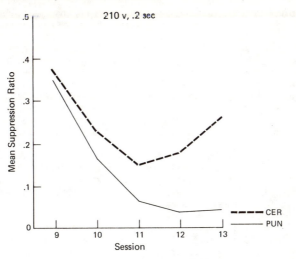

rence of a signal, an aversive event is contingent upon lever responding, subsequent occurrences of the signal will lead to a substantially greater suppression of lever responding than of other responses, such as chain pulling, panel pressing, etc. There will be some suppression of these other responses, because of the contingency between the signal and the aversive event, but the magnitude of suppression of the punished response will be substantially greater. In anthropomorphic terms one may say that the rat is afraid of the signal, and it is also afraid of making the specific responses during the signal.

A response-shift procedure was used to assess the accuracy of these statements. Forty-eight rats were trained to press a lever and also to pull a bead chain. Half the subjects received a discriminative punishment procedure, and the other half received a conditioned emotional response procedure. A given subject received the treatment either with the lever or the chain response, and it was tested either with the lever or chain response. A change in the response was expected to attenuate the magnitude of suppression in the discriminative punishment group markedly, but such a change was not expected to produce a substantial change in the magnitude of suppression in the CER group.

Procedure

Reinforcement training (Session 1–10). In the first five sessions the lever was inserted in the box, and lever responses were reinforced on a 1-min variable-interval schedule. In Sessions 6–10 the lever was removed and the chain was inserted in the box. Chain responses were now reinforced on a 1-min variable-interval schedule.

Treatment (Sessions 11–15). The subjects were randomly partitioned into four groups of 12 subjects each. Two of the groups had a lever inserted in the box, and the other two groups had a chain inserted in the box. All groups continued to receive the same schedule of reinforcement as during reinforcement training. During Minutes 6–8 and 21–23 of the 30-min sessions, however, a white noise signal sounded continuously. During these two 3-min periods, the treatment conditions differed among groups. Two groups (one lever and one chain) received a discriminative punishment treatment; the remaining two groups received a conditioned emotional response treatment. During these two 3-min periods a shock was primed on a 1-min random-interval schedule. The same random schedule was used for all subjects in a particular session, but a different schedule was used for each session. The shock was 160 V in intensity for a duration of 0.2 sec. These shocks could be delivered either as soon as they were primed (CER) or immediately following the first response after they were primed (discriminative punishment).

Extinction testing (Sessions 16–20). During extinction testing responses produced reinforcements, but no shocks were given. The signal was still presented during Minutes 6–8 and 21–23 of the 30-min sessions. Half the subjects in each of the four groups received extinction testing with the same manipulandum in the box as was used during treatment; the other half of the subjects received extinction testing with the other manipulandum.

Treatment (Sessions 21–32). After two sessions of continued extinction testing, the two groups of subjects that had received extinction testing with the same manipulandum that was used in treatment, continued the conditions of treatment for ten additional sessions. During Sessions 23–27 the shock was 250 V for 0.2 sec; during Sessions 28–32 the shock was 250 V for 1.0 sec. The shock was primed on a 6-min random schedule, so that only a single shock would be expected during the 6 min of signal. The purpose of this infrequent, but severe, shock was to increase the resistance to extinction.

Extinction testing (Sessions 33–37). The procedure was identical to that employed during the first period of extinction testing. Half the subjects in each of the two groups received extinction testing with the same manipulandum in the box that was used during treatment; the other half of the subjects received extinction testing with the other manipulandum.

Results

Reinforcement Training. The mean rate of pressing the lever and the mean rate of pulling the chain increased on successive sessions of reinforcement training, and the two functions were not radically different. For example, after five sessions of training, the mean rate of pulling the chain was 15.2 responses per minute and the mean rate of pressing the lever was 17.4 responses per minute. This small difference was significantly different from chance ($F_{1,47} = 7.6$; $p < .01$), but it accounted for only about 6% of the variance. The procedure of training the lever response first, however, may overemphasize the similarity between the two responses. First, the lever pressing response was more easily acquired than the chain pulling response. All except two of the 48 rats made 30 reinforced lever responses within 1 hr on the first session following magazine training (median time was 11.5 min), whereas few pilot subjects made chain pulling responses after similar pretraining. After five sessions of lever pressing on a 1-min variable-interval schedule of reinforcement, however, subjects quickly learned to pull the chain. All except one of the 48 rats made 30 reinforced chain responses within 1 hr on the first session of training (median time was 6.2 min). Secondly, under comparable conditions the lever pressing on the tenth session would have been somewhat greater than on the fifth session. Thirdly, the distribution of interresponse times may differ even when the rates are identical. Thus, although the two responses were similar, they are distinguishable.

Treatment (Sessions 11–15). In the absence of the signal the mean rate of lever responding was somewhat greater than the mean rate of chain responding (15.5 and 11.4 responses per minute, respectively; $F_{1,44} = 5.4$, $p < .025$), but the response rates of the subjects in the discriminative punishment group and the CER group were indistinguishable (13.6 and 13.3 responses per minute, respectively; $F_{1,44} = .03$, $p > .05$). Figure 2 shows the mean suppression ratio as a function of sessions of treatment and extinction testing. Although the mean suppression ratio of subjects with the chain response was slightly lower than that of subjects with the lever response, the difference did not depart significantly from chance ($F_{1,44} = 4.58$, $p > .05$). The basic treatment effect replicated the results reported in Experiment 1: Punishment produced greater suppression than the CER treatment ($F_{1,44} = 40.1$, $p < .001$). The treatment accounted for 43% of the variance.

Extinction testing (Sessions 16–20). The major problem was to determine whether the amount of response suppression was greater for subjects in the discriminative punishment group that were tested on the same response used in training than for the other groups. By a method of planned comparisons, this group was significantly more suppressed than the remaining groups ($F_{1,44} = 14.2$, $p < .001$, $\omega^2 = .21$), and the differences among the remaining three groups did not depart significantly from chance ($F_{2,44} = 1.19$, $p < .05$).

FIGURE 2

Mean suppression ratio as a function of sessions of discriminative punishment and CER treatment (Sessions 11–15), and of sessions of extinction (Sessions 16–20) in which the manipulandum was either the same as or different from the one used in training.

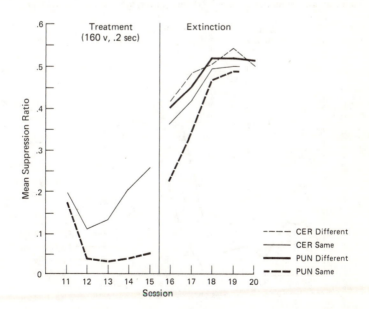

Treatment (Sessions 28–32).   In the absence of the signal the mean rate of lever responding was similar to the mean rate of chain responding (12.6 and 11.3 responses per minute respectively; $F_{1,20} = 0.3, p > .05$), and the mean rate of subjects in the discriminative punishment group and the CER group were similar (10.7 and 13.1 responses per minute, respectively; $F_{1,20} = 0.9, p > .05$). Figure 3 shows the mean suppression ratio as a function of sessions of treatment and extinction testing. Once again, punishment produced greater suppression than the CER treatment ($F_{1,20} = 13.2, p < .001, \omega^2 = .35$). The response, and the response by treatment interaction, did not approach statistical significance.

Extinction testing (Sessions 33–37).   Resistance to extinction was greater on the second extinction test than on the first, perhaps because the probability of a shock was lower (an average of once each 6 min instead of once each minute), and the severity of the shock was greater (250 V for 0.2 and 1.0 sec instead of 160 V for 0.2 sec). Again, the major problem was to determine whether the amount of response suppression was greater for subjects in the discriminative punishment group that were tested on the same response used in training than for the other groups. By a method of planned comparisons, this group again was significantly more suppressed than the remaining groups ($F_{1,19} = 7.03, p < .025, \omega^2 = .21$), and the differences among the remaining three groups did not depart significantly from chance ($F_{2,19} = 0.73, p > .05$).

The actual level of supression of the discriminative punishment group

---

FIGURE 3

Mean suppression ratio as a function of sessions of discriminative punishment and CER treatment (Sessions 28–32), and of sessions of extinction (Sessions 33–37) in which the manipulandum was either the same as or different from the one used in training.

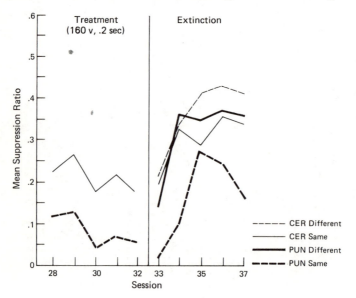

that was tested on the response different from the one used in training is informative. This group shows substantial response suppression, indistinguishable from that of the CER groups, and radically below .500.

Discussion

The results of these experiments support the working assumption that the suppression produced by the CER procedure is independent of any particular response but that the suppression produced by the discriminative punishment procedure involves response specificity. Because the discriminative punishment procedure involves a contingency between an aversive event and a response, as well as a contingency between an aversive event and a signal, a change in the response was expected to substantially attenuate the suppression produced by the stimulus. There were, however, two plausible degrees of attenuation.

Discriminative punishment may be considered as a situation involving a single contingent relationship between an aversive event and a response in the presence of a signal. Aversive events have occurred when the response has been made in the presence of the signal; they have not occurred when the response has been made in the absence of the signal or when the response has not been made in the presence of the signal. Because of this discrimination training the alteration of the response might leave the subject without a basis for fear. Therefore, a discriminative punishment procedure might be expected to lead to fear of the signal-response combined factor, but not to either of its elements alone.

On the other hand, discriminative punishment may be considered as a situation involving two separate contingent relationships. One of them is between an aversive event and a response in the presence of a signal; the other is between an aversive event and a stimulus (CER). Under this hypothesis, the alteration of the response leaves only the contingent relationship between the aversive event and the signal. Since this is the same relationship that defines the CER procedure, the magnitude of suppression of an unpunished response to a signal might be expected to be equivalent to that of a CER group.

All of the data from the present experiments support this second interpretation. On the first test session with the different response in Experiment 2, the magnitude of suppression of a discriminative punishment group on a new response was approximately the same as that of the CER groups, but it was also not far from .500. Thus, the group may not have been less suppressed than the CER groups only because of a ceiling effect. For this reason the additional sessions of treatment were with an intense electric shock and a sparse schedule of reinforcement designed to increase resistance to extinction. The discriminative punishment subjects with the different response again were indistinguishable from the CER subjects, and this time they were substantially suppressed.

In classical conditioning the experimenter specifies the relationship between a signal and an aversive (or reinforcing) event; in instrumental training the experimenter specifies the relationship between a response and an aversive (or reinforcing) event. A discriminative instrumental training procedure involves both of these contingencies, and a noncontingent control group involves neither of these contingencies. Thus, the present experiments may be considered a comparison between a procedure that involves both a classical and an instrumental contingency (discriminative punishment) and a procedure that involves only a classical contingency (CER). The results of an analogous experiment in which brief presentations of a second stimulus were used instead of responses might have been similar. By convention most experimenters have made use of signals that last for several minutes and responses that are of short duration. Evaluation of the equivalence of the principles of association for signals and responses would be facilitated by the comparison of the conventional signals with behavior sequences that last for several minutes or the comparison of conventional responses with signals that are of short duration.

References

Azrin, N. H. Some effects of two intermittent schedules of immediate and non-immediate punishment. *Journal of Psychology,* 1956, **42,** 3–21.

Boe, E. E., & Church, R. M. Permanent effects of punishment during extinction. *Journal of Comparative and Physiological Psychology,* 1967, **63,** 486–492.

Camp, D. S., Raymond, G. A., & Church, R. M. Temporal relationship between response and punishment. *Journal of Experimental Psychology,* 1967, **74,** 114–123.

Church, R. M. The varied effects of punishment on behavior. *Psychological Review,* 1963, **70,** 369–402.

Church, R. M. Response suppression. In B. A. Campbell & R. M. Church (Eds.), *Punishment and aversive behavior.* New York: Appleton-Century-Crofts, 1969.

Estes, W. K. An experimental study of punishment. *Psychological Monographs,* 1944, **57** (3, Whole No. 263).

Hays, W. L. *Statistics for psychologists.* New York: Holt, Rinehart, & Winston, 1963.

Hunt, H. F., & Brady, J. V. Some effects of punishment and intercurrent "anxiety" on a simple operant. *Journal of Comparative and Physiological Psychology,* 1955, **48,** 305–310.

Overmier, J. B., & Seligman, M. E. P. Effects of inescapable shock upon subsequent escape and avoidance responding. *Journal of Comparative and Physiological Psychology,* 1967, **63,** 28–33.

4/ Extinction

Extinction is a topic in learning research that is studied almost as extensively as is the acquisition process. It is clear that an extinction procedure (the withholding of all rewards following the execution of the CR) leads to a reduction in responding. Furthermore, we know a great deal about the paramaters of extinction, such as, for example, the decline of response rate as a function of the prior reward magnitude or schedule. And yet there are a number of issues relating to extinction that continue to pose challenging problems for learning researchers. Among these is the mechanism for extinction. For example, does nonreward reduce responding by "disconnecting" the habits learned during acquisition, or does it produce its effect indirectly by eliciting, say, frustration? The answers to these and other questions are still unresolved, although appreciable understanding has been achieved primarily through the study of the partial reinforcement effect. Here, one observes that subjects who were intermittently reinforced during acquisition are more persistent in their responding during extinction than subjects who previously received constant reward. This major phenomenon, to which the first paper (Capaldi and Capaldi, 1970) in this chapter is addressed, has provided a useful model of extinction that draws on a number of complex psychological processes including inhibition, discrimination, frustration, and memory retrieval.

A second, more practical aspect to the study of extinction involves the programmatic reduction of fear-motivated behavior such as avoidance responding. The techniques for eliminating such behaviors have importance for the treatment of certain psychological disorders. That is, many of the techniques in behavior therapy are aimed at eliminating unwanted or maladaptive behaviors which often originated from aversive or painful situations. By clarifying the factors that promote rapid extinction of fear-motivated avoidance responses, as in the second paper in this chapter by Schiff, Smith, and Prochaska (1972), we can presumably improve our treatment of disorders in the real world.

MAGNITUDE OF PARTIAL REWARD, IRREGULAR REWARD SCHEDULES, AND A 24-HOUR ITI: A TEST OF SEVERAL HYPOTHESES

E.J. Capaldi and Elizabeth D. Capaldi

The first paper in this chapter on extinction is by E. J. Capaldi and Elizabeth D. Capaldi (1970). It is a particularly valuable paper because it uses an interesting phenomenon to test several of the major theories of extinction. The phenomenon involves the persistence of a response during extinction as a function of the magnitude of the reward previously used during acquisition: greater resistance to extinction occurs following large (versus small) intermittent rewards. Frustration and cognitive dissonance theories attempt to explain this phenomenon in terms of the discrepancy between the anticipated reward and no reward on the nonreinforced trial. By contrast, Capaldi's *sequential theory* suggests that the important determinant of resistance to extinction is the magnitude of reward following a nonreward trial.

Four groups of rats were trained to run down a straight alleyway to a goal box. The groups differed only in terms of the magnitude of reward on the reinforced trials and the pattern of reinforced trials. The specific group assignments were as follows: LNL, LNS, SNL, and SNS (where S = small reward, L = large reward, and N = no reward). Note that the reward magnitude after nonreward (the parameter important to Capaldi's sequential theory) is the same in Groups SNL and LNL and in Groups SNS and LNS, but the expected reward level (the parameter important to frustration theory) is different in these pairs of groups. In other words, Groups SNL and LNL and Groups SNS and LNS expect different levels of reward on the N trial because of their first encounter with reward; those pairs of groups, however, should not differ during extinction if the only important factor were the level of reward following the N trial.

After training, all the subjects were given twenty-six extinction (unreinforced) trials. The results of this phase were quite clear: groups LNL and SNL did not differ from each other, but both those groups were significantly more resistant to extinction than Groups SNS and

LNS. In conclusion, these data clearly support the notion that resistance to extinction is a function of the magnitude of reward following a nonrewarded trial (Capaldi's sequential theory), not a function of the anticipated reward discrepancy (frustration theory).

Investigations attempting to determine the effects of magnitude of partial reward on resistance to extinction (R to E) have employed either a 24-hr. intertrial interval (ITI) and irregular reward schedules (Hulse, 1958; Wagner, 1961) or relatively massed trials and regular reward schedules (Capaldi & Lynch, 1968; Capaldi & Minkoff, 1969; Leonard, 1969). Whether the results produced by these two "kinds" of investigations may be interpreted in terms of a single theory, and thus in terms of common variables, or whether they demand two entirely different sorts of explanation is at present an open question.

According to one general interpretation of reward-magnitude extinction effects, expectancy (Lawrence & Festinger, 1962) and r_g (Amsel, 1962) are increasing functions of reward magnitude, and dissonance and frustration, respectively, are increasing functions of the discrepancy between anticipated reward and reward received on nonrewarded trials. The greater the anticipated reward discrepancy (ARD), the greater is the amount of dissonance reduced (Lawrence & Festinger, 1962), or the greater is the intensity of r_f–s_f conditioned to the instrumental reaction (Amsel, personal communication, 1967a), and, thus, the greater is R to E. Note that the amount of dissonance reduced or the intensity of r_f–s_f ultimately depends upon the ARD. The sequential hypothesis (Capaldi, 1966), on the other hand, suggests that R to E is an increasing function of the reward magnitude which occurs on rewarded trials which follow nonrewarded trials (MNR). In the Hulse (1958) and Wagner (1961) investigations, ARD and MNR increased together. Separating these (Capaldi & Lynch, 1968; Capaldi & Minkoff, 1969) suggests that R to E is independent of ARD and is an increasing function of MNR. These findings may be interpreted in a variety of ways, however, given other positions which have been entertained with respect to regularity of reward schedules and ITI.

Lawrence and Festinger (1962) have suggested that under regular reward schedules nonreward may be anticipated. On such nonrewarded trials, obviously, the usual ARD would be absent and R to E would not be increased. According to this argument, the ARD did not influence R to E in the regular schedules investigations cited earlier because none occurred, and thus the results of these studies are, practically speaking, irrelevant (see pp. 158–159). Amsel (1967b) and Gonzalez and Bitterman (1969) have suggested that while sequential variables such as MNR may regulate R to E under massed trials, other variables most certainly regulate R to E under spaced trials. According to Amsel's version of this view (see also Surridge & Amsel, 1966), at a 24-hr. ITI, R to E would be regulated by the ARD and would be independent of MNR. Another view (Capaldi, 1966) is that variables such as MNR regulate R to E under both massed and spaced trials and under both regular and irregular reward schedules.

The deficiencies of previous magnitude investigations with respect to the various hypotheses described above are perhaps clear. Either they did not separate the effects of ARD and MNR or, if they did, they employed relatively short ITIs and regular reward schedules. In the present investigation as MNR increased, the ARD either increased or decreased and, depending upon what assumptions are made, possibly remained constant as well. However, in this investigation the ITI was 24 hr. and the reward schedule was irregular.

METHOD

Subjects   The 36 male rats, obtained from the Holtzman Co., Madison, Wisconsin, were about 90 days old upon arrival at the laboratory.

Apparatus   The gray wood straight alley was 82 in. long, 4 in. wide, and enclosed by 9-in.-high sides, covered with hinged ½-in. hardware cloth. It had three basic sections: start 14 in., middle or run 52 in., and goal 16 in. When a 10-in. start treadle was depressed by the rat, whose front paws were always placed on the treadle's extreme forward edge, a .01-sec. clock started. This clock stopped and a second started when the rat broke an infrared beam 4 in. from the treadle's tip (start time). Interrupting the second beam, 52 in. from the first, stopped the second clock (run time) and started a third clock. Twelve inches from the second beam and 2 in. from the front edge of a brass 2 × 4¼ × 1¼ in. food cup, covered by a tightly fitting, automatically controlled sliding metal lid operated by an electric motor, was a third infrared beam. Interrupting it stopped the third and last clock (goal time) and opened the lid covering the food cup. When the rat broke the third beam, a brass guillotine door 12 in. from the alley's distal end was lowered manually. The elapsed time on the three clocks was summed and is termed "total."

Preliminary Training

Upon arrival at the laboratory the rats were housed in group cages and given free access to food and water for 5 days. On Day 6 (Day 1 of pretraining) all rats were placed in individual cages and restricted to a 12 gm/day maintenance diet of Wayne Lab Blox, with water ad lib. All animals were handled daily during pretraining and were habituated to the unbaited apparatus in groups of four for 5 min. on Days 7 and 9. On Days 7 through 10 of pretraining each rat received 10 .045-gm. Noyes pellets in the home cage. The rats were randomly divided into four groups of nine each before the start of experimental training.

TABLE 1

Reward Schedules for the Four Groups

Group	Trial										
	1	2	3	4	5	6	7	8	9	10	11
LNL	L	L	L	N	N	N	L	N	N	L	N
SNL	S	S	S	N	N	N	L	N	N	L	N
LNS	L	L	L	N	N	N	S	N	N	S	N
SNS	S	S	S	N	N	N	S	N	N	S	N

Group	Trial										
	12	13	14	15	16	17	18	19	20	21	22
LNL	N	N	L	L	L	L	L	N	N	L	L
SNL	N	N	L	S	S	S	L	N	N	L	L
LNS	N	N	S	S	L	L	L	N	S	S	S
SNS	N	N	S	S	S	S	S	N	N	S	S

Acquisition training began following Day 10 of pretraining. There was one trial per day in acquisition (22 days) and in extinction (26 days). Reward magnitude was either large (L), 22 .045-gm. Noyes pellets, or small (S), 2 pellets. On rewarded trials the rat was removed from the goal box immediately after all pellets had been consumed. On all nonrewarded (N) trials, the rat was confined to the goalbox for 30 sec. The 22 days of acquisition training were administered to each group on the basis of the reward schedules shown in Table 1. Groups SNS and LNL correspond directly to the groups employed by Hulse (1958) and Wagner (1961), i.e., total magnitude of reward and MNR increase together. Groups SNL and LNS allowed a test of the hypothesis that differences in the Hulse-Wagner situation were unrelated to total reward magnitude per se and were regulated, in fact, by MNR, i.e., N-L vs. N-S. Note in Table 1 that over days Groups SNL and LNS received the same magnitude of reward. However, Group SNL, like Group LNL (which received overall greater reward magnitude), received N-L transitions, while Group LNS, like Group SNS (which received overall lesser reward magnitude), received N-S transitions.

The rats were run in squads of four composed of one animal from each group. The within-squad running order was varied daily. On all trials the rat was placed in the apparatus as described above and given 60 sec. to traverse each alley section. If the rat failed in this, it was assigned a time score of 60 sec. for that alley section and all not yet traversed alley sections and was placed in the goal box. Following a trial, the animal was returned to the home cage where, about 15 min. later, it received the 12-gm. daily ration minus the amount eaten in the apparatus.

Results

Acquisition   Total speeds for each of the four groups on each day of acquisition are shown in Figure 1. As can be seen, on the final days of acquisition all groups which received a large magnitude of reward were running equally rapidly and faster than the group which received only a small magnitude of reward, Group SNS. An analysis of total speeds on the last day of acquisition indicated that the differences were highly significant ($F = 10.18$, $df = 3/32$, $p < .001$). A second, perhaps more important, feature of the running speeds shown in Figure 1 is that none of the groups showed any tendency to anticipate either rewarded or nonrewarded trials. This may be easily ascertained by comparing speed on a particular trial with the reward actually occurring on that trial (see Table 1). It can be seen employing this method that the dominant tendency early in training was to run relatively fast following rewarded trials and relatively slow following nonrewarded trials. This tendency produced some "errors" from an anticipatory standpoint in that speeds were sometimes higher on nonrewarded than on rewarded trials. For example, on Trial 4, a nonrewarded trial (which followed three rewarded trials), speeds were higher than on Trial 7, a rewarded trial (which followed three nonrewarded trials). Later on in training, after the animals had more or less overcome the tendency to slow down following nonrewarded trials, i.e., from about Trial 14 onward, speeds appear nondifferentiated on rewarded and nonrewarded trials. Thus, as would be expected in view of the irregularity of the schedules employed, there was no indication that the animals learned to anticipate reward or nonreward.

Because of the terminal acquisition differences, the speed scores were transformed into rate measures as recommended by Anderson (1963).

FIGURE 1

Mean total speed for each of the four groups on each trial of acquisition.

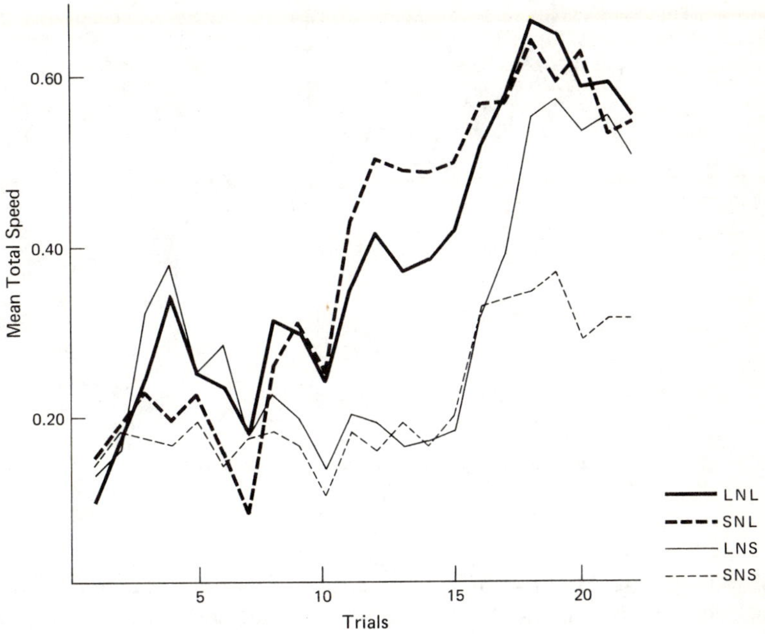

Employed as the estimate of the acquisition asymptote were the speeds on the last 6 days of acquisition and the first day of extinction, while the extinction asymptote was taken to be the reciprocal of 60 sec. in each alley section and 180 sec. in total.

Extinction   The rate measures for total for each of the four groups on each day of extinction are shown in Figure 2. As can be seen, Groups LNL and SNL differed from each other only negligibly and showed greater R to E than Groups LNS and SNS. As can also be seen, the rate measures for Group LNS tended to fall below those of Group SNS from about Trial 10 onward. The lesser R to E of Group LNS relative to Group SNS was largest in the run section where it approached but did not reach significance, and reflects differences in acquisition asymptote. On the basis of the speed scores themselves, Groups SNS and LNS were quite comparable following the initial extinction trials.

A simple analysis of variance employing the rate measures over all of the extinction trials indicated that differences for total were significant ($F = 11.87, p < .001$), as they were in the run section ($F = 11.40, p < .001$), and the goal section ($F = 9.12, p < .001$), but not the start section ($F =$

FIGURE 2

Rate measures for each of the four groups on each trial of extinction.

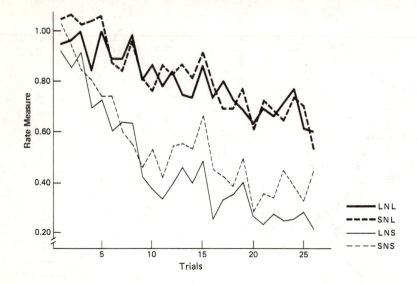

2.65, .05 $< p <$ .10; df = 3/32 in all cases). Subsequent Duncan's range tests indicated that neither in total nor in any alley section did Group LNL differ from Group SNL. Similarly, Groups SNS and LNS failed to differ, except as previously mentioned, in the run section, where differences approached but did not reach significance (.05 $< p <$ .10). In total, run, and goal, but not start, Groups LNL and SNL differed significantly from Groups SNS and LNS ($p <$ .01).

Discussion

In this investigation if R to E were an increasing function of MNR, then the groups would have been ordered in terms of greatest to least R to E as follows: LNL = SNL > LNS = SNS. The only departure from this expected ordering was the lesser, but not significantly lesser, R to E of Group LNS relative to Group SNS. The present results, then, are consistent with the view that R to E is an increasing function of MNR when the ITI is 24 hr. and the reward schedule is irregular. However, if the present results are to be convincingly ascribed to MNR, then it must be demonstrated that they were independent of the ARD. A demonstration of this sort, if satisfactorily accomplished, would also have important implications for understanding the effects of ITI and regularity of reward schedules on R to E. The reward schedule employed here, it should be noted, differs substantially from those employed in the earlier massed trial MNR investigations. Consequently, the attempt to demonstrate that the present results were independent of ARD involves considerations different from those advanced in connection with the massed trial studies.

From the standpoint of frustration theory and dissonance theory, expectancy or r_g, and thus the ARD, must have been greater in Group LNL than in Group SNL. Why then did Group LNL fail to show greater R to E than Group SNL? One possibility is that in Group SNL an ARD occurred on small-reward trials as well as on nonrewarded trials. Thus, while on nonrewarded trials the ARD was greater in Group LNL than in Group SNL, the latter group had more such experiences, i.e., the additional ones occurring on small-reward trials. On this basis, Groups LNL and SNL might not be expected to differ in extinction from both a dissonance and frustration standpoint. The difficulty with this line of argument, and presumably others like it, is perhaps apparent. It is this: Any set of assumptions within these frameworks which would tend to predict LNL = SNL in extinction would tend also to predict greater R to E in Group LNS than in Group SNS. Thus, in terms of the specific argument employed above, Group LNS would have experienced not only a greater number of ARDs than Group SNS, but some of these, i.e., those on nonrewarded trials, would necessarily have been of greater intensity. Thus, Group LNS should have shown greater R to E than Group SNS, which is contrary to the present results.

Perhaps the above difficulty could be avoided by demonstrating that the ARD was greater in Group SNL than in Group LNS. Unfortunately for frustration and dissonance, the opposite, if anything, seems to be the case. Note first of all, by consulting Table 1, that the nonrewarded trials of Group LNS follow without exception a greater number of large reward trials than do the nonrewarded trials of Group SNL. On any nonrewarded trial, then, expectation or r_g must have been at least as great in Group LNS as in Group SNL, and thus so must have been the ARD. Taking small-reward trials into consideration, where as previously indicated, ARDs may also have occurred, fails to alleviate this difficulty; on the contrary, it appears to exacerbate it. Note in Table 1 that the first three acquisition trials consisted of small reward in Group SNL and large reward in Group LNS. Group SNL should not have experienced frustration or dissonance on these initial small-reward trials. Thus, if anything, Group SNL had three fewer ARDs than did Group LNS, and those it did have were of lesser intensity. Accordingly, both frustration and dissonance would appear to predict, if anything, greater R to E in Group LNS than in Group SNL, or the opposite of the present results. It appears that in this investigation R to E was independent of the ARD and consequently of either the amount of dissonance reduced or the intensity of $r_f - s_f$ conditioned to the instrumental reaction.

The present results taken in conjunction with earlier ones (Capaldi & Lynch, 1968; Capaldi & Minkoff, 1969; Leonard, 1969) suggest that the MNR variable produces similar effects over two experimental conditions regarded by some as extremely critical, long vs. short ITIs and irregular vs.

regular reward schedules. Regarding ITI, classical interest in this variable (e.g., Weinstock, 1954) has been of late revived (e.g., Capaldi & Minkoff, 1967; Gonzalez & Bitterman, 1969; Surridge & Amsel, 1966). The issues, however, have changed somewhat. In the older literature a spaced-trial partial-reinforcement effect was taken to mean that sequential variables were not operative either under short or long ITIs (e.g., Weinstock, 1954). At present the operation of sequential variables under massed trials is considered either definite (e.g., Gonzalez & Bitterman, 1969) or possible (e.g., Amsel, 1967b). Under spaced trials, however, the presence of sequential variables is either affirmed (e.g., Capaldi, 1966) or denied (e.g., Amsel, 1967b; Gonzalez & Bitterman, 1969). In any event, the present results being consistent with previous massed trial findings for MNR suggests the appropriateness of the view that similar variables and processes operate under all conditions of trial spacing.

Lawrence and Festinger's (1962) position on the role of anticipation is as follows. Prior to the anticipation of nonreward, R to E will be an increasing function of the number of dissonance-producing experiences. After the development of anticipation, however, nonreward is no longer dissonance producing and R to E will be reduced in those groups manifesting such anticipation. In Lawrence and Festinger's view, it is because R to E is reduced in anticipating groups that R to E "appears" to be regulated by sequential variables. First of all, the present results are not favorable to their view that sequential variables fail to regulate R to E under nonanticipatory conditions. Or to put it differently, R to E was regulated by MNR here when reward was anticipated on nonrewarded trials, which is contrary to Lawrence and Festinger's view on anticipation (as distinguished from the dissonance hypothesis generally). Moreover, the present results clearly suggest that sequential variables do not achieve their effects through the complicated route suggested by Lawrence and Festinger, i.e., through a reduction in R to E in anticipating groups. Consistent with this observation are the results of two investigations by Grosslight and Radlow (1956, 1957). Both of these investigations compared the effects on response reversal of partial-reinforcement schedules which either contained or failed to contain a transition from nonrewarded to rewarded trials. The group having a nonreward-reward transition did not show anticipation in either investigation. In the first investigation, however, there was behavioral evidence that the group lacking a nonreward-reward transition anticipated nonreward, whereas in the second investigation, specifically designed to preclude such anticipation, this group did not appear to anticipate nonreward. However, in *both* investigations the group lacking a nonreward-reward transition reversed more rapidly than the other partial group. Recently another sort of anticipatory condition has been reported by Campbell (1969). In previous sequential investigations, as shown above, either neither group anticipated nonreward prior to extinction (or reversal) or one group anticipated nonreward while the other did not. In Campbell's study, which employed delay of reward, both groups anticipated delayed reward prior to extinction. Under these conditions, too, R to E was regulated by a sequential variable. Thus the present results, along with the others which have been described, suggest strongly that the influence of sequential variables is independent of the presence or absence of anticipation, i.e., sequential variables have been shown to regulate R to E or reversal when none of the groups discriminated nonrewarded from rewarded trials (Grosslight & Radlow, 1957; the present data), when both groups discriminated (Campbell, 1969), and when one group discriminated but the other did not (Grosslight & Radlow, 1956).

References

Amsel, A. Frustrative nonreward in partial reinforcement and discrimination learning: Some recent history and a theoretical extension. *Psychological Review*, 1962, **69**, 306–328.

Amsel, A. Personal communication. Cited by Leonard, D. W. Amount and sequence of reward in partial and continuous reinforcement. Unpublished doctoral dissertation, University of Texas at Austin, 1967. (a)

Amsel, A. Partial reinforcement effects on vigor and persistence. In K. W. Spence & J. T. Spence (Eds.), *The psychology of learning and motivation: Advances in research and theory.* Vol. 1. New York: Academic Press, 1967. (b)

Anderson, N. Comparison of different populations: Resistance to extinction and transfer. *Psychological Review*, 1963, **70**, 162–179.

Campbell, P. E. Sequences of delayed reward and extinction confinement: Effects on pattern running and extinction performance. *Psychonomic Science*, 1969, **17**, 34–35.

Capaldi, E. J. Partial reinforcement: A hypothesis of sequential effects. *Psychological Review*, 1966, **73**, 459–477.

Capaldi. E. J., & Lynch, A. D. Magnitude of partial reward and resistance to extinction: Effect of N-R transitions. *Journal of Comparative and Physiological Psychology*, 1968, **65**, 179–181.

Capaldi, E. J., & Minkoff, R. Reward schedule effects at a relatively long intertrial interval. *Psychonomic Science*, 1967, **9**, 169–170.

Capaldi, E. J., & Minkoff, R. Influence of order of occurrence of nonreward and large and small reward on acquisition and extinction. *Journal of Experimental Psychology*, 1969, **81**, 156–160.

Gonzalez, R. C., & Bitterman, M. E. Spaced-trials partial reinforcement effect as a function of contrast. *Journal of Comparative and Physiological Psychology*, 1969, **67**, 94–103.

Grosslight, J. H., & Radlow, R. Patterning effect of the nonreinforcement-reinforcement sequence in a discrimination situation. *Journal of Comparative and Physiological Psychology*, 1956, **49**, 542–546.

Grosslight, J. H., & Radlow, R. Patterning effect of the nonreinforcement-reinforcement sequence involving a single nonreinforced trial. *Journal of Comparative and Physiological Psychology*, 1957, **50**, 23–25.

Hulse, S. H. Amount and percentage of reinforcement and duration of goal confinement in conditioning and extinction. *Journal of Experimental Psychology*, 1958, **56**, 48–57.

Lawrence, D. H., & Festinger. L. *Deterrents and reinforcement.* Stanford: Stanford University Press, 1962.

Leonard, D. W. Amount and sequence of reward in partial and continuous reinforcement. *Journal of Comparative and Physiological Psychology*, 1969, **67**, 204–211.

Surridge, C. T., & Amsel, A. Acquisition and extinction under single alternation and random partial reinforcement conditions with a 24-hour intertrial interval. *Journal of Experimental Psychology*, 1966, **72**, 361–368.

Wagner, A. R. Effects of amount and percentage of reinforcement and number of acquisition trials on conditioning and extinction. *Journal of Experimental Psychology*, 1961, **62**, 234–242.

Weinstock, S. Resistance to extinction of a running response following partial reinforcement under widely spaced trials. *Journal of Comparative and Physiological Psychology*, 1954, **47**, 318–322.

EXTINCTION OF AVOIDANCE IN RATS AS A FUNCTION OF DURATION AND NUMBER OF BLOCKED TRIALS

Robert Schiff, Nelson Smith, and James Prochaska

The second paper in this chapter, by Robert Schiff, Nelson Smith, and James Prochaska (1972), deals with the extinction of aversively motivated behaviors through flooding—the technique whereby avoidance or escape responses are prevented while the subject is being exposed to the fear CS. Normally, flooding (also called response blocking) facilitates later extinction; that is, extinction takes place more quickly after flooding. Some theorists claim that this happens because Pavlovian fear is eliminated during the flooding phase; less fear, of course, would mean less motivation for the avoidance response during extinction. Other theorists, however, believe that the flooding session produces freezing behaviors which are incompatible with running; during extinction, then, the decrease in avoidance is really due to the execution of these competing responses, and not to a reduction in fear.

This particular study does not deal directly with the theory of flooding, but rather with two important variables—the number and the duration of flooding trials. Presumably, the greater the exposure to the fear CS, either in terms of length or number of exposures, the greater the impact of flooding on extinction. As the authors point out,

From "Extinction of Avoidance in Rats as a Function of Duration and Number of Blocked Trials" by Robert Schiff, Nelson Smith and James Prochaska in *Journal of Comparative and Physiological Psychology*, Volume 81, Number 2, 1972. Copyright 1972 by the American Psychological Association. Reprinted by permission.

a clear understanding of such basic variables of flooding is essential if therapists are to use the flooding procedure as a treatment model.

In the first phase of this study, rats were trained to avoid shock by running down a straight alleyway during a 10-second noise. Then, each animal was blocked (or flooded) in the start box, but the number of trials and the duration of each trial varied for different groups. Specifically, subjects were given either 1, 5, or 12 trials that lasted either 0, 5, 10, 50, or 120 seconds. Finally, in the third phase, extinction of the avoidance response was assessed. The results indicated that both the number of flooding trials, as well as the duration of each trial, contributed to extinction. Neither was the more dominant factor; the total exposure time (duration times number) appeared to be critical in facilitating later extinction.

A great deal of what has been called psychopathology can be characterized as some form of avoidance responding. Several clinicians, such as White (1964), Wolpe (1958), and Stampfl (1967), have stated that avoidance learning is often the primary aspect of neurosis. If this analysis is valid it is quite important for the effective treatment of psychopathology to develop effective ways to extinguish avoidance behavior.

One successful technique which has been used to eliminate avoidance responding in animals has been called flooding, blocking, or response prevention. Briefly, the procedure consists of detaining the subject in the presence of the CS without the US being presented. This prevents the subject from performing the learned operant response and thus prevents escape from the CS. Baum (1966), Black (1958), Coulter, Riccio, and Page (1969), Page and Hall (1953), and others have demonstrated that subjects whose avoidance responses have been blocked stop emitting the avoidance response more quickly during extinction trials than subjects whose responses have not been blocked.

Two variables of the blocking procedure which have not been adequately studied are the effect of the length of each blocked trial and the effect of the number of blocked trials upon later extinction. Weinberger (1965) varied the length of each blocked trial in several steps between 2, 5, and 20 sec. He found a linear relationship between reduction of avoidance response strength and length of each blocked trial. Baum (1969) found that while blocking for 1 min. did not produce any significant effects, blocking for 3 min. was effective. In addition, he found that added blocking beyond 3 min. was not any more effective. One of the aims of this study was to attempt to more fully determine the nature of the relationship between extinction rate and length of each blocked trial.

Another important parameter which this study explored was the effect of number of blocked trials on extinction rate. Benline and Simmel (1967) did not find any clearcut relationship when they blocked their subjects 40,

80, or 160 times. It is possible that even their lowest number of blocked trials (40) was enough for the effect to reach an asymptotic level. In the present study, because fewer blocking trials were used, it was hypothesized that there would be a significant negative relationship between number of blocked trials and resistance to extinction.

A third goal of this study was to determine the relative contribution of length of each blocked trial compared with the number of blocked trials. This comparison is important from a theoretical point of view. One position holds that for blocking to be effective each blocking trial must be long enough so that anxiety has sufficient time to build up and then begin to extinguish (Stampfl, 1967). What constitutes sufficient blocking time depends on many factors, but it seems reasonable to conclude that from this viewpoint fewer blocking trials but for longer periods of time would be more effective than shorter but more numerous blocking trials. However, if, as the other position suggests, the avoidance response is initiated by a classically conditioned response, then if that response is extinguished, the avoidance response should also be eliminated (Mower, 1951). By definition, the way to extinguish a respondent is to repeatedly present the CS without presenting the US. The larger the number of blocking trials, the more times the CS would be presented without the US. Thus, from the second point of view the number of blocked trials should be more important in facilitating extinction than the length of each blocking trial. To explore this question three sets of comparison cells were built into the design of the study. Each set had two groups with an equal amount of total blocking time, but one group had more blocked trials of shorter duration while the other had fewer blocked trials of longer duration.

METHOD

Subjects

The subjects were 120 experimentally naive rats, of the Sprague-Dawley strain, 84 of which were obtained from Charles River Breeding Laboratories and 36 from litters bred in the University of Rhode Island Comparative Psychology Laboratory. There were 98 males and 22 females. All subjects were maintained on an ad-lib schedule of both food and water. The subjects were approximately 120 days old when used in the study. Twelve subjects were replaced because they failed to learn the avoidance response within a 60-trial criterion.

Apparatus

The apparatus consisted of a straight-alley runway 48 in. long, 5 in. wide, and 7 in. high divided so that there was an 11-in. start box and an 11-in. goal box separated from the main runway by guillotine doors. The walls of the runway were aluminum, and the floor was stainless-steel grids spaced ½ in. apart. The US was a 175-v. ac shock from a matched-impedance source with 150 K ohm in series with the rat, and the CS was white noise at a 73-db. level.

Procedure

The procedure was divided into three phases: avoidance training, response blocking, and extinction. The subjects were randomly assigned to 15 groups of eight subjects each.

Avoidance training phase. Each subject was placed in the runway start box with the guillotine door shut. When the door opened, the CS was presented; after 10 sec. the shock began. Both the white noise and the shock terminated when the subject entered the goal box. The criterion for avoidance was that the rat entered the goal box before the shock began. Training continued until the subject made 10 consecutive avoidance responses.

Blocking phase. After each subject was trained, it was exposed to 1 of 15 different blocking treatments. A subject received either 1, 5, or 12 blocked trials, each lasting for either 0, 5, 10, 50, or 120 sec. The blocking consisted of placing the subject in the start box; the CS was then presented, but the guillotine door remained shut. After the appropriate interval, the CS was shut off and the rat was removed from the apparatus and the procedure was repeated for the appropriate number of blocking trials. Those rats receiving 0 sec. of blocking were placed in the start box and immediately removed.

Extinction phase. This phase was the same as the training phase in that subjects were placed in the start box, and when the door of the start box was opened the white noise was presented. However, no shock followed. When the subject entered the goal box, the CS shut off and the trial terminated. After a 30-sec. intertrial interval, another extinction trial was begun. Extinction procedures were stopped when the time to reach the goal box exceeded 120 sec. for 3 consecutive trials or 50 extinction trials were completed, whichever came first (the 50-trial criterion was reached for only 4 of the 120 rats).

All subjects were run individually with the three phases following in immediate succession.

Results

Table 1 shows the means and standard deviations of the number of trials to meet the extinction criterion for each group. The numbers shown include the three 120-sec. extinction trials.

The results supported the hypothesis of a negative relationship between the number of blocked trials and the number of trials to reach the extinction criterion. Table 1 indicates that, except for the control group, the number of trials necessary to reach the extinction criterion decreased as the number of blocked trials increased. An analysis of variance showed this main effect was significant ($F = 9.81$, $df = 3/105$, $p < .001$). A negative relationship was also found between the length of blocked trials and the trials-to-extinction criterion. Table 1 also shows that as the length of each blocked trial was increased, the number of trials to reach the extinction criterion decreased.

To determine if there was a differential effect between the number of blockings and length of blocking, three sets of groups were compared.

TABLE 1

Means and Standard Deviations of Trials-to-Extinction Criterion as a Function of Number and Length of Blocking Trials

No. of blocked trials	Seconds of blocking per blocking trial				
	0	5	10	50	120
1					
M	24.1	23.0	19.2	10.6	8.4
SD	14.4	11.2	15.1	15.1	4.8
5					
M	17.8	17.2	5.8	6.4	3.1
SD	7.05	16.4	2.8	6.4	.3
12					
M	20.7	7.1	4.4	4.0	3.0
SD	6.7	4.4	1.6	2.8	.0

FIGURE 1

Mean number of trials-to-extinction criterion as a function of total blocking time.

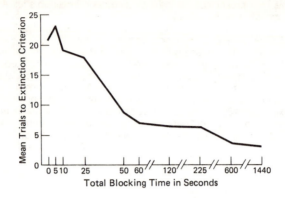

One set (10 blockings of 5 sec. and 1 blocking of 50 sec.) had a total blocking time of 50 sec., a second set had a total blocking time of 120 sec. (12 blockings of 10 sec. and 1 blocking of 120 sec.), and the third set a total blocking time of 600 sec. (5 blockings of 120 sec. and 12 blockings of 50 sec.). The results of t tests performed comparing the number of trials to extinction for each pair showed no difference within any of the three pairs. This suggests that if the total amount of blocking time is constant, then resistance to extinction was similar whether more blocking trials of shorter duration or fewer blocking trials of longer duration were administered.

Figure 1 shows the mean number of trials to extinction criterion as a function of the total blocking time. The figure illustrates that the greatest reduction in resistance to extinction occurred between 25 and 50 sec. of total blocking time.

A Newman-Keuls analysis showed that the only statistically significant change in resistance to extinction occurred between 25–50 sec. of accumulated blocking time. With those subjects blocked for one trial, the only significant differences occurred between the group blocked 10 sec. per blocked trial and those blocked 50 sec. per blocked trial. Likewise, with those subjects blocked for five trials the only significant differences occurred between the 5- and 10-sec. points. Finally, with those subjects blocked 12 times only the difference between the 0-sec. and 5-sec. points was significant.

Discussion

The results of this study are consistent with the literature that finds that blocking the avoidance response facilitates the extinction of that response (Baum, 1966; Black, 1958). The present results further extend this literature and indicate that when the number of blocked trials is relatively few (up to 12), the greater the number of blocked trials, the less the resistance to extinction. Furthermore, within a relatively short range of time (0–120 sec.), the greater the length of each blocked trial, the less the resistance to extinction.

The present results did not support the prediction based on the theory that length of blocked trial rather than number of blocked trials would be the critical variable. Nor did the results support the prediction based on the theory that number of blocked trials would be most important. The results of this study suggest that the key variable in determining response strength during extinction was the total blocking time as opposed to either number of blocked trials or length of each blocked trial. In addition, it appears that there may be a critical amount of blocking time during which the majority of reduction in response strength occurs.

Both of the theoretical positions being considered would hold that the reason avoidance behavior is extinguished by blocking is that the classically conditioned fear response is extinguished because the CS is no longer paired with the US. However, observations in the present study strongly suggest that even though the blocked animals did not perform the avoidance response during the extinction phase, they still showed clear signs of fear, especially freezing behavior. These observations are consistent with the findings of Page (1955) and Coulter et al. (1969) who found that with a limited amount of blocking, the avoidance behavior diminished but not the fear component. They suggest that an alternative avoidance response (for example, nonrunning) is counterconditioned during blocking, and thus the subject may be still performing an avoidance response, but one that is different and possibly incompatible with the originally conditioned avoidance response.

References

Baum, M. Rapid extinction of an avoidance response following a period of response prevention in the avoidance apparatus. *Psychological Reports*, 1966, **18**, 59–64.

Baum, M. Extinction of an avoidance response following response prevention: Some parametric investigations. *Canadian Journal of Psychology*, 1969, **23**, 1–10.

Benline, T. A., & Simmel, E. C. Effects of blocking of the avoidance response on the elimination of the conditioned fear response. *Psychonomic Science*, 1967, **8**, 357–358.

Black, A. H. The extinction of avoidance responses under curare. *Journal of Comparative and Physiological Psychology*, 1958, **51**, 519–524.

Coulter, X., Riccio, D. C., & Page, H. A. Effects of blocking an instrumental avoidance response, facilitated extinction but persistence of "fear." *Journal of Comparative and Physiological Psychology*, 1969, **68**, 377–381.

Mower, O. H. Two-factor learning theory: Summary and comment. *Psychological Review*, 1951, **58**, 350–354.

Page, H. A. The facilitation of experimental extinction by response prevention as a function of the acquisition of a new response. *Journal of Comparative and Physiological Psychology*, 1955, **48**, 14–16.

Page, H. A., & Hall, J. F. Experimental extinction as a function of the prevention of a response. *Journal of Comparative and Physiological Psychology*, 1953, **46**, 33–34.

Stampfl, T. G. Implosive therapy: The theory, the subhuman analogue, the strategy and the technique. In S. G. Armtage (Ed.), *Behavior modification techniques in the treatment of emotional disorders*. Battle Creek, Mich.: Veterans Administration Publication, 1967.

Weinberger, N. M. Effects of detainment on extinction of avoidance responses. *Journal of Comparative and Physiological Psychology*, 1965, **60**, 135–138.

White, R. W. *The abnormal personality*. New York: Ronald Press, 1964.

Wolpe, J. *Psychotherapy by reciprocal inhibition*. Stanford: Stanford University Press, 1958.

5/ Generalization and Discrimination

Generalization and discrimination are often thought of as representing "higher-order" psychological processes and, thus, as providing mechanisms for certain complex behaviors that cannot be explained by appealing to simple conditioning models. Certainly, this belief is founded to some degree; in fact, research on discrimination in animals has traditionally provided an interface to research on concept formation and problem solving in humans (see also Chapter 12).

Generalization, on the one hand, occurs when subjects respond to stimuli that were not involved in the original training, but that are *similar* to the CS along some dimension (either a physical dimension such as pitch or loudness, or an acquired dimension such as meaning). Discrimination, on the other hand, refers to the finding that subjects may learn to react to the *differences* between two stimuli. Thus, generalization and discrimination are "reciprocal" processes (although, in reality, they may not be causally related) in that as discrimination improves, generalization declines. The relationship, therefore, between levels of training (one basis for discrimination) and the degree of generalization is an important focus of study. Accordingly, we have included a well-known paper on this topic, by Hearst and Koresko (1968).

The literature on discrimination also involves interesting and varied phenomena. Integral to many of these phenomena is Mackintosh's attention theory (1965) which claims that attentional responses underlie the choice (or differential response) of the subject. By appealing to such a mediational theory, one is better able to account for certain findings, such as the overlearning-reversal effect, where an overtrained subject learns to choose the previously unreinforced stimulus more easily than a subject originally trained to a lower criterion. The second paper in this chapter illustrates this finding.

STIMULUS GENERALIZATION AND AMOUNT OF PRIOR TRAINING ON VARIABLE-INTERVAL REINFORCEMENT

Eliot Hearst and Minnie B. Koresko

This paper by Eliot Hearst and Minnie B. Koresko (1968) is an important contribution to the literature on generalization because it clarifies the relationship between generalization and the degree of training, a relationship that is important to several theories of generalization. Central to this paper is the distinction between absolute and relative generalization. Absolute generalization is the habit strength expressed in absolute terms (i.e., the number of responses) to each stimulus on the generalization test. In contrast, relative generalization is the level of responding expressed in relative terms; it is the proportional response rate to each stimulus.

In this study pigeons were trained to peck an illuminated plastic disk to obtain food on a variable interval schedule. Food was available when the subject pecked during the CS presentation (a vertical line projected onto the disk). The birds were grouped according to the number of training sessions they received: either 2, 4, 7, or 14. In the final phase of the study, a generalization test was given. Here, eight different lines, varying in their degree of slant from the vertical, were used as stimuli. Hearst and Koresko found that greater training affected both the absolute and relative gradients; specifically, the slope of both these gradients was increased. What this means is that with continued practice, the subjects came to execute a greater number of total responses to all stimuli and a greater proportion of those responses to the original CS.

Although the effect of number of reinforced trials (amount of training) on generalization gradients around the training stimulus is a question that has naturally interested behavior theorists for a long time (e.g., Estes, 1959; Hull, 1943, 1952; Razran, 1949), there is a distinct lack of agreement in the results and interpretation of prior experiments on this problem. De-

From "Stimulus Generalization and Amount of Prior Training on Variable-Interval Reinforcement" by Eliot Hearst and Minnie B. Koresko in *Journal of Comparative and Physiological Psychology*, Volume 66, Number 1, 1968. Copyright 1968 by the American Psychological Association. Reprinted by permission.

pending upon which summary of the literature one refers to (e.g., Hall, 1966; Kalish, in press; Kimble, 1961; Mednick & Freedman, 1960; Razran, 1949), one can find support for virtually any possible conclusion, i.e., that generalization to test stimuli increases, decreases, or remains the same with increases in the amount of training to the CS. Very often these reviewers refer to the same group of prior studies in reaching their different conclusions.

Some of the confusion seems to result from the failure of many workers to make a clear distinction between measures of absolute generalization and relative generalization in summarizing experimental findings. Conclusions could certainly differ depending on which of these measures was emphasized, and on whether amount of generalization or slope of generalization functions was used in analyzing the results.

The present set of experiments compared both absolute and relative generalization gradients following different numbers of sessions devoted to variable-interval (VI) reinforcement in the presence of a single stimulus (a vertical line on a pigeon's response key). In view of the popularity of such free operant techniques for studying stimulus generalization ever since the initial work of Guttman and Kalish (1956), it is somewhat surprising that basic parametric data on the amount-of-training variable are not available for this type of test situation. Olson and King (1962) did publish some data relating number of days of training to the slope of luminosity gradients in pigeons, but their experiment focused on the luminosity variable and, insofar as amount of training was concerned, was marred by a relatively small n and their elimination of Ss with low response rates in the group with the smallest amount of training (2 days).

METHOD

Subjects. Sixty-four experimentally naive hen pigeons, obtained from the Palmetto Pigeon Plant, Sumter, S. C., were maintained at 75% of their free-feeding weights throughout the study. Thirty-two White Carneaux pigeons were used in Experiment 1 and 32 White King pigeons in Experiment 2.

Apparatus. A standard (Foringer) key-pecking apparatus for pigeons was used. Details of this chamber, the method for varying the tilt of a white line projected on the dark key, and the programming and recording equipment have been reported elsewhere (Hearst, Koresko, & Poppen, 1964). A 5-sec. presentation of grain served as reinforcement. All Ss learned to peck the key when a vertical line (0°) was projected on it. The following line orientations were also presented in a randomized order during generalization testing: 22.5°, 45°, 67.5°, 90° (horizontal line), 112.5°, 135°, and 157.5°, designated in a clockwise sequence from the vertical.

Procedure. The study was comprised of two subexperiments. Experiment 2 was an exact replication of Experiment 1, except that a different type of pigeon was used. Experiment 1 was completed first and we wanted to determine whether the anomalous generalization gradient for 2-day Ss in that experiment (see Figure 2) was actually a reliable finding which would hold up in a replication of the entire experiment. Although we intended to use the same type of birds in the replication, White Carneaux Ss were not available from the supplier at that time and we used White King pigeons instead. The procedure described below applies to either experiment.

Training. On Days 1–3 Ss were given magazine training followed by 100–140 reinforcements on a continuous reinforcement (CRF) schedule for pecking the response key. During magazine training the key was covered with tape; during CRF a vertical line was projected on it.

The Ss were divided on a random basis into four groups of eight Ss for 2, 4, 7, or 14 days training on a 1-min. VI schedule. One day of training consisted of a 50-min. session. Sessions were scheduled Monday through Friday throughout the study. All VI training and generalization testing were given to the 2-day and 4-day Ss within one Monday-to-Friday span.

During training sessions, 30-sec. stimulus-on periods alternated with 10-sec. stimulus-off periods. During stimulus-on periods the vertical line was projected on the key, a dim house light came on, and reinforcement was possible for key pecks on a 1-min. VI schedule. During stimulus-off (blackout) periods, both the CS and the house light were turned off. Blackouts were included during training to make the situation as similar as possible to the forthcoming generalization test, where blackouts are necessary between stimulus presentations in order to provide time for E to record data and change the stimulus on the key.

Testing. On the day following the last day of training, tests for stimulus generalization were given to all Ss. Each S was first given a 10-min. warmup period under the same reinforcement and stimulus conditions as before. Then the generalization test began and was conducted under extinction conditions. Each of the eight orientations of the stimulus line was presented ten times. These 80 presentations were arranged in ten blocks, each of which included the eight different stimuli in a randomized order. As before, stimulus-on periods lasted 30 sec. and alternated with 10-sec. stimulus-off periods. The number of key pecks in each 30-sec. stimulus-on period was recorded.

Results

Gradients of absolute generalization, which plot total number of responses made to each test stimulus by the different groups of Ss, are shown in Figure 1. On the abscissa the stimulus line that was 157.5° from the training stimulus (CS) in a clockwise direction is indicated as $-22.5°$, the line that was 135° from CS is indicated as $-45°$, etc. Since a line 157.5° from CS is physically as close to CS as a line 22.5° from CS, both these values are plotted at the same absolute distance from CS, in a positive or negative direction. For purposes of symmetry the same response measure was plotted at $+90°$ and $-90°$.

Effects of amount of training on absolute generalization were quite similar for both experiments. As the number of days of VI training was increased, the total responses made to each of the different test stimuli increased. Thus amount of absolute generalization was a direct function of number of days of training.

Since this finding may merely reflect the greater overall resistance to extinction of groups trained for longer periods of time, a more interesting question is whether there are significant differences in the slopes of the absolute gradients for the different groups. If additional training merely added a constant number of responses to each value on the separate gradients (additive relation), then all the gradients in Figure 1 would be parallel. Inspection of Figure 1 suggests that this is not the case, since gradients become steeper with increased amount of training. Analyses of variance of the data in Figure 1 (two types of pigeons, four amounts of training, and five stimuli analyzed separately for the left and right sides of the gradient) support this conclusion strongly; besides the significant main effects of amount of training and stimuli at well beyond the .01 level ($F = 9.97$, $df = 3/56$, and $F = 40.04$, $df = 4/224$, respectively, for the left side of the

FIGURE 1

Gradients of absolute generalization for groups receiving 2, 4, 7, or 14 days of VI training. The training stimulus for all Ss was a vertical line [0°] on the response key. White Carneaux [WC] birds are shown on the left, White King [WK] on the right.

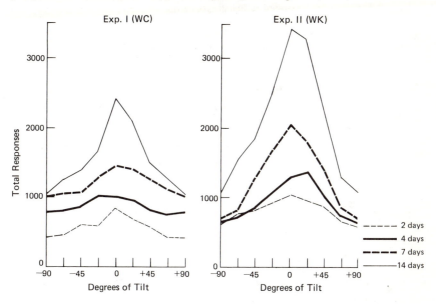

gradient; $F = 10.82$, $df = 3/56$, and $F = 40.81$, $df = 4/224$, respectively, for the right side), there was a highly significant Amount of Training × Stimuli interaction for both the left side ($F = 5.35$, $df = 12/224$, $p < .01$) and right side ($F = 5.69$, $df = 12/224$, $p < .01$) of the gradients. The main effect of type of pigeon (White Carneaux vs. White King) was not significant for either side of the gradient ($p > .05$), but there was a significant Type of Pigeon × Stimuli interaction on both sides ($F = 4.80$, $df = 4/224$, $p < .01$, on the left side; $F = 5.75$, $df = 4/224$, $p < .01$, on the right side).

Since slopes differ significantly, these statistical tests indicate that the relationship between absolute generalization and amount of training is not an additive one. From the gradients of Figure 1 it is not easy to make a decision about an alternative possibility, that of a multiplicative relation (i.e., each value on one gradient is multiplied by a constant to obtain the values on the other gradients). If the relationship were multiplicative, the gradients of Figure 1 would steepen with higher overall response levels. This is in fact the general trend in Figure 1, since the 14-day Ss responded the most during testing and had the steepest gradients. However, such a result could occur even if the relation were not multiplicative. Therefore, an examination of relative gradients, in which each value in Figure 1 is converted to a percentage of total response output over its entire gradient,[1]

[1] If relative gradients are plotted in another conventional manner, viz., by scaling the response output to each test stimulus as a fraction of the response output to the training stimulus, the same conclusions would be obtained as for the results shown in Figure 2.

FIGURE 2

Gradients of relative generalization for groups receiving 2, 4, 7, or 14 days of VI training.

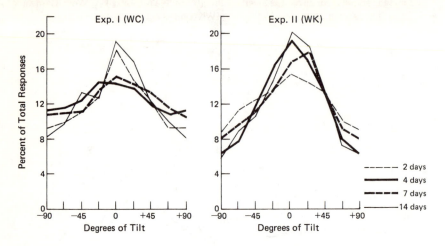

was undertaken. If the relationship in Figure 1 were a simple multiplicative one, all relative gradients would be essentially the same.

Figure 2 presents relative generalization gradients derived from the data of Figure 1. Inspection of Figure 2 shows that with only one exception (the 2-day group in Experiment 1) the relative gradients steepened systematically as a direct function of number of days of training; the 14-day gradient was the steepest of all in both experiments. To put it another way, the relative proportion of responding to the CS increased with increases in the number of days of VI training.

The most appropriate statistical test for evaluating the significance of the slope differences in Figure 2 is not easy to decide upon. When the relative scores were subjected to the same type of analysis of variance as were the absolute scores above, the Amount of Training × Stimuli interaction (i.e., slope differences) failed to reach an acceptable level of significance for either the left or right side of gradients ($F = 1.4$, on each side, $df = 12/224, p > .10$). But the analysis was continued to examine linear components (Edwards, 1964, p. 233), and the linear component of the Amount of Training × Stimuli interaction proved to be statistically significant ($F = 4.87, df = 3/224, p < .01$, for the right side; $F = 3.37, df = 3/224, p < .05$, for the left side). The significance of this interaction presumably reflects the steepening of the slopes of relative gradients with increases in the amount of VI training.

Therefore, the relationship displayed in Figure 1 is not a simple multiplicative one. Figures 1 and 2, taken together, show that gradients of both absolute and relative generalization steepen with increased training in a free operant situation.

Discussion

As Brown (1965) has also pointed out, one of the problems in analyzing the effects of various independent variables on stimulus generalization involves the appropriateness of using absolute or relative gradients in summarizing the results. These two types of gradients may change in different directions, the slope of one varying systematically in a different way from the slope of the other as a function of a given independent variable. In our experiment, however, the slopes of both absolute and relative gradients became steeper as a function of amount of VI training. The first of these results indicates that extended training does not merely add on a constant number of responses to each value on the absolute gradients, whereas the results from the relative gradients imply that a simple multiplicative relation is not appropriate for summarizing the absolute gradients either. The steepening of relative gradients could be interpreted as an increase in discriminability or "discrimination" with added training, since the proportion of total responding to the CS systematically increases.

Another source of confusion in studies of this kind lies in the distinction between amount and slope of absolute and relative generalization. Figure 1 does show that the amount of absolute generalization (i.e., total number of responses to non-CS values) increased with increased training (which, if phrased this way, is the consistent conclusion from all the studies summarized in the review articles on stimulus generalization mentioned in the introduction to the present paper), whereas Figure 2 shows that the amount of relative generalization (i.e., the percentage of total responses to non-CS values) generally decreased with increased VI training. Therefore, different conclusions regarding the interrelationships between absolute and relative generalization might be drawn in our study depending on whether one uses amount or slope as a criterion; the amounts varied in opposite directions, the slopes in the same direction as a function of extended training. A failure to be specific about this distinction is apparently one of the reasons why there has been so much disagreement in the interpretation of prior results concerning the effects of amount of training on stimulus generalization.

Our results appear to support some of the theoretical predictions of Hull (1952, Chap. 3) and Estes (1959) regarding the effect of practice on changes in the form of generalization gradients. Hull predicted that relative gradients should steepen with practice because of the loss of power of incidental irrelevant stimuli to control the CR. Estes' statistical theory implies that added practice is likely to increase the probability of S's responding to relevant stimulus elements, which presumably would be reflected in a steepening of relative gradients. In connection with these theoretical notions it is worth pointing out that we utilized the so-called nondifferential procedure (Jenkins & Harrison, 1960) during training, where a response is merely reinforced in the presence of a single stimulus; the differential procedure, on the other hand, involves reinforcement in one stimulus condition and extinction in another. Since discrimination training is suppos-edly absent during the nondifferential procedure, some workers (e.g., Thompson, 1958) have justifiably wondered how discrimination learning (i.e., steepening of relative gradients) could occur on such a procedure. Perhaps the blackouts in our study, or the intertrial intervals which are usually interspersed with stimulus presentations in other studies, are among the important procedural aspects which enable discrimination learning to develop, possibly in the manner Hull suggested.

Despite our finding that the slopes of both absolute and relative gra-dients steepen with increased training, it is possible that even further VI training (e.g., more than 20 days) would have produced an eventual de-crease in the slope of relative gradients. Friedman and Guttman (1963) observed that Ss tested for generalization after 30 days of VI training yield flatter relative gradients than Ss trained for the usual 1–2 wk. Possibly "proprioceptive control" and "locked rates" (Blough, 1963) become a fac-tor after very extended training, which in turn weakens the control by external stimuli.

References

Blough, D.S. Interresponse time as a function of continuous variables: A new method and some data. *J. Exp. Anal. Behav.*, 1963, **6**, 237–246.

Brown, J. S. Generalization and discrimination. In D. Mostofsky (Ed.), *Stimulus generalization*. Palo Alto: Stanford University Press, 1965.

Edwards, A. L. *Experimental design in psychological research*. New York: Holt, Rinehart, & Winston, 1964.

Estes, W. K. The statistical approach to learning theory. In S. Koch (Ed.), *Psychology: A study of a science*. Vol. 2. New York: McGraw-Hill, 1959.

Friedman, H., & Guttman, N. A further analysis of the effects of discrimination training upon stimulus generalization. Paper presented at the Conference on Stimulus Generalization, Boston University, 1963.

Guttman, N. & Kalish, H. I. Discriminability and stimulus generalization. *J. exp. Psychol.*, 1956, **51**, 79–88.

Hall, J. F. *The psychology of learning*. New York: J. B. Lippincott, 1966.

Hearst, E., Koresko, M. B., & Poppen, R. Stimulus generalization and the re-sponse-reinforcement contingency. *J. Exp. Anal. Behav.*, 1964, **7**, 369–380.

Hull, C. L. *Principles of behavior*. New York: Appleton-Century, 1943.

Hull, C. L. *A behavior system*. New Haven: Yale University Press, 1952.

Jenkins, H. M., & Harrison, R. H. Effects of discrimination training on auditory generalization. *J. Exp. Psychol.*, 1960, **59**, 246–253.

Kalish, H. I. Stimulus generalization. In M. Marx (Ed.), *Learning processes*. New York: Macmillan Company, in press.

Kimble, G. A. *Hilgard and Marquis' conditioning and learning*. New York: Apple-ton-Century-Crofts, 1961.

Mednick, S. A., & Freedman, J. L. Stimulus generalization. *Psychol. Bull.*, 1960, **57**, 169–200.

Olson, G., & King, R. A. Stimulus generalization gradients along a luminosity continuum. *J. Exp. Psychol.*, 1962, **63**, 414–415.

Razran, G. Stimulus generalization of conditioned responses. *Psychol. Bull.*, 1949, **46**, 337–365.

Thompson, R. F. Primary stimulus generalization as a function of acquisition level in the cat. *J. comp. physiol. Psychol.*, 1958, **51**, 601–606.

OVERTRAINING, REVERSAL, AND EXTINCTION IN RATS AND CHICKS

N. J. Mackintosh

The paper on overtraining and discrimination reversal by N. J. Mackintosh (1965) represents a brilliant piece of detective work. Two puzzles confronted Mackintosh at the outset. First, the overlearning-reversal effect (ORE—the paradoxical finding that extra training on a discrimination problem facilitates, rather than retards, later learning of the reversal problem) was thought to be elusive. Second, and more relevant to these studies, the ORE didn't seem to occur in chicks; in fact, extra training on a discrimination problem appeared to retard their learning of the reversal problem. This specific issue, how to resolve the discrepancy between ORE studies using rats and chicks, and the more general issue, how to explain the elusiveness of the ORE, provided the impetus for Mackintosh's work.

The first study reported by Mackintosh was a replication of the phenomenon described above. Rats and chicks had to choose the correct goal box (either black or white) to get food. Each subject was trained until it chose correctly on 18 of the 20 daily trials. After reaching this criterion of learning, half the subjects were given extra training (100 more trials). Finally, all of the subjects were given the reversal problem; that is, they had to choose the *opposite* goal box to obtain food. Mackintosh found that extra training caused the rats to learn the reversal problem more quickly, but it retarded reversal learning in the chicks.

Experiment 2 was similar except that the responses in all the subjects were extinguished just before reversal learning to the point where the subjects were choosing both alternatives equally often. The results showed that non-overtrained rats, like overtrained chicks, began their reversal learning task by incorrectly choosing the former correct choice.

Mackintosh's attention theory provides a way to explain these findings. Briefly, he argues that when subjects are mastering a discrimination problem, they strengthen their attention to the relevant stimulus dimensions and, at the same time, acquire a specific response to the correct stimulus based on their attention. Overtraining may strengthen either the attention response (if it is not already at maximum strength) or the specific response. Since birds are already so sensitive to visual stimuli, Mackintosh claims that overtraining merely strengthens their specific response choice. During reversal learning, then, the chicks switch their attention to other stimulus dimensions, but continue to make the formerly correct response. Rats, on the other hand, are not as sensitive to visual stimuli, so extra training tends to strengthen their attention to the stimulus dimension but not the specific response. During reversal, even though the specific choice response is readily extinguished, the attention response continues to be strong. Note that this theory is best expressed in the discussion of Experiment 2 and the introduction to Experiment 3.

The support for Mackintosh's theory is found in Experiments 3 and 4. These studies essentially replicate Experiments 1 and 2 with one important exception: a very difficult visual discrimination was used for the chick subjects. Mackintosh speculated that if the chick's attention to the simple black/white discrimination was already so high that it couldn't be strengthened by extra trials, then by using a very difficult discrimination, where attention strength is initially low, chicks should behave like rats in showing the ORE. This is precisely what Mackintosh found, and it led him to conclude that the ORE is not at all elusive; the phenomenon simply depends on the difficulty of the discrimination task.

Brookshire, Warren, and Ball (1961) have shown that the effect of overtraining on reversal learning differs for rats and chicks: Among other results, they found that rats (as was already well established) learned the reversal of a simultaneous brightness discrimination faster if overtrained on the initial problem, whereas chicks learned the reversal more slowly after initial overtraining.

From "Overtraining, Reversal, and Extinction in Rats and Chicks" by N. J. Mackintosh in *Journal of Comparative and Physiological Psychology*, Volume 59, Number 1, 1965. Copyright 1965 by the American Psychological Association. Reprinted by permission.

The present paper reports an attempt to investigate the basis of this apparent difference in the behavior of the rat and the chick. The first experiment repeated that of Brookshire et al. (1961) in a slightly different apparatus, partly in order to check the replicability of their results but largely in order to discover which stage of reversal learning was impeded by overtraining in chicks. In the case of rats, overtraining facilitated reversal learning, because although it slightly retarded extinction, it greatly reduced the number of trials during which Ss responded consistently to position cues (Mackintosh, 1962; Reid, 1953). Overtraining might retard reversal in chicks *either* because it so greatly retarded extinction that any savings in number of trials spent responding to position was outweighed, *or* because although it did not greatly increase resistance to extinction, it either did not decrease or actually increased the tendency to respond to position.

Experiment 1

METHOD

Subjects. Twenty-four male chicks (White Leghorn, Light Sussex cross) were obtained from a commercial hatchery when 1-day-old. At the age of 6 days they were put on a feeding schedule of 1½-hr. free access to food every 24 hr. Twelve Ss (overtrained group) started training when 10 days old, the remainder (nonovertrained) when 16 days old. The reason for starting training at different ages is that Warren, Brookshire, Ball, and Reynolds (1960) have shown that there is a considerable age effect on rate of reversal learning in young chicks; the present arrangement ensured that both groups began reversal at approximately the same age.

The other Ss were 12 naive female hooded rats 3 mo. old, from the colony maintained at the Institute of Experimental Psychology, Oxford. They were maintained on a 1½-hr. feeding schedule beginning a week before the start of the experiment.

Apparatus. A Grice-type discrimination box had an 8×4 in. start box leading into a choice area 12 in. long, 4 in. wide at the near end, and expanding to 12 in. wide at the far end. The choice area led straight to two 12×6 in. goal boxes side by side, each containing a $2 \times 2 \times 2$ in. feeding box at the far end. The start box and choice area were painted gray, one goal and feeding box black, and the other white. The lateral arrangement of the two goal boxes could be varied. The apparatus was 6 in. high and covered with hinged transparent Perspex. Transparent Perspex guillotine doors separated the start box from the choice area, and the choice area from the two goal boxes (these last were used to prevent retracing).

Procedure. For pretraining the two goal boxes were lined with gray cardboard, and Ss, first introduced into the apparatus in groups of four, were given a number of rewarded trials. For the chicks, pretraining was completed in a single day: they were given 20-min. exploration followed by two rewarded runs (the second forced to the opposite side). More extensive pretraining, spread over 5 days, was necessary for the rats: two 30-min. exploration periods were followed by 20 rewarded trials (with a sufficient number forced to equalize experience with either side).

Ten noncorrection trials were given on the first 2 days of training, thereafter 20 trials were run each day. A correct response was rewarded with 10-sec. eating for rats, and 5-sec. eating for chicks (hungry chicks peck at a remarkable rate). In each case appropriate commercial food was used. After incorrect responses, Ss were detained in the negative goal box for 10 and 5 sec., respectively. The position of the positive and negative goal boxes was varied in accordance with prepared random orders. The intertrial interval (during which Ss were kept in individual detention cages) was 3–6 min. The criterion of learning was 18 correct responses out of any 20 consecutive trials.

Experimental design. All Ss initially learned a brightness discrimination, half with black, half with white positive. Upon reaching criterion, half of each group was reversed immediately, while the other half was given 100 overtraining trials before reversal.

TABLE 1

Means and Standard Deviations of Trials to Criterion in Experiment 1

Groups	N	Original learning Trials to criterion		Reversal Initial errors		Position responses		Trials to criterion	
		M	SD	M	SD	M	SD	M	SD
Rats									
Overtrained	6	35.00	12.58	4.00	1.15	0.50	0.50	33.83	3.39
Nonovertrained	6	36.67	9.43	3.17	2.67	2.33	1.25	43.33	6.11
Chicks									
Overtrained	12	24.17	5.00	30.17	17.07	1.42	1.32	65.50	13.37
Nonovertrained	11	25.45	6.59	14.18	8.90	0.54	0.50	49.18	14.21

The results for both rats and chicks are shown in Table 1. One chick (black positive) died before the end of the experiment, so that there are only 11 Ss in the nonovertrained chick group.

Three scores are given for reversal learning: (a) as a measure of extinction, number of initial consecutive errors; (b) number of runs of five consecutive responses to one or other position (position responses); (c) overall trials to criterion. The rat results are closely similar to those of earlier experiments (e.g., Mackintosh, 1962): overtraining increased initial errors (but here not significantly: $t = .66$), decreased number of responses to position ($t = 2.77, df = 10, p < .02$), and significantly facilitated reversal ($t = 2.39, p < .05$).

As in the Brookshire et al. experiment (1961) reversal of a simultaneous brightness in chicks was retarded by overtraining ($t = 2.73, df = 21, p < .02$). The extinction scores show that this is partly because overtraining retarded extinction ($t = 2.20, p < .05$) but it also seems that overtraining increased the number of trials of position responses ($t = 2.00, df = 21, p < .06$). Thus the critical difference between rats and chicks in the effect of overtraining on reversal is that in rats overtraining reduced the tendency to respond to the irrelevant cue of position, while in chicks it seemed to increase it.

Experiment 2

Having established that there is indeed a difference in the behavior of rats and chicks in this situation, the logical next step was to attempt to correlate this difference with others; in this way it may be possible to achieve understanding of the differences in the mechanisms underlying the behavior of the two species.

If rats are trained on a simultaneous brightness discrimination, then extinguished until they choose S+ and S− equally often, and finally reversed, a striking difference appears between overtrained and nonovertrained Ss during early reversal trials (Mackintosh, 1963b); overtrained Ss show an orderly increase in their choice of the new S+, but nonovertrained Ss initially show an orderly increase in their choice of the *former* S+. The interpretation offered for this effect (discussed below) is that it is due to the same factor that reduces position responses during reversal after initial overtraining. If this suggestion is correct, since chicks show an increase in position responding after overtraining, it follows that overtrained chicks should show a greater tendency than nonovertrained to revert to selecting their former S+ in early reversal trials after extinction.

Since these earlier rat results (1963b) were obtained in a jumping stand, a group of rats was run in the same apparatus as the chicks in the present experiment, to ensure that any species difference that might appear could not be due simply to a difference in apparatus.

METHOD

Subjects and apparatus. The Ss were 24 male chicks and 12 female rats of the same age and from the same stock as those used in Experiment 1. The same apparatus was used.

Procedure. All details of feeding schedule, pretraining, and training were the same as in Experiment 1. During extinction, both feeding boxes were empty, and Ss were detained in the goal box (chicks for 5 sec., rats for 10 sec.) whichever side they chose.

Experimental design. All Ss initially learned a brightness discrimination, half with black, half with white positive. Half of each group was trained to criterion, half was given 100 overtraining trials. After initial training all Ss were extinguished until they selected S+ and S− five times each over any 10 consecutive trials. After reaching this criterion of extinction, all Ss learned the reversal of their initial brightness discrimination.

TABLE 2

Means and Standard Deviations of Trials to Criterion in Experiment 2

Groups	Original learning		Extinction		Reversal	
	M	SD	M	SD	M	SD
Rats						
Overtrained	40.00	10.00	35.50	10.24	25.17	2.96
Nonovertrained	35.00	5.00	27.33	8.06	42.00	10.68
Chicks						
Overtrained	26.66	6.24	66.33	24.60	30.08	6.20
Nonovertrained	28.33	6.89	61.66	25.44	22.58	3.76

FIGURE 1

Reversal learning curves in Experiment 2. (Last 10 trials of extinction are depicted at 0.)

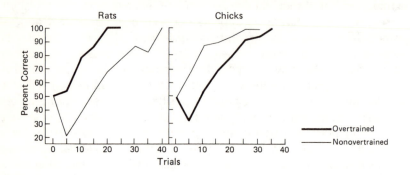

Results

Trials to criterion for initial learning, extinction, and reversal are shown in Table 2. For both rats and chicks, overtraining increased resistance to extinction, but in neither case was the difference significant (for rats, $t = 1.37$, $df = 10$, $p > .10$; for chicks, $t = .44$). In rats, overtraining led to significantly faster reversal ($t = 3.40$, $df = 10$, $p < .01$), in chicks to significantly slower reversal ($t = 2.72$, $df = 22$, $p < .02$).

The course of reversal learning is shown in Figure 1. The rat results confirmed those of the earlier experiment: nonovertrained Ss showed an initial drop in their choice of the new S+. Over Trials 1–10, they scored significantly below chance ($t = 3.32$, $df = 5$, $p < .05$), and made significantly more errors than overtrained Ss ($t = 4.98$, $p < .001$). In chicks, by contrast, it is the overtrained Ss who showed a drop (although a more transient one) in their choice of the new S+: over Trials 1–5, they scored significantly below chance ($t = 3.25$, $df = 11$, $p < .01$), and made more errors than nonovertrained Ss ($t = 4.26$, $p < .001$). As in Experiment 1, overtrained chicks made more position responses than nonovertrained chicks (1.00 against .58); if the results for the two experiments are combined, the difference was significant ($t = 2.22$, $df = 45$, $p < .05$).

Discussion

These two experiments confirm one previous finding about reversal learning in chicks: that reversal of a simultaneous brightness discrimination is retarded by overtraining. They also establish two new points: that overtraining increases the tendency to respond to position cues during reversal, and that correlated with this increase in position responses is a tendency to revert to selecting the former S+ upon reversal after extinction. In all three cases, overtraining has precisely the opposite effect on rats.

Any explanation of these differences must presumably depend upon a prior understanding of the cause of these effects in rats. Sutherland (1959) and Mackintosh (1962) have suggested the following explanation of the overtraining reversal effect in rats. In order to solve a discrimination problem, rats must learn first to switch in that analyzer which detects differences between S+ and S−, and secondly to attach appropriate responses to the outputs of the analyzer. If overtraining increases the strength with which the relevant analyzer is switched in without causing a corresponding increase in response strength, then upon reversal overtrained Ss will extinguish their original responses but still retain the relevant analyzer. They will therefore not switch in other analyzers (show little tendency to respond to irrelevant cues), and after extinction will merely have to learn to attach new responses to the analyzer (show an orderly increase in choice of the new S+). Nonovertrained Ss, however, will extinguish the relevant analyzer at an early point in reversal, and will therefore switch in other analyzers (respond to irrelevant cues). If after extinction they are rewarded for choice of their former S−, they will switch back in the relevant analyzer with its original responses still attached, and thus will increase their choice of their former S+.

The crucial assumption in this explanation is that overtraining strengthens the relevant analyzer without producing a corresponding increase in response strength. Thus perhaps the simplest explanation of the different behavior of the chicks is that overtraining increases response strength more than it increases analyzer strength. This is not an entirely implausible suggestion. Chicks are markedly more visual animals than rats; in the present experiments they learned the initial brightness discrimination with an average of only 3.32 errors (while the rats made 6.83; the difference is highly significant—$t = 4.98$, $df = 69$, $p < .001$). This would imply that the brightness analyzer has a high priority for the chick in this situation, and that it cannot therefore be greatly strengthened by increased training. If overtraining has only a small effect on the probability of switching in the brightness analyzer, but does increase response strength, then it will now be overtrained Ss that extinguish the analyzer before its response attachments, and nonovertrained Ss that extinguish the responses but retain the analyzer.

Experiment 3

This account is speculative; it does, however, provide a possible *explanation* of differences in the behavior of rats and chicks. It is also testable: if chicks are trained on a sufficiently difficult discrimination, where the initial probability of switching in the relevant analyzer is low, then there is no reason why overtraining should not benefit reversal. In the Brookshire et al. experiment (1961), when chicks were trained on a relatively difficult "response learning" problem, overtraining did not in fact retard reversal at all, so that there is already some support for the hypothesis. The following two experiments provide a direct test. In the first, chicks were trained on an orientation discrimination involving two irrelevant cues, and it was predicted that overtraining would now facilitate reversal. The final experiment investigated the effect of extinction on reversal learning in this more complex situation.

METHOD

Subjects and apparatus. The Ss were 20 naive male chicks from the same stock as those used in the previous experiments. The apparatus was an enclosed Y maze, painted flat gray throughout. The start arm was 8 in. long and separated from the two 11 in. long goal arms by a transparent guillotine door. The two goal arms were set at an angle of 90° to one another, and 135° to the start arm. The arms were 6 in. wide, and 8 in. high; the whole maze was covered with a hinged transparent lid. At the end of each goal arm was a gray goal box, 7 × 7 × 3 cm.; the stimuli (7 × 2 cm. rectangles cut from black or white ¼-in. Perspex) were glued to the front face of the goal boxes.

Procedure. Details of feeding schedule, pretraining and training were the same as for Experiment 1. All Ss initially learned a horizontal-vertical discrimination, half with horizontal, half with vertical positive. The stimuli were changed from side to side in a random order, thus position acted as one irrelevant cue. A second irrelevant cue was the brightness of the rectangles: on half the trials S+ was black and S− white, on remaining trials S+ was white and S− black.

Ten Ss began training when 10 days old, and received 100 overtraining trials after reaching criterion; 10 Ss began training when 16 days old, and were trained to criterion only. After initial learning, all Ss were reversed.

Results

The results are shown in Table 3. There was some sign that nonovertrained Ss learned the initial problem faster (presumably because they were older), but the difference fell short of significance ($t = .99$). In reversal, however, overtrained Ss, in spite of taking somewhat longer to extin-

TABLE 3

Means and Standard Deviations of Trials to Criterion in Experiment 3

Groups	Original learning:		Reversal					
	Trials to criterion		Initial errors		Position response [a]		Trials to criterion	
	M	SD	M	SD	M	SD	M	SD
Overtrained	152.00	12.20	18.70	13.11	7.10	3.05	138.10	26.27
Nonovertrained	136.00	9.30	10.40	9.22	10.10	3.11	177.50	42.50

[a] Block of 10 trials with 8 or more responses to irrelevant cues.

TABLE 4

Means and Standard Deviations of Trials to Criterion in Experiment 4

Groups	Original learning		Extinction		Reversal	
	M	SD	M	SD	M	SD
Overtrained	132.00	13.38	83.00	31.29	92.80	24.44
Nonovertrained	119.00	8.06	48.60	13.57	129.10	33.95

guish ($t = 1.53$, $df = 18$, $p > .10$), made fewer responses to irrelevant cues ($t = 2.07$, $p < .05$), and reached criterion significantly sooner than nonovertrained Ss ($t = 2.97$, $p < .01$). Thus a clear-cut overtraining reversal effect can be demonstrated in chicks, and the manner in which it is shown is precisely the same as in rats.

Experiment 4

Since in this situation, overtraining does significantly facilitate reversal learning in chicks, the extinction procedure of Experiment 2 should also show results similar to those of the rats—and unlike those of the chicks in that experiment. That is to say, if chicks are extinguished and then reversed on this discrimination, then nonovertrained Ss should show a greater drop than overtrained Ss in choice of the new S+ during early reversal trials.

METHOD

The Ss were 20 male chicks; the apparatus and discriminanda the same as in Experiment 3, and the training and extinction procedures the same as in Experiment 2.

Results

Trials to criterion for original learning, extinction, and reversal are shown in Table 4. Although overtrained Ss were again slightly slower in original learning ($t = .79$), and took longer to extinguish ($t = 3.17$, $df = 18$, $p < .01$), they learned the reversal significantly faster than nonovertrained Ss ($t = 2.60$, $p < .02$). The course of reversal learning is shown in Figure 2. It is apparent that nonovertrained Ss now showed the larger drop in choice of the new S+ during early reversal trials; over Trials 1–20, they scored significantly below chance ($t = 5.58$, $df = 9$, $p < .001$), and made significantly more errors than overtrained Ss ($t = 2.16$, $p < .05$). Overtrained Ss also scored below chance ($t = 2.41$, $p < .05$)—unlike overtrained rats. Before concluding that this shows a small quantitative difference between rats and chicks, it should be pointed out that relative to original learning

FIGURE 2

Reversal learning curves in Experiment 4 for Days 1–5. (Last 10 trials of extinction are depicted at 0.)

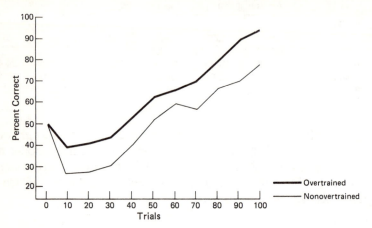

speed, the amount of overtraining given to the chicks in this experiment was very much less than that given to the rats in the earlier experiment.

Discussion

The results of the four experiments provide impressive support for the explanation of the overtraining reversal effect discussed earlier. As has been pointed out elsewhere (Mackintosh, 1963a; Mackintosh & Mackintosh, 1963); this account predicts that the magnitude of the effect will vary directly with the complexity of the discrimination problem. It also predicts (Mackintosh, 1963b) that where the effect is found, if Ss are extinguished before reversal, nonovertrained Ss will show an initial increase in choice of their former S+ upon reversal. The confirmation of this prediction for rats did not rule out the possibility that this difference between overtrained and nonovertrained Ss was only a coincidence and not causally related to the difference in overall rate of reversal learning. The chick results make this very much less likely: in a situation in which overtraining retards reversal for chicks, it is overtrained Ss who show the drop in choice of the new S+, whereas when overtraining facilitates reversal, it is nonovertrained Ss who show the larger drop.

The results of Experiments 1 and 3, that in chicks overtraining retarded the reversal of a brightness discrimination, but facilitated the reversal of a more complex orientation discrimination, reinforces one rather general impression about the overtraining reversal effect. On the basis of several failures to find the effect in position reversal studies with rats, some writers (D'Amato & Jagoda, 1962; Hill, Spear, & Clayton, 1962) have concluded that it is an elusive phenomenon. What in fact they have shown is that with rats as with chicks the effect will only appear if the discrimina-

tion is one in which the relevant dimension is not a "perceptually dominant" one for the animal concerned. For the rat a brightness discrimination
usually satisfies these conditions, for the chick it does not. But just as in
rats (Mackintosh, 1963a) and octopuses (Mackintosh & Mackintosh, 1963)
a greater effect appeared in a more complex situation, so in chicks a more
complex situation was necessary for the effect to appear at all.

References

Brookshire, K. H., Warren, J. M., & Ball, G. G. Reversal and transfer learning
following overtraining in rat and chicken. *J. comp. physiol. Psychol.*, 1961,
54, 98–102.

D'Amato, M. R., & Jagoda, H. Overlearning and position reversal. *J. exp. Psychol.*, 1962, **64**, 117–122.

Hill, W. F., Spear, N. E., & Clayton, K. N. T maze reversal after several different
overtraining procedures. *J. exp. Psychol.*, 1962, **64**, 533–540.

Mackintosh, N. J. The effects of overtraining on a reversal and a nonreversal shift.
J. comp. physiol. Psychol., 1962, **55**, 555–559.

Mackintosh, N. J. The effect of irrelevant cues on reversal learning in the rat. *Brit.
J. Psychol.*, 1963, **54**, 127–134. (a)

Mackintosh, N. J. Extinction of a discrimination habit as a function of overtraining.
J. comp. physiol. Psychol., 1963, **56**, 842–847. (b)

Mackintosh, N. J., & Mackintosh, J. Reversal learning in *Octopus vulgaris* Lamarck
with and without irrelevant cues. *Quart. J. exp. Psychol.*, 1963, **15**, 236–
242.

Reid, L. S. The development of noncontinuity behavior through continuity learning. *J. exp. Psychol.*, 1953, **46**, 107–112.

Sutherland, N. S. Stimulus analysing mechanisms. In, *Proceedings of a symposium
on the mechanisation of thought processes.* Vol. 2. London, England: Her
Majesty's Stationery Office, 1959. Pp. 575–609.

Warren, J. M., Brookshire, K. H., Ball, G. G., & Reynolds, D. V. Reversal learning
by white leghorn chicks. *J. comp. physiol. Psychol.*, 1960, **53**, 371–375.

6/ Biological Perspectives in Animal Learning

In recent years a number of psychologists have posed a serious challenge to basic learning research: laws of learning may be specific to the type of species and stimuli used to study learning. Stated somewhat differently, the explication of a universal set of principles of learning may be impossible to achieve; principles by which organisms learn may depend, to a very large degree, on the specific characteristics of the subject. Indeed, the ability to learn about certain things may have evolved differently among species, not to mention the sensory-motor differences that necessarily limit, or at least modify, commonly shared learning abilities.

The importance of maintaining a biological perspective in learning research has not been fully resolved. Some psychologists claim that although we do not know all the laws of learning, there is little evidence to suggest that the principles or laws of which we are aware differ qualitatively between species. However, many others now agree that at least the unique sensory-motor capabilities of each species must be seriously considered in any analysis of the learning process. The rate at which a given organism will learn a particular response does appear to be related to its biological endowment.

The evidence suggesting that a biological perspective is required for learning research originated in a number of different areas of inquiry, three of which are illustrated in this chapter. Perhaps the foremost area has been in research on acquired taste aversions. As shown in the first paper, by Wilcoxon, Dragoin, and Kral (1971), the degree to which an aversion is learned depends largely on the sensory capacity of the organism which, in turn, reflects the evolutionary development of the species. A second field that has provided support for a biological approach has been in the area of avoidance learning. Some types of avoidance responses are, paradoxically, more difficult to learn than others, even though the response itself is well mastered in other situations. The second paper chosen here, by Grossen and Kelley (1972), suggests that the ease with which an instrumental avoidance response is acquired may also reflect the evolutionary development of the animal. Finally, humans also might be relatively indifferent (or sensitive) to certain learning situations. The last paper, by Öhman, Eriksson, and Olofson (1975), suggests, for example, that humans learn to fear phobic stimuli more easily than neutral stimuli.

ILLNESS-INDUCED AVERSIONS
IN RAT AND QUAIL: RELATIVE SALIENCE
OF VISUAL AND GUSTATORY CUES

Hardy C. Wilcoxon, William B. Dragoin,
and Paul A. Kral

The first selection in this chapter, by Hardy C. Wilcoxon, William B. Dragoin, and Paul A. Kral (1971), is a widely cited article on taste aversion learning in rats and quail. The "special" characteristics of taste aversion learning (including the fact that poison is an effective US even when it is given hours after the flavor CS) have prompted many psychologists to consider more carefully the relationship between learning and evolution. Indeed, the authors of this paper note that their ". . . experiments came from a general view that the behavior of an organism, including what it can and cannot readily learn, is largely a product of its evolutionary history." In the case of taste aversion, these specialized learning abilities presumably evolved because it was highly adaptive for the rats to be able to associate flavor and malaise despite an interval of hours between the two events.

In this paper the authors provide dramatic support for the idea that learning abilities do reflect evolutionary development. They hypothesized that if a rat has an affinity for associating flavors and poison because of a reliance on its keen sense of taste for feeding, then quail should demonstrate an affinity for associating visual stimuli and poison. After all, the quail's learning ability, too, should reflect its specialized evolutionary development—particularly in the area of visual sensitivity, given its reliance on vision during foraging.

In the most important groups of Experiment 1, both rats and quail were given blue sour water followed by poison. Then, during the test, the aversion to each component was measured. As shown in panels D and E of Figure 1, rats showed a strong aversion to the flavor component whereas quail found the blue color to be the more aversive stimulus.

Earlier work on illness-induced aversions to eating and drinking shows rather clearly that the rat, at least, must have either a gustatory or an olfactory cue in order to learn to avoid ingesting a substance if the illness that follows ingestion is delayed by ½ hour or more. Visual, auditory, and tactual cues, even though conspicuously present at the time of ingestion, do not become danger signals for the rat in such circumstances (Garcia and Koelling, 1966; Garcia, McGowan, Ervin, and Koelling, 1968; Rozin, 1969). On the other hand, blue jays (*Cyanocitta cristata bromia* Oberholser, Corvidae) easily learn to reject toxic monarch butterflies (*Danaus plexippus* L., subfamily Danainae) on sight, although the model suggested for this learning gives emetic reinstatement of taste during illness a prominent, mediating role (Brower, Ryerson, Coppinger, and Glazier, 1968; Brower, 1969).

Impetus for our experiments came from the general view that the behavior of an organism, including what it can and cannot readily learn, is largely a product of its evolutionary history. In view of the rat's highly developed chemical senses, nocturnal feeding habits, and relatively poor vision, its ability to learn to avoid toxic substances on the basis of their taste or smell, rather than their appearance, is not surprising. But how general is this phenomenon across species? Might we not expect a diurnal bird, with its superior visual equipment and greater reliance upon vision in foraging for food and drink, to show a different pattern? Perhaps such birds, even in situations involving long delay between the time of ingestion of some food and the onset of illness, can learn to avoid ingesting substances that are distinctive in appearance only.

We report here two experiments which show that bobwhite quail (*Colinus virginianus*) can associate a purely visual cue with a long-delayed, illness consequence. In the first experiment we investigated the relative salience of a visual cue and a gustatory cue in both rats and quail. In the second experiment, in which we used quail only, we controlled for two variables which, unless accounted for, would not have allowed clear-cut interpretation of the first experiment.

Forty 90-day-old male Sprague-Dawley rats and 40 adult male bobwhite quail were subjects in the first experiment. All were caged individually and had free access to food throughout the experiment. At the start, both species were trained over a period of several days to drink all of their daily water from 30-ml glass Richter tubes. Water was presented at the same time each day, and the time allowed for drinking was gradually reduced to a 10-minute period. Baseline drinking was then measured for 1 week, after which experimental treatments were imposed.

On treatment day, subgroups of each species received an initial 10-minute exposure to water that was either dark blue ($N = 8$), sour ($N = 8$), or both blue and sour ($N = 24$). Water was made blue by the addition of three drops of vegetable food coloring to 100 ml of water. Sour water consisted of a weak hydrochloric acid solution (0.5 ml per liter). One-half hour after removal of the distinctive fluid all subjects were injected intra-

From "Illness-Induced Aversions in Rat and Quail: Relative Salience of Visual and Gustatory Cues" by Hardy C. Wilcoxon, William B. Dragoin and Paul Kral in *Science*, Volume 171, February 26, 1971. Copyright 1971 by the American Association for the Advancement of Science. Reprinted by permission.

FIGURE 1

Comparison of the amount of water consumed by quail (solid lines) and rats (dashed lines) expressed as a ratio of the amount consumed on a given day to the amount consumed on treatment day (TD); E_1 through E_5 are the five extinction trials given at 3-day intervals after the single conditioning trial on TD. (A) Group S : S; (B) group B : B; (C) group BS : BS; (D) group BS : S; (E) group BS : B.

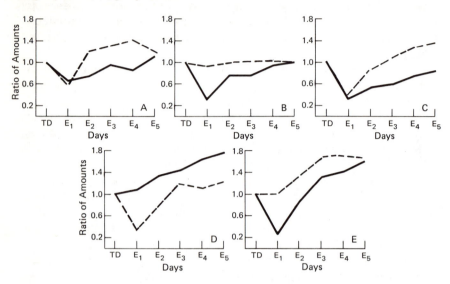

peritoneally with the illness-inducing drug, cyclophosphamide. The dosage for the rats was 66 mg/kg, a dosage known to be effective for establishing one-trial aversions to distinctive tastes in the rat. We used a larger dose (132 mg/kg) for the quail, however, because exploratory use of the drug with the birds showed that the larger dose was necessary in order to produce the primary symptom of illness that rats exhibit, namely, extensive diarrhea.

For 2 days after treatment all subjects drank plain water at the regular 10-minute daily drinking period. This allowed them time to recover from the illness, as evidenced by remission of diarrhea and a return to baseline amounts of water consumption. Extinction tests were then begun to determine whether aversive conditioning had been established to the cues present in the water on treatment day. Five 10-minute tests were conducted, one every third day, with 2 days intervening between tests during which subjects were allowed to drink plain water to reestablish the baseline.

Animals that drank sour water on treatment day were tested with sour water (S : S); those that drank blue water on treatment day received blue water in the extinction tests (B : B). However, the 24 animals of each species that had drunk blue-sour water on treatment day were divided into three subgroups for testing. One group of each species was tested on blue-sour water (BS : BS), another on sour water (BS : S), and the third on blue water (BS : B).

Figure 1 shows a comparison of the amount of water drunk by rats and quail over five extinction trials for each of the five treatment : test conditions. Differences between mean drinking scores on treatment day and the first extinction trial (E_1) were assessed for statistical significance by the t-test. Results in the S : S condition show that the sour taste by itself was an effective cue for avoidance in both rat ($P < .02$) and quail ($P < .05$). Only the quail, however, showed reduced drinking ($P < .01$) of water that was colored blue on treatment and test days (B : B). In the BS : BS condition, both species again showed significantly reduced drinking in the tests ($P < .001$).

Perhaps the most striking results were shown by the last two subgroups for which the compound cue (BS) of the treatment day conditioning trial was split for separate testing of each component. In the latter two conditions (BS : S and BS : B) rats and quail showed a remarkable difference with respect to the salience of gustatory and visual cues. When the sour element of the compound conditioning stimulus was the test cue (BS : S), rats avoided it ($P < .001$) but quail did not. On the other hand, when the blue color was the element tested (BS : B), quail avoided it ($P < .01$) but rats did not. The behavior of the quail in these split-cue tests is especially informative. Although the quail learned the aversion to taste alone (S : S condition), removal of the visual element from the compound conditioning stimulus (BS : S condition) apparently constituted such a radical change in stimulus for them that it rendered the remaining taste element ineffective. The results demonstrate, therefore, not only that quail can associate a visual cue with long-delayed illness, but also that a visual cue can be so salient as to overshadow taste when the two cues are compounded.

The most important result of this experiment is that quail were somehow able to associate blue water with a subsequent illness which we induced arbitrarily ½ hour after removal of the drinking tube. Failure of the rats used in our experiments to do so does not, of course, constitute a powerful argument that this species cannot associate a visual cue over a long delay. It is conceivable, although we think it unlikely, that rats see no difference between plain and dark blue water. In any event, Garcia and his co-workers have reported much more convincing evidence than ours that rats do not utilize a visual cue in delayed-illness avoidance learning. Thus, our main concern after the first experiment was whether the results for quail were unequivocal, rather than whether rats could actually see our visual cue.

In the second experiment we attempted to answer two questions: (i) Could the quail have been relying on some subtle taste of the dyed water rather than solely upon its appearance?; and (ii) Was the effective consequence that produced aversion to blue water really the drug-induced illness, or was it the considerable trauma of being caught, handled, and injected?

Birds from each of the five earlier subgroups were assigned to one of two groups, assignment being random except for the restriction that the groups be balanced with respect to prior treatment and test conditions. Procedural details were the same as in the first experiment. On treatment

FIGURE 2

A comparison of the amount of plain water drunk from tinted tubes by drug-treated quail (solid line) and saline-treated quail (dashed line). The amount drunk is expressed as a ratio of the amount ingested on a given day to the amount consumed on treatment day (TD).

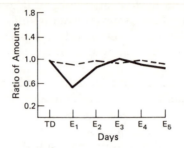

day, however, both groups drank from tinted blue tubes filled with the same plain water to which they were accustomed. One group ($N = 20$) was then injected with cyclophosphamide ½ hour after drinking, whereas the other group ($N = 20$) was injected with normal saline.

Figure 2 shows the result. Birds that received the illness-inducing drug drank less from the tinted tube when they next encountered it ($P < .001$), whereas those injected with saline did not.

Although Figures 1 and 2 give a clear picture of the relative changes

TABLE 1

Means and standard deviations (S.D.) of drinking scores in all groups of both experiments from the last baseline day through the first extinction test (E_1). Probabilities (P) of differences between means of the treatment day (TD) and E_1 were calculated by the t-test for repeated measures.

Group	N	Last baseline day Mean (ml)	S.D.	TD Mean (ml)	S.D.	First recovery day Mean (ml)	S.D.	Second recovery day Mean (ml)	S.D.	E_1 Mean (ml)	S.D.	P
Experiment 1												
S : S quail	8	12.9	3.16	9.1	3.24	9.8	4.49	12.6	3.75	6.0	3.77	< .05
S : S rat	8	17.8	4.60	10.6	2.31	17.6	2.04	19.0	3.16	6.2	3.99	< .02
B : B quail	8	12.4	2.52	14.1	2.83	9.5	4.50	11.4	1.90	5.1	3.66	< .01
B : B rat	8	17.4	2.71	19.6	3.70	13.1	2.60	17.6	2.27	18.1	3.71	
BS : BS quail	8	13.0	1.80	6.8	2.49	12.2	3.03	13.0	2.35	2.2	2.68	< .001
BS : BS rat	8	20.4	2.30	13.1	2.29	15.9	3.38	19.4	3.09	5.0	2.92	< .001
BS : S quail	8	13.2	3.07	6.6	3.03	13.2	4.81	12.2	2.59	7.1	3.61	
BS : S rat	8	17.9	2.90	12.0	2.24	17.6	2.53	17.8	2.17	4.5	2.96	< .001
BS : B quail	8	11.5	2.55	8.8	3.19	11.8	3.70	11.9	2.06	2.2	3.19	< .001
BS : B rat	8	18.5	3.08	12.2	3.73	15.9	1.93	17.5	2.96	12.2	4.35	
Experiment 2, quail only (tinted tube)												
Drug-treated	20	14.1	2.61	13.2	3.58	9.5	3.24	11.4	3.44	7.0	3.63	< .001
Saline-treated	20	13.3	2.86	13.5	3.98	13.0	3.87	13.5	3.30	12.5	3.10	

in drinking occasioned by treatment-day and test conditions, they give no information on the absolute amounts ingested or the degree of variability. Accordingly, means and standard deviations are shown in Table 1 for all groups each day from the last baseline day through the first extinction test. Comparison of baseline scores with those of treatment day shows that sour water, whether blue or not, was somewhat aversive to both species at first encounter, that is, before induction of illness; blue water alone was not. The amount of plain water drunk on the two recovery days after treatment shows a return to baseline levels. Effects of the delayed-illness conditioning trial are seen best by comparing scores of treatment day with those of the first extinction test.

Despite the controls introduced in the second experiment, it could be argued that the results represent not true associative learning but only the birds' increased wariness of strange-looking fluids as a result of recent illness. However, studies now completed in our laboratory show that, although such sensitization or heightened neophobia contributes to the effect, there is a significant associative learning component as well. We are confident, therefore, that at least one avian species can associate a purely visual cue with a delayed illness without mediation by means of peripheral mechanisms such as reinstated taste.

It seems reasonable to expect that this capacity will be widespread among animals whose visual systems are highly developed and whose niches demand great reliance upon vision in foraging. If so, the implications for ecology, behavior theory, and evolutionary theory are of considerable importance.

References

Brower, L. P. *Scientific American*, 1969, **220**, 22.

Brower, L. P., Ryerson, W. N., Coppinger, L. L., & Glazier, S. C. *Science*, 1968, **161**, 1349.

Garcia, J. & Koelling, R. A. *Psychonometric Science*, 1966, **4**, 123.

Garcia, J., McGowan, B. K., Ervin, F. R., & Koelling, R. A. *Science*, 1968, **160**, 794.

Rozin, P. *J. Comp. Physiol. Psychol.*, 1969, **67**, 421.

SPECIES-SPECIFIC BEHAVIOR AND ACQUISITION OF AVOIDANCE BEHAVIOR IN RATS

Neal E. Grossen and Michael J. Kelley

The second paper in this chapter is by Neal E. Grossen and Michael J. Kelley (1972). It is considered one of the best articles addressing Bolles' species-specific defense reaction (SSDR) theory of avoidance learning. Bolles claimed that avoidance in the natural environment is not an arbitrary behavior that is learned gradually through the presentation of rewards. Rather, it is a preprogrammed behavior that occurs reflexively when the animal is threatened. Avoidance in the laboratory, therefore, should occur more or less readily depending on the degree to which the required laboratory response (such as running, jumping, lever pressing) is compatible with the naturalistic, species-specific defense pattern. This is exactly what Grossen and Kelley demonstrate in their paper.

In Experiment 1, the authors showed that rats will become *thigmotatic* (that is, they will remain in close contact with objects) when given shock stress. This is the animal's natural SSDR. Grossen and Kelley then reasoned that since thigmotaxis reflexively occurs during shock, an avoidance response that is compatible with the SSDR should be learned more readily than one that is not. To prove their point, they allowed the subjects in Experiment 2 to avoid shock by jumping onto a platform located either in the center of the cage (incompatible with thigmotaxis) or at the periphery of the cage (compatible with the SSDR). Their results supported Bolles' theory: the peripheral SSDR behavior was learned faster. The third experiment was a control study to show that the rats had no affinity towards the peripheral platform except when stressed. Here, no differences were observed when groups were trained to obtain food rewards from either the central or the peripheral platform. In conclusion, Grossen and Kelley's paper is an excellent example of how avoidance learning has been viewed from a biological perspective.

Bolles (1970) has recently suggested that one of the most important variables in the acquisition of avoidance behavior is the nature of the avoidance response (R_A)itself. His analysis of the acquisition of avoidance learning requires that R_As are more rapidly acquired to the extent that they are related to subjects' species-specific defense responses (SSDRs).

For example, Bolles (1969) has demonstrated that rats will readily acquire a running R_A, but will not learn to avoid if the required R_A is rearing on the hind legs. Bolles (1969) hypothesizes that the failure to acquire the rearing R_A is due to the competition of the rat's natural defensive behavior (running) with the rearing response in the situation.

Barnett (1963) has indicated that rats show positive thigmotaxis (i.e., tend to run in contact with objects) within their free-ranging environment. Such a thigmotactic tendency could be interpreted as a part of the rat's defensive repertoire, since it would be more difficult for predators (especially predatory birds) to attack the rat if the rat remained close to a wall as opposed to its venturing out into an open area.

The above is at best a tenuous post hoc hypothesis in lieu of any direct experimental data. However, if a rat became more thigmotactic under defensive rather than appetitive motivational conditions, we might tentatively conclude that thigmotactic behavior in the rat was more probably under aversive motivation.

Experiment 1

Experiment 1 was concerned with demonstrating that the rat becomes more thigmotactic under aversive conditions, e.g., shock, than under conditions which involved less aversion, e.g., being placed in a large open field while food deprived.

METHOD

Subjects. The subjects were 10 female rats of the Long-Evans strain approximately 90 days old at the beginning of the experiment. The subjects were housed in individual cages 2 wk. prior to the experiment and were 48-hr. food deprived at the onset of the experimental session.

Apparatus. The apparatus was a large box 152.4 × 152.4 × 91.44 cm. The floor of the box was made of .32-cm.-diam. stainless-steel grids placed 1.27 cm. from center to center. Shock could be supplied to the grids from a 1,000-v. dc source through a current-limiting resistor in series with a set of nine neon bulbs in series with the grids, so that the voltage drop between any adjacent grids was 58 v. Current delivered to the subject was somewhat variable but averaged 1.2 ma., with a minimum value of .9 ma. and a maximum of 1.4 ma.

Procedure. Each rat was placed into one corner of the box and allowed a 10-min. adaptation period. For the next 30 min. two observers recorded the percentage of time the rat engaged in thigmotactic behavior and freezing behavior during each 1-min. period. Thigmotactic behavior was defined as the rat being in actual contact with the wall. Freezing behavior was defined as the rat being immobile without movement of the vibrisa. In addition, locomotion and general location of the rats were noted.

Following this 30-min. period the subjects were then given one .2-sec. shock each minute for 30 min. The observers again recorded the percentage of time during each minute that the rat engaged in thigmotactic behavior.

Results and Discussion

The pattern of thigmotactic behavior was the same within each of the 30-min. periods under no-shock and shock conditions, so overall means for each period are reported. During the no-shock phase of observation, the subjects spent 61% of their time engaged in thigmotactic behavior, while during the shock period the subjects spent 82% of their time engaged in thigmotactic behavior. A Wilcoxon signed-ranks test indicated these differences were reliable ($T = 0, p < .01$).

The rats froze on an average of 12% of the time during the no-shock period. During the shock period this behavior became the predominant behavior with the rats freezing 82% of the time. These differences were highly reliable ($p < .01$).

The type of thigmotactic behavior engaged in during the shock period was dramatically different from that shown during the no-shock period. During the no-shock period 67% of the thigmotactic behavior consisted of the rat running around the perimeter of the field, next to the wall, while in the shock period 91% of the rats' thigmotactic behavior consisted of freezing next to the wall, typically in one corner. In addition, rats during the shock period almost never strayed more than 30 cm. from the wall, while in the no-shock period the rats spent some 7% of their time further than 30 cm. from the wall.

The results of this experiment are consistent with those of Blanchard and Blanchard (1969). These investigators found that rats in situations where no explicit moving CS (a prod which also delivered the shock) was present tended to engage in immobility reactions. This tendency to freeze to the situational cues of the apparatus was also observed in the rats during the shock phase of Experiment 1. There was also a marked tendency to freeze in these animals after a single shock. These observations tend to confirm those reported by Blanchard and Blanchard (1969) that fear may be conditioned to situational cues after a single shock.

The present results also support the suggestion that rats increase their thigmotactic behavior in defensive as compared to nondefensive motivational conditions. It would seem to follow from Bolles' (1970) position, then, that a rat should learn an R_A which exploited this thigmotactic tendency more rapidly than a comparable R_A which did not exploit this tendency.

Experiment 2

The second experiment was concerned with demonstrating that an R_A which took advantage of the rat's thigmotaxis would be acquired faster than one which did not. More specifically, a rat should learn to jump onto a ledge on the side of the box more rapidly than a comparable ledge placed in the center of the box.

METHOD

Subjects. The subjects were 32 female rats of the Long-Evans strain approximately 90 days old at the beginning of the experiment. All subjects were housed in individual cages 2 wk. prior to and during the experiment. Food and water were always available in the subjects' home cages.

Apparatus. The same box and shock parameters employed in the previous study were used here.

Two block-like platforms were constructed so that the total area of each was nearly equal.[1] One platform was 10.16 cm. wide, 22.86 cm. above the floor of the box, and could be placed so that it ran continuously around the perimeter of the box. This perimeter platform reduced the dimensions of the grid area, then, to 132.08 × 132.08 cm. or a loss of 5,780.63 sq. cm. The second platform was 78.74 × 78.74 × 22.86 cm. and could be placed in the center of the box. This center platform reduced the area of the grid by 6,200 sq. cm.

Procedure. The rats were assigned randomly to one of three groups. These groups differed only with respect to the nature of the R_A required of the subjects. The rats in Group P had only the outer platform avilable during avoidance training. The rats in Group C had only the center platform available, and the rats in Group PC had a choice of jumping to either the center or perimeter platform.

An avoidance trial was initiated by placing the rat in one corner of the jump-out box about 17.8 cm. from the outer wall, or 7.6 cm. from the wall of the side platform when it was present. No explicit CS was used. The rats were allowed 10 sec. to make an R_A (jumping onto a platform) after being placed in the jump-out box. If a subject failed to respond within 10 sec., it was required to jump onto the platform to escape the shock which was discontinuous (.2-sec.-on time and 2-sec.-off time). If the subject failed to escape shock, the trial was terminated after 30 sec. and the subject was picked up and held for 20 sec. prior to starting a new trial. The subject was allowed to remain on the ledge for 20 sec. following either an R_A or an escape response and was then picked up and placed in a small cardboard box for 10 sec. prior to replacing it in the apparatus for the next trial. Thus, the intertrial interval was about 30–40 sec. All subjects were given 30 acquisition trials.

Results and Discussion

Group P avoided on 77% of the trials during acquisition, while Group C avoided only 57 of the trials during acquisition. These differences were reliable ($p < .01$). The subjects in Group PC, having a choice of R_As, chose the R_A of jumping onto the side platform 92% of the trials on which they avoided. Overall, they avoided on 72% of the trials.

The results of this experiment are consistent with Bolles' (1970) SSDR hypothesis that animals will readily learn an avoidance response only if this response is closely related to the animals species-specific defensive behavior. Hence, the group of rats in Experiment 2 whose required R_A was jumping onto a platform at the perimeter of a large open field learned in a relatively efficient manner, while the group whose R_A was jumping onto a similar platform in the center of the open field demonstrated great difficulty with this task requirement.

---

[1] In subsequent pilot work we matched ledges in terms of perimeter length rather than their areas and obtained similar results.

Although these results tend to support the notion that the acquisition of an R_A is enhanced if the R_A is related to the subject's species-specific defensive behavior, it may be that the difference is mainly a difference in operant level since thigmotactic behavior is to begin with a high-probability response in the rat. Specifically, the rat's propensity to go to a side platform may be a higher probability response than going to a center ledge. In order to demonstrate that the differences observed under defensive motivation were not entirely due to operant rate per se for the two responses, we would have to show that under appetitive motivation (food reward) either the response of going to the side platform or center platform could be readily acquired.

Experiment 3

Experiment 3 was similar to Experiment 2 except that food was used as the reinforcer instead of shock avoidance.

METHOD

Subjects. The subjects were 12 female rats of the Long-Evans strain approximately 90 days old at the experiment. The subjects were housed individually and reduced to 80% of their ad-lib weight, by food restriction, before the start of the experiment and maintained at that weight throughout the experiment. Water was always available in the subjects' home cages.

Apparatus. The apparatus was the same large box used in the previous experiment. Two small block-like platforms 31 × 31 × 13 cm. were constructed so either of them could be placed in a corner of the box or the center of the box. A small glass food cup was attached to the center of these platforms.

Procedure. The subjects were gentled and adapted to the apparatus for 10 min. each day for 1 wk. Following this period the subjects were randomly assigned to three groups of four each.

One group was rewarded for going to the platform placed in the corner, while another group was rewarded for going to the platform placed in the center. A third group was rewarded for going either to the platform in the corner or the platform in the center (this was the only group which had both platforms present). The subjects in this latter group were forced to go to the center platform or the side platform (order determined randomly) on either Trial 1 or Trial 2. These subjects were then allowed to make their own choice on the remainder of the trials. The reward for all subjects was four .045-mg. Noyes pellets.

Each subject was placed in the corner of the box at the start of a trial. The subjects in each group were placed so that each had a comparable distance to run in order to gain reward. Latency measures for the amount of time from placement until eating were taken. Each subject was given four such trials each day for 5 days with about 1 min. between trials.

Results and Discussion

An analysis of variance of the center and side group latencies by trials indicated no reliable effect due to the response requirement ($F < 1$) nor was there any interaction of Type of Response × Trials ($F < 1$). The two groups of subjects readily acquired the required response and appeared to do so at nearly the same rate.

The subjects in the group which had a choice between the side and center response showed no clear-cut preference. Two of the four subjects almost always went to the center and the other two almost always went to the side. All subjects performed each response at least three times on the free-choice trials. This would seem to indicate that if the motivation is appetitive, there is little difference in the rats' choice of these two responses.

General Discussion

The results of the present experiments indicate that the range of available responses that a rat will acquire in learning situations is greatly restricted under defensive motivation. This response restriction appears to be directly related to the animals' species-specific behavior.

An alternative way of looking at these results, rather than invoking an SSDR concept, is to assume that shock and other stressful stimuli change the operant rate of the responses emitted by the animal. This change in operant rate can be observed, as was the case in Experiment 1, and from these observations it is possible to predict what responses a particular animal will readily acquire under particular motivational conditions.

References

Barnett, S. A. *The rat: A study in behaviour*. London: Metheun, 1963.

Blanchard, R. J., & Blanchard, D. C. Passive and active reactions to fear-elicited stimuli. *Journal of Comparative and Physiological Psychology*, 1969, **68**, 129 –135.

Bolles, R. C. Avoidance and escape learning: Simultaneous acquisition of different responses. *Journal of Comparative and Physiological Psychology*, 1969, **68**, 355–358.

Bolles, R. C. Species-specific defense reactions in avoidance learning. *Psychological Review*, 1970, **77**, 32–48.

ONE-TRIAL LEARNING AND SUPERIOR RESISTANCE TO EXTINCTION OF AUTONOMIC RESPONSES CONDITIONED TO POTENTIALLY PHOBIC STIMULI

Arne Öhman, Anders Eriksson, and Claes Olofsson

The final paper in this chapter, by Arne Öhman, Anders Eriksson, and Claes Olofsson (1975), was selected because it applies a biological perspective of learning to the issue of fear conditioning in humans. The traditional theory of phobias has assumed that virtually any stimulus would become fear-evoking if paired with trauma. Öhman and his colleagues, however, show that this notion is questionable. In their study two kinds of CSs (pictures of snakes versus pictures of "neutral" objects) were paired with a shock US. Using the skin conductance CR to measure strength of aversion, the authors found that the snake stimuli were more strongly conditioned than the neutral CSs. The implication is that many of the phobic stimuli that exist in the everyday world are not arbitrary stimuli that have become dominant through protracted conditioning, but are stimuli that have a special propensity for becoming phobic. This notion has very important implications, not only for our methods of therapy, but also for our general understanding of the nature of humankind.

Ever since its inception as an experimental field of investigation, the psychology of learning has been dominated by associationistic theories. A fundamental assumption within this theoretical framework has been that associations can be studied independent of the associated elements. In other words, the laws of learning have been regarded as valid without qualifications in terms of the kinds of stimuli, responses, or reinforcements involved. Recently, this "premise of equipotentiality" has been persuasively challenged by Seligman (1970), and the argument is substantiated by readings compiled by Seligman and Hager (1972).

The main point in Seligman's alternative to the equipotentiality premise (Seligman, 1970; Seligman & Hager, 1972) is that learning must be viewed from a biological perspective, which is taken to imply that evolution has prepared a certain species to form some associations more easily than others. Thus, he postulates a dimension of preparedness that is defined in terms of "how degraded the input can be before that output reliably occurs which means that learning has taken place [Seligman & Hager, 1972, p.4]," claiming that traditional learning theory has dealt only with the middle, unprepared region of the continuum. Highly prepared learning like, for instance, the acquisition of taste aversion in rats (see reviews by Garcia, McGowan, and Green, 1972, and Rozin and Kalat, 1971) is supposed to be very rapid, whereas extinction is quite slow; it is established even at very long interstimulus intervals (ISIs); it is not mediated by cognitive activity; and it seems to be dependent upon a physiological mechanism different from that of ordinary learning (Seligman & Hager, 1972).

This theory of prepared learning has been based entirely on animal data. However, starting from a suggestion by Seligman (1971) that phobias may be viewed as instances of prepared learning, Öhman, Erixon, and Löfberg (1975) attempted to test the applicability of the theory to human classical conditioning. They presented sets of pictures of snakes, human faces, and houses to human subjects, while measuring skin conductance. One group of subjects was shocked on snakes and another on either faces or houses. The 2 groups did not differ during 10 acquisition trials, but the subjects shocked on snakes showed clear evidence of superior resistance to extinction. Furthermore, this group was not affected by instructions about extinction, in contrast to conventional electrodermal conditioning results (e.g., Grings & Lockhart, 1963). This study, then, lends support to Seligman's prepared learning theory of phobias, and offers the possibility of comparing prepared and unprepared human classical autonomic conditioning.

The present study was planned in order to extend the results of Öhman et al. (1975), and, specifically, to study extinction after different amounts of training. The hypothesis was that autonomic responses to phobic stimuli should appear full blown after only one pairing of conditioned stimulus (CS) and unconditioned stimulus (US), whereas a number of pairings should be necessary to establish conditioned responses to neutral stimuli.

In order to optimalize the conditions for observing the effect of phobic stimuli, a number of modifications of the previous procedure (Öhman et al., 1975) were introduced. First, in the previous study, sets of stimuli were used, which implies that concept learning was part of the conditioning procedure. In the present experiment, learning was facilitated by exposing each subject to one stimulus only. Thus, there were different groups of subjects given potentially phobic and supposedly neutral stimuli. To avoid incidental influences unrelated to the central theme of a set of phobic or neutral pictures, it was necessary to present different pictures of the same type to the different subjects in a certain group. Second, there were 3 modes of stimulus presentations, with different groups of subjects exposed to either paired CS–US presentations, random noncontingent stimulus presentations, or CS-alone presentations. Thus, associative effects and effects of sensitization could be separated from each other and from effects of the phobic stimulus alone, in contrast to the previous study where only associative and sensitization effects could be differentiated. This modification is essential, since noncontingent presentations of CS and US may be sufficient to produce prepared learning (Garcia et al., 1972), thereby invalidating a sensitization control group as a baseline for the assessment of conditioning effects. Third, vasomotor activity measured as finger pulse volume changes was introduced as an additional dependent variable in order to obtain more extensive information about prepared autonomic conditioning.

METHOD

Subjects. A total of 131 students attending introductory courses in psychology at the University of Uppsala were paid to participate as subjects. There were 66 males and 65 females, with a mean age of 24.1 yr. (*SD* of 4.4 yr.). Eleven subjects were excluded because of apparatus failure or experimenter error, leaving 12 groups with 10 subjects each.

Apparatus. Skin conductance was measured by a constant voltage circuit (Hagfors, 1970) through Beckman-Offner silver/silver chloride electrodes, which had a diameter of 8 mm. and were enclosed in a plastic cup filled with Beckman-Offner electrode paste. Finger pulse volume was measured by a transilluminated photoplethysmograph, set at a time constant of .1 sec. Respiration, which was used as a control variable, was measured by a strain gage fastened around the subject's chest. Output from the various transducers was amplified and recorded on a Hewlett-Packard 7700 polygraph. Electric shock USs were delivered through silver electrodes from a capacitor, which was charged by a stabilized dc current, whose voltage could be manipulated.

Color slides, 24 × 36 mm., were projected from a Sawyer projector onto a milk-glass screen placed approximately 2 m. in front of the subject, which resulted in a visible picture of 38 × 56 cm. The exposure time was controlled by an electronic timer, and the interval between successive exposures, as well as between USs, was programmed on a 2-channel Tandberg tape recorder, which started the timer controlling the exposures and discharged the shock capacitor by activating relay detectors.

The visual stimuli consisted of 10 different pictures of snakes and 10 different pictures of houses. Thus, the 10 subjects in a group had 10 different pictures, each subject seeing a different picture.

Design. Basically, a conpletely randomized factorial 3 × 2 × 2 design was used. The first factor consisted of conditioning, sensitization, and CS-alone treatments. The second factor was phobic (snakes) vs. neutral (houses) CSs, and the third factor was 1 vs. 5 reinforcements. Thus, there were 12 groups with 10 subjects each. In some analyses a trial factor with repeated measurement was added.

Procedure. The subject was seated in a comfortable armchair in a room separated from the experimenter and the apparatus. He was then shown 5 pictures of snakes and 5 pictures of houses presented in randomized order, and was asked to rate each picture on a discomfort scale ranging 1–9. A second rating of the same pictures was performed after the conditioning session. The pictures used differed for different subjects, and in no case was the CS for a particular subject among the pictures he rated.

The second phalanges of the subject's right first and second finger were washed with distilled water, and the skin conductance electrodes were applied with the help of adhesive electrode collars. The electric shock electrodes were taped to the dorsal side of the right third and fourth fingers. The plethysmograph was attached to the second finger of the left hand, and the respiration strain gage was put in place around the subject's chest. The functions of the different transducers were informally explained while they were being applied.

The intensity of the US was individually decided by exposing the subject to gradually increasing intensities until a sensation level defined as "definitely unpleasant but not painful" was reached. This procedure was not carried out on the 4 groups of subjects in the CS-alone treatments.

The subject was instructed that he would be shown a picture a number of times, and, if he belonged to the conditioning or sensitization treatments, that a few shocks would be given. The door to the subject's room was then closed, and the subject was allowed to rest for a few minutes while the experimenter calibrated the apparatus.

The duration of the picture CSs was 8 sec., and when reinforcement was given the US followed immediately at CS offset, giving an ISI of 8 sec. In the sensitization treatments, the USs were interspersed in the intervals between successive CSs according to a random schedule.

Five initial habituation trials and 10 extinction trials were common for all 12 groups. For the conditioning groups, 1 or 5 reinforced acquisition trials were interspersed between the habituation and extinction phases. The sensitization groups had 1 or 5 CSs and 1 or 5 USs in the corresponding part of the experiment, and the CS-alone groups were merely given 1 or 5 CSs.

Response definitions. Skin conductance multiple responses were defined according to the criteria proposed by Lockhart (1966). Thus, CS responses were scored in the interval 1−4 sec., and pre-US responses in the interval 4−9 sec., after CS onset. During extinction "post-US" responses were scored 1−4 sec. after CS offset. If more than one response occurred in an interval, the one having the most typical latency for the subject was scored. The responses were directly obtained in conductance, with micromhos as units.

Finger pulse volume responses were scored according to the method proposed by Furedy (1968). Thus, the scoring interval was 2−10 sec. after CS onset, and the responses were expressed as percentage of volume pulse change.

Trials with respiratory irregularities were excluded from further analyses.

During extinction, trials were grouped in blocks of 2 trials each.

Results

Habituation

The skin conductance responses showed a decrease over trials during the initial habituation to CS alone ($F = 24.90$, $df = 4/432$, $p < .001$), as well as significantly larger responses to phobic than to neutral stimuli ($F = 14.67$, $df = 1/108$, $p < .001$). The groups having a shock level determined before the experiment showed larger responses than the CS-alone groups, as revealed by the main effect ($F = 3.73$, $df = 2/108$, $p < .05$) and follow-up Tukey tests. For finger pulse volume responses there was only a significant decrease over trials ($F = 13.63$, $df = 4/432$, $p < .001$).

Acquisition

The effects of acquisition were tested in 2 different ways. First, the first extinction trial was taken as a test trial for acquisition, and completely randomized $3 \times 2 \times 2$ analyses of variance were carried out. Second, within-subjects acquisition curves were examined for the subjects given 5 reinforcements, which resulted in a $5 \times 3 \times 2$ split plot type of analysis with 10 subjects in each of the 6 groups. Tukey tests were used to further analyze significant effects.

Skin conductance responses. The mean response magnitudes dur-

TABLE 1

Mean Skin Conductance (in μmhos) and Finger Pulse Volume Responses (% Volume pulse change) during the First Extinction Trial as a Function of Stimulus and Treatments

| | Skin conductance | | | | | | Finger pulse volume | |
| | CS response | | Pre-US response | | Post-US response | | | |
Treatment	Phobic	Neutral	Phobic	Neutral	Phobic	Neutral	Phobic	Neutral
Conditioning	.533	.333	.342	.140	.365	.222	.086	.106
Sensitization	.265	.235	.111	.069	.135	.130	.074	.073
CS alone	.045	.019	.014	.008	.003	.003	.089	.015

Note. Abbreviations: CS = conditioned stimulus; US = unconditioned stimulus.

ing the first extinction trials are shown in Table 1. Since there was no effect of the number-of-reinforcements factor, data have been collapsed over this variable. The conditioning groups exceeded the sensitization and CS-alone groups for all 3 response components. The difference between the conditioning group on the one hand and the sensitization and CS-alone groups on the other tended to be larger for the phobic stimuli, indicating better conditioning in the latter case. Table 2 shows the F ratios for the stimulus, conditioning, and Stimulus × Conditioning effects. For the CS response, the significant effect of conditioning was due to larger responses in the conditioning and sensitization groups as compared to the CS-alone groups. The tendency toward better conditioning to phobic stimuli was not significant. For the pre-US response, all 3 effects shown in Table 2

TABLE 2

F Ratios for the Stimulus, Conditioning, and Stimulus × Conditioning Effects during Acquisition

| | Between-subjects analysis | | | | | Within-subjects analysis | | | |
| | | Skin conductance response | | | Finger pulse volume | | Skin conductance response | | Finger pulse volume |
Source	df	CS	Pre-US	Post-US		df	CS	Pre-US	
Stimulus (S)	1/108	2.02	6.52[1]	1.05	1.07	1/54	4.66[1]	2.57	3.21
Conditioning (C)	2/108	13.52[3]	17.13[2]	12.04[3]	2.10	2/54	6.40[2]	3.61[1]	1.10
S × C	2/108	.97	3.40[1]	.95	2.57	2/54	.88	.53	.10

Note. Abbreviations: CS = conditioned stimulus, US = unconditioned stimulus.
[1]$p < .05$.
[2]$p < .01$.
[3]$p < .001$.

FIGURE 1

Skin conductance conditioned stimulus (CS) and pre-unconditioned-stimulus (pre-UCS) response acquisition curves for the phobic and neutral conditioning, sensitization, and CS-alone groups ($n = 10$).

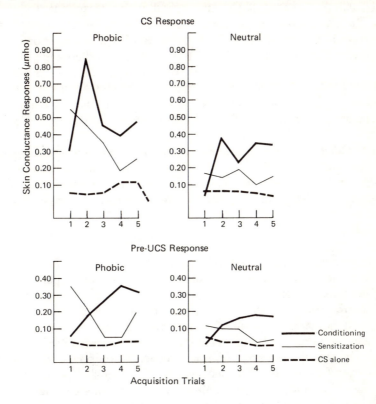

were significant. The interaction between stimulus and conditioning was due to better conditioning to phobic stimuli. Thus, the phobic conditioning groups exceeded both the phobic sensitization and CS-alone groups, which did not differ, whereas there were no significant differences between the neutral groups. Furthermore, the phobic conditioning group showed significantly larger responses than the neutral conditioning group, whereas no difference emerged between the sensitization and CS-alone groups for the 2 types of stimuli. The significant main effect of conditioning on the post-US response, finally, was due to larger responses in the conditioning than in the sensitization and CS-alone groups.

The results for the within-subjects acquisition analyses are shown in Figure 1. The CS responses were larger to phobic than to neutral stimuli, and the conditioning groups tended to exceed the sensitization and CS-alone groups in response magnitude. Table 2 shows that the stimulus effect was significant, but the significant conditioning effect pertained to larger responses in the conditioning and sensitization groups as compared with the CS-alone group. In addition, the effect of trials was significant ($F = 2.81$, $df = 4/126$, $p < .05$), as well as the Trials × Conditioning interaction ($F = 3.74$, $df = 8/126$, $p < .01$), the latter being due to the initial rise in the acquisition curves for the conditioning groups as compared with the falling or flat functions for the other treatments.

The pre-US responses showed tendencies similar to those of the CS response, but as shown in Table 2 only the effects of conditioning were significant. Follow-up tests showed that only the conditioning groups differed from the CS-alone groups. As was the case with the CS response, there was a Trials × Conditioning interaction ($F = 5.00$, $df = 8/216$, $p < .01$), which was due to the increasing trends over trials in the conditioning groups in contrast to the falling trends of the sensitization and CS-alone groups.

Finger pulse volume responses.   Data from the between-subjects acquisition analysis are shown in Table 1, and those from the within-subjects analysis in Table 3. As can be seen in Table 2 there were only very weak effects of stimulus pairing, and in no case was there any significant effect.

Extinction

Separate analyses of variance with a split plot 5 × 3 × 2 × 2 design were carried out for each response measure during extinction. As before, Tukey tests were used in followups.

Skin conductance responses.   The mean response magnitudes for the skin conductance measures are shown in Figure 2. Since there were no effects of number of reinforcements, the data were collapsed for this factor. The results were similar for all 3 response components: There was a slow overall decrease with extinction trials, the overall responding tended to be higher to phobic than to neutral stimuli, and whereas there was an immediate and rather abrupt extinction effect in the neutral groups, the phobic conditioning groups continued to respond throughout the extinc-

TABLE 3

Mean Finger Pulse Volume Responses (% volume pulse change) during Acquisition and Extinction

Treatment	Acquisition (n = 10)		Extinction (n = 20)	
	Phobic	Neutral	Phobic	Neutral
Conditioning	.095	.066	.080	.073
Sensitization	.080	.040	.064	.046
CS alone	.062	.040	.049	.033

Note. Data are collapsed over number of reinforcements. Abbreviation: CS = contitioned stimulus.

FIGURE 2

Skin conductance conditioned stimulus (CS), pre-unconditioned-stimulus (pre-UCS), and post-UCS response extinction functions for the phobic and neutral conditioning, sensitization, and CS-alone groups. (Data were collapsed for the number of reinforcements factor; $n - 20$.)

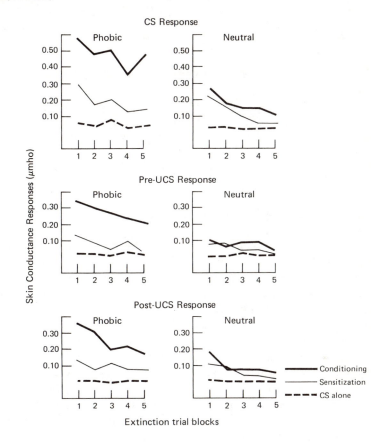

tion period. The relevant statistics are given in Table 4. Follow-up tests showed that the conditioning groups differed from both the sensitization and CS-alone groups in the phobic condition, whereas no significant differences between groups emerged with the neutral stimulus. The effect of the phobic stimulus was a specific associative one, since the phobic conditioning groups exceeded the neutral conditioning groups, whereas the phobic sensitization and CS-alone groups did not differ from the neutral sensitization and CS-alone groups. The post-US response was the only one to show a genuine extinction effect since, according to the Trial × Conditioning interaction ($F = 3.60$, $df = 8/432$, $p < .001$), the conditioning groups tended to converge with the sensitization and CS-alone groups as a function of extinction trials.

Finger pulse volume responses.   The means for finger pulse vol-

TABLE 4

F Ratios for the Trials, Stimulus, Conditioning, and Stimulus × Conditioning Effects during Extinction

Source	df	Skin conductance response			Finger pulse volume
		CS	Pre-US	Post-US	
Trials (T)	4/432	8.24[3]	4.66[3]	10.27[3]	5.36[3]
Stimulus (S)	1/108	10.09[2]	8.46[2]	8.14[2]	2.24
Conditioning (C)	2/108	15.15[3]	12.72[3]	15.35[3]	4.81[2]
S × C	2/108	4.31[1]	5.06[2]	3.91[1]	.13

Note. Abbreviations: CS = conditioned stimulus; US = unconditioned stimulus.
[1] $p < .05$.
[2] $p < .01$.
[3] $p < .001$.

ume responses collapsed over trials and number of reinforcements are shown in Table 3.

The response magnitude diminished as a function of trials and there were overall differences between the different modes of stimulus presentation (see Table 4). Follow-up tests showed that the conditioning groups definitely exceeded the CS-alone groups ($p < .01$), and that they tended to exceed also the sensitization groups ($p < .10$).

Ratings of discomfort. The subject's ratings of discomfort produced by the type of stimulus he had as CS were summed over the 5 stimuli, and a difference between the ratings before and after the conditioning session was computed. Conditioning, sensitization, and CS alone were compared pairwise with t tests for phobic and neutral stimuli. The groups conditioned to snakes had a significantly higher difference than those conditioned to houses ($t = 2.14$, $df = 18$, $p < .05$), with means of 2.05 and .35, respectively. For sensitization and CS-alone groups there were no significant differences.

Discussion

The present data show unequivocally that electrodermal responses conditioned to phobic stimuli are much more resistant to extinction than responses conditioned to neutral stimuli. Whereas all response components showed immediate and complete extinction in the latter case, they showed rather complete resistance to extinction in the former. This effect, furthermore, was a specific associative one, since the phobic conditioning groups differed from the phobic sensitization and CS-alone, and from all the neutral, groups. The ineffectiveness of the number-of-reinforcements factor indicates that the responses to phobic stimuli reached full resistance to extinction after only one CS–US pairing, whereas for the neutral stimuli there was no resistance to extinction even after 5 CS–US pairings. In conclusion, then, it can be stated that the expectations from prepared learning theory were fully confirmed for the extinction electrodermal data.

The electrodermal acquisition data were less consistent. For the CS response, the conditioning and sensitization groups exceeded the CS-alone groups, but did not differ between themselves in either of the 2 analyses; and there was no effect of type of stimulus, although the tendency was in the direction of the hypothesis. The post-US response, too, failed to show superior conditioning to the phobic stimuli, although there were overall effects of conditioning. For the pre-US response, finally, there was a discrepancy between the results from the between- and within-subjects analyses. In the former, there was a significant conditioning effect to the phobic but not to the neutral stimuli, and, as in the case of the extinction data, this effect was specifically associative. In the within-subjects analysis, the tendencies were in the same direction, but only the overall difference between the conditioning and CS-alone groups was significant. Thus, the prepared learning hypothesis was only partially confirmed for the pre-US response and clearly disconfirmed for the CS and post-US responses.

The finger pulse volume responses showed no significant effects during acquisition, and during extinction the conditioning groups exceeded only the CS-alone groups. Although it is possible to condition this response system in a single cue paradigm (Öhman, 1974b), very few conditioning trials were used in the present study, which might prevent the possibility of observing a conditioning effect. Furthermore, peripheral vasomotor changes are less sensitive to psychological impact than are electrodermal responses (Furedy & Gagnon, 1969). Therefore, the present negative findings may indicate that vasomotor responses are less sensitive than electrodermal ones, and that the situation was nonoptimal for learning, rather than being a source of evidence against the prepared learning theory.

The results for the remaining dependent variable, the subjective ratings of discomfort, were positive to the prepared learning hypothesis. Thus, there were differences between the conditioning groups given phobic and neutral stimuli, but not between any other groups. This means that there were detectable subjective effects of the phobic conditioning procedure. Since there was very little extinction of the electrodermal responses to phobic stimuli, but rather complete disappearance of responses to neutral ones, the results from the ratings are in good agreement with those for the autonomic measure.

In comparing the present results with those of the previous study (Öhman et al., 1975), 3 points appear to be especially relevant. First, the objective of optimalizing the conditions for observing the effects of phobic stimuli obviously was successfully fulfilled. Thus, in the previous data, there were clear-cut effects of the phobic stimulus only on the CS responses during extinction, whereas, in the present instance, the effects were quite clear for all 3 response components during extinction, and, to a lesser extent, for the pre-US response during acquisition.

Second, the very rapid extinction to the neutral CSs was of some importance to the success in demonstrating differences between phobic and neutral stimuli in both the previous and the present study. In conventional situations with tone or light CSs, about 10 trials seem to be needed for complete extinction (e.g., Öhman, 1974a; Öhman & Bohlin, 1973), whereas the responses to the supposedly neutral house stimuli disappeared instantly when the US was discontinued. Therefore, it is tempting to speculate that the so-called "neutral stimuli" in effect come from the contraprepared side of the preparedness continuum. These speculations open the possibility of turning the preparedness concept into a true dimension by comparing prepared, unprepared, and contraprepared human autonomic conditioning in the same experimental situation.

Third, the conclusion regarding preparedness differed in both studies according to whether it was based on acquisition or extinction data. This finding restricts the generality of the preparedness concept (cf. Seligman & Hager, 1972, p. 5) in demonstrating that acquisition and extinction data are independent, the latter fulfilling the criterion of prepared learning, whereas the former does not.

A couple of more general problems with the preparedness concept are raised by the present project. First, one may not legitimately conclude that our results show that phobias are based on an inherited disposition to associate fear with certain situations. This is clearly implied in the theory, but this assumption was not tested in either of the 2 studies, nor can it ever be directly tested in the present context. This is, in fact, a fundamental weakness in Seligman's theory, since, instead of suggesting a "resolution of the instinct-learning controversy [Seligman & Hager, 1972, p. 1]," the preparedness concept leaves us with the problem of determining the genetical or experiential basis for the preparedness. A monkey with a well-learned learning set certainly shows "preparedness" when faced with a new discrimination problem, but it is only through knowledge of the background factors that we can explain this behavior in terms of more complex learning rather than in terms of genetical endowment.

For the present data, it remains to be shown that it is the *content* of the snake pictures, as required by the prepared learning theory, and not some abstract property such as attensity, novelty, or complexity, that is effective in producing the superior resistance to extinction. A plausible line of reasoning is to argue that the snake pictures for such reasons (but cf. Klimova, 1965) provoke more orienting responding which in turn gives better conditioning (cf. Öhman & Bohlin, 1973), and in this case there is no need to invoke genetical–evolutionary concepts in the explanation. Such an argument is strengthened by the observation of larger orienting responses to phobic than to neutral stimuli during the initial habituation trials.

A second problem with the preparedness concept is that it runs the danger of becoming circular. This is so since evolution is open to speculative interpretations, rather than presenting a well-established theory from which preparedness can be predicted. Thus, the preparedness concept is anchored primarily on the dependent variable side, and from the history of psychology we know that this might be a paramount problem. The present results, for instance, may be taken as support for the proposition that phobias are instances of prepared learning. If they are interpreted as supporting the notion that prepared learning is very slow to extinguish, however, the circle is completed.

Thus, it appears that the theory of prepared learning is faced with a number of important problems. Nevertheless, it has pointed out the significance of biological context for learning, and it has suggested a number of significant problems for empirical analysis. A more careful evaluation of the theory, therefore, must wait for the accumulation of further knowledge.

References

Furedy, J. J. Human orienting reaction as a function of electrodermal versus plethysmographic response modes and single versus alternating stimulus series. *Journal of Experimental Psychology*, 1968, **77**, 70–78.

Furedy, J. J., & Gagnon, Y. Relationships between and sensitivities of the galvanic skin reflex and two indices of peripheral vasoconstriction in man. *Journal of Neurology, Neurosurgery, and Psychiatry*, 1969, **32**, 197–201.

Garcia, J., McGowan, B. K., & Green, K. F. Biological constraints on conditioning. In A. H. Black & W. F. Prokasy (Eds.), *Classical conditioning II: Current research and theory.* New York: Appleton-Century-Crofts, 1972.

Grings, W. W., & Lockhart, R. A. Effects of "anxiety-lessening" instructions and differential set development on the extinction of GSR. *Journal of Experimental Psychology*, 1963, **66**, 292–299.

Hagfors, C. *The galvanic skin response and its application to the group registration of psychophysiological processes.* (Jyväskylä Studies in Education, Psychology, and Social Research, No. 23) Jyväskylä, Finland: University of Jyväskylä, 1970.

Klimova, V. I. The character of the components of some orientational reactions. In L. G. Voronin, A. N. Leontiev, A. R. Luria, E. N. Sokolov, & O. S. Vinogradova (Eds.), *Orienting reflex and exploratory behavior.* Washington, D. C.: American Institute of Biological Sciences, 1965.

Lockhart, R. A. Comments regarding multiple response phenomena in long interstimulus interval conditioning. *Psychophysiology*, 1966, **3**, 108–114.

Öhman, A. Orienting reactions, expectancy learning, and conditioned responses in electrodermal conditioning with different interstimulus intervals. *Biological Psychology*, 1974, **1**, 189–200. (a)

Öhman, A. The relationship between electrodermal and digital vasomotor responses in aversive classical conditioning. *Biological Psychology*, 1974, **2**, 17–31. (b)

Öhman, A., & Bohlin, G. Magnitude and habituation of the orienting reaction as predictors of discriminative electrodermal conditioning. *Journal of Experimental Research in Personality*, 1973, **6**, 293–299.

Öhman, A., Erixon, G., & Löfberg, I. Phobias and preparedness: Phobic versus neutral pictures as conditioned stimuli for human autonomic responses. *Journal of Abnormal Psychology*, 1975, **84,** 41–45.

Rozin, P., & Kalat, J. Specific hungers and poison avoidance as adaptive specialization of learning. *Psychological Review*, 1971, **78,** 459–486.

Seligman, M. E. P. On the generality of the laws of learning. *Psychological Review*, 1970, **77**, 406–418.

Seligman, M. E. P. Phobias and preparedness. *Behavior Therapy*, 1971, **2,** 307–321.

Seligman, M. E. P., & Hager, J. E. (Eds.) *Biological boundaries of learning.* New York: Appleton-Century-Crofts, 1972.

7/ Cognitive Perspectives in Animal Learning

Perhaps the most fruitful trend in current learning research is the increased use of cognitive language in learning theory. Some claim that the movement began with Rescorla's theory of classical conditioning (see the first paper in Chapter 1 of this volume), which emphasized that the predictability of the CS was the underlying mechanism for conditioning. Predictability on the part of the stimulus, of course, suggests expectancy or cognition on the part of the animal. Regardless, many psychologists have recently appealed to expectancy theory in discussing a wide range of phenomena—from avoidance learning and extinction, to models of depression, to the nature of the learning process itself.

It is useful to emphasize that the new cognitive perspective in animal learning relies heavily on the notion that stimuli highly correlated with particular outcomes predict those outcomes and, in turn, are assumed to produce appropriate expectations for the outcome in the subject. As shown in the first paper of this chapter by Rescorla (1967), the outcome may be unusually "complex," in which case the animal comes to expect more than simply the onset or offset of the US.

Another line of research in this area has focused on compound conditioning where two CSs are used instead of one. The important conclusion reached by Rescorla (1971), in the second paper, is that the "meaning" or predictability of one stimulus profoundly affects conditioning to other cues in the environment.

Finally, some researchers have claimed that learning occurs, or expectancies are generated, even when the response and the US are uncorrelated (that is, when the response is a poor predictor of reinforcement). The expectancy that responding is unrelated to subsequent US presentations, in turn, prevents the subject from learning at some later time when the response would, in fact, lead to reward. This inability to learn is termed *learned helplessness*, and is the subject of the third paper in this chapter, by Seligman, Rosellini, and Kozak (1975).

INHIBITION OF DELAY IN
PAVLOVIAN FEAR CONDITIONING

Robert A. Rescorla

The following article by Robert Rescorla (1967) is one of the most elegant examples of a class of experiments typically called "interaction studies." In these studies, a Pavlovian CS is presented while the animal is engaged in the performance of some ongoing instrumental behavior. By observing changes in the instrumental response rate, one can assess the cognitive or emotional meaning of the Pavlovian stimulus. For example, if the animal were making an avoidance response and a Pavlovian fear CS (a stimulus that had previously been paired with shock) is introduced, the avoidance rate would increase, indicating that the fear added by the superimposed CS was compatible with the fear that underlined the avoidance response.

Interaction studies have gone well beyond simple demonstrations such as the one cited above. In fact, rather specific Pavlovian phemenona have been studied using an interaction design. In this paper, for example, Rescorla first established a baseline level of avoidance responding. Then, in a second phase of the experiment, he instituted a Pavlovian inhibition of delay procedure. In such a situation, a relatively long-lasting CS is followed by a shock US; the subject gradually comes to inhibit the CR during the early part of the CS, but responds with an excitatory CR just prior to the US presentation. In the third phase of the study, when Rescorla presented the CS during avoidance responding, he observed that the response rate changed over the course of the CS. In the early portions, the rate declined (indicating Pavlovian inhibition of delay), whereas during the latter part of the CS, the rate increased (indicating augmentation of instrumental responding due to Pavlovian excitation).

The paradigm of fear conditioning is the same as that used by Pavlov for salivary conditioning—the CS and US are paired independently of S's behavior. But to what degree are similar laws involved? If the laws of fear conditioning are similar to those which Pavlov described for salivary con-

From "Inhibition of Delay in Pavlovian Fear Conditioning" by Robert Rescorla, in *Journal of Comparative and Physiological Psychology*, Volume 64, Number 1, 1967. Copyright 1967 by the American Psychological Association. Reprinted by permission.

ditioning, we should be able to produce not only conditioned elicitors but also conditioned inhibitors of fear. Pavlov found that stimuli which bore certain temporal and logical relations to the US for salivation came to inhibit the flow of conditioned salivation. Following similar Pavlovian paradigms, Rescorla and LoLordo (1965) were able to demonstrate conditioned and discriminative inhibitors of the fear reaction.

The experiments reported here attempt to produce the phenomenon of inhibition of delay for fear conditioning. Pavlov observed that with an extended CS-US interval conditioned salivation was confined (after many trials) to the later part of the reinforced CS. Further, the early portion of such a CS actively reduced the salivary flow which would otherwise have been elicited by other stimuli. Thus the phenomenon of inhibition of delay consists of three separate observations: (a) reduction, as conditioning progresses, in the CR elicited by the early portion of the CS; (b) confinement of the CR to the later part of the CS—resulting in a gradually increasing flow of saliva through the CS-US interval; and (c) the ability of the early part of the CS to inhibit CRs elicited by other stimuli. The question of the present report is whether these observations can be made with fear conditioning.

The fear-eliciting and -inhibiting properties of the CS were assessed by the changes it induced in ongoing Sidman avoidance responding. Increases in rate of avoidance were interpreted as indicating increases in fear, and depressions in rate as indicating inhibition of fear.

Experiment 1

METHOD

Subjects and apparatus. The Ss were 17 mongrel dogs obtained from a local supplier and maintained in individual cages on ad-lib food and water throughout the experiment. The apparatus was a two-compartment shuttle box for dogs described in detail by Solomon and Wynne (1953). The two compartments were separated by a barrier of adjustable height and by a drop gate which, when lowered, prevented S from crossing from one compartment into the other. The floor was composed of stainless steel grids which could be electrified through a scrambler. Speakers, mounted above the hardware-cloth ceiling, provided a continuous white noise background and permitted the presentation of tonal stimuli. The general noise level in the box, with the white noise and ventilating fans on, was about 80-db. SPL; the tones added 10 db. to this level. All stimulus events were automatically controlled and recorded together with response events in an adjoining room.

Procedure. The training procedure was similar to that described by Rescorla and LoLordo (1965). Each S was trained to jump the barrier separating the two sides of the shuttle box to avoid electric shock. Brief (.25-sec.), intense shocks were programmed on a Sidman avoidance schedule; the shock-shock interval was 10 sec. and the response-shock interval 30 sec. The Ss received 3 initial days of avoidance training; on the first day the barrier height was 9 in. and the shock level 6 ma.; on all subsequent days the barrier height was 15 in. and the shock set at 8 ma. Several Ss, reluctant to make initial responses on Day 1, were coaxed by E's calling to them across the barrier.

Beginning with the fourth experimental day, S was confined to half of the shuttle box and given Pavlovian fear conditioning. For the 10 experimental Ss in Group D (delay) a tone CS was presented for 30 sec., and was coterminous with a 5-sec., 3-ma. electric shock. For 5 Ss the CS was a 1,200-cps tone and for 5 a 400-cps tone. Twenty-four trials were given in each Pavlovian conditioning session; the mean intertrial interval was 2 min. For the 7 control Ss, Group DCR (delay control: random), 24 30-sec. tones occurred with a mean intertrial interval of 2 min., and 24 5-sec., 3-ma. shocks were programmed randomly during the session. This was arranged by a series of independent VI tapes begun at random for each S on each day. Shocks could occur during the CS as well as during the intertrial interval, so that CS occurrences provided no information about subsequent US occurrences. For 4 Ss in Group DCR, the CS was a 400-cps tone, and for 3 a 1,200-cps tone.

Following the 3 initial avoidance training days, Pavlovian conditioning and avoidance training days were alternated until S had received a total of 5 avoidance training and 3 conditioning sessions. Pavlovian conditioning sessions were conducted alternately on the two sides of the shuttle box. On the ninth experimental day, the first test session was given. During this session, S performed the avoidance response under extinction conditions; imposed upon this performance were 24 nonreinforced presentations of the 30-sec. CS. The intertrial interval was 1.5, 2, or 2.5 min., with a mean of 2 min. Then Ss received 2 additional days of avoidance training, each of which was followed by another day of Pavlovian conditioning. On the next day a second test session, identical to the first, was given. The avoidance rates during the CS in the two test sessions were examined for evidence of inhibition of delay of the fear reaction.

Results

Avoidance acquisition.   All Ss attained stable avoidance responding by the third day of training. However, records of 3 Ss were discarded, 2 because of illness and 1 because of a procedural error; this resulted in an experimental group of 8 Ss and a control group of 6 Ss.

Effect of the CS upon avoidance.   The mean number of responses in successive 5-sec. periods prior to, during, and following CS presentation during the first test session are shown in the top panel of Figure 1. Little change was noted over the course of the test session, so all CS presentations were combined.

Prior to the onset of the CS, both groups had relatively stable response rates of about 6.5 per minute. With the onset of the CS, Group D showed little change in rate; however, as the CS continued there was a gradual increase in response rate to a maximum during the final 10 sec. With the termination of the CS, there was an abrupt decrement in response rate, followed by a recovery to pre-CS levels. The response rate during the final 10 sec. of the CS was reliably greater than either the rate during the 30 sec. prior to CS onset or the rate during the initial 5 sec. of the CS (Wilcoxon $T = 3, 1.5; p < .05, .02$). The rate during the 5-10 sec. after CS termination was reliably below the rate prior to CS onset ($T = 0$, $p < .01$). Thus on Test Day 1, Group D showed inhibition of delay in the second sense of a confinement of the CR to the end of the CS-US interval.

In contrast, Group DCR showed relatively little change in rate with the introduction and removal of the CS. There was only a slight, but nonsignificant, rate increase with CS onset. To assess the importance of the conditioning contingencies in producing the results for Group D, comparisons were made with Group DCR. Use was made of suppression ratios of the form $A/(A + B)$ where B is the rate prior to CS onset and A is the rate during the period on which we wish to compare the two groups. Use of this ratio provides a partial solution to the problem of individual differ-

FIGURE 1

Mean number of responses in successive 5-sec. periods prior to, during, and following CS presentation on Test Days 1 and 2 of Experiment 1.

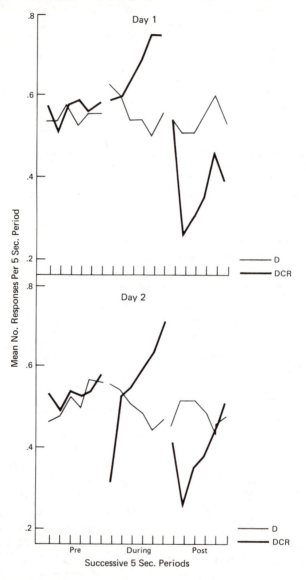

ences in pre-CS response rate. Group D showed a greater increase during the final 10 sec. of the CS than did Group DCR (Mann-Whitney $U = 7$, $p < .02$); the depression in rate following CS termination was greater for Group D ($U = 0$, $p < .01$). However, the two groups did not differ reliably in the rate during the initial 5 sec. of the CS.

The results of the second test session are shown in the lower panel of Figure 1. The two groups responded similarly prior to CS onset. However, with the onset of the CS, Group D showed a marked drop in response rate. This was followed by a gradual growth in response rate until it reached a maximum at the end of the CS. As on Day 1, CS termination led to a sharp rate reduction. For Group DCR, CS presentation resulted only in a slight decrease in rate throughout the trial.

An overall Friedman analysis of variance by ranks substantiated the growth in response rate during the CS for Group D ($\chi r^2 = 13.45, p < .02$). Further individual Wilcoxon tests showed both that the rate during the initial 5 sec. of the CS was below the pre-CS rate and that the rate during the final 5 sec. of the CS was above the pre-CS rate ($T = 1, 2; p < .02$).

Between-group comparisons of suppression ratios confirmed the fact that the two groups differed markedly in their response to the CS. Group D showed a lower response rate during the initial 5 sec. of the CS ($U = 3, p < .01$) but a higher rate during the final 5 sec. of the CS ($U = 4, p < .01$). The rate during the period 5-10 sec. after CS termination was lower for Group D than for Group DCR ($U = 1, p < .01$).

Discussion

The results of this experiment provide evidence for all three senses of inhibition of delay. (a) There was a reduction, as conditioning continued, in the response rate elicited by the early portion of the CS. On Test Day 1 the first 5 sec. of the CS produced no change over the pre-CS response level; however, after 48 additional trials, the rate during this period was depressed below the pre-CS level. However, only two levels of conditioning were examined here; Experiment 2 provides more evidence on this point. (b) On both Test Days 1 and 2, the increase in response rate produced by the CS was largely confined to the later part of the CS. This is in marked contrast to the abrupt increase in response rate found by Rescorla and LoLordo (1965) with short CS-US intervals. (c) On Test Day 2, the onset of the CS produced a decrement in response rate. Thus the early portion of the CS inhibited the ambient level of fear maintaining the avoidance response. During the initial 5 sec. of the CS, Ss showed typical signs of relaxing, raising their tails and panting.

When measured against the results of the control group, both the excitatory effect of the later part of the CS and the inhibitory effect of the onset of the CS are due to the Pavlovian conditioning contingency. It should be noted that the control procedure used here is one not typically employed, it has been argued elsewhere that the arrangement of a truly random relation between CS and US such as that of Group DCR provides the most appropriate control procedure for both inhibitory and excitatory Pavlovian conditioning (Rescorla, 1967).

One of the most striking results of this experiment was the rate depression following CS termination. This result confirms the similar finding by Rescorla and LoLordo (1965) with short CS-US intervals. There are several possible explanations for this finding. It may be, for instance, that it results from the failure to deliver the US during the test session; *S* may be "surprised" or "relieved." Experiment 2 provides some evidence on this point.

Experiment 2

In this experiment inhibition of delay was again measured as it affected operant behavior. However, unlike Experiment 1, the Pavlovian conditioning trials were presented while *S* was responding on the Sidman avoidance schedule. This change in procedure has several advantages for answering questions raised by Experiment 1. First, Experiment 1 provided only a crude estimate of the growth of inhibition of delay over conditioning trials. Performing the Pavlovian conditioning while the operant was occurring allowed assessment of conditioning on each trial, thereby providing a detailed record of the development of both inhibition and excitation. Secondly, the technique of this experiment allowed us to look for rate depression following CS termination when the US continued to be presented.

This experiment also employs a different response, the panel press. This has the advantage of yielding higher response rates, thereby permitting more sensitive measurement.

METHOD

Subjects. Eight mongrel dogs, obtained from a local supplier, were maintained on ad-lib food and water in individual cages throughout the experiment.

Apparatus. The apparatus was a modification of that described by Black (1958). The *S* was placed in a Pavlov-type harness, supported beneath by a rubber sling through which its legs extended. The *S*'s four legs were secured to the frame of the harness by tie ropes and its head rested on a metal tray. On either side of *S*'s head, and approximately 2 in. from it, was mounted a Lucite panel 8 in. square. The depression of either panel for approximately ½ in. served as the avoidance response. When additional restraint was necessary, a metal yoke was placed over *S*'s neck and secured to the panel frames. Shock electrodes, consisting of brass plates, were smeared with electrode paste and mounted directly on the hind paws of *S*.

The apparatus was positioned in a sound-attenuating booth with a continuous white noise at 80-db. SPL. Speakers mounted behind and slightly above *S* permitted presentation of a 400-cps tone from an Eico tone generator, which added approximately 10 db. to the ambient noise level. A single 50-w. bulb mounted approximately 4 ft. in front of *S* and 1 ft. above its head provided the illumination for the chamber. Experimental events were automatically programmed with relays and timers located outside the experimental chamber.

Procedure. All Ss were first given three 1-hr. sessions of Sidman avoidance training. The shock-shock interval was 10 sec. and the response-shock interval 30 sec. Shocks were 0.25 sec. long at 4–6 ma. (the minimum in this range that maintained initial avoidance). Presses on either panel postponed shock for 30 sec. with one further restriction: responses within 0.5 sec. following a shock were ineffective. Only the initial panel depression postponed shock; holding the panel down had no effect upon shock delivery.

On Days 4–10, avoidance training was continued but 24 30-sec. presentations of the 400-cps tone were superimposed on the behavior. The intertrial interval was 1.5, 2, or 2.5 min., with a mean of 2 min. Shocks, at 8 ma., could be received according to the Sidman avoidance contingencies at any time during these sessions, including the periods during which the tones were presented. These sessions provided an estimate of the unconditioned reaction to repeated presentations of the tone.

On Day 11, Pavlovian fear conditioning was begun. The procedure was identical to that of pretest days except that each 30-sec. CS terminated with a 0.25-sec., 8-ma. shock. Delivery of the CS and US was independent of S's panel pressing. Conditioning continued for 300 trials.

The first 12 trials of Day 23 continued Pavlovian conditioning. However, superimposed upon conditioning were presentations of a flashing light stimulus. On each trial the light illuminating the chamber was flashed at a rate of 1 per second for 5 sec. The time during the CS that the light occurred was determined by S's behavior on Day 22. On 6 trials the light flashed during the 5-sec. period of minimum rate on Day 22, while on the other 6 trials the light flashed during the period of the CS of maximum response rate on Day 22. The order of presentations of the light was random and counterbalanced across Ss. It was hoped that the use of this procedure would make it possible to observe both disinhibition of the inhibition early in the CS and external inhibition of the excitation late in the CS.

Beginning with Trial 13 of Day 23 and continuing through Day 35, extinction conditions were in effect (300 trials). Tone CSs continued to be presented as in conditioning, except that now the shock US was omitted. Through extinction, as on all other days, the Sidman avoidance schedule remained in effect.

Results

Avoidance acquisition. Training of the panel-press response was somewhat more difficult than training barrier hurdling; however, terminal response rates were higher. By the final pretest day the mean rate was 15.9 per minute; the earned shock frequency was reduced to 1.6 per session.

Pretest. Although the initial presentations of the CS often produced disruption of the avoidance response, by the final pretest session the CS had little effect. The upper left panel of Figure 2 shows the mean response

FIGURE 2

Mean number of responses in successive 5-sec. periods prior to, during, and following CS presentation on 6 selected days from Experiment 2.

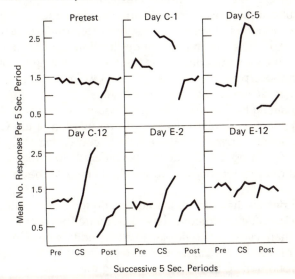

rate during successive 5-sec. periods prior to, during, and after tone presentation on the final pretest day (Day 10). Onset and continuation of CS produced no noticeable change in response rate; however, termination of the CS produced a slight rate depression (Wilcoxon $T = 1, p < .02$).

Conditioning and extinction. The top middle panel of Figure 2 shows the results of the first conditioning session (C-1). The introduction of conditioning trials raised the overall response rate both in the presence and absence of the CS. The rate in the 30 sec. prior to CS onset was 21.1 per minute on Day 11 compared to 16.7 per minute on Day 10. The response rate during the CS increased to 29.4 per minute, so that the rate during the CS was reliably greater than that prior to CS onset ($T = 2, p < .02$).

As is evident from Figure 2, responses were not uniformly distributed throughout the CS on the first conditioning day. Onset of CS produced an abrupt increment in rate, but the rate fell off as the CS continued ($\chi r^2 = 12.34, p < .05$). A more detailed examination of the results reveals that this decline was largely due to the first 12 trials; by Trials 13–24 the response rate during the CS was more uniform.

Delivery of the US did not produce an immediate, reliable increase in response rate. Although the response rate in the 5 sec. following the very first US delivery was not different from pre-CS levels, by the third conditioning trial the rate in the 5 sec. after the US was only 6 per minute while that prior to CS onset was 27.5 per minute.

As conditioning continued, the pre-CS rate remained fairly stable. However, the rate early in the CS declined progressively while the rate late in the CS increased. The results of the fifth conditioning day, shown in the top right panel of Figure 2, represent an intermediate stage in this change. The maximum response rate has moved toward the end of the CS but still occurred well prior to the time of the US; the rate early in the CS had declined to the level of pre-CS responding.

The results of the twelfth conditioning day (lower left panel of Figure 2) showed a monotonic increase in response rate during the CS ($\chi r^2 = 21.95, p < .001$). The maximum rate occurred in the final 5-sec. period of the CS and the minimum during the first 5 sec. These rates both differed reliably from those prior to CS onset ($T = 3, 0; p < .05, .01$) The rate continued to be depressed at CS termination.

The remaining two panels of Figure 2 show the results of the second and twelfth extinction sessions. Repeated presentation of the CS without the US considerably attenuated the effects of conditioning. By Day E-12 the overall rate during the CS no longer differed from the rate prior to CS onset, as did neither the rate during the initial nor the final 5 sec. of the CS.

Figure 3 depicts the changes in rate for selected 5-sec. periods of each trial over the last 32 experimental days. This figure shows more clearly the progressive changes which took place with conditioning and extinction. The pre-CS rate was fairly stable across days except for the brief increase on the first conditioning day. The rate during the initial 5 sec. of the CS

FIGURE 3

Mean number of responses per 5-sec. block for sessions from selected periods during a trial in Experiment 2.

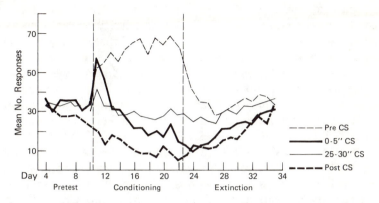

showed an abrupt increase on the first conditioning day, followed by a gradual decline to below pre-CS levels during conditioning. With extinction, the rate during the initial 5 sec. of the CS slowly returned to pre-CS rates.

The rate during the final 5 sec. of the CS grew rapidly on the first conditioning day and then more slowly throughout the remainder of conditioning. With extinction, the rate during this period returned to baseline. The response rate in the 5 sec. following CS termination declined even during pretest. This decline continued through conditioning; but with extinction, this depression was attenuated.

External inhibition and disinhibition.   The effect of the introduction of the novel flashing light during the CS was confined to the first two presentations of each type. The first 2 trials presenting the light early in the CS did not change the relative distribution of responses during the CS but produced a uniform rise in response rate. During the CS on these trials, the response rate was 2.55 per 5 sec. compared to 1.77 per 5 sec. for the comparable trials on the previous day. Presentation of the light late in the CS-US interval had no effect upon response rate. After six presentations of each type of extraneous stimulus, the effect of presentation early in the CS had vanished. Thus only disinhibition, but no external inhibition, was observed; the disinhibition declined as the novelty of the stimulus was reduced.

Discussion

The results of this experiment support those of Experiment 1. The end product of long-delay conditioning was initial inhibition of conditioned fear to CS onset followed by a change into excitation as the CS continued. The present experiment, however, showed more clearly the first sense of inhibition of delay, a progressive decrease in the CR elicited by the early portion of the CS. Together these two experiments provide strong evidence for inhibition of delay in fear conditioning in all three senses. Taken together with the earlier experiments of Rescorla and LoLordo (1965), these results strongly support the proposition of two-process theories that fear conditioning obeys the laws of Pavlovian salivary conditioning.

In this experiment CS-termination produced rate depression even in pretest. Nevertheless, the fact that this depression was enhanced by conditioning and attenuated by extinction indicates that removal of the US during test sessions does not account for the post-CS depression observed in Experiment 1. Two further explanations of the post-CS depression remain. One possibility is that it is an example of Pavlovian induction; a period of high excitation may reflexively be followed by a period of inhibition. Another possibility is that CS termination signals a period free from the US, the intertrial interval. Termination of CS may become a conditioned inhibitor of fear; similar relations between stimuli and shock have been shown by Rescorla and LoLordo (1965) to produce inhibitors of fear.

Finally, the possibility of instrumental effects of the Pavlovian US should be mentioned. A few Ss in this experiment showed abrupt rate decreases just prior to the delivery of the Pavlovian US. Observation of the dogs indicated that this was due to punishment of the higher rate of responding during the CS; during Pavlovian extinction such behavior typically disappeared. This kind of effect raises a general question. If we present a Pavlovian CS while an animal is performing an instrumental response, do we continue to follow the CS with the US (as in Experiment 2) or leave the CS unreinforced (as in Experiment 1)? If we continue to deliver the US, we may punish the baseline operant. Thus in Experiment 2, we may be attenuating the fear-eliciting effects of the CS. But if we do not continue to reinforce the CS we introduce other instrumental contingencies. Suppose that the initial reaction to a CS after conditioning is a rate increase; this will be followed in the test session by failure of the aversive US to occur. This is clearly a condition of avoidance training and we are providing reinforcement for the baseline operant.

Thus it seems obvious that neither procedure is to be strongly preferred. Rather, the most conservative approach is to try to study the effects of Pavlovian CSs with both procedures. If the observed effects occur with both procedures, as in the present experiments, it can be reasonably asserted that they are not produced by unwanted instrumental contingencies.

References

Black, A. H. The extinction of avoidance responses under curare. *J. Comp. Physiol. Psychol.*, 1958, **51,** 519–525.
Rescorla, R. A. Pavlovian conditioning and its proper control procedures. *Psychol. Rev.*, 1967, **74,** 71–80.

Rescorla, R. A., & LoLordo, V. M. Inhibition of avoidance behavior. *J. Comp. Physiol. Psychol.*, 1965, **59,** 406–412.

Solomon, R. L., & Wynne, L. C. Traumatic avoidance learning: Acquisition in normal dogs. *Psychol. Monogr.*, 1953, **67**(4, Whole No. 354).

VARIATION IN THE EFFECTIVENESS OF REINFORCEMENT AND NONREINFORCEMENT FOLLOWING PRIOR INHIBITORY CONDITIONING

Robert A. Rescorla

This paper by Robert A. Rescorla (1971) deals with a topic that has received much attention in the last decade—the conditioning of compound CSs. The reason underlying this interest was a discovery by Kamin that conditioning to a cue could be blocked if that cue was combined with one already strengthened (an outcome that was not compatible with traditional theory). Among the many important theories of this phenomenon is a model of compound conditioning by Rescorla and Wagner. The basic idea of the model is that each US will support only a fixed amount of conditioning; if much of that conditioning strength has already been relegated to one CS, then little remains for additional CSs and conditioning to the added cue will thus be blocked. If, however, one CS becomes "weak" due to inhibitory conditioning, then conditioning to the added CS will be even stronger than usual. In short, cues "compete" for strength; one becomes extra strong (or weak) as a result of the existing weakness (or strength) of the other. In this particular paper, Rescorla confirms these basic predictions.

In both experiments reported here, a CER procedure was used in which rats were taught to press a lever for food and then were given Pavlovian conditioning. Groups of subjects varied according to whether the cue A was given extra reinforcement trials or extra nonreinforcement trials. The results showed that conditioning to the target CS (cue X) increased when cue A was extra "weak" through nonreinforcement, or decreased when cue A was extra "strong" through reinforcement. Similarly, in Experiment 2, Rescorla demonstrated that X would become excitatory if both A were inhibitory and if the AX compound were not reinforced. This finding too is accommodated by the Rescorla/Wagner model.

Recently, Rescorla (1969), Wagner (1969a,b) and Rescorla and Wagner (1970) have put forth several versions of a theory of the operation of reinforcement in Pavlovian conditioning. According to that theory, the effectiveness of a reinforcement or nonreinforcement in increasing or decreasing, respectively, the associative strength of a stimulus which it follows depends upon the total associative strength evoked during the presentation of that stimulus. If that total associative strength is high, then reinforcements will be relatively ineffective, but nonreinforcements will be especially potent. Conversely, a stimulus complex evoking low associative strength will be highly susceptible to increments by reinforcements but relatively immune to decrements when followed by nonreinforcement. The unique feature of the theory is that the increases and decreases in associative strength of a given stimulus depend not only upon the associative strength of that stimulus but upon the *total* associative strength evoked during the stimulus. Thus if a compound stimulus AX is followed by reinforcement or nonreinforcement, changes in the associative strength of X will depend upon the total associative strength of both A and X, not simply that of X. Consequently, a given pairing of X and reinforcement may have quite different consequences depending upon the associative strength of stimuli present simultaneously with X.

This theory has been given a somewhat more formal statement by Rescorla and Wagner (1970). According to that version, the separate changes in associative strengths of two stimuli A and X, as a consequence of a reinforced presentation of the AX compound, are both linearly related to $(\lambda - (V_A + V_X))$. In this expression λ is the asymptote of conditioning supportable by the given US and depends entirely upon that US, whereas V_A and V_X are, respectively, the associative strengths of A and X prior to the trial. Notice that increments to each component stimulus can be modified by the values of the other component as well as by their own current associative strength.

One implication of this model is that if an AX compound is followed by reinforcement, then the resulting conditioning of X depends upon any prior treatments given to A. For instance, if A has itself a history of reinforcement when presented alone, the V_A will be relatively large (in the limit, λ); consequently, $V_A + V_X$ will only be a little discrepant from λ. Since that discrepancy determines the magnitude of increments to V_X on a reinforced AX trial, the possible conditioning to X will be severely limited. Several recent reports by Kamin (1968, 1969) indicate that this is the case in a conditioned suppression situation; reinforcement of AX produces little conditioning of X if A has itself previously been followed by that same reinforcement.

The model also makes a symmetrical prediction. If *A* has received a prior treatment making it a conditioned inhibitor (that is, giving V_A a negative value), then $V_A + V_X$ should be especially discrepant from λ and the ability of a reinforcement following *AX* to increase V_X should be particularly *enhanced*. The first experiment reported here attempts to replicate the findings of Kamin and extend them to this symmetrical case. A conditioned suppression procedure was employed.

Experiment 1: Reinforcement of AX

METHOD

Subjects and apparatus. The *Ss* were 56 Sprague-Dawley male rats about 100 days old at the start of the experiment. They were maintained throughout the experiment at 80% of their normal body weight.

The experimental chambers were eight identical Skinner boxes 22.9 × 20.3 × 20.3 cm. Each chamber had a recessed food magazine in the center of the end wall and a bar to the left of the magazine. The floor of the chamber was composed of 1.9-mm stainless-steel rods, spaced 19.0-mm apart. This grid could be electrified through a relay-sequence scrambler (Hoffman & Fleshler, 1962) from a high-voltage high-resistance shock source. The two end walls of the chamber were aluminum; the side walls and top were clear Plexiglas. Each Skinner box was enclosed in a sound- and light-resistant shell. Mounted on the rear wall of this shell was a 6.5-W bulb and two speakers. The speakers permitted the presentation of a constant white masking noise and a 1800-Hz tone CS. During Phase II conditioning sessions a chamber similar to the Skinner boxes but without a lever was used. Experimental events were controlled and recorded automatically by relay equipment located in an adjoining room.

Procedure. The procedure consisted of four phases. Phase I established the baseline bar-press response. In the first session, *S* was magazine trained automatically with food pellets delivered on a VI 1-min. schedule. In addition, each bar-press yielded a food pellet. This session continued until *S* had emitted 50 bar-presses; shaping was used if necessary. Starting with Experimental Day two, all sessions were 2 hr long and *S* was placed on a VI schedule of reinforcement. For the first 20 min of this session the schedule was VI 1 min; thereafter it was VI 2 min. Phase I VI training continued for six daily 2-hr sessions. During Session six, the two stimuli subsequently to be used in conditioning were pretested. Two 2-min presentations of the 1800 Hz tone and of a 2-Hz flashing of the normally off houselight were superimposed on the bar-pressing behavior.

The next day began Phase II, which was designed to establish various values of associative strength to the tone CS (*A*). The conditioning chambers were substituted for the Skinner boxes and four groups of animals formed. Group 8-0 received a treatment designed to establish the tone as an elicitor of fear. Twelve 2-min tones were given in each session with a mean intertone interval of 8 min. During tone presentations, electric foot-shocks, 0.5 sec long at 1 mA were delivered at a rate of 0.8 per 2-min interval. Shocks were programmed in such a way as to be equiprobable at any time during the CS; however, no shocks were delivered in the absence of the CS. Group 0-8 received a comparable treatment designed to establish the tone as a conditioned inhibitor of fear. Tone presentations occurred as in the previous group; however, shocks were programmed to occur only in the *absence* of the CS. Shocks occurred at a rate of 0.8 per 2 min throughout the session except for the 4-min period initiated by the onset of a 2-min CS. During that period no shocks were delivered. Group 0-8 Control received the same number of shocks and tones as Group 0-8 except that the shocks were randomly distributed throughout the session, entirely independently of the occurrence of tones. This treatment has been found by Rescorla (1969) to yield a relatively neutral tone (i.e., with *Va* about zero). Finally, Group Shock received a treatment identical to that of Group 0-8 Control except that all tone presentations were omitted. This treatment, too, was designed to yield a *Va* of approximately zero. Phase II conditioning continued for five daily 2-hr sessions. Group Shock contained 8 animals; the others 16 each.

Immediately following Phase II, *Ss* were returned to the Skinner boxes and given 3 days of additional VI 2-min training. This permitted recovery of the base-line bar-press rate which is typically depressed following experience with shock. The next day began Phase III, during which all groups received 2-min presentations of the tone (A) in compound with the flashing houselight (X), followed by shock. During each of two 2-hr sessions, four 2-min AX compounds were presented. Four of these trials, two on each day, terminated in a 0.5-sec 1-mA foot-shock. These trials were superimposed upon the bar-pressing behavior which continued to be reinforced on a VI 2-min schedule throughout this phase.

Finally, in Phase IV, the light was presented alone during bar-pressing to assess the amount of suppression controlled by it. Again, each 2-hr session contained four nonreinforced presentations of the light. Phase IV continued for four test sessions.

The measure of conditioning to the light was the amount of suppression of bar-pressing produced by its presentation. In order to attenuate the effects of individual differences in overall rate of responding, the results of the test sessions are plotted in terms of a suppression ratio. This ratio has the form $A/(A + B)$, where A is the rate of responding during the CS and B is the rate of responding in a comparable period prior to the CS onset. Thus a suppression ratio of zero indicates no responding during the CS (good conditioning) while one of 0.5 indicates similar rates of responding during the CS and pre-CS periods (little conditioning).

Results

Following conditioning in Phase II, the overall level of barpressing was depressed; however, by the third VI recovery day response rates were high enough to begin Phase III. During this phase and Phase IV the groups did not differ in response rates in the absence of the CS. The conduct of Phase III, while the animal engaged in bar-pressing, permitted observation of the development of suppression to the light – tone compound. Figure I shows the mean suppression ratios for each of the four groups during Phase III. It is clear that Group 8-0 was suppressed during the light – tone compound from the outset, while Group 0-8 took considerably longer to acquire

FIGURE 1

Phase III of Experiment 1. Acquisition of suppression to the tone-light (AX) compound following different treatments of tone (A) in Phase II.

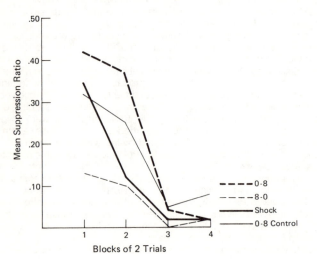

FIGURE 2

Phase IV of Experiment I. Suppression to the light (X) presented alone

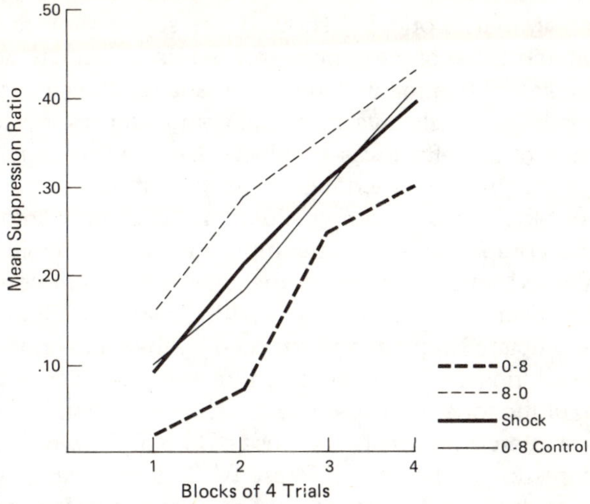

suppression to the compound. The two control groups were intermediate in suppression to the compound. These differences are confirmed by an overall Kruskal–Wallis analysis of variance by ranks ($H(3) = 34.11, p < .001$). Individual Mann–Whitney U tests indicated that Groups 8-0 and 0-8 each differed reliably from the control groups which in turn were not reliably different from each other. Since none of the groups had received prior treatment with the light, the differences presumably reflect the treatments of Phase II in conditioning the tone. They suggest that Phase II was effective in making the tone a conditioned excitor for Group 8-0 and a conditioned inhibitor for Group 0-8.

The results of presenting the light alone in Phase IV are shown in Figure 2. Since the light was presented without shock, all of the groups showed extinction of suppression across trials. However, throughout extinction Group 0-8 showed the greatest suppression to the light and Group 8-0 the least. The two control groups were intermediate and about equal. These observations were confirmed by an overall Kruskal–Wallis analysis ($H(3) = 19.74, p < .001$) and by individual Mann–Whitney U tests which indicated that only the two control groups failed to differ reliably from each other.

Discussion

The results of conditioning in Phase III confirm the expectation that conditioning in Phase II would establish different reactions to the tone. They suggest that the addition of the light to the tone CS did not disrupt the conditioned excitation established in Group 8-0 or the conditioned inhibition established in Group 0-8. Furthermore, the slower acquisition of fear during Phase III in Group 0-8 supports Rescorla's (1969) finding that inhibitory stimulus complexes are more difficult to condition as excitors.

The finding that Group 8-0 showed less suppression to the light in Phase IV than did either of the control groups is in agreement with Kamin's data; prior excitatory treatment of the tone made reinforcement of the light –tone compound less effective in conditioning suppression to the light. The magnitude of this effect was somewhat less than that typically found by Kamin. In the present experiment initial conditioning of the tone was conducted outside the barpressing situation; however, reinforcement of the light-tone compound was superimposed on bar-pressing. It seems likely that the excitation elicited by the tone underwent some stimulus generalization decrement, thereby permitting some conditioning of the light. The incomplete suppression produced by the light –tone compound in Group 8-0 during the early trials of Phase III, despite extensive prior conditioning of the tone, is in agreement with this possibility.

The most interesting results are those of Group 0-8 which showed the greatest suppression to the light in Phase IV. This indicates a symmetry in the effects of pretraining to the tone. Just as prior excitatory training of the tone can reduce the effectiveness of subsequent reinforcement of the light– tone compound, so prior inhibitory training of the tone can apparently *increase* the effectiveness of reinforcement of that compound. This procedure yields what might be termed "superconditioning" of the light. In terms of the model presented by Rescorla and Wagner (1970), these prior treatments of the tone simply yield positive or negative V values. These values for V_A in turn either decrease or increase the expression $\lambda - (V_A + V_X)$ and therefore modulate the degree of conditioning to the light (X).

Experiment 2: Nonreinforcement of AX

The previous experiment indicates that prior excitatory or inhibitory treatment of A modifies the effectiveness of subsequent reinforcement of AX in increasing V_X. The present model also indicates that these prior treatments should modify the effectiveness of subsequent *nonreinforcement* in decreasing V_X. Within the model, variations in magnitude of the US are expressed as changes in the value of λ, the asymptote of conditioning which that US will support. Presumably nonreinforcement will support an asymptote which is low; for convenience we will assume that the λ associated with nonreinforcement is zero. In that case, the changes in V_A and V_X as a result of a nonreinforcement of the AX compound would be decrements, linearly related to $-(V_A + V_X)$. Consequently, the degree to which a nonreinforcement can decrease the associative strength of a stimulus, X, is dependent upon the V values of other stimuli simultaneously present, much in the same way that the ability of a reinforcement to increase associative strength is so modulated.

Rescorla and Wagner (1970) report a number of experiments supporting this modulation of the effectiveness of nonreinforcement. One simple case is the conditioned inhibition paradigm of Pavlov (1927). In that paradigm one stimulus, A, is repeatedly reinforced while a compound, AX, is nonreinforced. An X so treated becomes a conditioned inhibitor whereas simple nonreinforcement of AX is inadequate to produce that result. In terms of the model, the conditioned inhibition procedure results in a large positive value for V_A and hence a large negative value for $-(V_A + V_X)$ on the compound trials. Consequently, an X which has an initial V value of zero will receive only decrements and take on negative V values, i.e., become a conditioned inhibitor. In the absence of a positive value for V_A, as in simple repeated nonreinforced presentation of AX, this consequence would not be expected.

One other case of nonreinforcement of AX is particularly interesting. Instead of prior excitatory conditioning of A, consider the case of prior inhibitory training of A, followed by nonreinforcement of AX. If A has become a conditioned inhibitor, then V_A is negative but $-(V_A + V_X)$, the quantity determining changes in V_A and V_X on nonreinforced AX trials, will be positive for values of V_X close to zero. The consequence is that V_X will be *increased* on nonreinforced AX presentations. That is, prior inhibitory training of A followed by nonreinforcement of AX should transform a formerly neutral X into a conditioned excitor, even though it is never paired with reinforcement. This experiment is an initial attempt to examine that prediction.

METHOD

Subjects and apparatus.   The Ss were 64 Sprague–Dawley male rats about 100 days old at the start of the experiment. They were maintained throughout the experiment at 80% of their normal body weight. The apparatus was identical to that of Experiment 1.

Procedure.   The Ss were trained to bar-press and given 6 days of VI 2 min training as in Experiment 1. On the final day of VI training, two 2 min presentations each of a steady 1800-Hz tone and of a 250-Hz tone interrupted at a rate of 1 Hz were superimposed on the bar-pressing behavior. The third stimulus to be subsequently used in conditioning, a 2-Hz flashing of the houselight, was not pretested. This initial VI training was followed by two phases of conditioning and one of testing.

Phase I: For conditioning in Phase I, the conditioning chambers replaced the Skinner boxes. The animals were divided into four equal-sized groups, which were labeled such that the letters before the hyphen refer to the treatment of Phase I and those after the hyphen to the treatment of Phase II. Groups I-P (Inhibitory-Paired) and I-U (Inhibitory-Unpaired) received a standard Pavlovian conditioned inhibition procedure. During each 2-hr session, they received 12 2-min trials; on six trials the 1800-Hz tone was presented singly and terminated with a 0.5-sec 1-mA foot-shock; on the other six trials the 1800-Hz tone was presented in conjunction with the flashing houselight (A) and no shock was given. The animals in Group NL-P (No Light-Paired) received exactly the same treatment, except that the light was never presented. This resulted in partial reinforcement of the 1800-Hz tone. Finally, animals in Group NS-P (No Shock-Paired) also received a treatment identical to that of I-P and I-U except that no shocks were administered. The latter two treatments were designed to leave the light (A) relatively valueless, while nevertheless presenting portions of the events administered to the two inhibitory groups. Phase I continued for six daily 2-hr sessions.

Phase II: Phase II of conditioning began on the following day, retaining the conditioning chambers in place of the Skinner boxes. Three groups (I-P, NL-P, and NS-P) received, during each of two 2-hr sessions, 12 paired presentations of the light (A) in compound with the 250-Hz tone (X). Each stimulus presentation was 2-min long and the two components were coterminous. Group I-U also received 12 presentations of the light and of the 250-Hz tone, but the two stimuli were never paired; they were presented in random order with a mean interstimulus interval of 3 min. As a consequence of these treatments, only Group I-P had its nonreinforced presentations of the 250-Hz tone occur in conjunction with the light conditioned inhibitor. Groups NL-P and NS-P had the tone presented in conjunction with the light during Phase II, but had not received prior inhibitory conditioning to that light in Phase I. Group I-U had received prior inhibitory training to the light but in Phase II received nonreinforced presentations of the tone alone.

On the day immediately following Phase II, all animals were returned to the Skinner boxes and given 1 day of VI 2-min bar-press training. The next 2 days constituted Phase III, designed to assess the degree to which the tone was excitatory in the various groups. During each session, four 2-min presentations of the 250-Hz tone were superimposed on the bar-pressing. Trials 2 and 4 of each session terminated in a 0.5-sec, 1-mA shock. This "savings" test was selected as a sensitive procedure for evaluating any conditioned excitation to the tone.

Results

The primary results of this experiment are from Phase IV, shown in Figure 3. This figure indicates that throughout Phase IV Group I-P showed somewhat greater suppression than did the other groups. However, the initial differences were small and the rate of conditioning rapid in all groups. Consequently, the more rapid acquisition of suppression in Group I-P is most readily assessed in the second block of trials, at an intermediate conditioning level. At this point Group I-P was suppressed reliably more than each of the other groups ($H = 11.42, p < .01$).

Discussion

The results of this experiment suggest that if a stimulus A has been established as a conditioned inhibitor, then simple nonreinforcement of AX is sufficient to give X some small amount of excitatory strength. Neither simple nonreinforcement of AX when A has not received prior inhibitory training nor simple inhibitory training of A without subsequent AX presentation will alone accomplish this. However, the effect observed here was relatively small, reliably showing itself only in the faster acquisition of fear by Group I-P but not in differences in initial level of suppression produced by the CS.

The small magnitude of the excitation observed to X was not unexpected for a number of reasons. First the nonreinforcement of AX was conducted in a situation somewhat different from that in which X was subsequently tested. This situational change has been observed in other experiments in our laboratory to result in stimulus generalization decrement of conditioned excitation. Secondly, the nonreinforcement of AX should, according to the present theory, result in an increase of excitation which is shared by A and X; although the AX compound should be increased in value toward zero, X will only receive a portion of that increment. If A and X are equally salient, then X will attain an asymptotic V value equal to $-V_{AO}/2$, where V_{AO} is the value of A just prior to nonreinforcement of the AX compound. Roughly speaking, X can be expected only to become half as excitatory as A was inhibitory. Finally, it is not unreasonable to expect that

FIGURE 3

Phase IV of Experiment 2. Acquisition of suppression to the 250-Hz tone.

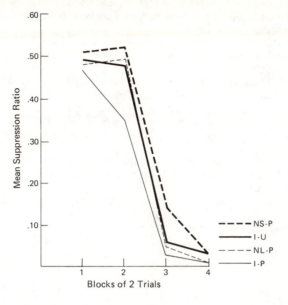

the salience of A would be enhanced by prior inhibitory training. If A is considerably more salient than X, then X will receive an even smaller portion of the excitation conditioned on the nonreinforced AX trials (Rescorla & Wagner, 1970). For these reasons the present small effect may be interpreted as encouraging for the theory. Nevertheless, it is clear that considerable additional work is needed to determine whether manipulation of appropriate variables will increase the size of the observed excitation.

The experiments presented here, taken together with others reported by Kamin (1967, 1968), Rescorla (1969, 1970), Rescorla & Wagner (1970), Wagner (1969a,b), and others, provide general confirmation for the kinds of propositions embodied in the present model. It is clear that the effectiveness of both reinforcement and nonreinforcement in producing conditioning of a stimulus is importantly dependent upon the total amount of conditioning evoked during that stimulus. To reiterate, if that total level of conditioning is high, the ability of a reinforcement to increase associative strength will be reduced while the ability of a nonreinforcement to decrease associative strength will be enhanced; when the level of conditioning is low, these relations are reversed.

References

Hoffman, H. S. & Fleshler, M. A relay sequencing device for scrambling grid shock. *Journal of the Experimental Analysis of Behavior*, 1962, **5**, 329–330.
Kamin, L. J. Attention-like processes in classical conditioning. In M. R. Jones (Ed.),

Miami Symposium on the Prediction of Behavior: Aversive Stimulation. Coral Gables: University of Miami Press, 1968.

Kamin, L. J. Predictability, surprise, attention, and conditioning. In R. M. Church & B. A. Campbell (Eds.), *Punishment and aversive behavior.* New York: Appleton-Century-Crofts, 1969.

Rescorla, R. A. Conditioned inhibition of fear. In W. K. Honig & N. J. Mackintosh (Eds.), *Fundamental issues in associative learning.* Halifax: Dalhousie University Press, 1969.

Rescorla, R. A. Reduction in the effectiveness of reinforcement following prior excitatory conditioning. *Learning and Motivation,* 1970, **1,** 372–381.

Rescorla, R. A., & Wagner, A. R. A theory of Pavlovian conditioning: Variations in the effectiveness of reinforcement and nonreinforcement. In A. H. Black & W. F. Prokasy (Eds.), *Classical conditioning II.* New York: Appleton-Century-Crofts, 1970.

Wagner, A. R. Stimulus validity and stimulus selection. In W. K. Honig & N. J. Mackintosh (Eds.), *Fundamental issues in associative learning.* Halifax: Dalhousie University Press, 1969a.

Wagner, A. R. Stimulus selection and a "modified continuity theory." In G. H. Bower & J. T. Spence (Eds.), *The psychology of learning and motivation,* Vol. 3. New York: Academic Press, 1969b.

LEARNED HELPLESSNESS IN THE RAT: TIME COURSE, IMMUNIZATION, AND REVERSIBILITY

Martin E. P. Seligman, Robert A. Rosellini, and Michael J. Kozak

The final paper in this chapter, by Martin E. P. Seligman, Robert A. Rosellini, and Michael J. Kozak (1975), was selected because it demonstrates several interesting facets of the helplessness phenomenon. Helplessness, according to Seligman and his colleagues, is a cognitive state induced by inescapable shock. The result of helplessness is a reduction in future escape learning. In other words, during the initial inescapable shock phase the subjects perceive that their behavior is independent of punishment and reward; it is this perception that later interferes with their learning, when reward and punishment are not independent of behavior.

For several years the helplessness phenomenon could not be demonstrated in rats. Not only is that problem resolved in this paper, but the authors have gone further to show that many of the aspects of the phenomenon are the same for rats as for dogs. For example, Experiment 1 indicates that helplessness does not wear off after a week: rats were no more able to learn a lever press escape response after they had received inescapable shock one week earlier than they were after receiving it five minutes earlier.

Experiment 2 illustrates the important phenomenon of immunization. Experimental rats were first trained on a jump-up response; then they were given the inescapable shock phase and, finally, the lever press escape test. The results indicated that these subjects were immunized to the effects of inescapable shock. That is, the initial ability to control shock during the jump-up phase protected the rats from becoming helpless during phase 2.

The final study shows yet another facet of helplessness—that of reversibility. After being given inescapable shock, rats were tested on the lever press escape response and all exhibited helplessness. Two weeks later, while still showing an inability to learn the escape response, the experimental subjects were literally dragged onto the lever. This procedure, in essence, forced the animals to respond, and it resulted in the reversibility of the helplessness condition.

When a dog receives inescapable shock in a Pavlovian harness and is later tested for escape–avoidance in a shuttle box, striking interference with performance occurs. In contrast, dogs that receive equivalent amounts of shock they can escape, or no shock, later escape and avoid efficiently. Occasionally, such a dog will escape by jumping the barrier and then revert to failing to escape. This phenomenon has been dubbed "learned helplessness" (Maier, 1970; Overmier, 1968; Overmier & Seligman, 1967; Seligman & Groves, 1970; Seligman & Maier, 1967; Seligman, Maier, & Geer, 1968; and see Maier, Seligman, & Solomon, 1969, and Seligman, Maier, & Solomon, 1971, for reviews). This phenomenon has been observed in other species besides the dog: Thornton and Jacobs (1971), Hiroto (1974), and Hiroto and Seligman (in press) have reported it in humans; Thomas (1974) and Seward and Humphrey (1967) in cats; Padilla, Padilla, Ketterer, and Giacalone (1970) in goldfish; and Braud, Wepmann, and Russo (1969) in mice.

Looney and Cohen (1972), Maier, Albin, and Testa (1973), and Seligman and Beagley (1975) have reported behavior in rats apparently parallel to learned helplessness in the dog. Rats pretreated with inescapable

From "Learned Helplessness in the Rat: Time Course, Immunization, and Reversibility" by Martin E. P. Seligman, Robert A. Rosellini and Michael J. Kozak in *Journal of Comparative and Physiological Psychology*, Volume 88, Number 2, 1975. Copyright 1975 by the American Psychological Association. Reprinted by permission.

shock fail subsequently to escape shock. In addition, such rats occasionally make successful responses but then revert to taking the shock. Rats that receive equivalent but escapable preshock, or no preshock, escape efficiently. This study further explores the parallels between rat and dog helplessness by examining the time course, the prevention, and the reversibility of the effects of inescapable shock on the rat.

Experiment 1: Time Course

Learned helplessness in the dog has a time course. Following a single session of inescapable shock in the harness, dogs will fail to escape in a shuttle box up to 24–48 hr. later (Overmier, 1968; Overmier & Seligman, 1967). Following multiple sessions of inescapable shock, however, dogs fail to escape up to 1 wk. later; furthermore, dogs reared in the laboratory from birth tend not to show a time course (Seligman & Groves, 1970). Does the disruptive effect on later escape behavior of one session of inescapable shock dissipate in time in the rat?

METHOD

Subjects and apparatus. The subjects were 80 male albino rats of the Sprague-Dawley strain obtained from the Holtzman Co., Madison, Wisconsin. They arrived at the laboratory when 90–110 days old and were housed individually for at least 3 wk. before being run. They were on ad-lib food and water and were run during their light cycle, with a 12-hr.-light–12-hr.-dark schedule.

Two test chambers 20.5 cm. wide, 19 cm. high, and 30 cm. long, in sound-attenuating cubicles, were used for both training and testing. The 2 long sides of the chambers were made of Plexiglas; the ends were made of plywood. The floor had .5-cm.-diameter stainless steel grids. Centered on the right-hand wall was a lever (6 × 7.5cm.) which was 6 cm. off the floor and was the testing manipulandum. The chambers were illuminated by 1.5-w. red light bulbs and had peepholes through which the subjects could be observed. White masking noise provided a background.

FIGURE 1

Mean bar-press escape latency in seconds for the 20 test trials of the 10 treatment groups.

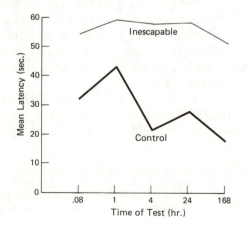

Each rat's back was shaved and a safety pin electrode was mounted subcutaneously in the upper back of the rat and suspended from the ceiling. A constant current 1.0-ma. shock delivered from a 600-v. transformer through a limiting resistor was the unconditioned stimulus. Shock pulsated on and off 5 times a second. All programming and recording were carried out automatically in an adjacent room.

Procedure. The 80 subjects were randomly assigned to 10 groups of 8. The 5 experimental groups received a single session of inescapable shock and the 5 control groups were pinned, shaved, and placed in the chamber, but received no shock. At 5 different times following the pretreatment, all groups were tested on a fixed ratio (FR) of 3 bar presses to escape. The pretreatment—test intervals were 5 min., 1 hr., 4 hr., 24 hr., and 168 hr.

The inescapable shock session consisted of 80 15-sec. inescapable shock trials programmed on a variable interval (VI) 1-min. schedule (range 10–110 sec.). The session lasted approximately 90 min. The bar was not present in the chamber. In the test procedure each rat was placed in the test chamber at the designated time after pretreatment. Twenty unsignaled escape trials were run on a VI 1-min. schedule. Pressing the bar 3 times terminated the shock. If the rat failed to escape, shock terminated automatically after 60 sec. So there were 10 groups: 5 inescapably shocked groups tested at 5 min., 1 hr., 4 hr., 24 hr., and 168 hr., and 5 nonshocked control groups tested at the same intervals.

Results[1]

The groups receiving inescapable shock failed to escape at all intervals following pretreatment. The controls escaped shock at all intervals following pretreatment. Learned helplessness in the rat does not dissipate in time after a single session of inescapable shock, at least for the temporal intervals tested. Figure 1 presents the mean latency of escape for each of the 10 groups. Each inescapable group differed significantly from its control group. All *ps* were less than .01 (Mann-Whitney *U* test) except in the case of inescapable – 1 hr. vs. control – 1 hr. ($p < .05$, Mann-Whitney *U* test). No differences were significant among the inescapable groups. Among the control groups the escape latency was faster for the 1-hr. than for the 4-hr. group ($p < .05$, Mann-Whitney *U*. No other differences were significant. Overall, the inescapable groups failed to escape on 78% of the test trials and the control groups failed to escape on 34% of the test trials.

Discussion

Learned helplessness in the rat, in contrast to that in the dog, does not dissipate in time following one session of inescapable shock. What could be responsible for this difference? The dogs whose helplessness dissipated in time were of unknown past history (Overmier & Seligman, 1967). When dogs are raised in the laboratory, however, they are more vulnerable to helplessness: a higher percentage fail to escape following inescapable shock, and helplessness does not dissipate in time (Seligman & Groves, 1970). The reason for the presence of a time course in dogs of unknown past history thus appears to be immunization: During their pre-laboratory history such dogs probably have escaped natural aversive events.

---

[1] All tests are 2 tailed.

Such escape experience proactively interferes with inescapable shock experience, and proactive interference increases in time (Maier & Gleitman, 1967). Cage-reared dogs are relatively deprived of escape experience, and so do not have proactive interference to immunize them against the effects of inescapable shock. Our rats are cage reared and may likewise lack immunizing experience. If this is so, it is not surprising that the effects of inescapable shock do not dissipate in time in laboratory rats.

Weiss, Stone, and Harrell (1970) have suggested that the behavioral effects of inescapable shocks may be due to the depletion of brain norepinepherine caused by experience with inescapable shocks. Recently, Weiss (1974) has attempted to account for the time course of learned helplessness in dogs by proposing that failure to escape 24 hr. following inescapable shock could be due to norepinephrine depletion, with the normal escape behavior seen in dogs after 48 hr. resulting from a repletion of norepinephrine. The results of the present study indicate that a norepinephrine depletion that is repleted in 48 hr. cannot account for the fact that rats are helpless 1 wk. after one session of inescapable shock.

The basis of our reasoning concerning the time course of learned helplessness is that prior escapable shock prevents inescapable shock from disrupting escape behavior in the dog (Seligman & Maier, 1967). Dogs that escape shock in the shuttle box and are then given inescapable shock in the harness do not subsequently exhibit helplessness in the shuttle box. If our reasoning is correct, immunization should also occur in the rat. Does learning that shock is escapable via a jumping response prevent inescapable shock from disrupting the bar press escape response?

Experiment 2: Immunization

METHOD

Subjects and apparatus. Subjects were 24 rats of the same age and strain as those used in Experiment 1. The same apparatus was used, except that during escape immunization training for the immunized group, a motor-operated platform entered the chamber to start each trial. This platform (18.5 cm. long, 7.5 cm. wide, and 6.5 cm. high) could be inserted rapidly into the chamber through an opening in the wall opposite the wall with the bar. When retracted, the shelf was flush with the wall. Jumping on the platform activated a system of microswitches that terminated shock during the training phase. The bar was not present except during the training phase. The platform was not present during the inescapable shock and during the test phase.

Procedure. The 24 rats were randomly assigned to 3 groups of 8: the immunized group, the inescapable group, and a no-shock control group. The immunized group received jump-up escape training followed by inescapable shock, followed by bar-press escape testing. Jump-up escape training was conducted according to the procedure of Seligman and Beagley (1975, Experiment 4). On the first 2 trials, the rats were given 2 60-sec. shocks with the platform withdrawn from the chamber. On the next 20 trials the platform was inserted at the start of each trial. If the rat failed to escape on its own in 20 sec., the experimenter pulled the rat up to the platform by the electrode that was attached to its back. On the rest of the trials (to make a total of 80) the rat responded on its own with no pulling. Twenty-four hours later each rat in the immunized group received 80 trials of 15-sec. inescapable shock, as described previously. The platform as well as the bar was absent from the chamber. Twenty-four hours following this, each rat in the immunized group was given 20 trials of unsignaled, escapable shock with the FR-3 bar-press as the

FIGURE 2

Mean bar-press escape latency in seconds as a function of blocks of 5 trials for the 3 treatment groups (I = inescapable group; 0 = no-shock control group; EI = immunized group.)

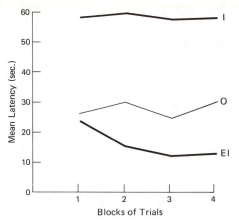

escape response. Other parameters were the same as in Experiment 1. The inescapable group received only the 80 trials of inescapable shock followed 24 hr. later by FR-3 bar-press escape testing. The control group received FR-3 bar-press escape testing following equivalent exposure to the training chambers but without shock.

Results

Immunization training successfully prevented inescapable shock from disrupting later escape behavior. Rats (immunization group) that learned to jump up to escape and were then given inescapable shock learned the FR-3 bar-press escape response as well as the nonshock controls did. All 8 animals given inescapable shock failed to learn the FR-3 response. Figure 2 presents these results. The immunization group performed the FR-3 response significantly faster than the inescapable group ($p < .001$, Mann-Whitney U). The immunization and control groups did not differ significantly, and the control group performed better than the inescapable group ($p < .001$, Mann-Whitney U) Finally, the shorter the escape latency in jump-up immunization, the shorter was the FR-3 bar-press escape latency ($p < .05, r = .65$).

Discussion

If rats first experience escapable shock followed by inescapable shock they do not become helpless, even though the inescapable shock experience is sufficient to produce helplessness in an untreated group of rats. Experience with escapable shock effectively immunizes the rats against the effects of inescapable shock, even though the original escape response is of a considerably different topography from that of the response the animals are subsequently required to perform during escape testing. In addition to being topographically different, the immunizing manipulandum is on the opposite wall from the test manipulandum. So rats, like dogs, can be immunized against the disruptive effects of inescapable shock by pretreatment with escapable shocks.

The final similarity between dog and rat helplessness that will be investigated is its reversibility.

Experiment 3: Reversibility

Seligman et al. (1968) reported one procedure that reliably "cured" dogs that repeatedly failed to escape in the shuttle box following exposure to inescapable shock. These dogs were dragged by leashes back and forth across the shuttle box to "show" them that responding terminated shock. This form of "putting through" was successful in all cases, but required 20–200 draggings before the dogs responded reliably on their own. If learned helplessness in the rat parallels learned helplessness in the dog, forcible exposure to an escape contingency following inescapable shock should produce reliable escape learning. Seligman and Beagley (1975, Experiment 4) successfully used a dragging procedure to produce reliable escape learning in naive rats that received escapable shock. In Experiment 3 we used a similar procedure to break up failure to escape resulting from prior inescapable shock.

METHOD

Subjects and apparatus. The subjects were 17 rats as described above. The apparatus was also the same, with the FR-3 bar-press used as the escape response.

Procedure. The rats were divided into 3 groups: a forced escape group, a dragging control group, and a yoked control group. All 3 groups first received 80 15-sec. trials of inescapable shock on a VI 1-min schedule. All the rats were subsequently tested on FR-3 bar-press escape (Seligman & Beagley, 1975), and all failed to escape. Two–six weeks later the animals were retested for helplessness. Twenty trials of 60-sec. escapable shock, with an FR-3 bar-press as the escape response, were given to each rat. If the animal escaped more than 2 times in 20 trials it was discarded. Two animals did so, leaving 15 rats with 5 in each group. Thereupon the experimental procedures were instituted.

Forced escape training began on the twenty-first trial. Shock came on. If after 20 sec. the animal had not escaped, the experimenter dragged it by the electrode lead onto the bar until 3 bar presses resulted and shock terminated. This procedure continued through 80 forced escape trials per day until the animal escaped on 10 successive trials without experimenter intervention. The intertrial interval continued on a VI 1-min. schedule.

In the dragging control group, each rat was yoked to a member of the forced escape grc 'o and received an equivalent amount of trials, shock, and dragging. The only difference was that the dragging was nondirected; on each trial that the forced escape animal was dragged onto the bar, the dragging control animal was dragged back and forth until shock was programmed to terminate. In the rare event that these subjects pressed the bar 3 times, shock terminated. Thus, the dragging control animal differed from the forced escape animal only in that it was not forcibly exposed to the FR-3 bar-press–escape contingency.

In the yoked control group, each rat was matched with a forced escape and a dragging control animal. Each rat in the triad received the same number of trials and the same shock duration. For all 3 groups shock was escapable, and when FR-3 bar presses were made, shock terminated.

Results

Each rat in the forced escape group began to respond on its own and reached the criterion of 10 consecutive FR-3 bar-press escapes. No rat in either the dragging control or the yoked control groups acquired the escape response. Table 1 presents the number of trials and the number of escape responses for each of the 5 triads.

The forced escape group made more escape responses than the 2 control groups ($p < .008$, Mann-Whitney U test), which did not differ from each other.

The behavior of the individual animals is worth noting. Like dogs, rats in the forced escape group are progressively easier to drag with progressively more trials. Typically, the experimenter begins by dragging the entire "dead" weight of the animal. After a number of forced escapes, however, the animal becomes more active and dragging requires less effort. Finally, each animal escapes without dragging. Rats in the dragging control group become more active but do not acquire the bar-press escape response.

TABLE 1

Number of Trials, Escape Responses, and Escape Responses in the Last 10 Trials for Each Triad

Subject	Trials	Escapes	Escapes in last 10 trials
FE1	135	27	10
DC1	135	7	0
YC1	135	1	0
FE2	309	44	10
DC2	309	12	0
YC2	309	4	0
FE3	111	43	10
DC3	111	1	0
YC3	111	0	0
FE4	92	34	10
DC4	92	0	0
YC4	92	0	0
FE5	120	25	10
DC5	120	0	0
YC5	120	0	0

Note. A triad consists of a forced escape (FE), a dragging control (DC), and a yoked control (YC) rat.

General Discussion

The learned helplessness in the rat can be reversed by forcible exposure to the response–shock-termination contingency. Rats that previously failed to escape shock as a result of inescapable shock learn the FR-3 bar press to escape shock when dragged repeatedly onto the bar. Control groups that receive the same dragging and the same shock do not learn to escape. These findings wholly parallel those on the reversibility of learned helplessness in the dog (Seligman et al., 1968). Forced exposure to the response–shock-termination contingency "cures" helpless dogs and they become progressively more active en route with dragging.

It has been suggested that the failure to escape produced by repeated exposure to inescapable shock is mediated by competing motor responses (e.g., Anisman & Waller, 1973; Miller & Weiss, 1969). Such a view would hold that forcible exposure to the escape contingency works because it breaks up a competing motor pattern. This view has been criticized at length elsewhere (e.g., Seligman et al., 1971) and will not be reviewed here. It should be noted, however, that merely breaking up the motor pattern of the rats that fail to escape is insufficient to produce escape learning—the dragging control animals do not learn the escape response even though they become active. Only forced exposure to the bar-press–escape contingency reverses learned helplessness in the rat. It has been suggested that learned helplessness results from norepinephrine depletion (Weiss et al., 1970). It seems unlikely that forcibly showing a rat that bar pressing terminates shock would suddenly replete norepinephrine or that immunizing a rat with prior escapable shock would prevent norepinephrine depletion.

In conclusion, learned helplessness in the rat as shown by Seligman & Beagley (1975) shows 6 similarities to learned helplessness in the dog. (a) Like dogs, rats receiving inescapable shock fail to escape later on. (b) Like dogs, rats receiving inescapable shock sometimes respond successfully during escapable shock but revert to passively taking the shock. (c) Like dogs, yoked rats receiving identical escapable shocks do not become helpless. We have shown that (d) like cage-reared dogs, cage-reared rats show failure to escape that does not dissipate in time; (e) like dogs, rats receiving prior escapable shock are immunized against becoming helpless when faced with inescapable shock; and (f) like dogs, rats given forced exposure to the response–shock-termination contingency learn to escape on their own.

References

Anisman, H., & Waller, T. G. Effects of inescapable shock on subsequent avoidance performance: Role of response repertoire changes. *Behavioral Biology*, 1973, **9**, 331–355.

Braud, W., Wepmann, B. & Russo, D. Task and species generality of the 'helplessness' phenomenon. *Psychonomic Science*, 1969, **16**, 154–155.

Hiroto, D. S. Locus of control and learned helplessness. *Journal of Experimental Psychology*, 1974, **102**, 187–193.

Hiroto, D. S. & Seligman, M. E. P. Generality of learned helplessness in man. *Journal of Personality and Social Psychology*, in press.

Looney, T. A. & Cohen, P. S. Retardation of jump-up escape responding in rats pretreated with different frequencies of noncontingent electric shock. *Journal of Comparative and Physiological Psychology*, 1972, **78**, 317–322.

Maier, S. F. Failure to escape traumatic shock: Incompatible skeletal motor responses or learned helplessness? *Learning and Motivation*, 1970, **1**, 157–170.

Maier, S. F., Albin, R. W., & Testa, T. Failure to learn to escape in rats previously exposed to inescapable shock depends on nature of escape response. *Journal of Comparative and Physiological Psychology*, 1973, **85**, 581–592.

Maier, S. F., & Gleitman, H. Proactive interference in rats. *Psychonomic Science*, 1967, **7**, 25–26.

Maier, S. F., Seligman, M. E. P., Solomon, R. L. Pavlovian fear conditioning and learned helplessness. In B. A. Campbell & R. M. Church (Eds.), *Punishment and aversive behavior*. New York: Appleton-Century-Crofts, 1960.

Miller, N. E., & Weiss, J. M. Effects of somatic or visceral responses to punishment. In B. A. Campbell & R. M. Church (Eds.), *Punishment and aversive behavior*. New York: Appleton-Century-Crofts, 1969.

Overmier, J. B. Interference with avoidance behavior: Failure to avoid traumatic shock. *Journal of Experimental Psychology*, 1968, **78**, 340–343.

Overmier, J. B., & Seligman, M. E. P. Effects of inescapable shock upon subsequent escape and avoidance learning. *Journal of Comparative and Physiological Psychology*, 1967, **63**, 23–33.

Padilla, A. M., Padilla, C., Ketterer, T., & Giacalone, D. Inescapable shocks and subsequent escape/avoidance conditioning in goldfish, *Carassius auratus*. *Psychonomic Science*, 1970, **20**, 295–296.

Seligman, M. E. P., & Beagley, G. Learned helplessness in the rat. *Journal of Comparative and Physiological Psychology*, 1975, **88**, 534–541.

Seligman, M. E. P., & Groves, D. Non-transient learned helplessness. *Psychonomic Science*, 1970, **19**, 191–192.

Seligman, M. E. P., & Maier, S. F. Failure to escape traumatic shock. *Journal of Experimental Psychology*, 1967, **74**, 1–9.

Seligman, M. E. P., Maier, S. F., & Geer, J. The alleviation of learned helplessness in the dog. *Journal of Abnormal and Social Psychology*, 1968, **73**, 256–262.

Seligman, M. E. P., Maier, S. F., & Solomon, R. L. Unpredictable and uncontrollable aversive events. In F. R. Brush (Ed.), *Aversive conditioning and learning*. New York: Academic Press, 1971.

Seward, J., & Humphrey, G. L. Avoidance learning as a function of pretraining in the cat. *Journal of Comparative and Physiological Psychology*, 1967, **63**, 338–341.

Thomas, E. Experimental neurosis as a motivational deficit. Paper presented at the meeting of the American Psychological Association, New Orleans, August 1974.

Thornton, J. W., & Jacobs, P. D. Learned helplessness in human subjects. *Journal of Experimental Psychology*, 1971, **87**, 367–372.

Weiss, J. M. Learned helplessness: Does it exist? Paper presented at the Columbia University Colloquium, New York, March 1974.

Weiss, J. M., Stone, E. A., & Harrell, N. Coping behavior and brain norepinephrine level in rats. *Journal of Comparative and Physiological Psychology*, 1970, **72**, 153–160

8/ **Verbal Learning**

How is information retrieved from memory? Let's look at a typical example. Suppose you are walking down the street and meet a young man about your age. He looks familiar, but you cannot "place" him. You think you may know him from a previous psychology course and search your memory for his name. Then, a second person suggests that he might be someone you knew in high school; in a flash, you recall this familiar face from your home room. Of course, it's Joe; how could you have forgotten?

In this example, recognition memory for a stimulus depended on identifying the appropriate context—that is, finding the same context that was present at the time of initial learning. This type of phenomenon could be called *context-based retrieval,* and it is of interest to psychologists because it suggests that memory retrieval processes rely partly on context cues. Indeed, one line of research has drawn attention to a new theory of forgetting called *retrieval failure theory,* which postulates that information may be available in long-term memory but cannot be remembered if there is no retrieval route to it. Similarly, when items are stored in long-term memory within certain contexts, placing several items in the same context may cause memory interference. Following our example, you might confuse the name of the "familiar face" with the name of someone else you knew in high school.

The studies presented in this section were designed to test the theory that retrieval from memory involves finding the retrieval route to the correct context. Tulving and Thomson (1973) investigated the *encoding specificity hypothesis* by constructing a situation in which cued recall performance was higher than recognition. Wickens and Clark (1968) explored the role of word categories in proactive interference, and Underwood (1965) studied a related issue by noting the errors that subjects made on word recognition tests.

ENCODING SPECIFICITY AND
RETRIEVAL PROCESSES IN EPISODIC MEMORY

Endel Tulving and Donald M. Thomson

Endel Tulving and Donald Thomson (1973) tested several theories of
the retrieval processes involved in word recognition from a list. Their
own theory, called the *encoding specificity hypothesis,* postulates that
in learning a given item, the subject also stores information about the
learning situation. Later recognition of the item depends on the learner's
reestablishing the memory for the specific input context of the learning experience. Thus, cues that lead to the original context of the
learning should facilitate recognition. An alternative theory is the *generation-recognition theory* which postulates that retrieval involves the
subject's generating various possible responses and then deciding
which one of these is actually the item to be retrieved. This theory
predicts that recall tasks should always be more difficult than recognition tasks, given that the former requires two stages whereas the
latter requires only one stage.

To test these and other theories of retrieval, Tulving and Thomson
asked their subjects to learn and recall word lists. The general procedure was as follows: First, the subjects learned a list of 24 target words
(printed in capital letters). A weakly associated cue word (printed in
lowercase letters) was presented with each target word. Next, the subjects were given words strongly associated with each target word and
asked to write any freely associated words that came to mind. They
were then asked to indicate which of these generated words they had
learned as target words in the original list. Although the subjects frequently generated target words, they recognized very few of them as
such. Finally, the subjects were given the original input cues (the lower
case words) and asked to recall the target words; in this case, they
performed quite well, recalling 63 percent in a typical study.

Tulving and Thomson described this result as "recognition failure
of recallable words": the subjects failed to recognize words that they
were able to recall. This finding is inconsistent with the generation-
recall theory (in that recall was better than recognition), but it can be
explained in terms of encoding specificity: the subjects did not recognize many of the words they had generated because the cues they used
to generate them differed from those established during learning.

The current transition from traditional associationism to information processing and organizational points of view about human memory manifests itself in many ways. One of the clearest signs of change has to do with the experimental and theoretical separation between storage and retrieval processes. In an important early paper, Melton (1963), for instance, pointed out that "the principal issues in theory of memory . . . are about either the storage or the retrieval of traces [p. 4]." Only 10 years before Melton made the statement, it would have puzzled most students of verbal learning. At that time memory was still a matter of acquisition, retention, transfer, and interference of associations between stimuli and responses. While everyone was aware of the logical distinction between acquisition and retention on the one hand and retention and recall on the other hand, these distinctions shaped neither experiment nor theory. At the level of conceptual analysis, the mechanism of recall was included in the concept of association; at the level of experimental operations, recall was observable behavior whose measurable aspects simply served to provide evidence about strength of associations. Moreover, the act of recall was empirically neutral in that it did not affect the state of the system; it was theoretically uninteresting because it could not be studied independently of acquisition.

The last 10 or 15 years have changed the ideational framework for studying memory. Today the orienting attitudes clearly include the notion that both recall and recognition are more or less complex retrieval operations or processes that can be studied and analyzed in some sense separately of storage operations or processes. Retrieval operations complete the act of remembering that begins with encoding of information about an event into the memory store. Thus, remembering is regarded as a joint product of information stored in the past and information present in the immediate cognitive environment of the rememberer. It is also becoming increasingly clear that remembering does not involve a mere activation of the learned association or arousal of the stored trace by a stimulus. Some sort of a more complex interaction between stored information and certain features of the retrieval environment seems to be involved in converting a potential memory into conscious awareness of the original event and corresponding behavior.

Relations between the effects of the past and present inputs and the interaction of the memory trace with the retrieval environment constitute the domain of theories of retrieval. Although the important issues are not yet entirely clear, many questions do seem to be central to the understanding of retrieval processes and are likely to come more directly under experimental and theoretical scrutiny. What, for instance, determines the high degree of selectivity of retrieval, the fact that at any given moment a person can only remember one discrete event? Is the output mode of the memory system different from the input mode? Can information be retrieved at the same time that some other information is stored, or does storage always involve retrieval, and retrieval storage? How do we conceptualize the nature of the effect of a retrieval cue on stored information? Does it activate the trace, does it elicit it directly or indirectly, does it provide access to it, does it restrict the size of the search set, does it somehow complement the information contained in the trace, or what? Is there a fundamental difference between recall and recognition, or do these two retrieval operations differ only in terms of the nature of retrieval cues present at output? What controls retrieval in a situation in which no specific cues seem to be present, such as in free recall? What makes some stimuli effective cues for retrieval of a given event and others not?

Since the separation of the total act of remembering into storage and retrieval processes has only recently been translated into experimental observations and theoretical speculations, there are as yet no theories of retrieval that provide satisfactory answers to these and many other possible questions one might want to ask. The development of these theories is one of the important objectives of research on memory. But a modest beginning has been made, and it is the purpose of the present paper to examine and describe the early state of the art.

In the first part of the paper, we describe a familiar phenomenon that has recently been brought into the laboratory and that has become the source of a minor theoretical controversy. This is the so-called extralist cuing effect, facilitation of recall of a list item by a retrieval cue that was not explicitly a part of the input list. We summarize and briefly evaluate seven theories that have been advanced to explain the effect. In the second major section of the paper, we present some new data from experiments that were initially designed to test the most popular and widely accepted explanation of the extralist cuing effect, the generation-recognition theory. Somewhat unexpectedly, the results of the experiments showed large superiority of recall over recognition, a state of affairs that cannot occur according to the generation-recognition theory as well as most other extant theories of retrieval. In the third and final section, we consider several possible interpretations of the new data and subsume them, together with other data already in the literature, under the encoding specificity principle: What is stored is determined by what is perceived and how it is encoded, and what is stored determines what retrieval cues are effective in providing access to what is stored.

The present analysis applies to memory for simple events of the kind frequently used in laboratory studies. A familiar word or some other object is presented as a member of an unfamiliar collection or list, and the subject's task is to remember that he saw that particular word or object in that particular list in that particular situation. In such a list-item task, the subject may be instructed to retrieve the whole set of presented items, some particular subset thereof, or a single item. At the time of retrieval, he is given general instructions as to the set or subset of items to be retrieved, and sometimes the instructions are supplemented with specific cues. The cues may be units of material that were presented as a part of the input list (intralist cues). They may also be items not explicitly present at the time of the study (extralist cues). An intralist cue to aid retrieval of List Item B may be another List Item A, or it may be a literal copy of the Target Item B. In the former case, it is customary to refer to the subject's task as that of cued recall; in the latter we say that the task is one of recognition. (Despite the apparent differences in the nature of these two kinds of cues, we assume that the processes involved are essentially the same in both cases, and we make no theoretical distinction between recall and recognition. The subject's task is the same in both cases, namely to utilize the information provided in the retrieval environment to select some specific stored information.)

The paper is about retrieval processes in episodic rather than semantic memory. The distinction between these two memory systems has been described in detail elsewhere (Tulving, 1972). It forms part of the general background of the present analysis. Briefly, episodic memory is concerned with storage and retrieval of temporally dated, spatially located, and personally experienced events or episodes, and temporal-spatial relations among such events. Appearance of a word in a to-be-remembered list in an experimental task is such an event. (In typical laboratory experiments the spatial coordinates of events to be remembered are held constant, hence the focus on their temporal dates and relations only.) Semantic memory is the system concerned with storage and utilization of knowledge about words and concepts, their properties, and interrelations. Thus, episodic information about a word refers to information about the event of which the word is the focal element, or one of the focal elements, while semantic information about a word is entirely independent of the word's occurrence in a particular situation or its temporal co-occurrence with some other words.

We agree with the widely held pretheoretical assumption that the central representation of the to-be-remembered event, the memory trace, is a multidimensional collection of elements, features, or attributes (e.g., Bower, 1967; Norman & Rumelhart, 1970; Posner & Warren, 1972; Underwood, 1969; Wickens, 1970). We also assume along with many other contemporary students of memory (e.g., Bower, 1967, 1972; Martin, 1968, 1972; Melton & Martin, 1972; Underwood, 1969, 1972; Wickens, 1970) that an encoding process intervenes between the perception of an event and the creation of the corresponding trace, a process of as yet unknown nature that converts the stimulus energy into mnemonic information. The concern with retrieval processes in the present paper necessarily means that we must take an interest in the nature of stored information and in conditions determining the format of this information, that is, in encoding processes. It makes little sense to talk about retrieval without knowing something, or at least making some assumptions, about what it is that is being retrieved.

One term that we will use rather frequently in the paper is "effectiveness of retrieval cues." By this we mean the probability of recall of the target item in the presence of a discretely identifiable retrieval cue. Effectiveness, as thus defined, can always be expressed in absolute terms, but for certain reasons it is more convenient to describe the effectiveness of any specific cue in relation to the basic reference level of retrieval observed in absence of any specific cues. An effective cue, in this sense, is one whose presence facilitates recall in comparison with free or nominally non-cued recall.[1]

Generation-Recognition Models

At the present time the most widely accepted theories of retrieval are various versions of the generate-test model of information processing. The generation-recognition models assume that retrieval of stored information consists of two successive or overlapping stages: (a) implicit generation of possible response alternatives and (b) recognition of one of the generated alternatives as meeting certain criteria of acceptability. The generation phase is frequently guided by semantic information the system possesses about the cue word: given *table* as cue, the implicitly generated responses consist of words semantically related to it, including CHAIR. The operations in the recognition phase, on the other hand, can be successful only to the extent that relevant episodic information is available. The generated response alternative CHAIR would be identified as the desired word if its internal representation carries an appropriate "occurrence tag" (Mandler, 1972) or "list marker" (Anderson & Bower, 1972), information about the membership of the word in a particular list in a particular situation.

Effective retrieval cues of all sorts, including extralist cues, facilitate recall (to follow the reasoning of generation-recognition models) because they reduce the probability that the desired information, although available in the memory store, cannot be found. Cued recall, in this view, produces a higher level of retrieval than does noncued recall for the same reason that recognition is higher than recall. Bahrick (1969), in one of the most explicit accounts of the workings of the generation-recognition mechanism, said that a cue or a prompt

> is likely to produce a hierarchy of responses as a result of past learning. . . . One of these responses is likely to be the training response. *S* is thus unburdened of the search strategy involved in unaided recall tasks. He continues to produce responses associated with the prompt until he can identify one of them as the response presented during training. This portion of the prompted recall task functionally approximates a recognition task [Bahrick, p. 217].

---

[1] Subjects may retrieve items through schemes other than those suggested by the experimenter, and match the item to the cue after retrieval has occurred. Such cases could distort and inflate the absolute measures of effectiveness, and this is why measures relative to the noncued base line are preferred. One can then talk about inhibiting effects of specific cues, although it only means that cues assumed to be present in the nominally noncued situation are more effective in absolute terms than those the subject attempts to use at the experimenter's request (e.g., Earhard, 1969; Postman, Adams, & Phillips, 1955; Slamecka, 1969).

In Bahrick's formal model (1970), the probability of recall of the target item in response to the extralist cue is the product of the probability of its implicit generation and the probability of its recognition.

Many other contemporary thinkers advocate, or at least approvingly mention, the generation-recognition model as an appropriate explanation of cuing effects (e.g., Bower, 1970; Bower, Clark, Lesgold, & Winzenz, 1969; Fox & Dahl, 1971; Kintsch, 1970; Murdock, in press; Norman, 1968; Shiffrin & Atkinson, 1969; Slamecka, 1972; Underwood, 1972). The terminology used by different theorists is not always the same, but the basic ideas are identical.

Encoding Specificity Principle

The encoding specificity principle is the final idea about retrieval and extralist cuing effects we discuss. In its broadest form the principle asserts that only that can be retrieved that has been stored, and that how it can be retrieved depends on how it was stored. In its more restricted senses, the principle becomes less truistic and hence theoretically more interesting. For instance, we assume that what is stored about the occurrence of a word in an experimental list is information about the specific encoding of that word in that context in that situation. This information may or may not include the relation that the target word has with some other word in the semantic system. If it does, that other word may be an effective retrieval cue. If it does not, the other word cannot provide access to the stored information because its relation to the target word is not stored.

Thus, the effectiveness of retrieval cues depends on the properties of the trace of the word event in the episodic system. It is independent of the semantic properties of the word except insofar as these properties were encoded as a part of the trace of the event. The distinction between semantic characteristics of words as lexical units and words as to-be-remembered events can be readily demonstrated with homographs—for instance, if VIOLET is encoded and stored as a color name, it normally cannot be retrieved as an instance of the category of flowers, or girls' names—but the same principle presumably holds for all verbal items. The cue *table* facilitates recall of the target word CHAIR if the original encoding of CHAIR as a to-be-remembered word included semantic information of the kind that defines the relation between two objects in the same conceptual category. Most intelligent subjects in episodic memory experiments routinely encode to-be-remembered words semantically, and hence words meaningfully related to target items will serve as effective retrieval cues.

A recent application of the encoding specificity principle to the interpretation of effectiveness of retrieval cues appeared in a study by Tulving and Osler (1968); one of its more interesting implications was explicitly tested in three experiments by Thomson and Tulving (1970); and its bearing on results from intralist cuing experiments has been discussed by Postman (1972). Since the principle asserts that it is the encoded trace of the target word rather than the characteristics of the target word in semantic memory that determines the effectiveness of extralist retrieval cues, as well as all other cues, it can be experimentally contrasted with theories that attribute the effectiveness of extralist cues to their preexperimental relations with target words. Such contrasts, however, are possible only under special conditions.

Logic of Experimental Comparison between Theories

The main difference between the generation-recognition models of retrieval and the encoding specificity principle that is subject to test lies in the encoding stage of an item's processing as the locus of the effect of cues. According to the generation-recognition models the encoding stage is not important, as long as it does not disturb the capacity of the extralist cue to produce the target item as an implicit response. According to the encoding specificity principle, the target item must be encoded in some sort of reference to the cue for the cue to be effective.

Both theories can account equally well for the finding that a given cue in fact is effective. Thus, for instance, if *table* does facilitate the recall of the target word CHAIR, it is possible that an implicit response "chair" was made to the cue at retrieval and subsequently recognized. It is also possible that the target CHAIR was semantically encoded at the time of presentation in a specific way that rendered the cue word *table* effective. Experiments in which specific encoding conditions are unknown cannot provide critical data for evaluation of theories that differ in claims that they make about the importance of these conditions.

The comparison of effectiveness of extralist cues under conditions in which the subjects were free to encode the target item in any way they wished and in which they were induced to encode the target item in the context of a specific list cue was undertaken by Thomson and Tulving (1970). Target words such as CHAIR were presented either alone or in the context of list cues such as *glue*, and the effectiveness of extralist cues such as *table* was observed under the two types of encoding condition. The results showed that extralist cues did facilitate recall of target words, but only if the target words appeared in the list as single items. In this case (Experiment II, Groups 1 and 3) cued recall was on the order of 70% as compared with the values in the neighborhood of 45% in the nominally noncued test. Under the conditions in which the target word occurred at input with, and was presumably stored in some relation to another word (Experiment II, Groups 5 and 6), cuing with extralist cues resulted in a much lower recall level of some 23%. Noncued recall of target words encoded in presence of specific list cues (Experiment II, Group 4) was approximately 30%. These data seem to be more compatible with the encoding specificity principle than with the generation-recognition theory. It is not known, however, to what extent the pairing of target words with specific list cues at input may have reduced the capacity of extralist cues to produce targets as implicit responses, and therefore the results of the Thomson and Tulving experiment are not entirely unequivocal.

We next report data from three experiments in which the two phases of retrieval as envisioned by generation-recognition theories, generation and recognition, could be directly observed. The experiments were patterned after the Thomson and Tulving study, except that we did not test the effectiveness of extralist retrieval cues under conditions where target words were presented in absence of any specific intralist context. Previous experiments have made it quite clear that extralist associates of target words would be quite effective retrieval cues under these conditions. This kind of result, as we have seen, would not distinguish among theories.

When Retrieval Cues Fail: Three Experiments

In the experiments to be described, subjects studied a list of target words, such as CHAIR, each presented in the company of a specific input cue, such as *glue*. Since the subjects expected to be tested with these cues, they presumably encoded target words in an appropriate relation to the input cue. After studying the list, the subjects were asked to produce free association responses to strong extraexperimental associates of target words such as *table*. The probability of generation of target words (CHAIR) in response to the extralist cues was one observation of interest. Next, subjects were asked to identify those generated words that they remembered having seen in the input list, their success in doing so being another observation of interest. Finally, a cued recall test involving input cues (*glue*) was given to the subjects in an attempt to estimate the extent to which information about target words (CHAIR) was available in the memory store.

GENERAL METHOD

In all three experiments the same procedure was used up to a critical point in time when different treatments and tests were administered to subjects. The procedure common to all experiments follows.

Every subject was shown and tested on three successive lists. The sole purpose of the first two lists was to induce subjects to encode each target word with respect to, or in the context of, another word. The word pairs in these two set-establishing lists were comparable to weak-cue input lists used by Thomson and Tulving (1970). The target words, each paired with its cue word, were shown visually, one at a time, at the rate of three seconds/pair. Immediately at the end of the presentation of the list the subjects were provided with 24 haphazardly ordered input cue words on a recall sheet and instructed to write down the target words. Three minutes were given for the recall of the list. The mean number of words recalled for these two lists were 14.3 and 17.6 in Experiment 1; 15.7 and 18.3 in Experiment 2; and 14.4 and 17.7 in Experiment 3.

The third list in each experiment was the critical list, providing the data of interest. This list, too, consisted of 24 cue-target pairs, with the material presented exactly as in the first two lists.

The target words in the third list in each experiment were those designated as such in Table 1. The two sets, A and B, were used equally frequently with two subgroups of subjects in each of the three experiments; otherwise, all subjects in a given experiment were treated identically. In Table 1, each target word is accompanied by two cue words, one "weak" and the other one "strong." These triplets were selected from free-association norms (Bilodeau & Howell, 1965; Riegel, 1965) to conform to the following criteria: (a) the

TABLE 1

Materials Used in the Construction of Critical Lists in Experiments 1, 2, and 3

List A			List B		
Weak cue	Strong cue	Target word	Weak cue	Strong cue	Target word
ground	hot	COLD	hope	low	HIGH
head	dark	LIGHT	stem	long	SHORT
bath	want	NEED	whiskey	lake	WATER
cheese	grass	GREEN	moth	eat	FOOD
stomach	small	LARGE	cabbage	square	ROUND
sun	night	DAY	glass	soft	HARD
pretty	sky	BLUE	country	closed	OPEN
cave	dry	WET	tool	finger	HAND
whistle	tennis	BALL	memory	fast	SLOW
noise	blow	WIND	covering	lining	COAT
glue	table	CHAIR	barn	clean	DIRTY
command	woman	MAN	spider	eagle	BIRD
fruit	bloom	FLOWER	crust	bake	CAKE
home	bitter	SWEET	deep	bed	SLEEP
grasp	infant	BABY	train	white	BLACK
butter	rough	SMOOTH	mountain	leaf	TREE
drink	tobacco	SMOKE	cottage	hate	LOVE
beat	ache	PAIN	art	boy	GIRL
cloth	lamb	SHEEP	adult	labor	WORK
swift	stop	GO	brave	strong	WEAK
lady	king	QUEEN	door	color	RED
blade	scissors	CUT	roll	carpet	RUG
plant	insect	BUG	think	dumb	STUPID
wish	soap	WASH	exist	human	BEING

target word is a low-frequency (mean of 1% for the whole set) associate to its weak cue; (b) the target word is a high-frequency associate to its strong cue (mean of 52%), and (c) weak and strong cues of a given target word are not associatively related to each other in the norms.

The 24 pairs of words in critical lists consisted of weak cues and their corresponding target words. The strong cue words were not shown at the time of the presentation and were used only as extralist retrieval cues in the subsequent test phase. For instance, subjects tested with List A saw the pairs, ground COLD, head LIGHT, bath NEED, and so on, one pair at a time, for all 24 pairs, the cue word appearing in lower-case letters above the capitalized target word. The same instructions that had been given to the subjects in the first two lists were routinely repeated: their task was to remember the capitalized words, but paying attention to cues might help them at the time of the subsequent test. No mention was made of any change in the procedure between Lists 2 and 3. Each pair was again shown visually for three seconds. After all 24 pairs had been presented once, subjects received different treatments in different experiments, as described below.

Experiment 1

After the presentation of the third, critical list—henceforth referred to as "the list"—all 40 subjects, undergraduates at Yale University, were given the same four successive tasks.

First, each subject received a sheet of paper listing 12 extralist cues corresponding to one half of the to-be-remembered words from the list. For instance, subjects tested with List A were given the words hot, dark, want, and so on. They were told that each of the listed cue words was related to one of the capitalized words in the list that they had just studied, and that their task was to write down as many of the capitalized words as they remembered, each one beside its related cue word. Three minutes were allowed for this task. The mean number of target words recalled in this extralist-cue test was 1.8 (15%).

Second, subjects were given the remaining 12 extralist cues, briefly told about the free association procedure, instructed to look carefully at each cue word, produce free associates to each mentally, and then, "if one of the words you generate as a free association is a word from the list that you have just studied," to write it down beside its stimulus word. Again, three minutes were given for this task. The mean number of target words recalled in this test was 3.6 (30%). This figure was significantly higher than the 15% recall level in the first phase.

Third, all 24 extralist cue words, that is, the cues that the subjects had just seen in the first and second phase of testing, were presented to the subjects once more, listed on a sheet of paper, together with instructions to "write down all the words that you can generate as free associations" to these stimulus words. Beside each stimulus word were six blank spaces for up to six responses. Twelve minutes were allowed for this task. Each subject generated, on the average, 104 free association responses to the 24 stimulus words, a mean of 4.4 response words. Among the 104 responses thus generated there were, on the average, 17.7 (74% of the 24) words matching the target words of the list. Of these words, 70% were given by subjects as the primary response to the stimulus words. Thus, the proportion of target words generated as primary responses to the high-frequency stimuli was 52% (70% of the 74%), matching the normative data exactly.

Fourth, the subjects were instructed to look over all their generated responses and to circle all words that they recognized as target words from the list they had learned last. They were given as much time as they needed for this task. The mean number of words circled was 4.2, out of the maximum of 17.7, producing a hit rate of 24%. The percentage of false positives, circled words that were not target words from the list, was 4.5%

A fifth task in Experiment 1 was an afterthought whose relevance became clear after we had tested and seen the results from 30 subjects. It was administered to the final 10 subjects. (Their performance on the first four tasks was not distinguishable from that of the first 30 subjects.) These 10 subjects were provided, on two sheets of paper, with the 24 input cues from the list and were instructed to recall the capitalized words from the list they had seen last. The mean number of target words recalled on this cued recall test was 15.2, for a hit rate of 63%. Further analysis of the data from these 10 subjects revealed that in their fourth and fifth tasks, they both recognized and recalled a total of 43 words; recognized but did not recall 4 words; and recalled but did not recognize 69 words.

These data can be summarized as follows: (a) Pairing of to-be-remembered words at input with cue words associatively unrelated to subsequently presented extralist cues has no adverse effect on subjects' ability to utilize these extralist cues in generating target words from semantic memory. (b) Regardless of whether subjects are or are not instructed to use the generate-recognize strategy, under conditions where cues are switched from input to output, the level of their recall performance in presence of extralist cues does not materially exceed that expected under noncued conditions (cf. Thomson & Tulving, 1970). (c) Under the experimental conditions as described, subjects cannot recognize many generated copies of target words, although they can produce these words in presence of what appear to be more effective cues, context items from the input list. The recognition hit rate of 24% contrasted with the hit rate of 63% in the cued recall test.

Experiment 2

One purpose of Experiment 2 was to replicate Experiment 1; another was to find out to what extent the low hit rate in the recognition of generated free association responses was attributable to the source of the recognition test items. In Experiment 1, each subject generated the "old" items and distractors for the recognition test. In Experiment 2 this procedure was replicated with one half of the list items, while for the other half of the list the source of "old" test items and distractors for a given subject was the free association protocol of a yoked subject.

Twenty-two subjects, undergraduate students of both sexes at Yale University, participated in this experiment. Again, they were divided into two groups for the sole purpose of using both Lists A and B, as shown in Table 1, in the critical, third list position. Otherwise, all subjects were administered an identical sequence of tasks.

Each subject was again first tested with two successive set-establishing lists, and then the third list was presented, as in Experiment 1. Following the presentation of the list, subjects were given five successive tasks.

1. They were asked to generate and write down six free association responses to each of the 12 extralist cue words corresponding to the target words. The mean number of words generated was 54 per subject, of which 9.6 (80% of the 12) matched target words in the list. Primary responses coincided with target words 53% of the time.

2. Subjects were asked to examine all the words they had generated in the free association test and to write down, on a separate piece of paper, all those words they recognized as target words from the list. On the average, 1.8 target words were thus recognized, for a hit rate of 18%. The false positive rate was 2.8%.

3. Each subject was given the free associates generated by another subject to the remaining 12 extralist cues, and instructed to perform the same kind of recognition test on these words that they had performed on their own. This time the 22 subjects correctly identified 51 out of the total of 204 copies of target words, for a hit rate of 25%, a score not significantly different from the 18% hit rate of subjects' own generated responses, $t = 1.18$, $df = 21$.

4. Subjects were asked to write down, beside each of the recognized target words from the second set (yoked subjects' free association responses), the corresponding input cues they remembered from the list. The 22 subjects could provide 36 (71%) such cues for the 51 targets.

5. Finally, all subjects were given all 24 original input cues from the list and were asked to recall as many target words as they remembered. The mean number of words recalled on this test was 14.1, for a hit rate of 59%. Again, as in Experiment 1, there were very few words that were recognized in the second task but not recalled in the fifth task (a total of 5 for all 22 subjects), and there were numerous words recalled in the fifth task but not recognized, although generated, in the second task (total of 73 for 22 subjects).

The results of Experiment 2 thus confirmed the results of Experiment 1: when provided with strong extraexperimental associates of target words as stimuli, subjects generated many responses matching the target words but they did rather poorly in identifying these as target words from the list. In Experiment 2, the hit rate in the recognition test of generated target words was, on the average, 22%, while the false positive rate was 2.8%. The source of the "old" test words and distractor items in the recognition test—whether the subject's own semantic memory or that of another subject—did not seem to be an important determinant of the recognition performance under these conditions, although the confounding of order of tests with experimental treatment may have contributed to the absence of a significant difference between the two conditions. Subjects also remembered a sizable proportion of input cues for the target words they correctly identified from among those generated by their yoked partners. Finally, the data from Experiment 2 confirmed those from Experiment 1 in showing that a low hit rate in the recognition test on generated target words did not prevent subjects from doing reasonably well in recalling these words in presence of the original input stimuli. The mean recognition rate of 22% in Experiment 2 again contrasted starkly with the cued-recall hit rate of 59%.

While the data in these experiments were averaged over all target words in the two critical lists, A and B, as shown in Table 1, it may be of some interest that large differences in recognition of individual words occurred. The words in both lists in Table 1 are ordered from least to most recognizable, on the basis of data in Experiments 1 and 2. Target words at the top of each list (COLD, LIGHT, HIGH, SHORT, WATER) were never recognized, even though each was generated by anywhere from 13 to 21 subjects; words in the middle (BALL, WIND, CHAIR, MAN, FLOWER, SLOW, COAT, DIRTY) showed individual hit rates of .14 to .16; words at the bottom (QUEEN, CUT, BUG, WASH, STUPID, BEING) were correctly recognized over 50% of the time.

Experiment 3

A possible interpretation of the very low recognition hit rates of generated to-be-remembered words in Experiments 1 and 2 might be provided by invoking the concept of "high criterion": for reasons unknown, the subjects adopt a very cautious attitude in the recognition test and check off only those words that they are extremely confident about as being identical with target words from the list. While the observed false positive rates, in relation to the observed hit rates, are sufficiently high to weaken the force of this argument, we made a more direct attempt to evaluate this interpretation in Experiment 3.

Fourteen subjects, from the same source as those in Experiments 1 and 2, served in this experiment. Again, they were divided into two groups for the sole purpose of counterbalancing materials in the critical test conditions. The materials and other conditions of the experiment were identical with those used in Experiments 1 and 2.

Subjects were again given two set-establishing lists first. The third list was then presented under the same instructions and conditions as Lists 1 and 2, and followed by three tasks. First, subjects were provided with two sheets of paper, listing the 24 extralist cues corresponding to the target words from the list. They were instructed to write down four free association responses to each of the 24 cue words, words that the cue words "made them think of."

Second, a forced-choice recognition test was given. Subjects were instructed to look at the four words they had generated for each of the stimulus words and circle the word that appeared to be the most likely member of the set of target words in the last list they had learned, guessing whenever necessary. In addition, the subjects were asked to indicate their confidence in the correctness of the response, on a scale on which the three values, 1, 2, and 3, were labeled as "guessing," "reasonably sure," and "absolutely sure."

The 14 subjects generated a total of 221 target words in the free association test, or an average of 15.8 (66%) of the possible 24. The proportion of target items among primary responses was 46%, only a little less than the normative value of 52%. In what was effectively a four-alternative forced-choice recognition test, the subjects correctly circled 118 out of the 221 copies of target words and failed to recognize the other 103 words, for a hit rate of 53%. Of the 118 to-be-remembered words correctly circled in the recognition test, 47 were labeled as guesses, while the remaining 71 were given confidence ratings of 2 or 3. The standard guessing correction yields a corrected recognition score of 38%. Alternatively, if we consider only those to-be-remembered words as recognized for which the subjects gave confidence ratings of 2 or 3, we obtain a recognition score of 71/221, or 32%.

In the third and final task, subjects were tested for recall of target words in presence of their original input cues, as in Experiments 1 and 2. The mean number of target words recalled was 14.2, for a hit rate of 61%, considerably higher than the recognition scores of 32% or 38%.

The major finding in Experiment 3 was that the failure to recognize recallable words also occurs, perhaps in a somewhat attenuated form, under the conditions of the forced-choice recognition test. It rules out the response bias as the sole explanation of the similar results obtained under free-choice recognition procedure in Experiments 1 and 2.

General Results

A summary of the data from the three experiments, together with those from Experiment II in the Thomson and Tulving (1970) paper, is presented in Table 2. Table 2 shows probability of recall of target words in presence of three kinds of specific cues: (a) input cues, (b) copies of target words generated by subjects in free association tests, and (c) strong preexperimental associates of target words used as extralist retrieval cues.

TABLE 2

Probability of Recall of the Target Word in the Presence of Three Kinds of Retrieval Cues

Cue	Tulving & Thomson (1970)[2] Exp. II	Exp. 1	Exp. 2	Exp. 3
Input cue	.65	.63	.59	.61
Extraexperimental associate	.23	.15, .30	—	—
Copy of target	—	.24	.22	.32, .38

[2]Data are from Group 6, Experiment II, by Thomson and Tulving (1970).

The importance of the data pertaining to recall in presence of input cues is twofold: the observed levels of recall in various experiments indicate the extent of effectiveness of input cues in relation to other cues, and they provide a lower-bound estimate of the availability of information about target words in memory. The data thus constitute a critical link in the argument that takes us from the results to the general conclusion of the experiments: conditions can be created in which information about a word event is available in the memory store in a form sufficient for the production of the appropriate response and yet a literal copy of the word is not recognized. This phenomenon of recognition failure was a striking one. Ignoring words that could be recalled and recognized and those that could be neither recognized nor recalled—response categories defining theoretically uninteresting outcomes—we found, in Experiments 1 and 2, that the number of words that were recalled but not recognized exceeded the number of words that could be recognized but not recalled by a ratio of approximately 15:1.

The phenomenon of recognition failure of recallable items is not a novel one. Other experiments have been reported in which learned materials were recalled at higher levels than they were recognized (Bahrick & Bahrick, 1964; Lachman & Field, 1965; Lachman, Laughery, & Field, 1966). But in these experiments the subjects were given only a limited amount of time to make the recognition judgments, and it is not known to what extent the outcome was a consequence of time pressure. It is quite likely that if the subjects in the Lachman and Field (1965) experiment, for instance, in which the learned material was a meaningful prose passage, would have been given more time, they might have been able to recognize all words that they could recall, simply by reproducing each word as an element of the learned passage and matching it with the test word. This strategy may not have been feasible under the conditions of Lachman and Field's recognition task in which subjects only had 1.5 seconds to make the decision about each word.

Failure of Recognition of Generated Words

The recognition failure of recallable words is an empirical phenomenon that cannot occur according to the two-process theory of recall and recognition (Kintsch, 1970) and other versions of the generation-recognition model of retrieval (e.g., Bower et al., 1969; Murdock, in press; Norman, 1968; Shiffrin & Atkinson, 1969; Slamecka, 1972; Underwood, 1972). Recovery of information through two bottlenecks (generation and recognition) in a recall situation cannot be more effective than that through only one of the two (recognition). Since the experimental data show that under certain conditions generation and recognition produce a higher level of retrieval than recognition alone, existing generation-recognition models require revision.

At the present time, it is possible only to point once more to the encoding specificity principle as a general answer to the questions. What produced the asymmetry of associations between list cues and target items in our experiments? What determined the functional memory units and their relations to the nominal units? Why was one of the two nominal units embedded in the whole complex more readily recognized when it appeared alone than was the other? Why did the list cue serve the function of a control element or code of the stored cue-target trace while the target item did not? Why was the information contained in the input cue sufficient to complement the stored information while that in the extralist cue and the copy of the target item was not?

A general answer to all these questions is provided by the encoding specificity principle: Specific encoding operations performed on what is perceived determine what is stored, and what is stored determines what retrieval cues are effective in providing access to what is stored.[3]

References

Anderson, J. R., & Bower, G. H. Recognition and retrieval processes in free recall. *Psychological Review*, 1972, **79**, 97–123.

Asch, S. E. Reformulation of the problem of association. *American Psychologist*, 1969, **24**, 92–102.

Atkinson, R. C., & Shiffrin, R. M. Human memory: A proposed system and its control processes. In K. W. Spence & J. T. Spence (Eds.), *The psychology of learning and motivation*. Vol. 2. New York: Academic Press, 1968.

Bahrick, H. P. A two-phase model for prompted recall. *Psychological Review*, 1970, **77**, 215–222.

Bahrick, H. P., & Bahrick, P. O. A re-examination of the interrelations among measures of retention. *Quarterly Journal of Experimental Psychology*, 1964, **16**, 318–324.

Bartlett, F. C. *Remembering: A study in experimental and social psychology*. Cambridge, England: University Press, 1932.

Bilodeau, E. A., & Howell, D. C. *Free association norms*. (Catalog No. D210.2:F87) Washington, D. C.: U.S. Government Printing Office, 1965.

Bobrow, S. A. Memory for words in sentences. *Journal of Verbal Learning and Verbal Behavior*, 1970, **9**, 363–372.

Bower, G. H. A multicomponent theory of the memory trace. In K. W. Spence & J. T. Spence (Eds.), *The psychology of learning and motivation*. Vol. 1. New York: Academic Press, 1967.

Bower, G. H. Organizational factors in memory. *Cognitive Psychology*, 1970, **1**, 18–46.

Bower, G. H. Stimulus-sampling theory of encoding variability. In A. W. Melton & E. Martin (Eds.), *Coding processes in human memory*. Washington, D. C.: Winston, 1972.

---

[3] Although we have emphasized the importance of encoding conditions at input, we do not wish to imply that once an event has been encoded its trace does not undergo further changes. Among many possible modifications of stored information, those produced through active recoding of the trace are most relevant to determining its subsequent retrievability in different retrieval environments. For our present purposes, encoding processes are considered always to subsume recoding processes that occur prior to the act of implicit retrieval of interest.

Bower, G. H., Clark, M. C., Lesgold, A. M., & Winzenz, D. Hierarchical retrieval schemes in recall of categorized word lists. *Journal of Verbal Learning and Verbal Behavior*, 1969, **8**, 323–343.

Bregman, A. S. Forgetting curves with semantic, phonetic, graphic, and contiguity cues. *Journal of Experimental Psychology*, 1968, **78**, 539–546.

Broadbent, D. E. *In defence of empirical psychology.* London: Methuen, 1973.

Craik, F. I. M. A "levels of analysis" view of memory. In P. Pliner, L. Krames, & T. M. Alloway (Eds.), *Communication and affect: Language and thought.* New York: Academic Press, 1973.

Craik, F. I. M., & Lockhart, R. S. Levels of processing: A framework for memory research. *Journal of Verbal Learning and Verbal Behavior*, 1972, **11**, 671–684.

Cramer, P. Magnitude and selectivity as independent factors in semantic generalization. *Journal of Verbal Learning and Verbal Behavior*, 1970, **9**, 509–524.

DaPolito, F., Barker, D., & Wiant, J. The effects of contextual changes on the component recognition. *American Journal of Psychology*, 1972, **85**, 431–440.

Earhard, M. Storage and retrieval of words encoded in memory. *Journal of Experimental Psychology*, 1969, **80**, 412–418.

Estes, W. K. An associative basis for coding and organization. In A. W. Melton & E. Martin (Eds.), *Coding processes in human memory.* Washington, D. C.: Winston, 1972.

Fox, P. W., & Dahl, P. R. Aided retrieval of previously unrecalled information. *Journal of Experimental Psychology*, 1971, **88**, 349–353.

Freund, J. S., & Underwood, B. J. Restricted associates as cues in free recall. *Journal of Verbal Learning and Verbal Behavior*, 1970, **9**, 136–141.

Frost, N. Encoding and retrieval in visual memory tasks. *Journal of Experimental Psychology*, 1972, **95**, 317–326.

Gardiner, J. M. Studies of word retrieval in human memory. Unpublished doctoral dissertation, University of London, 1972.

Ghatala, E. S., & Hurlbut, N. L. Effectiveness of acoustic and conceptual retrieval cues in memory for words at two grade levels. *Journal of Educational Psychology*, 1973, **64**, 347–352.

Harrower, M. R. Organization in higher mental processes. *Psychologische Forschung*, 1933, **17**, 56–120.

Hollingworth, H. L. *Psychology: Its facts and principles.* New York: Appleton, 1928.

Hyde, T. S., & Jenkins, J. J. Differential effects of incidental tasks on the organization of recall of a list of highly associated words. *Journal of Experimental Psychology*, 1969, **82**, 472–481.

James, W. *Principles of psychology.* New York: Holt, 1890.

Johnson, N. F. The role of chunking and organization in the process of recall. In G. H. Bower (Ed.), *The psychology of learning and motivation.* Vol. 4. New York: Academic Press, 1970.

Johnston, C. C., & Jenkins, J. J. Two more incidental tasks that differentially affect associative clustering in recall. *Journal of Experimental Psychology*, 1971, **89**, 92–95.

Kintsch, W. Models for free recall and recognition. In D. A. Norman (Ed.), *Models of human memory.* New York: Academic Press, 1970.

Koffka, K. *Principles of Gestalt psychology.* New York: Harcourt, Brace & World, 1935.

Köhler, W. *Gestalt psychology.* New York: Liveright, 1947.

Lachman, R., & Field, W. H. Recognition and recall of verbal material as a function of degree of training. *Psychonomic Science*, 1965, **2**, 225–226.

Lachman, R., Laughery, K. R., & Field, W. H. Recognition and recall of high frequency words following serial learning. *Psychonomic Science*, 1966, **4**, 225–226.

Lauer, P. A., & Battig, W. F. Free recall of taxonomically and alphabetically organized word lists as a function of storage and retrieval cues. *Journal of Verbal Learning and Verbal Behavior*, 1972, **11**, 333–342.

Light, L. L. Homonyms and synonyms as retrieval cues. *Journal of Experimental Psychology*, 1972, **96**, 255–262.

Light, L. L., & Carter-Sobell, L. Effects of changed semantic context on recognition memory. *Journal of Verbal Learning and Verbal Behavior*, 1970, **9**, 1–11.

Mandler, G. Organization and memory. In K. W. Spence & J. T. Spence (Eds.), *The psychology of learning and motivation*. Vol. 1. New York: Academic Press, 1967. (a)

Mandler, G. Verbal learning. In, *New directions of psychology, III*. New York: Holt, Rinehart & Winston, 1967. (b)

Mandler, G. Organization and recognition. In E. Tulving & W. Donaldson (Eds.), *Organization of memory*. New York: Academic Press, 1972.

Martin, E. Stimulus meaningfulness and paired-associate transfer: An encoding variability hypothesis. *Psychological Review*, 1968, **75**, 421–441.

Martin, E. Stimulus component independence. *Journal of Verbal Learning and Verbal Behavior*, 1971, **10**, 715–721.

Martin, E. Stimulus encoding in learning and transfer. In A. W. Melton & E. Martin (Eds.), *Coding processes in human memory*. Washington, D. C.:Winston, 1972.

McCormack, P. D. Recognition memory: How complex a retrieval system? *Canadian Journal of Psychology*, 1972, **26**, 19–41.

McLeod, P. D., Williams, C. E., & Broadbent, D. E. Free recall with assistance from one and from two retrieval cues. *British Journal of Psychology*, 1971, **62**, 59–65.

Melton, A. W. Implications of short-term memory for a general theory of memory. *Journal of Verbal Learning and Verbal Behavior*, 1963, **2**, 1–21.

Melton, A. W., & Martin, E. (Eds.), *Coding processes in human memory*. Washington, D. C.: Winston, 1972.

Mikula, G. Der Einfluss mnemotechnischer Hilfen auf das Erlernen und Behalten verbalen Materials. *Psychologische Forschung*, 1971, **34**, 312–324.

Murdock, B. B. *Human short-term memory*. Potomac, Md.: Lawrence Earlbaum Associates, in press.

Murdock, B. B., Jr., & Babick, A. J. The effect of repetition on the retention of individual words. *American Journal of Psychology, 1961*, **74**, 596–601.

Norman, D. A. Toward a theory of memory and attention. *Psychological Review*, 1968, **75**, 522–536.

Norman, D. A., & Rumelhart, D. E. A system for perception and memory. In D. A. Norman (Ed.), *Models of human memory*. New York: Academic Press, 1970.

Paivio, A., & Csapo, K. Picture superiority in free recall: Imagery or dual coding? (Research Bulletin No. 243) London: University of Western Ontario, Department of Psychology, 1972.

Posner, M. I.,   Warren, R. E. Traces, concepts, and conscious constructions. In A. W. Melton & E. Martin (Eds.), *Coding processes in human memory*. Washington, D. C.: Winston, 1972.

Postman, L. Short-term memory and incidental learning. In A. W. Melton (Ed.), *Categories of human learning*. New York: Academic Press, 1964.

Postman, L. A pragmatic view of organization theory. In E. Tulving & W. Donaldson (Eds.), *Organization of memory*. New York: Academic Press, 1972.

Puff, C. R. Clustering as a function of the sequential organization of stimulus word lists. *Journal of Verbal Learning and Verbal Behavior*, 1966, **5**, 503–506.

Riegel, K. F. Free associative responses to the 200 stimuli of the Michigan restricted association norms. (USPHS Tech. Rep. No. 8, Grant MH 07619) Ann Arbor: University of Michigan, 1965.

Schulman, A. J. Recognition memory for targets from a scanned word list. *British Journal of Psychology*, 1971, **62**, 335–346.

Shiffrin, R. M. Memory search. In D. A. Norman (Ed.), *Models of human memory*. New York: Academic Press, 1970.

Shiffrin, R. M., & Atkinson, R. C. Storage and retrieval processes in long-term memory. *Psychological Review*, 1969, **76**, 179–193.

Slamecka, N. J. Testing for associative storage in multitrial free recall. *Journal of Experimental Psychology*, 1969, **81**, 557–560.

Slamecka, N. J. The question of associative growth in the learning of categorized material. *Journal of Verbal Learning and Verbal Behavior*, 1972, **11**, 324–332.

Thomson, D. M. Context effects in recognition memory. *Journal of Verbal Learning and Verbal Behavior*, 1972, **11**, 497–511.

Thomson, C.M., &Tulving, E. Associative encoding and retrieval: Weak and strong cues. *Journal of Experimental Psychology*, 1970, **86**, 255–262.

Tulving, E. Theoretical issues in free recall. In T. R. Dixon & D. L. Horton (Eds.), *Verbal behavior and general behavior theory*. Englewood Cliffs, N. J.: Prentice-Hall, 1968. (a)

Tulving, E. When is recall higher than recognition? *Psychonomic Science*, 1968, **10**, 53–54. (b)

Tulving, E. Episodic and semantic memory. In E. Tulving & W. Donaldson (Eds.), *Organization of memory*. New York: Academic Press, 1972.

Tulving, E., & Osler, S. Effectiveness of retrieval cues in memory for words. *Journal of Experimental Psychology*, 1968, **77**, 593–601.

Tulving, E., & Pearlstone, Z. Availability versus accessibility of information in memory for words. *Journal of Verbal Learning and Verbal Behavior*, 1966, **5**, 381–391.

Tulving, E., & Psotka, J. Retroactive inhibition in free recall: Inaccessibility of information available in the memory store. *Journal of Experimental Psychology*, 1971, **87**, 1–8.

Tulving, E., & Thomson, D. M. Retrieval processes in recognition memory: Effects of associative context. *Journal of Experimental Psychology*, 1971, **87**, 116–124.

Tversky, B. Encoding processes in recognition and recall. *Cognitive Psychology*, in press.

Underwood, B. J. False recognition produced by implicit verbal response. *Journal of Experimental Psychology*, 1965, **70**, 122–129.

Underwood, B. J. Attributes of memory. *Psychological Review*, 1969, **76**, 559–573.

Underwood, B. J. Are we overloading memory? In A. W. Melton & E. Martin, (Eds.), *Coding processes in human memory*. Washington, D. C.: Winston, 1972.

Watkins, M. J. When is recall spectacularly higher than recognition? *Journal of Experimental Psychology*, 1973, in press.

Wickens, D. D. Encoding categories of words: An empirical approach to meaning. *Psychological Review*, 1970, **77**, 1–15.

Winograd, E., & Conn, C. P. Evidence from recognition memory for specific encoding of unmodified homographs. *Journal of Verbal Learning and Verbal Behavior*, 1971, **10**, 702–706.

Winograd, E., Karchmer, M. A., & Russell, I. S. Role of encoding unitization in cued recognition memory. *Journal of Verbal Learning and Verbal Behavior*, 1971, **10**, 199–206.

Wood, G. Category names as cues for the recall of category instances. *Psychonomic Science*, 1967, **9**, 323–324.

Yates, F. A. *The art of memory*. Chicago: University of Chicago Press, 1966.

Yntema, D. B., & Trask, F. P. Recall as a search process. *Journal of Verbal Learning and Verbal Behavior*, 1963, **2**, 65–74.

OSGOOD DIMENSIONS AS AN
ENCODING CLASS IN SHORT-TERM MEMORY

Delos D. Wickens and Sandra Clark

The paper by Delos Wickens and Sandra Clark (1968) provides a second line of support for the idea that the context at the time of encoding influences the subject's ability to retrieve information. Their work is aimed at determining "the dimensions along which words are encoded" — that is, the categories that humans use as context cues for the storage and retrieval of words.

For example, in a typical study, subjects were presented with a triad of words, asked to count backwards by 3's for 20 seconds (to prevent rehearsal), and then asked to recall the words. This was continued for five trials. For the control group, all five triads came from the same category (such as words rated positively like *true, enjoy, nice*; or words rated negatively like *kill, danger, worry*). For the experimental group, the first four trials were identical to those in the control group, but on the fifth trial the triad came from the opposite end of the category dimension (for example, positive words on trial 5 if trials 1 through 4 consisted of negative words, or negative words on trial 5 if trials 1 through 4 consisted of positive words).

The results, for many types of word categories, indicated that recall performance fell from trial 1 to trial 4 for both groups. This is an example of *proactive interference* (PI), the idea that prior learning interferes with memory for new material. However, the recall performance of the experimental group was much better on trial 5, although it continued to remain low for the control group. Wickens described the shift in performance for the experimental group as "release from proactive interference," because the subjects behaved as though they had been "freed" from the massive interfering effects of prior trials. In a subsequent review paper, "Encoding Categories of Words: An Empirical Approach to Memory" (1970), Wickens referred to many other shifts that produced release from PI. Examples included shifting between words and numbers, between one taxanomic class and another, between high and low frequency, and so on.

Why did a shift in word category result in better recall? Wickens and Clark suggest that incoming information was stored by category; thus, by trial 4, 12 possible word cues were connected to the same single retrieval cue. For the experimental subjects, the fifth trial provided a new and different retrieval cue, so the words could be stored and retrieved as a separate group.

In the short-term memory (STM) situation employing the Peterson and Peterson (1959) technique, proactive inhibition (PI) builds up rapidly (Keppel & Underwood, 1962), reaching a maximum after three or four trials. It has been shown by Wickens, Born, and Allen (1963), however, that the PI will be eliminated if the item presented is different from that used in the previous trials. In that experiment, one group of Ss was presented with a series of consonant trigrams (CCCs) and another group with a series of three-digit numbers (NNNs); each group was then shifted to a test item of the other class. Both groups showed a marked improvement on the shift trial, performing as well on that trial as on the first one of the experiment. Subsequently, Loess (1967) has demonstrated the same build-up and release of PI when Ss shift from a homogeneous class of word triads (such as species of birds) to a new class of word triads (species of trees).

Together these experiments indicate that in the STM situation, triads or trigrams, all elements of which are homogeneous with respect to conceptual class, seem to be encoded not only as unique items, but also as members of the same conceptual class. If another item is drawn from a different conceptual class, then competition no longer occurs or, at least, is minimal. A reduction in amount of retroactive inhibition is also found in long-term memory if the originally learned list and the interpolated list are composed of items drawn from different classes of material (Friedman & Reynolds, 1967; Postman, Keppel, & Stark, 1965).

The results of the Wickens et al. (1963) and of the Loess (1967) experiments suggest to the authors the possibility that the shift procedure may be used as something of a projective technique of organization in STM; a way of asking S what response classes are being employed without requiring him to identify and label them.

The semantic differential developed by Osgood, Suci, and Tannenbaum (1957) describes a three-dimensional verbal space identified by the three characteristics of Evaluation, Potency, and Activity. Using the Wick-

FIGURE 1

The results for the experimental and control groups on the Evaluation scale.

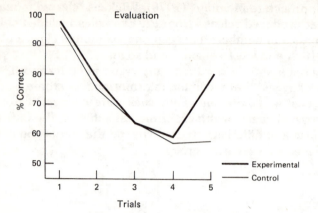

ens et al. method, the present experiment asks whether or not meaningful verbal materials are encoded in STM by the Osgood dimensions.

The general plan of the experiment consisted of presenting word triads drawn from one end of a scale and then shifting to the other end, for the experimental groups, while the control groups remained on triads drawn from the same scale end. If the two ends of the semantic scale represent different classes in STM storage, the accumulated PI should be reduced by a shift from one end of the scale to the other of the experimental groups, and the performance should be superior to that of the control groups. In this manner, the STM situation can be used as a partial validation of the Osgood semantic differential.

METHOD

Subjects. The Ss were 300 male and female introductory psychology students at Ohio State University who chose this experiment to meet part of their course requirement. There were 100 Ss, 50 experimental and 50 control, on each of the three Osgood scales.

Materials. Three separate experiments were conducted on each of the three semantic differential dimensions: Evaluation, Potency, and Activity. Fifteen words were selected from the extreme ends of each dimension according to the profile of the word obtained by Heise (1965). A word was chosen if it fell on the extreme end of one dimension and was relatively neutral on the other two dimensions. No synonyms or antonyms of any words were used. Because similarity of word sounds may be responsible for interference or noninterference effects (Conrad, 1964; Wickelgren, 1965), an effort was made to include only words with different initial sounds. However, to meet the criteria of extremity along the dimension and to avoid the use of synonyms or antonyms, a few words were included which contained the same initial letter. These words, however, neither appeared in the same group of three words on a single trial nor in the same position in the group of words (i.e., the first, second, or third word) on subsequent trials.

Apparatus. The equipment used in the experiment consisted of a Carousel slide projector, a Gerbrands tape timer, an electric metronome, and 2 × 2 in. slides on which the experimental material was printed.

Procedure. All materials were projected on a wall about 3 ft. in front of S. Following an asterisk which appeared for 2 sec., the triad was presented for about 1.5 sec. The S recited it twice, the numerical slide appeared, and S counted backwards by 3s from a three-digit number to the beat of a metronome at a 1-sec. rate. The three-digit numbers were selected so that a single digit never appeared in the same position in any three-digit sequence.

At the end of 15 sec. of counting, a question mark signaled the end of the retention interval and the beginning of the 10-sec. interval to recall the three words. After an inter-trial interval of 6 sec., an asterisk appeared for 2 sec., serving as a ready signal for the next trial.

On the fifth trial the experimental group was presented words (the critical test items) from the opposite end of the same differential scale. Equal numbers of Ss changed from the ends of each dimension, positive to negative and vice versa. The control group received five trials of words from the same end of the dimension.

Order of appearance of the trials was counterbalanced so that each group of words appeared equally as often on each of the five trials for different Ss. The appropriate control S was run after each experimental S (i.e., the same triad was presented on the critical fifth trial). To enable S to gain facility in counting backwards at the 1-sec. rate, a single three-digit number was given before the start of the experiment. The subtraction numbers were counterbalanced so that the same number was neither in the same ordered position throughout the experiment, nor followed the same triad.

Results

The results of the experiment on the Evaluation dimension are presented in Figure 1. As is usually true in these types of experiment, a reduction in accuracy of performance occurred progressively during the first four trials for the experimental group, followed by a marked increment in performance on the critical shift trial. The control group, on the other hand, showed no such increment.

A t test for independent groups with equal n's indicated a significant difference, t (98) = 3.39, $p < .005$, between performance on Trial 5 for the experimental group and for the control group. A t test for dependent groups indicated a significant difference, t (98) = 3.28, $p < .005$, between performance on Trial 4 and on Trial 5 for the experimental group and no difference for the control group, t (98) = .66.

The results for the Potency scale, shown in Figure 2, are essentially the same as for the Evaluation scale, resulting in a significant difference, t (98) = 3.27, $p < .005$, between retention on Trial 5 for the experimental group and for the control group; and a significant difference, t (98) = 4.23,

FIGURE 2

The results for the experimental and control groups on the Potency scale.

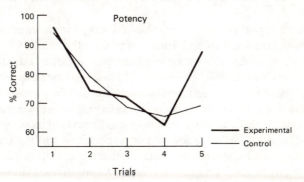

FIGURE 3

The results for the experimental and control groups on the Activity scale.

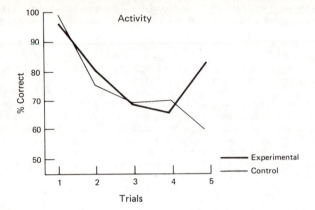

$p < .005$, between performance on Trial 4 and on Trial 5 for the experimental group and no difference for the control group, $t(98) = .47$.

The results for the Activity scale were similar with a significant difference, $t(98) = 4.15$, $p < .005$, between performance on Trial 5 for the experimental group and for the control group. These results are plotted in Figure 3. Again a significant difference, $t(98) = 3.13$, $p < .01$, was found between performance on Trial 4 and on Trial 5 for the experimental group. However, the results also indicated a significant fall, $t(98) = 1.87$, $p < .05$, in performance for the control group from Trial 4 to Trial 5. This latter result might be attributable to chance, or to some characteristic of the words chosen for this scale.

Discussion

Since the three dimensions of the scale show approximately the same results in this experiment, they will be discussed together. All groups show the usual PI effects found in similar experiments (Keppel & Underwood, 1962; Loess, 1967; Wickens et al., 1963). Specifically, for the three scales combined, the percentage correct on Trial 1 was 95, and it dropped to 65 on Trial 4.

All three experimental groups showed a significant increase in performance when they were shifted from one to the other end of the scale. This increase in performance is interpreted as evidence of a reduction in PI as a consequence of the shift. The sharp PI release associated with a change in class of material has been demonstrated in the Wickens et al. experiment where the shift was from consonants to numbers and vice versa; and also by Loess (1967) when a shift was made from classes such as birds, vegetables, and countries. It seems safe to conclude, on the basis of these experiments, that PI release will occur if there is a shift in materials from the class in which the PI had accumulated to another class. The results of the present experiment are, therefore, best interpreted by assuming that Ss will encode verbal materials by some meaning characteristic which is associated with the extremes on each of the Osgood scales. The finding further suggests that the dimensions of the scale are in fact bipolar or at least that the sample of words chosen from the two scale ends clearly represent different classes of connotative meaning.

The build-up of PI during the preshift trials, together with the performance change resulting from the shift, implies, in addition, that the words at each end of the scale are relatively homogenous with respect to at least a portion of their underlying meaning or the psychological process which represents this portion. Thus, in a sense, the results of the experiment offer some support for the validity of the bipolarity of the scale.

One possible interpretation of the increase in performance on the shift trial is that, because the material is new, it is perceived better and hence learned better. However, when Ss were questioned at the conclusion of the experiments on the Potency and Activity dimensions as to whether or not they perceived a difference in any of the trials, only a few of them answered in the affirmative. Thus, the improvement in performance consequent upon the shift was not usually associated with a mechanism of which S was aware, or, at least, which he could verbalize. In other words, the Wickens et al. technique is sensitive to psychological structures within the individual which he himself does not readily recognize.

The above fact seems to argue for an interference interpretation of the results rather than for a heightened perceptual interpretation, since one would expect that a perceptual heightening would be associated with an awareness of the external conditions responsible for the perceptual change.

References

Conrad, R. Acoustic confusion in immediate memory. *British Journal of Psychology*, 1964, **55**, 75–84.

Friedman, M. J., & Reynolds, J. H. Retroactive inhibition as a function of response-class similarity. *Journal of Experimental Psychology*, 1967, **74**, 351–355.

Heise, D. R. Semantic differential profiles for 1,000 most frequent English words. *Psychological Monographs*, 1965, **79**(8, Whole No. 601).

Keppel, G., & Underwood, B. Proactive inhibition in short-term retention of single items. *Journal of Verbal Learning and Verbal Behavior*, 1962, **1**, 153–161.

Loess, H. Short-term memory, word class, and sequence of items. *Journal of Experimental Psychology*, 1967, **74**, 556–561.

Osgood, C. E., Suci, G. J., & Tannenbaum, P. H. *The measurement of meaning.* Urbana: University of Illinois Press, 1957.

Peterson, L. R., & Peterson, M. J. Short-term retention of individual verbal items. *Journal of Experimental Psychology*, 1959, **58**, 157–173.

Postman, L., Keppel, G., & Stark, K. Unlearning as a function of the relationship between successive response classes. *Journal of Experimental Psychology*, 1965, **69**, 111–118.

Wickelgren, W. A. Acoustic similarity and retroactive interference in short-term memory. *Journal of Verbal Learning and Verbal Behavior*, 1965, **4**, 53–61.

Wickens, D. D., Born, D. G. & Allen, C. K. Proactive inhibition and item similarity in short-term memory. *Journal of Verbal Learning and Verbal Behavior*, 1963, **2**, 440–445.

FALSE RECOGNITION PRODUCED BY IMPLICIT VERBAL RESPONSES

Benton J. Underwood

The study by Benton J. Underwood (1965) differs from the first two papers within this section in that Underwood investigated errors in recognition as a means of testing the effects of encoding activity on retrieval. Although he described the task and results in terms of S-R associations, his study bears on some of the same issues addressed in the two studies previously cited.

Underwood's subjects listened to a list of 200 words, at the rate of one every ten seconds, and for each word had to decide whether it had been previously presented. The list consisted of 20 *critical stimulus* words (such as "rough") that were assumed to evoke particular *representational responses* (RR) when the learner read them. For each critical stimulus word, a specific experimental word ("smooth") and a control word ("weak") occurred later in the list; the experimental words were highly associated with the critical words and were thus likely to evoke the same RR, whereas the control words were not.

The results indicated that "false recognitions" — the tendency of subjects to say that a word had been presented earlier when it had not — were higher for experimental words than for control words. Why did the subjects tend to "recognize" the experimental words? According to Underwood, critical and experimental words may share the same RR; if they do, the subjects are more likely to think they have heard the experimental word before. The terminology here differs from that used by Tulving and Thomson, but to the extent that RRs and retrieval cues refer to a similar construct, the results are consistent with those presented in the two preceding papers. Underwood's work further suggests, as does the study by Wickens and Clark, that words associated with the same cue may become confused with one another.

In the development of conceptual schemes to incorporate verbal-learning phenomena, implicit responses are being given more and more prominent roles. Two examples may be cited. The studies of mediation in transfer evolved from two basic assumptions, namely, that implicit responses to verbal stimuli occur and that these implicit responses will serve as mediators. When conceptual similarity within a paired-associate list is found to produce interference it seems appropriate to account for this in part by assuming that the instances of a category (e.g., DOG, COW, HORSE) may all elicit the same implicit response (ANIMAL), which, in this situation, is a nondifferentiating response.

A distinction must be made between two kinds of implicit responses made to a verbal unit. There is first the response made to the unit itself as the act of perceiving it. This implicit response has been called the *representational response* by Bousfield, Whitmarsh, and Danick (1958), and will be abbreviated here as RR. The second kind of implicit response, the one with theoretical relevance, is produced by the stimulus properties of the RR. This implicit response may be another word which is associated with the actual word presented and will be called the *implicit associative response* (IAR). The particular IAR to a given word is often assumed to be the most frequent associate produced to the word in word-association procedures. Or, as in a mediating transfer situation, the IAR is assumed to be the word which S had learned as a response to a given stimulus in a previous list. That other nonverbal implicit responses (such as affective responses) may occur to the RR cannot be denied, but for the present purposes, need not be considered.

It must be clear that IAR, in most theoretical formulations, is conceived of as actually occurring. This is to say, it is not a hypothetical construct. It is hypothetical only in the sense that it is assumed to occur in a particular situation where it cannot be observed directly, and this assumption is made because it *has* been observed to occur overtly with a certain frequency in other situations (e.g., word-association procedures). The validity of the assumption is tested by experimental procedures wherein a given phenomenon is predicted *if* specific IARs are occurring. The present study fits into this framework.

The rationale of the experiment may be understood by examining the task presented Ss. A total of 200 words was read to S at a 10-sec. rate. As each word was read, S made a decision as to whether or not the word had been read to him earlier in the list. Thus, the general procedure is that devised by Shepard and Teghtsoonian (1961) in their study of memory for 3-digit numbers. In the present list of 200 words were critical words assumed to elicit particular IARs. At a later point in the list, therefore, the

From "False Recognition Produced by Implicit Verbal Responses" by Benton Underwood in *Journal of Experimental Psychology*, Volume 70, Number 1, 1965. Copyright © 1965 by the American Psychological Association. Reprinted by permission.

words assumed to be IARs to earlier RRs were in fact presented to S. If S responded by saying that these words had been read earlier in the list we would conclude that the IARs had occurred to the critical words at the time these critical words were read. For example, if a critical stimulus word is UP, and if later the assumed IAR (DOWN) is presented and S indicates that DOWN had occurred earlier in the list, we assume that DOWN had occurred as an IAR to the RR to the word UP, and that S subsequently confused an IAR with an RR.

METHOD

Words.   Four different types of words must be distinguished.
   Critical Stimulus Words (CS Words): These words were assumed to elicit particular IARs.
   Experimental Words (E Words): These were the words representing the assumed IARs to the CS Words.
   Control Words (C Words): These words were used as controls for the E Words and were assumed not to have been preceded in the list by words for which they were IARs.
   Filler Words (F Words): These words were presumed to be neutral with regard to the E Words and were used to build up a specific repetition frequency.
   There were 20 E Words (hence, 20 C Words) as may be seen in Table 1. There were five different classes of CS Words, labeled A1, A3, CV, SO, and SI in Table 1. Each of these classes must be explained. Classes A1 and A3 consisted of words for which the E Word (assumed IAR) was an antonym of the CS Word. Thus, TOP is assumed to be the IAR to BOTTOM, TAKE to GIVE, and so on. In forming A1 and A3, 16 pairs of antonyms were divided randomly into four subgroups of four pairs each. Two of these subgroups were then assigned randomly to A1 and A3 as CS Words and E Words, the second member of the pairs of the other two subgroups as C Words. However, for these C Words, no CS Word appeared earlier in the list. Thus, when S was confronted with the C Word DOWN, this had not been preceded by UP. On the other hand, when S was confronted with the E Word TOP, it had been preceded by the CS Word, BOTTOM. The rationale of the study predicts that S will be more likely to say that TOP rather than DOWN had occurred earlier in the list.
   The CS Words for the A1 class were presented only once; those for the A3 class were each presented three times prior to the appearance of the E Word. A comparison between these two classes will provide evidence on the role of frequency of IARs.
   The third class of CS Words in Table 1 is CV, an abbreviation for converging associations. Each of the CS Words on a line is known to elicit the E Word with appreciable frequency in word-association norms. Thus, BREAD is a frequent response to both BUTTER and CRUMB, SLEEP a frequent response to both BED and DREAM, and so on. In selecting words for the first three classes in Table 1, major use was made of the Connecticut word-association norms as given by Bousfield, Cohen, Whitmarsh, and Kincaid (1961) with minor use of the Minnesota norms (Russell & Jenkins, 1954).
   The fourth class of CS Words in Table 1 is labeled SO (superordinates). Each of the CS Words on a given line is a specific instance of the category which becomes the E Word. These Words were taken from Cohen, Bousfield, and Whitmarsh (1957). In actual fact these investigators asked Ss to give specific instances to the category name. However, we are assuming that the instances will in turn elicit the category name as an IAR with appreciable frequency. Some justification for this assumption is found in word-association norms. For example, the Connecticut word-association norms show that 50% of the Ss responded to the stimulus word CANARY with BIRD.
   The final class in Table 1 is SI (sense impressions). Taken from Underwood and Richardson (1956), each word on a line is known to elicit the E Word with appreciable frequency when the associations are limited to sense impressions by instructions and training.
   The CS Words on a given line are not completely without associates to E Words on other lines. There are two fairly obvious instances. The CS Word DOUGHNUT in the SI class also elicits the word SWEET with appreciable frequency, SWEET being an E Word in the CV class. So also SNOW leads to COLD. Such "contamination" would, according to the notions

TABLE 1

Critical Stimulus Words, Experimental Words, and Control Words

Class	Critical Stimulus Words	E Word	Position	C Word
A1	BOTTOM	TOP	113	DOWN
	GIVE	TAKE	135	GOOD
	DAY	NIGHT	170	LOW
	MAN	WOMAN	188	RICH
A3	ROUGH	SMOOTH	154	WEAK
	FALSE	TRUE	162	DIRTY
	HARD	SOFT	178	SHORT
	SLOW	FAST	192	GIRL
CV	BUTTER, CRUMB	BREAD	129	BRIDGE
	BED, DREAM	SLEEP	155	SMILE
	SUGAR, BITTER, CANDY	SWEET	147	SALT
	ANIMAL, CAT, BARK	DOG	182	HORSE
	DARK, HEAVY, LAMP, MATCH	LIGHT	175	LEG
	WARM, CHILL, FREEZE, FRIGID, HOT, ICE	COLD	196	CLOUD
SO	MAPLE, OAK, ELM, BIRCH	TREE	123	FISH
	COTTON, WOOL, SILK, RAYON	CLOTH	158	FRUIT
	ROBIN, SPARROW, BLUEJAY, CANARY	BIRD	189	FLOWER
SI	BARREL, DOUGHNUT, DOME, GLOBE, SPOOL	ROUND	146	SHARP
	ATOM, CABIN, GERM, GNAT, VILLAGE	SMALL	165	FAT
	BANDAGE, CHALK, MILK, RICE, SNOW	WHITE	179	RED

in the introduction, tend to increase the number of false recognitions of the appropriate E Words.

The column labeled "Position" in Table 1 represents the position in the series of 200 words occupied by each E Word. The position of a given C Word was always two positions away from the position of its corresponding E Word. Thus, the C Word DOWN occurred at Position 111. Taken as a whole, the C Words occurred after the E Words half the time and before the E Words half the time.

The CS Words were scattered throughout the positions with the last occurring at Position 151. However, it may be of value to indicate the number of positions between the last CS Words and the E Words of the classes. For A1, the range for the four words, was from 86 to 104 positions, with a mean of 96. For A3, the range was 36–89, with a mean of 53; for CV, a range of 30–60, with a mean of 42; for SO, from 27–68, with a mean of 50, and finally, for SI, 27–73, with a mean of 53.

There were 47 F Words. Of these 42 occurred twice, 4 occurred three times, and 1 occurred only once. Therefore, the 200 positions are accounted for as follows: CS Words, 63; E Words, 20; C Words, 20; and F Words, 97. The actual repetition was arranged so that in the first quarter (first 50 words) 5 words had occurred earlier, with 19, 16, and 18 having occurred earlier in each of the remaining three quarters.

Procedure and Ss. The instructions and the words were presented by a magnetic tape recorder. The *Ss* were given a single sheet of paper on which 200 numbered blanks occurred. The instructions required *S* to record a plus if he believed the word had occurred earlier in the list, a minus if he believed it had not. The instructions indicated that if *S* was in doubt a decision had to be made; a plus or minus had to be recorded for each blank. The words were read at a 10-sec. rate, each being spoken twice in immediate succession. The trial number was indicated after every tenth word to avoid any confusion as to the particular number of the word at the moment.

A total of 107 Ss records was completed in four group sessions. All Ss were college students taking introductory psychology courses at Northwestern. Seven of the records were eliminated on a random basis, so the data to be presented are based on 100 Ss.

Results

Table 2 shows the number of plusses (hence, percentage of Ss) recorded for each E Word and its corresponding C Word. Also shown are the subtotals for each class of words. Looking at these subtotals it may be quickly noted that for Classes A1 and SI, expectations are not supported but that for Classes A3, CV, and SO, frequency of plusses for the E Words is much greater than for the C Words. However, we may first make an overall statistical evaluation without regard to classes of words. For each S the total number of plusses made to the 20 E Words was determined and also the total number made to the 20 C Words. The E Words produced a mean

TABLE 2

Number of Plusses Given to Each E and C Word by 100 Ss with Subtotals for Each Class of Words

Class	E Word	No. of Plusses	C Word	No. of Plusses
A1	TOP	9	DOWN	20
	TAKE	11	GOOD	5
	NIGHT	24	LOW	27
	WOMAN	5	RICH	10
	Total	49		62
A3	SMOOTH	28	WEAK	9
	TRUE	12	DIRTY	9
	SOFT	37	SHORT	25
	FAST	49	GIRL	9
	Total	126		52
CV	BREAD	21	BRIDGE	28
	SLEEP	23	SMILE	10
	SWEET	24	SALT	11
	DOG	20	HORSE	7
	LIGHT	42	LEG	13
	COLD	39	CLOUD	15
	Total	169		84
SO	TREE	19	FISH	9
	CLOTH	18	FRUIT	11
	BIRD	38	FLOWER	11
	Total	75		31
SI	ROUND	7	SHARP	9
	SMALL	14	FAT	7
	WHITE	3	RED	8
	Total	24		24

FIGURE 1

False-alarm rate (number of plusses) within each successive block of 25 positions across the 200 words and number of plusses for each of the 20 E Words.

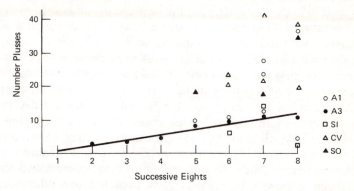

of 4.43 plusses, the C Words a mean of 2.53. The difference (1.90 ± .23) gives a t of 8.26. It must be concluded that Ss responded more frequently to the E Words than to the C Words.

A statistical analysis of differences in frequency for E and C Words by classes of items is difficult by conventional methods since many Ss did not respond with a plus to any of the words within a class. Even in the above analysis there were 8 Ss with a zero entry for the 20 E Words and 24 Ss with a zero entry for the C Words. However, certain simple computations allow some fairly firm conclusions about the statistical significance of the responses by classes of words, a matter to which we will turn shortly.

We may ask about the frequency of plusses for all words except E Words when they first occurred. This determination across the entire series of words provides a measure of the "false-alarm" or "false-positive" rate. The 200 words were divided into eighths and the number of false alarms determined for each of these eight sections. The number of words which first occurred (hence, could result in false alarms) in each successive eighth was 23, 22, 16, 15, 18, 9, 10, and 9. The mean numbers of plusses (false alarms) per word in each eighth are plotted as filled dots in Figure 1 with a straight line drawn through them. It is clear that there is an increase in false alarms as the number of prior words increases; in the eighth section for the 100 Ss averaged 11.2 false alarms for the nine words which first occurred in that section; in the first section the corresponding value was 0.5.

The plusses or false alarms for each E Word are also plotted in Figure 1, above the eighth in which it occurred. The statistical question is whether or not the E Words of various classes can be considered to come from the population of words represented by the false-alarm rate of all non-E Words when they first occurred. Clearly, Classes A1 and SI could come from this population. It can be shown, however, that it is highly improbable that the E Words in each of the other three classes could have come from this population of false alarms for control words. The sum of the plusses for the three E Words in the SO class is 75; how probable is it that this sum would be equaled by any three control words used to derive the false-alarm rate in Figure 1? To determine this the number of plusses for the 46 words used to derive the last half of the false-alarm curve were each listed. From this listing 100 samples of three each were drawn (using a table of random numbers) and the sum of the plusses for each sample determined. In drawing the samples, replacement was immediate; that is, the same value (representing the number of plusses for a given word) could have been drawn so as to constitute all three entries in a sample. The mean of this distribution of 100 sums was 30.71, with a standard deviation of 12.04. The maximum summed value obtained for any one sample was 71. Since the E Words in the SO class produced a sum of 75, we conclude that it is quite unlikely that these three E Words could come from the control population. This is to say, therefore, that the frequency of false alarms given to these E Words must have been influenced by the earlier presence of the CS Words. Or, to say this another way; S apparently confused the RR of the E Word with the IAR made earlier to the CS Word.

The above procedure could be repeated for the A3 and CV classes and the same conclusion would be reached. However, this is quite unnecessary. The maximum frequency of plusses for any word used in obtaining the control false-alarm rate was 28 (for BRIDGE, a C Word). Multiplying this value by 4 (112) does not yield a frequency as high (126) as the frequency produced by the four E Words in the A3 class. Multiplying 28 by 6 does not result in a frequency as high as that produced by the six E Words in the CV class.

In summary, therefore, the evidence indicates that RRs were confused with IARs for three classes of words. Among the 13 E Word-C Word comparisons in these three classes there is only one instance in which the frequency of the plusses for the C Word was higher than for the E Word (Class CV, BRIDGE VS. BREAD). The maximum frequency of false alarm for any E Word was 49; 49% of the Ss indicated that the word FAST had occurred earlier in the list when in fact it had not. It is of some interest to compare this value with that of the lowest frequency of detection of a repeated word. The F Word HOME appeared in Position 13 and again in Position 118 at which time only 51% of the Ss indicated it had occurred earlier. Overall, however, the correct detection of repeated words was 85.0%. It is evident, therefore, that S is far more likely to recognize a repeated word than to give a false alarm to a nonrepeated word even when we attempt to confuse him.

Other relationships. The Ss showed appreciable consistency in their tendency to report that a word had occurred earlier when in fact it had not. The product-moment correlation across the 100 Ss for number of plusses for the 20 E Words and for the 20 C Words was .62. A total of 102 of the 200 positions was held by CS Words and by the first occurrence of F Words. The correlation between the number of plusses made to these 102 words and the number made to the E Words was .60, and to the C Words, .67. On the other hand, the ability to detect a repetition is not related to the tendency to indicate that a word had occurred earlier when it had not. There were 58 positions held by repeated words. The correlation across the 100 Ss between the number of plusses assigned these 58 positions and the number of plusses assigned the 102 positions when words first occurred was −.02. A scatter plot gives no indication of curvilinearity.

Discussion

Three of the classes of E Words produced results in conformance with the notion that RRs may be confused with IARs that occurred earlier; two classes did not. The fact that words in the A1 class did not produce false alarms beyond the control rate while those in A3 did, indicates that frequency of IARs is a critical variable. It would seem quite reasonable to presume that if an IAR occurs three times it has more of the properties of an RR than if it occurs only once. Indeed, it is precisely this fact which Deese (1959) has demonstrated by a sharp relationship between the appearance of an intrusion (a word which had not appeared in the list) in recall and the associative strength of the intruding word to the words actually in the list. However, in the case of the A1 words vs. the A3 words in the present study, another factor might be involved. As noted in the procedure section, on the average the number of words occurring between the CS Words and the E Words was greater for A1 than for A3. Perhaps the IARs to the CS Words in A1 are, therefore, forgotten or interfered with more than those produced by the CS Words in A3. While this possibility cannot be ruled out entirely, there is evidence against it. In the A3 class a total of 89 words occurred between the last presentation of the CS Word HARD and its E Word SOFT, yet 37% of the Ss indicated they had heard the word earlier. For two of the cases in the A1 class, 86 and 89 words occurred between the CS Word and the E Word, yet the E Words produced only 11% and 5% plusses. Furthermore, an examination of the results for the CV class indicates that those cases where four and five CS words occurred (and were presumed to elicit a common associate) produced more false alarms than did the cases in the CV class where only two and three CS words were used, and this occurred when the number of words between the last CS and the E Word was essentially the same for all cases. Thus, the evidence points strongly to frequency of IAR as a variable in producing confusion between IARs and RRs.

 The SI class of words gave completely negative results; frequency of false alarms to the E Words in this class was no greater than for the C Words. As will be remembered, a given set of CS words in the SI class will, under appropriate instructions and training, elicit the common response which was here used as the E Word. It is possible that within the context of the present series of words these sense-impression responses occur as IARs with low frequency. However, in the Connecticut word-association norms (Bousfield et al., 1961) four of the five CS Words presumed to elicit the E Word ROUND do in fact elicit ROUND with some frequency (10%, 9%, 9%, and 28%). Nevertheless, these frequencies are much lower than the frequencies in the other classes. We may tentatively conclude that the negative results in the SI class are due to the failure of the CS words to elicit the common IARs with appreciable frequency.

The logic of the experiment was that the RR to the word of the moment would lead S to say that the word had occurred earlier if this RR was the same as an IAR produced by a word or words earlier in the list. This scheme might be reversed to say that the IAR to the word of the moment, if the same as an RR to an earlier word, would lead S to say that the present word had occurred earlier. Thus, if the word of the moment was DOWN, and if it elicits the IAR UP, and if UP occurred earlier in the list, S might believe that DOWN had occurred earlier. Such a mechanism might indeed handle the results for A3, for antonyms are bidirectionally associated. And, such a mechanism might account for the failure for the SI items, since the E Words do not elicit the CS Words with appreciable frequency in available norms. However, it cannot account for the results for the CV and SO classes. The positive effects produced in these classes must be due to the elicitation of the same IAR by two or more different CS Words, otherwise positive results would have been obtained in the A1 class. The IAR of the word of the moment cannot be confused with two or more different RRs of previous words such as would be necessary by the alternative scheme. Of course, it is possible that both mechanisms may be involved but until this is clearly demonstrated we will conclude that the original scheme presented is most appropriate; the RR to the word of the moment is confused with the common IAR produced by two or more previous words. This is essentially the same conclusion reached by Mink (1963) as a result of his studies on semantic generalization. And it should be noted that the present study could be classified as a study of secondary or semantic generalization.

Figure 1 showed that the frequency of false alarms increased throughout. Although this increase may be due to the same mechanisms presumed to operate for the E Words, another factor may be in part responsible. It is possible that the greater the number of words S heard the more likely he would believe that a repetition would occur. Thus, if in doubt late in the list he would be more likely to signify that a repetition had occurred than if in doubt early in the list. This could be true in spite of the fact that the objective repetition was held constant over the last three quarters of the list. Nevertheless, certain of the C Words produced false alarms with such high frequency that an examination of possible causes was made. Some may have been produced by high formal similarity of RRs. For example, LOW produced 27 false alarms. The word LAW occurred as an F Word earlier in the list. The high frequency for SHORT may have been due to the appearance of SHARP earlier in the list. The C Word which produced the highest number of false alarms was BRIDGE. No previous word has high formal similarity and, when BRIDGE is thought of as a structure spanning water, no previous word would seem to elicit it as an IAR. If these Ss are avid players and followers of the game of bridge, such words as MASTER and MAJOR (which occurred three times) may have elicited BRIDGE as an IAR. In any event, it is apparent that we were unsuccessful in the attempt to establish homogeneity in false-alarm rates to control words.

References

Bousfield, W. A., Cohen, B. H., Whitmarsh, G. A., & Kincaid, W. D. The Connecticut free association norms. Technical Report No. 35, 1961, University of Connecticut, Contract Nonr-631 (00), Office of Naval Research.

Bousfield, W. A., Whitmarsh, G. A., & Danick, J. J. Partial response identities in verbal generalization. *Psychol. Rep.*, 1958, **4**, 703–713.

Cohen, B. H., Bousfield, W. A., & Whitmarsh, G. A. Cultural norms for verbal items in 43 categories. Technical Report No. 22, 1957, University of Connecticut, Contract Nonr-631 (00), Office of Naval Research.

Deese, J. On the prediction of occurrence of particular verbal intrusions in immediate recall. *J. Exp. Psychol.*, 1959, **58**, 17–22.

Mink, W. D. Semantic generalization as related to word association. *Psychol. Rep.*, 1963, **12**, 59–67.

Russell, W. A., & Jenkins, J. J. The complete Minnesota norms for responses to 100 words from the Kent-Rosanoff Word-Association Test. Technical Report, No. 11, 1954, University of Minnesota, Contract N8 onr-66216, Office of Naval Research.

Shepard, R. N., Teghtsoonian, M. Retention of information under conditions approaching a steady state. *J. Exp. Psychol.*, 1961, **62**, 302–309.

Underwood, B. J., & Richardson, J. Some verbal materials for the study of concept formation. *Psychol. Bull.*, 1956, **53**, 84–95.

9/ Human Information Processing

MULTI-STAGE STORAGE

Consider the process by which you use the telephone book to find a friend's phone number. After you look up the number, your next step is to pick up the phone and start dialing. At this point, you may find yourself repeating the number over and over again to yourself. This process is called *rehearsal*. It is one way of keeping information active in your memory. Suppose the line is busy: you hang up and try to dial again, but as you start, you realize that you've forgotten the number. Now you have to look it up again and start over.

This phenomenon provides introspective support for the concept of short-term memory—a memory store that is limited and requires active rehearsal, and that loses information if rehearsal is prevented or too much information is entered. Note that short-term memory is quite different from long-term memory—a store that contains a permanent, organized record of experience. In our telephone example, rehearsal was needed to keep the phone number in short-term memory; but once information enters long-term memory, it needs no rehearsal. Moreover, information was lost from short-term memory within a brief period of time, whereas information in long-term memory persists indefinitely. And finally, short-term memory is quite limited: to remember three or four phone numbers in short-term memory would be a very difficult task. Yet we can recall long strings of numbers that have been encoded in long-term memory, such as our own phone number and those of our close friends.

The first three papers in this section explore the question of whether humans have one type of memory storage or several types. The *multi-stage storage theory* postulates that humans use several different memory stores—that is, stores that vary according to how exact they are, how long they can hold information, the form in which they hold information, the mechanism for losing information, and so on. On the other hand, the *single memory theory*, postulates that humans possess just one type of memory but that it is flexible. Specifically, the paper by Atkinson and Shiffrin (1968) presents the general multi-stage model of memory, consisting of a sensory store, a short-term store, and a long-term store. The paper by Averbach and Sperling (1960) provides a landmark study that suggests the existence of sensory memory. And the paper by Glanzer and Cunitz (1966) presents a test of the distinction between short-term and long-term stores.

LEVELS OF PROCESSING

The next three papers concern the relationship between learning and memory as a function of *levels of processing*. Imagine a lecture given by a professor on the subject of human memory. One student writes down every date and name mentioned. Another student writes down every sentence spoken by the professor. A third student writes down a paraphrased version of every sentence. These note-taking strategies represent three different levels of processing of the incoming information. The first student must pay attention only to the mention of a name or date; the second student must pay attention to the sound of every word and then convert that sound to a written word; the third student must pay attention to the *meaning* of each sentence so that it can be rewritten in different words. In fact, all note-taking strategies will require a certain degree of cognitive processing, but some require only the processing of sounds whereas others require the processing of sound plus meaning.

Instead of describing information processing as the movement of information from one discrete memory box to another, the levels of processing approach is concerned with the *type* of processing performed by the subject on incoming information. For example, one type of processing might be used to keep information temporarily in consciousness (corresponding to short-term memory), whereas another type of processing may be used to learn names that must be recalled later (corresponding to long-term memory). Does the levels of processing framework describe the same events as the multi-stage storage framework, using different terms? The following three papers may help to answer that question insofar as they provide a second approach to human memory and learning, and thus a more complete understanding of the processes involved.

HUMAN MEMORY:
A PROPOSED SYSTEM AND
ITS CONTROL PROCESSES

R. C. Atkinson and R. M. Shiffrin

The first selection in this chapter, by R. C. Atkinson and R. M. Shiffrin (1968), provides a general introduction to the concept of multi-stage storage. The authors describe a model of information flow consisting of environmental input moving from a sensory register to a short-term store, and finally to a long-term store. In addition, the flow of information among these memory stores is controlled by processes such as rehearsal, coding, decisions, retrieval.

Although other authors have presented the general information processing model using different terms and diagrams, this excerpt from Atkinson and Shiffrin presents the main assumptions and framework for this approach.

Structural Features of the Memory System

This section of the paper will describe the permanent, structural features of the memory system. The basic structural division is into the three components diagrammed in Figure 1: the sensory register, the short-term store, and the long-term store.

When a stimulus is presented there is an immediate registration of that stimulus within the appropriate sensory dimensions. The form of this registration is fairly well understood in the case of the visual system (Sperling, 1960); in fact, the particular features of visual registration (including a several hundred millisecond decay of an initially accurate visual image) allow us positively to identify this system as a distinct component of memory. It is obvious that incoming information in other sense modalities also receives an initial registration, but it is not clear whether these other registrations have an appreciable decay period or any other features which would enable us to refer to them as components of memory.

The second basic component of our system is the short-term store. This store may be regarded as the subject's "working memory." Information entering the short-term store is assumed to decay and disappear completely, but the time required for the information to be lost is considerably longer than for the sensory register. The character of the information in the short-term store does not depend necessarily upon the form of the sensory input. For example, a word presented visually may be encoded from the visual sensory register into an auditory short-term store. Since the auditory short-term system will play a major role in subsequent discussions, we shall use the abbreviation a-v-l to stand for auditory-verbal-linguistic store. The triple term is used because, as we shall see, it is not easy to separate these three functions.

The exact rate of decay of information in the short-term store is difficult to estimate because it is greatly influenced by subject-controlled processes. In the a-v-l mode, for example, the subject can invoke rehearsal mechanisms that maintain the information in STS and thereby complicate the problem of measuring the structural characteristics of the decay process. However, the available evidence suggests that information represented in the a-v-l mode decays and is lost within a period of about 15–30 seconds. Storage of information in other modalities is less well understood and, for reasons to be discussed later, it is difficult to assign values to their decay rates.

The last major component of our system is the long-term store. This store differs from the preceding ones in that information stored here does not decay and become lost in the same manner. All information eventually is completely lost from the sensory register and the short-term store, whereas information in the long-term store is relatively permanent (although it may be modified or rendered temporarily irretrievable as the result of other incoming information). Most experiments in the literature dealing with long-term store have been concerned with storage in the a-v-l mode, but it is clear that there is long-term memory in each of the other sensory modalities, as demonstrated by an ability to recognize stimuli presented to these senses. There may even be information in the long-term store which is not classifiable into any of the sensory modalities, the prime example being temporal memory.

The flow of information among the three systems is to a large degree under the control of the subject. Note that by information flow and transfer between stores we refer to the same process: the copying of selected information from one store into the next. This copying takes place without the transferred information being removed from its original store. The information remains in the store from which it is transferred and decays according to the decay characteristics of that store. In considering information flow in the system, we start with its initial input into the sensory register. The next step is a subject-controlled scan of the information in the register; as a result of this scan and an associated search of long-term store, selected information is introduced into short-term store. We assume that transfer to the long-term store takes place throughout the period that information resides in the short-term store, although the amount and form of the transferred information is markedly influenced by control processes. The possibility that there may be direct transfer to the long-term store from the sensory register is represented by the dashed line in Figure 1; we do not know whether such transfer occurs. Finally, there is transfer from the long-term store to the short-term store, mostly under the control of the subject; such transfer occurs, for example, in problem solving, hypothesis testing, and "thinking" in general.

This brief encapsulation of the system raises more questions than it answers. Not yet mentioned are such features as the cause of the decay in each memory store and the form of the transfer functions between the stores.

FIGURE 1

Structure of the memory system.

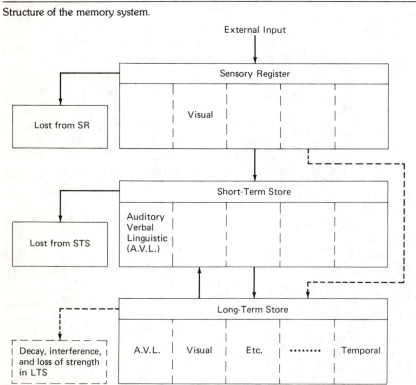

SHORT TERM STORAGE
OF INFORMATION IN VISION

E. Averbach and G. Sperling

The second selection, by E. Averbach and G. Sperling (1960), describes some of the major studies that led to the concept of sensory memory. The experimental procedure used in these studies involved the presentation of letters and/or numbers to a subject for a brief period. The subject was then asked to write answers to a recall test. The test was repeated over several trials involving different arrays. A method known as the *whole report procedure* was utilized in some experiments, in which subjects were required to write down as many of the presented items as they could recall. In other experiments utilizing the *partial report procedure*, the subjects were asked to write down just one row of the presented items. In this latter method, a tone was presented following each array: for example, a high tone signalled the subject to recall the top row of items whereas a low tone signalled recall of the bottom row. The subject did not know in advance which row would be requested. Furthermore, the delay of the tone was varied from zero to one second so that the subject had to retain the information in memory.

The results of the whole report procedure indicated that subjects could recall an average of 4.5 items regardless of the number presented. This is a typical finding, leading some researchers to postulate that immediate memory is limited. An alternative theory postulates that humans have a sensory image of what was presented, and that this image is complete. According to this latter theory, the reason that subjects are able to report only 4.5 items is that the image rapidly fades; thus, as subjects are "reading" off the items in their image, it has faded away in the short time it takes to write down 4 or 5 items. The concept of an exact, rapidly fading sensory memory predicts that subjects should perform at nearly 100 percent on the partial report procedure, but that performance should fall to the standard level (that is, 4.5 items out of the entire array) if the test is delayed.

The actual results support the predictions of the sensory memory theory. In the absence of a retention interval, the subjects' performance on partial report indicates that they know more than just 4.5 items from the array. However, when the retention interval is increased up to one second, performance falls to the standard level. Apparently, within one second's time, the information in the sensory memory has decayed and only some of that information (4.5 items) can be transferred to short-term memory.

There have been numerous estimates of human ability to extract information from brief visual presentations. The greatest information intake has been observed with exposures of items having high information content as compared to items of low information content, e.g., decimal digits and letters as opposed to binary digits. The limit of performance in these experiments, called the 'span of perception' or 'span of immediate memory', seems to be a limit on the number of items recalled rather than a limit on amount of information. A subject can report only about a half dozen items regardless of the ensemble from which these items were chosen.

'Span' experiments are very gross. They treat the observer as a transmission link without indicating where or how; information is lost between exposure of the stimulus and the subject's report. This paper describes some experiments that attempt to measure the characteristics of the early stages of the perceptual process. The classical 'span' technique of dealing with brief exposures is contrasted with a 'sampling' technique. It is shown that humans are able to store rather large amounts of information for short time periods. Experimental estimates are given of the amount and duration of the visual storage and of the rate at which visually stored information can be utilized.

The span type of experiment is an old one, and it is not surprising that it has many names. It has been called the span of apprehension, span of attention, span of perception, and span of immediate-memory experiment. In this kind of experiment the subject is briefly shown a stimulus containing a number of letters. He is asked to report as many letters as he can; that is, to make a *whole* report of the visual stimulus.

This whole report procedure was tried with a variety of different stimulus arrays (Sperling, 1960). Figure 1 shows some typical stimuli. These arrays vary in the number of items, in their spatial arrangement, and in their composition; that is, some arrays have letters alone, others have letters and numbers. The various stimuli were exposed for 50 msec (1/20th sec) individually to five highly trained subjects. Figure 2 shows the average number of letters that subjects were able to report correctly. The subjects reported nearly all the letters correctly so long as the number of letters in the stimulus did not exceed five. When stimuli contained five or more letters, subjects were able to report only about 4½ letters correctly on the average. These are the classical results. We would say that the span of immediate-memory for these stimuli is about four to five letters.

In order to find out if this five letter limit was determined by the short exposure time that was used, the exposure duration was systematically varied from 15 to 500 msec at the same intensity. Figure 3 shows the

FIGURE 1

```
R N F                    K L B
                         Y N X

X V N K H                X M R J
                         P N K P

L Q D K K J              T D R
                         S R N
                         F Z R

ZYVVFF                   7 I V F
                         X L 5 3
                         B 4 W 7
```

results. Apparently, within the limits of the conditions used, exposure duration does not influence the number of letters reported.

The span type of experiment may be summarized as follows: when the subjects are asked to report all the letters of a stimulus, they can report only about five letters on the average; this limit of 'immediate-memory' holds for a wide range of visual arrays and exposure durations.

In the whole report procedure observers often assert that they could *see* more letters than they were able to *report* later. They say that while they are reporting some letters, they forget others. This suggests that the immediate-memory span sets a limit on a process that is otherwise rich in available information. In other words, although an observer can correctly report only about five letters from the brief visual stimulus, he may nevertheless have chosen these five letters from a larger store of letters which were momentarily available to him. In the sampling type of experiment an attempt was made to ascertain how much information does, in fact, become available to the observer as a result of the stimulus.

FIGURE 2

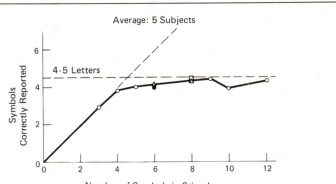

Average: 5 Subjects

4-5 Letters

Symbols Correctly Reported

Number of Symbols in Stimulus

FIGURE 3

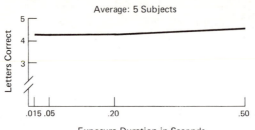

Average: 5 Subjects

In this experiment a sampling procedure which does not require a whole report is used in order to circumvent the immediate-memory span. This method requires the observers to report only a part (designated by location) of a letter array exposed for 1/20th sec. The part to be reported consists of just one out of three rows of letters. It is small enough (3–4 letters) to lie within the memory span. A tonal signal (high, medium or low frequency tone) was used to indicate which of the rows was to be reported. The subject did not know which signal to expect, and the indicator signal was not sounded until after the visual stimulus had been turned off. In this way, information available for report was sampled immediately after the termination of the stimulus.

There is an important procedural difference in the two kinds of experiments. In the first kind, the observer is required to report all the letters of the stimulus. He must give a 'whole' report. In the sampling experiment the observer reports only one row of letters of the stimulus, but he does not know which row of letters will be called for until after the stimulus has been turned off. We call this a 'partial' report.

Each observer, for each set of material tested (stimuli of 6, 8, 9 and 12 symbols), gave partial reports that were more accurate than whole reports for the same material (Sperling, 1960). These results are illustrated in Figure 4. The lower curve is the same immediate-memory data as that illustrated in Figure 2. These are obtained by a *whole* report. The upper curves represent the accuracy of *partial* reports. For example, following the exposure of stimuli consisting of 12 letters, 76 per cent of the letters called for in the partial report were given correctly by the observers. It is possible to calculate the total information available to the observer from which he draws his partial report. It is about 9·1 letters; namely, 76 per cent of 12 letters. The 9·1 randomly chosen letters are equivalent to 40·6 bits of information. This estimate of the information available in a brief exposure is considerably more than previous experimental estimates (20 to 25 bits) which were obtained using a whole report. Apparently, the subject's memory span was the limiting factor in these experiments. Further experiments with stimuli containing more than 12 letters showed that the 40-bit figure observed using partial report experiments was limited by the small amount of information in the stimuli rather than by the capacity of the observers.

These results show that immediately after the stimulus is turned off, observers have available at least two to three times more information than they can give in a whole report. In order to determine how this available information decreases with time, the instruction signal which indicates the row of the stimulus to be reported was delayed by various amounts.

Figure 5 shows data obtained with stimuli having 12 letters each. The light flash is schematically indicated at the lower left. The span of immediate-memory for this material is indicated by the bar at the right. Note that information in excess of the memory span is stored for less than a second. Both the whole report and the partial report procedure give exactly the *same* estimate of the number of available letters (namely four to five) when the instruction to report is delayed by more than a second. Only when the instruction is given within a second of the exposure do the results obtained by the two methods differ. That is why the results of this experiment are different from those of previous ones; in this experiment, unlike earlier ones, the instruction to give a partial report was coded so that it could be given at a precisely determined time, *within* one second of the exposure.

Summary and Conclusion

The work described in this paper shows that the visual process involves a buffer storage of relatively high capacity that can take in information virtually instantaneously and retain it to permit its relatively slow utilization. By making use of sampling techniques and the erasure characteristics of the storage, the following properties were demonstrated:

FIGURE 4

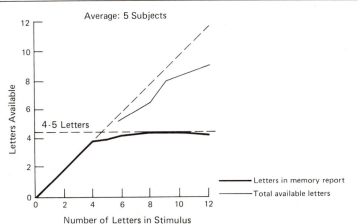

FIGURE 5

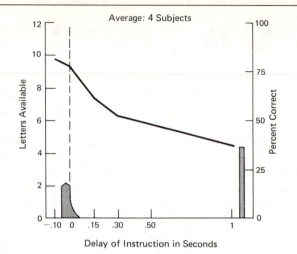

Delay of Instruction in Seconds

(1) The capacity of the storage is high compared to the 20–25 bits obtained in span of immediate-memory. The experiments showed that 70 bits could be stored, but this is still only a lower bound on the capacity since different arrangements might well have produced higher figures.

(2) The decay time depends upon pre- and post-exposure conditions as well as on the exposure itself. The measured decays varied from ¼ sec to several seconds.

(3) The spatial resolution of the storage is disturbed when too many letters are put in. A 2 × 8 array is enough to demonstrate this effect.

Reference

Sperling, G. 'The Information Available in Brief Visual Presentations'. *Psychol. Monogr.*, 1960, **74,** No. 11, Whole No. 498.

TWO STORAGE MECHANISMS
IN FREE RECALL

Murray Glanzer and Anita R. Cunitz

The previous paper by Averbach and Sperling presented some evidence for hypothesizing that there is a visual memory qualitatively different from other memory stores. The present selection, by Murray Glanzer and Anita R. Cunitz, deals with the question of whether it is also useful to make a further distinction between short-term memory and long-term memory. One way of testing the duplex theory—the idea that short- and long-term memory have qualitatively different characteristics—is to use experimental variables that should affect one of the memory stores but not the other. Glanzer and Cunitz use this strategy in the set of experiments that follow.

In both experiments, subjects were presented with a list of 20 words, one word at a time, and then were asked to recall as many of the words as they could (in any order). This method is called *free recall*, and the typical result is that subjects produce a serial position curve—that is, more words are recalled from the beginning and end of the list than from the middle. The superior performance at the beginning of the list is called the *primacy effect*, whereas the superior performance at the end of the list is called the *recency effect*. According to the duplex theory, when a word is presented it first enters a limited short-term memory and then may be coded into long-term memory. Thus, the recency effect may be due to the "disposal" of information from short-term memory, and the primacy effect may be related to the fact that more of the first words enter long-term memory due to less competition.

In Experiment 1, the rate at which new words were presented was varied. The duplex theory predicts that slower rates will allow more words to be coded into long-term memory; thus, the primacy part of the curve should be increased but the recency part should not. If memory consists of a single store, the manipulation should affect all parts of the curve equally. However, the results of this experiment indicated that the primacy effect was increased but the recency effect was not affected by the rate of presentation, as predicted by the duplex theory.

In Experiment 2 (reproduced here), the retention interval was varied. The duplex theory predicts that when the interval is increased from 0 to 30 seconds, and rehearsal is prevented, short-term memory will be erased; thus, increasing the retention interval should reduce the recency portion of the curve but not the primacy portion. Again, however, the results were consistent with the duplex theory: longer retention intervals affected mainly the recency portion of the serial position curve.

Although these results provide support for the concept of multi-stage storage, it must be noted that the support is far from universal. The next section on *levels of processing* (Craik and Lockhart) provides an alternative framework for discussing human memory processes.

In a free-recall task, S is presented with a series of words, which he then tries to recall. He is permitted to recall the words in any order that he wishes. The data obtained from this task characteristically show a pronounced serial position effect. The plot of the probability of recall as a function of the position of the word in presentation is U-shaped, with the beginning peak usually lower than the end peak.

The hypothesis proposed here is that the U-shaped serial position curve consists of two curves, each curve representing output from a separate storage mechanism. One is a long-term storage mechanism, the other is a short-term storage mechanism. It follows from the assumption of a long-term and short-term storage mechanism that the material recalled from the beginning of the list should be primarily output from long-term storage, that from the end of the list primarily output from short-term storage. From the initial decline in the serial position curve and the preceding statement, it may be further asserted that the capacity of long-term storage is limited. The more items that are already in, the less likely that there will be place for a new item. By definition, the short-term storage mechanism is limited not with respect to capacity but with respect to the amount of time it can hold an item.

The proposal then is to view the usual serial position curve as a composite of two output curves—one, declining from beginning to end of list, represents output from long-term storage. The other, rising from beginning to end of list, represents output from short-term storage. The amount of overlap between the two curves in a given set of data cannot be specified at present. It is, in part, the aim of this study to develop information on this point.

The distinction between long-term and short-term storage has been developed in the work of Hebb (1949) and Broadbent (1958). Experimental work on short-term storage has been carried out by a number of investigators, starting from the work of Broadbent (1958), Brown (1958), Conrad (1957), and Peterson and Peterson (1959). This work, including a study using a two-factor approach (Waugh, 1960) that has points of similarity with the one used here, has been concerned almost wholly with fixed-order recall.[1] Surveys of the developments in the area and the theoretical questions involved may be found in recent papers by Melton (1963) and Postman (1964).

In order to support the view proposed above, the attempt will be made here to separate the two hypothesized curves. This will be done by means of experimental operations which have a differential effect on the beginning and end sections of the serial position curve. As will be pointed out subsequently, some of these differential effects have already been demonstrated in the literature.

There are well-established procedures that are used to produce long-term storage. These are rote-learning procedures. The variables that affect the efficiency of rote learning—presentation rate, number of presentations, meaningfulness, etc.—suggest the operations that should have their effect on the beginning section of the serial position curve. Short-term storage should, by definition, be affected primarily by the amount of time which has elapsed since presentation. This variable, amount of time elapsed, should therefore have its effect on the end section of the serial position curve.

The aim of this study is, then, to test the hypothesis that there are two distinct storage mechanisms that produce the serial position curve in free recall. The strategy is to use variables which should have one effect on one storage mechanism and a different effect (either no effect or an opposed effect) on the other storage mechanism. These variables should give predictable changes in the shape of the serial position curve.

EXPERIMENT TWO

The purpose of this experiment was to study the separate output of the hypothesized short-term storage mechanism. The strategy again was to introduce a variable that would have a different effect on long-term and short-term storage and thus have a different effect on the beginning and end peak of the serial position curve. The variable selected was delay between the end of the list and start of recall.

Before determining the form in which this delay would be imposed, the effects of pure delay, i.e., delay without an interpolated task, were investigated further. The weight of evidence from the fixed-order recall experiments indicates that pure delay has no effect on short-term storage. The subsidiary evidence in Exp. I on the effects of pure delay also indicated that it had no effect. The effects of pure delay were, however, examined further because the interpretation of predicted differential effect of delay would be simplest if no interpolated task were used. There was reason to believe that the free recall task differed sufficiently from the fixed-

---

[1] The task used by Peterson and Peterson (1959) is viewed here as a fixed-order recall task, since S was required to recall the letters of the trigram in the order that they had been presented.

order recall tasks that had been used, to make it worthwhile to investigate the effects of pure delay on the free-recall task. Moreover, even for the fixed-order recall task there is at least one instance in which pure delay results in a drop in total amount recalled (Anderson, 1960).

A pilot study was, therefore, carried out in which two groups of Ss were each given four 30-word lists, one group with no delay before recall, the other group with 30-sec delay. There was no interpolated task during the delay. A significant reduction of the end peak was found with 30-sec delay, $F(1,233) = 37.00, p < .001$. There was no marked effect of delay on the beginning peak, $F(1,233) = 2.67, p > .10$. The effect on the end peak was, however, small in magnitude, with the serial position curve showing a clear end peak after a 30-sec delay.

It was therefore decided to require the Ss to carry out a minimal task during the delay periods used in this experiment. It was expected that, under these conditions, as the amount of delay increased, the height of the end peak would decrease but the beginning peak would remain unaffected.

METHOD

Subjects. The Ss were 46 Army enlisted men.

Materials and Equipment. The words were shown on a screen, with an automatic slide projector. The words were 240 AA monosyllabic nouns drawn from the Thorndike-Lorge list (1944). Each word was printed in black on a light blue background.

Procedure. The S was first shown three 5-word practice lists, and then fifteen 15-word lists. Each word was shown for 1 sec with a 2-sec interval between successive words. The E read each word as it appeared. After the last word in each list, the symbol # or a digit from 0 to 9 was shown. If the cross-hatch symbol appeared, E said "write,"

FIGURE 1

Serial position curves for 0-, 10-, and 30-sec delay. Each point represents the mean for five lists and 46 Ss.

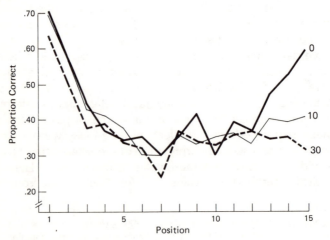

and the S immediately started writing all the words he could recall in his test booklet. If a number appeared, the S started counting out loud from that number until E said "write." While the S was counting, E would measure either 10 or 30 sec wth a stop watch before telling him to write. Each of the delay conditions was used with each of the three practice lists and with five of the main lists. The Ss were individually tested. For each S the words were assigned at random to the lists and order of the delay conditions within the three practice lists and within the fifteen main lists was assigned at random. This meant that each S received a different set of lists and a different sequence of delay conditions.

After each list, the S was given a minimum of 1 min and a maximum of 5 min to complete his recall of each list. After the completion of each session E went over the booklet with the S to make sure that all the words were legible.

Results

The results are summarized in Figure 1. Each curve represents 5 lists re-called by the 46 Ss. The 10-sec delay was sufficient to remove most of the end peak. With a 30-sec delay there is no trace at all of the end peak.[2]

Analysis of variance was carried with positions, and delay interval as within-subjects variables. Both variables and their interaction are signifi-cant at the .001 level or better—position $F (14,630) = 24.87$, delay inter-val, $F (2,90) = 19.75$, and their interaction, $F (28,1260) = 2.29$. Evaluation of the Fs with reduced degrees of freedom, here 1 and 45, leaves the effect of position and delay interval both significant at the .001 level. The inter-action, however, is not significant, under this conservative test. Since, however, the effect was specifically predicted for the end peak, a separate analysis was made of the effect of the delay condition on the sum of cor-rect responses for successive sets of five positions in the curves. The de-grees of freedom for these tests are 1/45. For the first five positions, $F = 3.60, p > .05$; for the second five positions $F = 1.44, p > .10$. The effect of delay is significant only in the last five positions—$F = 22.42, p < .001$.

There is one characteristic of the no-delay curve that makes it differ from the usual serial position curve—the end peak is lower than the begin-ning peak. This may be due to the special characteristics of this experi-ment, in which S was exposed to delay conditions that lowered the efficiency of recall of items from the end of the list. This could have led to a strategy for handling the lists that emphasized the beginning items of the list.

Discussion

The results of this experiment give further support to the hypothesis of two distinct storage mechanisms. Again, it was demonstrated that an experi-mental operation had a predicted, differential effect on the peaks of the serial position curve.

---

[2] Since the submission of this paper, similar results have been reported by Postman, L. and Phillips, L. W., *Quart. J. Exp. Psychol.* 1965, **17**, 132–138.

The hypothesis furnishes a simple explanation for the serial position curve in free recall. It also furnishes a basis for further assertions about free recall which are supported by findings in the literature. Or, to say the same thing another way, the hypothesis makes it possible to systematize a number of findings in the literature:

(1) Word frequency, a variable that has an effect on rote learning, and, therefore presumably on long-term storage, should have an effect on the beginning peak of the serial position curve. This assertion is supported by recent findings by Sumby (1963).

(2) Linguistic constraints in the words of the list, a variable that has an effect on rote learning, and therefore, presumably, on long-term storage should have an effect on the beginning peak of the curve. This assertion is supported by findings by Deese and Kaufman (1957).

(3) Requiring the S to recall the items in forward order should depress the end peak of the serial position curve. By requiring sequential recall, E imposes a delay with an interpolated task—recall of the early list items. This permits the loss of items from short-term storage. This assertion is supported by findings by Deese (1957) and Raffel (1936).

The approach used here is not presented as a complete theory for free recall. A complete theory would permit derivation of the exact form of each of the hypothesized component curves. Once such a derivation is available then it would be possible to move away from the gross distinction between short-term and long-term storage. In a complete theory, the derivation of the output curve for long-term storage would, moreover, be based on specific assumptions about the processing involved in long-term storage. This would make it possible to move away from the simple identification of long-term storage variables with those affecting rote learning. The assumptions should also permit derivation of the characteristics of recall under more complex conditions than those considered here—for example, repeated presentations of the same word list.

The attempt to build a complete theory could, of course, be based on a variety of other constructs. For example, an approach could be developed by using inhibition or interference constructs—more specifically the constructs of proactive and retroactive inhibition.

References

Anderson, N. S. Poststimulus cuing in immediate memory. *J. Exp. Psychol.*, 1960, **60**, 216–221.

Broadbent, D. E. *Perception and communication.* New York: Pergamon, 1958.

Conrad, R. Decay theory of immediate memory. *Nature*, 1957, **179**, 831–832.

Deese, J. Serial organization in the recall of disconnected items. *Psychol. Rep.*, 1957, **3**, 577–582.

Deese, J., & Kaufman, R. A. Serial effects in recall of unorganized and sequentially organized verbal material. *J. Exp. Psychol.*, 1957, **54**, 180–187.

Hebb, D. O. *The organization of behavior.* New York: Wiley, 1949.

Melton, A. W. Implications of short-term memory for a general theory of memory. *J. Verb. Learn. Verb. Behav.*, 1963, **2**, 1–21.

Peterson, L. R. & Peterson, M. J. Short term retention of individual verbal items. *J. Exp. Psychol.*, 1959, **58**, 193–198.

Postman, L. Short-term memory and incidental learning. In A. W. Melton (Ed.), *Categories of human learning.* New York: Academic Press, 1964. Pp. 145–201.

Raffel, G. Two determinants of the effect of primacy. *Amer. J. Psychol.*, 1936, **48**, 654–657.

Sumby, W. H. Word frequency and serial position effects. *J. Verb. Learn. Verb. Behav.*, 1963, **1**, 443–450.

Thorndike, E. L. & Lorge, I. *The teacher's word book of 30,000 words.* New York: Bureau of Publications, Teachers College, Columbia University, 1944.

Waugh, N. C. Serial position and the memory span. *Amer. J. Psychol.*, 1960, **73**, 68–79.

LEVELS OF PROCESSING:
A FRAMEWORK FOR MEMORY RESEARCH

Fergus I. M. Craik and Robert S. Lockhart

Fergus I. M. Craik and Robert S. Lockhart (1972) offer their framework as an alternative to the concept of multi-stage storage discussed in the previous study. Their selection outlines the concept of *levels of processing,* which postulates that deeper levels of processing and elaboration lead to better recall of presented material.

The levels of processing approach raises several additional testable questions. It predicts, for example, that the amount of time spent processing a stimulus will not affect later recall if the processing occurs at a single low level. Results by Craik and Watkins (1973) and Woodward, Bjork, and Jongeward (1973) seem to confirm this prediction. Furthermore, it might be suggested that deeper levels of processing in which information is elaborated upon by the subject may result in *poorer* performance on tasks requiring memory of low-level specifics such as the sound of the word or whether a letter was capitalized. This refinement of the levels of processing hypothesis is supported by the results of several recent studies (see Morris, Bransford, and Franks, 1977; and Stein, 1977).

Many theorists now agree that perception involves the rapid analysis of stimuli at a number of levels or stages (Selfridge & Neisser, 1960. Treisman, 1964; Sutherland, 1968). Preliminary stages are concerned with the analysis of such physical or sensory features as lines, angles, brightness, pitch, and loudness, while later stages are more concerned with matching the input against stored abstractions from past learning; that is, later stages are concerned with pattern recognition and the extraction of meaning. This conception of a series or hierarchy of processing stages is often referred to as "depth of processing" where greater "depth" implies a greater degree of semantic or cognitive analysis. After the stimulus has been recognized, it may undergo further processing by enrichment or elaboration. For example, after a word is recognized, it may trigger associations, images or stories on the basis of the subject's past experience with the word. Such "elaboration coding" (Tulving & Madigan, 1970) is not restricted to verbal material. We would argue that similar levels of processing exist in the perceptual analysis of sounds, sights, smells and so on. Analysis proceeds through a series of sensory stages to levels associated with matching or pattern recognition and finally to semantic—associative stages of stimulus enrichment.

One of the results of this perceptual analysis is the memory trace. Such features of the trace as its coding characteristics and its persistence thus arise essentially as byproducts of perceptual processing (Morton, 1970). Specifically, we suggest that trace persistence is a function of depth of analysis, with deeper levels of analysis associated with more elaborate, longer lasting, and stronger traces. Since the organism is normally concerned only with the extraction of meaning from the stimuli, it is advantageous to store the products of such deep analyses, but there is usually no need to store the products of preliminary analyses. It is perfectly possible to draw a box around early analyses and call it sensory memory and a box around intermediate analyses called short-term memory, but that procedure both oversimplifies matters and evades the more significant issues.

Although certain analytic operations must precede others, much recent evidence suggests that we perceive at meaningful, deeper levels before we perceive the results of logically prior analyses (Macnamara, 1972; Savin & Bever, 1970). Further elaborative coding does not exist in a hierarchy of necessary steps and this seems especially true of later processing stages. In this sense, "spread" of encoding might be a more accurate description, but the term "depth" will be retained as it conveys the flavor of our argument.

Highly familiar, meaningful stimuli are compatible, by definition, with existing cognitive structures. Such stimuli (for example, pictures and sentences) will be processed to a deep level more rapidly than less meaningful stimuli and will be well-retained. Thus, speed of analysis does not necessarily predict retention. Retention is a function of depth, and various factors, such as the amount of attention devoted to a stimulus, its compatibility with the analyzing structures, and the processing time available, will determine the depth to which it is processed.

Thus, we prefer to think of memory tied to levels of perceptual processing. Although these levels may be grouped into stages (sensory analyses, pattern recognition, and stimulus elaboration, for example) processing levels may be more usefully envisaged as a continuum of analysis. Thus, memory, too, is viewed as a continuum from the transient products of sensory analyses to the highly durable products of semantic–associative operations. However, superimposed on this basic memory system there is a second way in which stimuli can be retained—by recirculating information at one level of processing. In our view, such descriptions as "continued attention to certain aspects of the stimulus," "keeping the items in consciousness," "holding the items in the rehearsal buffer," and "retention of the items in primary memory" all refer to the same concept of maintaining information at one level of processing. To preserve some measure of continuity with existing terminology, we will use the term primary memory (PM) to refer to this operation, although it should be noted that our usage is more restricted than the usual one.

We endorse Moray's (1967) notion of a limited-capacity central processor which may be deployed in a number of different ways. If this processing capacity is used to maintain information at one level, the phenomena of short-term memory will appear. The processor itself is neutral with regard to coding characteristics: The observed PM code will depend on the processing modality within which the processor is operating. Further, while limited capacity is a function of the processor itself, the number of items held will depend upon the level at which the processor is operating. At deeper levels the subject can make greater use of learned rules and past knowledge; thus, material can be more efficiently handled and more can be retained. There is apparently great variability in the ease with which information at different levels can be maintained in PM. Some types of information (for example, phonemic features of words) are particularly easy to maintain while the maintenance of others (such as early visual analyses—the "icon") is apparently impossible.

The essential feature of PM retention is that aspects of the material are still being processed or attended to. Our notion of PM is, thus, synonymous with that of James (1890) in that PM items are still in consciousness. When attention is diverted from the item, information will be lost at the rate appropriate to its level of processing—slower rates for deeper levels. While PM retention is, thus, equivalent to continued processing, this type of processing merely prolongs an item's high accessibility without leading to formation of a more permanent memory trace. This Type I processing, that is, repetition of analyses which have already been carried out, may be contrasted with Type II processing which involves deeper analysis of the stimulus. Only this second type of rehearsal should lead to improved memory performance. To the extent that the subject utilizes Type II processing, memory will improve with total study time, but when he engages in Type I processing, the "total time hypothesis" (see Cooper

& Pantle, 1967) will break down. Stoff and Eagle (1971) have reported findings in line with this suggestion.

To summarize, it is suggested that the memory trace is better described in terms of depth of processing or degree of stimulus elaboration. Deeper analysis leads to a more persistent trace. While information may be held in PM, such maintenance will not in itself improve subsequent retention; when attention is diverted, information is lost at a rate which depends essentially on the level of analysis.

References

Cooper, E.H. & Pantle, A.J. The total-time hypothesis in verbal learning. *Psychological Bulletin*, 1967, **68**, 221–234.

James, W. *Principles of Psychology*. New York: Holt, 1890.

Macnamara, J. Cognitive basis of language learning in infants. *Psychological Review*, 1972, **79**, 1–13.

Moray, N. Where is capacity limited? A survey and a model. In A. Sanders (Ed.) *Attention and Performance*. Amsterdam: North-Holland, 1967.

Morton, J. A functional model of memory. In D.A. Norman (Ed.) *Models of Human Memory*. New York: Academic Press, 1970, pp. 203–254.

Savin, H.B. & Bever, T. G. The nonperceptual reality of the phoneme. *Journal of Verbal Learning and Verbal Behavior*, 1970, **9**, 295–302.

Selfridge, O.G. & Neisser, U. Pattern recognition by machine. *Scientific American*, 1960, **203**, 60–68.

Stoff, M. & Eagle, M.N. The relationship among reported strategies, presentation rate, and verbal ability and their effects on verbal recall learning. *Journal of Experimental Psychology*, 1971, **8**, 423–428.

Sutherland, N.S. Outlines of a theory of visual pattern recognition in animals and man. *Proceedings of the Royal Society. Series B*, 1968, **17**, 297–317.

Treisman, A. Monitoring and storage of irrelevant messages in selective attention. *Journal of Verbal Learning and Verbal Behavior*, 1964, **3**, 449–459.

Tulving, E. & Madigan, S.A. Memory and verbal learning. *Annual Review of Psychology*, 1970, **21**, 437–484.

RECALL FOR WORDS AS A FUNCTION OF SEMANTIC, GRAPHIC, AND SYNTACTIC ORIENTING TASKS

Thomas S. Hyde and James J. Jenkins

The experiment by Thomas S. Hyde and James J. Jenkins (1973) provides a test of the prediction that deeper processing during learning results in better recall. In this experiment, subjects listened to word lists with one word presented every three seconds. Several different groups were formed, based on instructions given to the subjects: for example, some subjects were given directions that required semantic processing of each word (that is, determining whether the word was pleasant or unpleasant) while other subjects were given directions that required nonsemantic processing (that is, determining whether the word contained an "e" or "g," or determining whether a word was a noun, verb, and so on). Certain subjects in each group were told to expect a recall test while the others were not.

According to the *levels of processing* hypothesis, tasks requiring semantic elaboration result in better permanent memory, whereas orienting tasks that require only low level processing yield less permanent results, insofar as the words in this latter case are not as well embedded in the memory. An alternative prediction assumes that because all groups spent the same amount of time (3 seconds) actively processing each word, recall should be about the same for all groups. This second prediction is based on a version of the *total time hypothesis* (see Baddeley, 1977), which postulates that the amount remembered depends on the *amount* of processing. The first prediction, however, is based on the level of processing concept that the amount remembered depends on the *depth* of processing.

The results of the study favor the levels of processing hypothesis in that more words were remembered after semantic processing than after nonsemantic processing, even when the subjects had been told to expect a test.

A natural way to study memory is one in which the subject is caught unprepared, so-to-speak, and asked to recall events he experienced at some point in time. Our distrust of such natural procedures usually stems from our concern with loss of control. We fear, on one hand, that the subject may have anticipated the experimenter's plan and invalidated the observation by learning the material when he was merely supposed to be experiencing it. On the other hand, we worry that the subject may not pay attention to the events that the experimenter has arranged and, thus, may not have had the experiences that the experimenter wants him to recall.

Out of this dilemma have grown the paradigms of incidental learning, or if one prefers, incidental memory. Since most natural memory is likely to be incidental, these designs may be viewed as furnishing rather important and realistic data concerning memory processes. The incidental learning paradigms, rather than being residuals of forgotten problems, may be especially appropriate to our revived interest in memory processes and their organizaton.

Hyde and Jenkins (1969), Johnston and Jenkins (1971), and Hyde (1973) recently studied the effects of a number of orienting tasks on the recall of lists of highly associated words. Their findings suggest that when a subject performs an orienting task which requires him to consider the meaning of the words in such a list (semantic task), his subsequent recall is as extensive and as highly structured as the recall of a subject who is instructed to learn the list without performing any orienting task. On the other hand, a subject who performs an orienting task which does not require a consideration of word meaning (nonsemantic task) shows remarkably poor recall and very little associative structure. The results of these experiments seem to indicate that when a subject performs a semantic orienting task, the semantic relationships between the stimulus words are available for the organization of his recall. If, on the other hand, a subject performs a nonsemantic orienting task, the existing semantic relationships between the words are not available and he shows poor recall with little associative structure.

All of these previous experiments have utilized conditions in which the subject knew he was going to have to recall the words (standard free recall paradigm) as well as conditions in which the subject was not prewarned about the recall task (standard incidental learning paradigm). The intention-to-learn dimension produced very little difference in either recall or associative structure, and the effects of the various semantic and nonsemantic tasks were relatively constant across the intentionality dimension. The results of the experiments, therefore, address themselves to both paradigms, the only difference being the prior instructions to learn the list.

While the results seem to be in reasonable accord with the accepted generalizations concerning studies of incidental learning (for example, Postman's review, 1964), our interpretation of the results departs from the traditional view in several important respects. For example, the traditional view has emphasized the relation between the orienting task and the criterion task that is used to assess learning. In doing so, it has focused attention on the responses made to the stimulus materials at the time of presentation as being important in determining whether appropriate learning takes place. Surely this emphasis on tasks is correct, but the generalization concerning responses is too limited to furnish guidance for the research worker because we do not know what constitutes a response in most tasks, nor do we know what kinds of responses are essential to different kinds of learning.

Traditional analysis works with a fairly literal notion of response. When the materials to be learned consist of nonsense syllables that are new to the subject, it seems reasonable to suppose, with Mechanic (1962a, b, 1964), that pronouncing responses constitute the minimal integrating activity that must take place if the subject is to reproduce these items. But when we are past this simple surface level, it is hard to describe responses in a convincing way and specify the relation of the hypothetical responses to the criterion behavior. Why, for example, should estimating the frequency with which one contacts a word (Postman, Adams, & Bohm, 1956) prove to be an effective orienting task with respect to organization of recall? And why should relating items to geometric figures be relatively efficient when one tries to recall adjectives, though the same task is obviously nonfacilitative when one tries to recall nonsense syllables (Postman & Adams, 1956)?

The usual escape clause for such anomalous findings has been a generalization with which we must argue. The traditional view has been that differences between orienting tasks (and between intentionality conditions) are minimal when stimulus materials are either very easy or very difficult to learn. Conversely, it is argued that stimulus material differences are minimal when the tasks are either very facilitative or very antagonistic to learning (Postman, 1964; Deese, 1964). While both of these contentions are psychometrically reasonable at the extremes, due to floor and ceiling effects, the generalizations are sometimes applied in *ad hoc* fashion to explain any outcome that is observed. The role of learning ease and difficulty in incidental learning is the least well-defined and most poorly defended portion of the traditional analysis. Indeed, if one takes seriously the traditional statements concerning the interaction of orienting tasks, criterion tasks, and the nature of the learning required by different kinds of materials, it is apparent that a task *per se* has no particular level of facilitation or inhibition independent of materials and criterion measures. Similarly, ease or difficulty of materials cannot be specified independently of other variables. If one had a better theory of tasks, materials, and interaction, the generalizations dealing with ease of learning could be dispensed with.

The writers want to suggest that the phenomena of memory, whether in a free recall or an incidental learning paradigm, can be approached from a process point of view. We will argue such a view can replace both the notion of hypothetical response and the discussion of difficulty of 'earning materials found in the incidental learning literature. What is sug ested is that the nature of the orienting task be described in terms of processes rather than responses, and that the processes engaged by the orienting task be related to those necessary for the recall and reproduction of the particular stimulus materials used.

Postman and his colleagues consider only three kinds of responses: naming or labeling, responses elicited by stimulus generalization, and responses which establish associative links among the items to be remembered. We think this treatment tends to focus attention on the superficial aspects of behavior. If the subject is asked whether *table* is pleasant or unpleasant, or whether *table* has an "e" in it, his observable response may be the same, a checkmark on a two-valued scale in front of him. We do not know what his hypothetical responses are, but, certainly, we can say what processes must be necessarily involved. In the first case he must access his knowledge of what the word *table* means and evaluate that knowledge against the pleasant–unpleasant dimension. In the second case he must recall the spelling of the word and evaluate that knowledge against the question. The first task activates the semantics of *table*; the second task need not. To the extent that recall processes normally depend on semantics and to the extent that the organization present in the materials is semantic, the first task will be superior to the second in producing recall in either an intentional or incidental learning paradigm.

E. J. Gibson (1971) discussed our first study (Hyde & Jenkins, 1969) in an even more general fashion. She argued that similar distinctive features of words (features of one type) are processed in parallel, while features of different sorts must be encoded sequentially. If this view is correct, then any semantic task allows for the encoding of semantic features of the stimulus words, even semantic features not involved in the task. If some semantic grouping strategy is required by subjects during recall, a subject who had performed a semantic task would have a set of semantic features available for such organizing. If this process is relatively automatic, prior knowledge of the recall task would be of little importance. If, however, the subject performed an orienting task that required him to utilize some other class of distinctive features (for example, graphic, phonetic, or syntactic features), then the semantic information would not be encoded at the same time and would not be available for organization during recall, regardless of the intention to learn.

The present study was designed for two purposes: First, to broaden the range of tasks we have examined in earlier studies, and second, to bring the processing point of view into contrast with some aspects of the traditional view of incidental learning. The contrast with the tradition is twofold. First, and most importantly, we wanted to show that different tasks, having little in common except a requirement for the subject to think about the meaning of the word, would produce very similar results in recall. Second, we wanted to show that processes and list structure, considered together, yield reasonable predictions about recall effects without the use of a dubious concept such as ease of learning.

In broadening the range of tasks we followed the hint from Gibson's (1971) analysis and devised two syntactic tasks to contrast with the semantic and graphic tasks that we had used previously. The syntactic tasks have the virtue that the word is considered as a whole and that a judgment is executed concerning it. Thus, superficially, the task is very similar to semantic rating tasks and quite unlike the graphic tasks that we have used (detecting particular letters and estimating the word length). Yet, if our hypotheses are correct, the syntactic tasks should produce little recall and poor organization, that is, they should function more like the graphic tasks than like the semantic tasks. Two different syntactic tasks were devised; one required a simple judgment as to the part of speech of the word, while the other asked which of two sentence frames each word would fit.

For an additional semantic task we turned to the Postman, Adams, and Bohm (1956) study. These writers found that an orienting task that required rating words for frequency of usage produced minimal differences between incidental and intentional learning for a list of associated words. They attributed the minimal effect to the materials themselves, arguing that the interconnections among the words were so strong and readily detectable that neither the intentionality nor task variables could have much effect. Our interpretation is that the frequency judgment task is essentially semantic: The subject must ask, "What does this mean and how often do I encounter whatever it means?" The orienting task thus automatically led to the encoding of the semantic features of the stimulus words.

The experiment calls for two types of material to be learned: A list of associated words and a list of semantically unrelated words. It calls for different orienting tasks varying in their abstract nature (semantic, graphic, and syntactic). Finally, to meet the traditional concerns of the field, it calls for intentional and incidental groups who perform each of the different orienting tasks, and two control groups who are asked only to recall the lists.

At this point we can hazard predictions, some of which are contrary to the traditional point of view. From the writers' current view we must predict that the groups performing the semantic orienting tasks will perform about as well as control groups in both amount and organization of recall and that the groups assigned to all types of nonsemantic tasks will perform poorly in both recall and organization. We must further predict that the differences between groups performing the semantic and nonsemantic tasks will be greater for the semantically related list (the easier list) than for the unrelated words.

METHOD

The experiment consists of two complete subexperiments differing only in the stimulus list used. Five different orienting tasks were employed. For each task there was one group of subjects who were informed as to the subsequent recall and one group of subjects who were not. In addition, for each subexperiment there was a control group that was simply instructed to listen to the material and attempt to recall it. The design can be described as a 2 (List) × 5 (Orienting Task) × 2 (Intentionality) design, plus the two Controls. The total experiment involved 22 groups.

Subjects

The subjects were undergraduate students enrolled in Introductory Laboratory Psychology at the University of Minnesota and in General Psychology at Case Western Reserve University. All experimental conditions were conducted in the classroom, each separate section making up one group. Assignment of students to sections is not made on any systematic basis and sections were taken to represent essentially random samples of students enrolled in these classes. Experimental conditions were assigned to classes on a random basis except that all the incidental conditions were run first.[1] The number of subjects per group ranged from 19 to 33.

Materials

The list of associated words consisted of 12 pairs of primary associates selected from the Palermo and Jenkins (1964) association norms for university students. Pairs were selected to represent medium-strength primary associates, with an average intrapair association strength of 43.5% (range, 34.5–57.6). Interpair associations were held to a minimum (less than 1%). The words were randomly ordered with the constraint that associates could not be adjacent in the list.

The list of unassociated words was chosen from the Palermo and Jenkins norms and D. G. Doren's unpublished norms for associations to the Palermo and Jenkins response words. Twenty-four words were selected which had no appreciable associative relationship to each other (less than .2%). This list was also screened by the investigators to eliminate any obvious relationships that might have survived the associative screening test. The words in the unassociated list were comparable to the words in the list of associates in terms of length, letter frequency, and frequency of usage. The words were randomly ordered in the list.

Four unassociated filler words were added to each list, two at the beginning and two at the end to minimize primary and recency effects. The filler words were not included in any of the data analysis.

Tasks

The five orienting tasks employed were:

Pleasant–unpleasant rating. This task involved rating the words as to their pleasantness or unpleasantness on a simple five-point rating scale. The task was essentially the same as the semantic task used by Hyde and Jenkins (1969).

Estimating the frequency of usage. This task involved rating the frequency with which the words are used in the English language. Each word was rated on a five-point rating scale, from very infrequent to very frequent. This task was adapted from Postman, Adams, and Bohm (1956).

E–G checking. This task consisted of detecting the occurrence of the letters "E" and "G" in the spelling of the stimulus words. Subjects were instructed to make a check on their rating sheet if either or both of these letters occurred in the word. This task was essentially the same as that used by Hyde and Jenkins (1969).

Parts of speech. On this task subjects were asked to record whether the words were nouns, verbs, adjectives, or "some other" part of speech. They were provided with a check sheet that had these categories labeled for each item. The subjects were told that if they were not certain about the particular part of speech, they were to guess, or put down whatever they thought best. Also, many of the words were ambiguous, in that they could be more than one part of speech. In this case subjects were instructed to put down whatever came to mind first.

Sentence frames. In this final orienting task subjects were presented with two sentence frames and a "does not fit" category. The two sentence frames were printed at the top of the rating sheet and were numbered "1" and "2." The third category was labeled

[1] The writers acknowledge the methodological inelegance involved in the random assignment of classes rather than subjects. The procedure was followed in this experiment for reasons of economy and convenience. Prior studies involving hundreds of subjects performing these tasks on similar and identical materials show no differences between comparable groups formed from laboratory sections and groups formed by random assignment of subjects. See Hyde and Jenkins (1969) and Hyde (1973) for comparable tasks and lists.

"does not fit." The sentence frames contained no words with semantic reference. They were, "It is ———" and "It is the ———." All mass nouns and adjectives fit into the first sentence and all count nouns fit into the second. Many of the words could be either mass nouns or count nouns and could, therefore, fit into either sentence. The subjects were told that if a word seemed to fit into both sentences they were to pick whichever seemed best.

Procedure

The words were recorded at a 3-sec interval. Each subject in a given list condition heard the same recording of the list. The list was presented only once to each group.

Each subject heard the instructions specific to his task. The list was played and he performed his task for each item as it occurred. Following the presentation, his task materials were removed and he was given instructions for the free recall task. All subjects were given 5 min for recall.

FIGURE 1

Number of words recalled by subjects performing each task under both conditions of intentionality for unrelated and associated word lists.

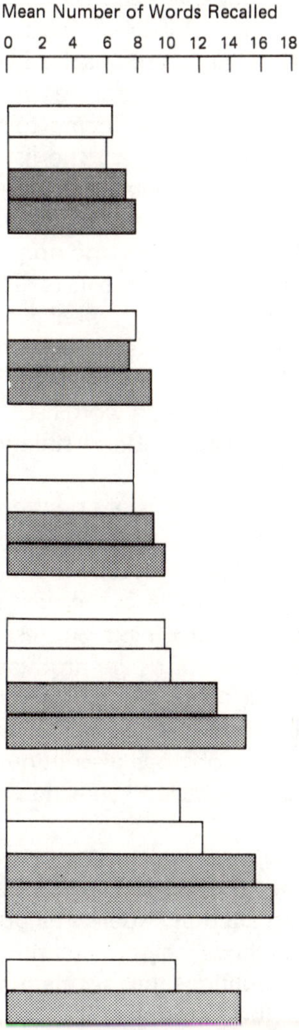

Task Material Condition		Mean Number of Words Recalled	$\bar{X}$	SD	N
Sentence Frame					
Unrelated	Incid		6.6	2.8	23
	Intent		6.2	2.8	25
Associated	Incid		7.3	2.2	19
	Intent		8.1	2.4	20
E-G Checking					
Unrelated	Incid		6.6	2.1	24
	Intent		8.2	2.9	33
Associated	Incid		7.8	2.9	31
	Intent		9.2	3.6	30
Part of Speech					
Unrelated	Incid		8.1	2.5	23
	Intent		8.1	2.2	20
Associated	Incid		9.3	3.1	21
	Intent		10.1	2.7	21
Frequency of Usage					
Unrelated	Incid		10.2	2.6	32
	Intent		10.4	2.9	30
Associated	Incid		13.6	3.2	31
	Intent		15.4	3.5	32
Pleasant-Unpleasant					
Unrelated	Incid		11.2	2.9	30
	Intent		12.7	2.2	33
Associated	Incid		16.2	3.6	30
	Intent		17.3	3.2	25
Control					
Unrelated			10.9	3.8	36
Associated			15.2	3.1	26

RESULTS

Mean Recall

Mean recall scores for all 22 groups are given in Figure 1. It is apparent that the list of associated words (shaded bars) is more readily recalled than the list of unrelated words (unshaded bars). It is also apparent that the semantic orienting tasks yield much more recall than the nonsemantic tasks and, in fact, compare favorably with the recall of the intentional control groups who had no orienting task to perform.

Analysis of variance for unequal Ns was conducted on the recall scores of the 20 groups that performed orienting tasks. The main effects were all significant beyond the .001 level: Intentionality, $F(1, 513) = 11.7$; Lists, $F(1, 513) = 102$; and Tasks, $F(4, 513) = 117$. None of the interactions were significant except the interaction of Lists and Tasks which was significant beyond the .01 level, $F(4, 513) = 9.30$.

Study of Figure 1 reveals the source of the List × Task interaction. The effects of the different orienting tasks on recall of the list of unrelated words are moderate, the semantic tasks being followed by good recall while the nonsemantic tasks were not. For the list of associated words, however, the task effects were appreciably enhanced; the semantic tasks enjoyed a greater advantage over the nonsemantic tasks than they did on the unrelated word list. Roughly speaking, the nonsemantic tasks allowed about the same level of recall for the two lists. The semantic tasks increased recall for both lists but to a much greater extent in the list of associates. With the list of associates the semantic tasks increase recall an average of 83% over recall produced by nonsemantic tasks, while there was only a 42% increase in the unrelated word list. Thus, as expected, the easier (semantically structured) list provided a situation where the relevant task differences were magnified.

The results with respect to the types of orienting tasks are remarkably clear. Across both Lists and conditions of Intentionality the ordering of the tasks in terms of amount recalled is virtually identical. The task yielding the least recall is the *Sentence frame* task, the next poorest recall is associated with *E–G checking*, and the next poorest follows the *Parts of speech* task. *Estimating frequency of usage* produced recall that was just about the level of the *Control* group that performed no orienting task, and *Pleasant–unpleasant* produced the highest recall, superior to the *Control* group in every case. There is an obvious discontinuity in amount of recall that separates the tasks we have called syntactic and graphic from tasks we have called semantic.

There are a variety of ways in which one may examine the data statistically. If one examines the contrasts between Tasks in each experimental condition separately in an attempt to detect all possible differences that might be worth pursuing, one finds that the semantic tasks and the *Control* group form one cluster of conditions that seems homogeneous with only marginal exceptions. With the associated list, the *Frequency of usage* group was different from the *Pleasant –unpleasant* group at the .05 level for both Intentional and Incidental conditions and it was different from the *Control* group at the .05 level for the Incidental condition. For the unrelated list the three tasks are nowhere statistically different. In all experimental conditions, however, these semantic tasks were found to be different from the nonsemantic tasks beyond the .001 level.

Similarly, the nonsemantic tasks tend to form a homogeneous block, with minor exceptions. In the conditions using the associated list, the *Parts of speech* and *Sentence frame* groups were different from each other at the .05 level of significance. With the unrelated word list in the Intentional condition the *Sentence frame* group was different from the *Parts of speech* and the *E–G checking* groups at the .05 level. Otherwise, these groups were not significantly different from each other, but were always different from the semantic and *Control* groups at the .001 level.

Since such minute comparisons leave true significance levels in doubt, it was decided to test the Task differences with the Bonferroni t procedure (Miller, 1966). This procedure, which is a very conservative one in this case, was applied to the Task analysis, with the data pooled across all other experimental conditions. The comparisons chosen for test were those which dictated the original choice of tasks, that is, the control, the semantic, and the nonsemantic conditions. All Bonferroni ts are based on 513 df and three comparisons. The semantic tasks were not different from the control tasks ($t = .18$, n.s.); while the nonsemantic tasks were reliably different ($t = 3.01, p < .01$). As expected, the semantic tasks were significantly different from the nonsemantic tasks ($t = 3.07, p < .01$).

Thus, statistical procedures at both extremes, individual comparisons within conditions, and very conservative multiple comparisons across groups of conditions yield the same general picture; the semantic orienting tasks produce as much recall as the control conditions which had no task to perform, and the nonsemantic tasks were reliably inferior in recall to both the semantic tasks and the Control groups.

A final interesting finding emerges when the Intentionality effect is examined within each list. For the unrelated words, there is no main effect of Intention, $F (1, 263) = 3.20, p > .05$, but there is a significant Task effect, $F (4, 263) = 38.4, p < .001$. For the easier (more structured) list of associated words, there is both an Intention effect, $F (1, 250) = 8.51, p < .01$, and a Task effect, $F (4, 250) = 77.3, p < .001$. Thus, we have the interesting case in which a list of comparatively easy materials (as judged by Postman, Adams, & Bohm, 1956) enhanced the differences between intentional and incidental learners over those observed on a list of unstructured materials of moderate difficulty.

Associative Clustering

For the groups using the associated list, it was possible to analyze the recall protocols for associative clustering as a function of orienting task. Clustering was scored as the percentage of clustering per opportunity (Jenkins,

Mink, & Russell, 1958). This index consists of the number of associated pairs that occurred together in recall divided by the number of opportunities for clustering (multiplied by 100). An opportunity for clustering was simply the appearance of one member of the pair occurring in recall; if the second member of the pair occurred later in the list, it was not counted as another opportunity for clustering. The values, reported in Table 1, are the mean values for the subjects in each group.

As can be seen in Table 1 the data for clustering look very much like the data for mean recall. The groups performing a semantic task or the control learning task show high proportions of clustering. These groups performing graphic or syntactic tasks show very low proportions of clustering.

Analysis of variance revealed no significant effect with respect to differences in clustering across the Intentionality conditions, but a highly significant effect with respect to the Task variable, $F (1, 250) = 58.2$, $p < .001$. The interaction of Intentionality and Task was not statistically significant.

Again, if one examines all comparisons under the Incidental and Intentional conditions, minor variations from the two major blocks of tasks (semantic and nonsemantic) can be detected. The *E-G checking* task was marginally different from the *Part of speech* task at the .01 level under both Intentional and Incidental conditions. The *Sentence frames* task was different at the .05 level from the *Parts of speech* task under the Intentional condition. Likewise the *Frequency of usage* task yielded more clustering than the *Pleasant-unpleasant* task under the Intentional condition, $p < .05$. However, the major differences, as before, were the contrasts between the semantic tasks and the *Control* condition on the one hand and the nonsemantic tasks on the other. All such contrasts are significant beyond the .001 level.

General Discussion

The data reported here support the guiding hypothesis that tasks which call for the processing of semantic features of words will make these features available during recall and that the subject can use this information to organize his recall in a semantic fashion. The present study has broadened the range of tasks that have been examined in exploring the effect of different kinds of orienting tasks on the amount and structure of recall of meaningful word lists. In general, semantic tasks are conducive to high levels of recall and high degrees of organization. Such tasks include pleasant-unpleasant ratings, finding nouns for adjectives and adjectives for nouns, estimating frequency of usage of the words, and active-passive ratings (see Hyde & Jenkins, 1969; Johnston & Jenkins, 1971; Postman, Adams, & Bohm, 1956; Hyde, in press, respectively). Tasks which require processing of the graphic or acoustic form of the stimulus words result in poor recall and little associative structure. Such tasks include letter check-

TABLE 1

Means and Standard Deviations for the Clustering Index for Each Group Using the Associated List

| | Conditions | | | |
| | Incidental | | Intentional | |
Tasks	Mean	SD	Mean	SD
Sentence frames	25.2	21.4	21.6	17.1
E-G checking	12.8	15.3	21.0	19.1
Part of speech	30.8	21.5	36.8	24.0
Frequency of usage	61.3	24.7	72.0	21.1
Pleasant-unpleasant	63.6	21.9	60.2	21.3
Control	–	–	63.3	27.1

ing, word length, rhyming, number of syllables, and voice of the speaker (see Hyde & Jenkins, 1969; Johnston & Jenkins, 1971; Walsh & Jenkins, 1973). The present study has added two new tasks to the list, namely, the assigning of parts of speech and fitting words into sentence frames. These tasks are especially important because they are unrelated to the acoustic or graphic form of the words. They force us then to consider semantic processing versus all kinds of nonsemantic processing, rather than restricting ourselves to meaning versus form of the stimulus, as we did in our earlier studies.

It is clear from the foregoing that tasks which have the same effects need not involve similar responses at any simple level of analysis and, conversely, that tasks which appear to involve identical superficial responses (say, checkmarks on a scale) may have radically different effects on subsequent performances. In short, these findings argue that a processing approach may be more adequate than a response approach in describing the nature of the tasks that result in good and poor recall of meaningful words.

If, as Gibson (1971) has argued, similar distinctive features of a word are processed in a parallel fashion, then an orienting task that focuses subjects on some semantic aspect of the words may allow for the processing of a general range of semantic characteristics of the stimuli. If semantics is essential to long-term memory or if some semantic strategy aids subjects in organizing their recall, then subjects who have performed semantic tasks of any sort will be in a favorable position. It is tempting to believe that other classes of orienting tasks may lead to the encoding of other classes of information which might be useful in different subsequent tasks or with different materials, but clearly, such tasks do not furnish an adequate preparation for the free recall of meaningful materials. The degree of failure of these tasks is all the more dramatic as the materials offer more possibilities of semantic organization.

Detailed examination of the results for the two lists clearly supports the claim that for the tasks that reduced recall and organization (nonsemantic tasks), there was about the same amount of recall for both the associated and unassociated lists. Across both the Incidental and Intentional conditions, these tasks produced recall of about seven words, regardless of the nature of the stimulus list. When subjects performed a task that required the processing of semantic information, there was greater recall for both the associated and unassociated lists. The associated words, however, showed a much greater increase in recall than the list of unassociated words. It would seem that the encoding of semantic information facilitates recall for any type of meaningful material, but the increases are much greater if there are obvious experimenter-imposed semantic relationships that can aid the subjects in organizing their recall.

If we read the older literature properly, it seems to us that it predicts that easy materials in themselves can eliminate task differences. This experiment serves as a demonstration that the effects of Task variables and Intentionality variables may actually be enhanced by the choice of appropriate materials that interact favorably with the processes involved in one set of tasks and unfavorably with the processes involved in others.

As the result of this and other experiments, we suggest that the traditional view of incidental learning be revised in two respects. First we urge that processes rather than responses be studied as the variables that exercise major control over the learning that we see evidenced in the criterion task. Of course, we do not pretend to understand processes better than responses nor do we argue that processes are more objective or more scientific. Indeed, we probably know as little about processes as we do about hypothetical responses. We do argue, however, that the notion of processes involved in a task offers more adequate, productive, and interesting experimental ideas than the relatively constricted (and equally hypothetical) notion of responses.

Second, we suggest that the "escape route" of ease or difficulty of learning as an explanation of unpredicted experimental effects be abandoned. While the inherent difficulty of materials may eventually be seen to play some role, in and of itself, it appears to us that the major part of the variance observed in the criterion task will be accounted for by the interaction of the materials with the processes required in the orienting and criterion tasks. Until we have explored these major contributions to variance we should not use difficulty to explain away our anomalous findings.

References

Deese, J. Behavioral effects of instruction to learn: Comments on Professor Postman's paper. In A. W. Melton (Ed.), *Categories of human learning.* New York: Academic Press, 1964. Pp. 202–209.

Gibson, E. J. Perceptual learning and the theory of word perception. *Cognitive Psychology*, 1971, **2**, 351–368.

Hyde, T. S. The differential effects of effort and type of orienting task on the recall and organization of highly-associated words. *Journal of Experimental Psychology*, 1973, **79,** 111–113.

Hyde, T. S. & Jenkins, J. J. Differential effects of incidental tasks on the organization of recall of a list of highly associated words. *Journal of Experimental Psychology*, 1969, **82,** 472–491.

Jenkins, J. J., Mink, W. D., & Russell, W. A. Associative clustering as a function of verbal association strength. *Psychological Reports*, 1958, **4,** 127–136.

Johnston, C. D. & Jenkins, J. J. Two more incidental tasks that differentially effect associative clustering and recall. *Journal of Experimental Psychology*, 1971, **89,** 92–95.

Mechanic, A. Effects of orienting task, practice, and incentive on simultaneous incidental and intentional learning. *Journal of Experimental Psychology*, 1962a, **64,** 393–399.

Mechanic, A. The distribution of recalled items in intentional and incidental learning. *Journal of Experimental Psychology*, 1962b, **63,** 593–600.

Mechanic, A. The responses involved in the rote learning of verbal materials. *Journal of Verbal Learning and Verbal Behavior*, 1964, **3,** 30–36.

Miller, R. G. *Simultaneous statistical inference.* New York: McGraw-Hill, 1966.

Palermo, D. S. & Jenkins, J. J. *Word association norms: Grade school through college.* Minneapolis: University of Minnesota Press, 1964.

Postman, L. Short-term memory and incidental learning. In A. W. Melton (Ed.), *Categories of human learning.* New York: Academic Press, 1964. Pp. 145–201.

Postman, L. & Adams, P. A. Studies in incidental learning: III. Interserial interference. *Journal of Experimental Psychology*, 1956, **51,** 323–328.

Postman, L., Adams, P. A., & Bohm, A. M. Studies in incidental learning: V. Recall for order and associative clustering. *Journal of Experimental Psychology*, 1956, **51,** 334–342.

Walsh, D. A. & Jenkins, J. J. Effects of orienting tasks on free recall in incidental learning: Difficulty, effort and process explanations. *Journal of Verbal Learning and Verbal Behavior*, 1973, **12,** 481–488.

NARRATIVE STORIES
AS MEDIATORS FOR SERIAL LEARNING

Gordon H. Bower and Michal C. Clark

The experiment by Gordon H. Bower and Michal C. Clark provides another piece of evidence concerning the effect of a subject's encoding strategy on later recall performance. There are many types of *elabo-*

From "Narrative stories as mediators for serial learning" by Gordon H. Bower and Michal C. Clark, PSYCHONOMIC SCIENCE, Vol. 14, 1969, pp. 181–182. Reprinted by permission.

ration processes, or encoding activities, that encourage the learner to actively relate new words to an existing set of meaningful knowledge. In this experiment Bower and Clark examine one such technique, which involves the relating of each word to a running story.

In this experiment, subjects were given 12 successive lists of 10 concrete nouns per list. Some subjects were asked to learn the words by making up a running story that incorporated each word in the list; the remaining subjects were given standard instructions to learn as many of the words as they could. That is, the first group performed deep elaborations on the words whereas the second group processed the words only to keep them for a short time (until the "immediate" test). An "immediate" recall test was given after each of the 12 lists, and a surprise delayed test for all 120 words was given at the end.

The levels of processing theory predicts that both groups should perform well on the immediate test, but only the first group should perform well on the surprise delayed test. The alternative theory based on the total time hypothesis predicts that both groups should perform at similar levels for both tests given that the time spent actively processing the words was equal for the two groups.

The results indicated no significant differences between the groups on the immediate tests: apparently the processing of both groups was sufficient to ensure short-term retention. At the same time, the performance on the delayed test was much better for the group that elaborated during learning.

A technique recommended by mnemonists (e.g., Young & Gibson, 1962) for learning serial lists is the "chaining" method, whereby S is enjoined to construct a narrative story around the critical words to be remembered. The critical words are to be woven into the story in the order they are to be recalled, and these words should be emphasized in some manner, e.g., by vocal stress, pausing, or by making them the main actors or objects in the narrative. The prescriptions permit a wide latitude in constructive details (e.g., the number of critical words per sentence) depending upon the ease of organizing the particular list of words to be learned. A common additional prescription is that S should try to visualize the scenes he is constructing for linking the successive words.

Such procedures request that S generate very many contextual verbal responses. And it is not at all obvious why these should aid memory rather than compete or interfere with recall of the critical words. Further, a prior study by Jensen & Rohwer (1963) found no effect of sentence mediators (linking words n and n + 1) upon rote learning by the serial anticipation method. However, the Jensen and Rohwer study had several features not conducive to showing verbal mediation effects: (a) successive linking sentences were unrelated and were provided by E only on the first trial, and (b) the Ss were mental retardates learning a picture series.

For several reasons, then, our initial study with the chaining technique was done simply to see whether it "worked" efficiently in circumstances for which it plausibly might be efficient. These circumstances were (a) self-paced exposure to the complete serial list, (b) the critical recall units were content words (nouns), and (c) S had a large number of lists to learn and remember, so that massive interference and forgetting would normally be expected for control Ss not using the narrative chaining technique.

METHOD

Each S studied and recalled 12 successive serial lists consisting of 10 concrete nouns chosen to be apparently unrelated. All Ss were run individually; they first received general instructions for the serial learning task. The Narrative Ss were then briefly instructed on the mnemonic technique, as follows: "A good way to learn a list of items is to make up a story relating the items to one another. Specifically, start with the first item and put it in a setting which will allow other items to be added to it. Then, add the other items to the story in the same order as the items appear. Make each story meaningful to yourself. Then, when you are asked to recall the items, you can simply go through your story and pull out the proper items in their correct order."

The Narrative S was handed the first list of 10 words and told to make up his story. He did not have to say his story aloud, and he could take as long as he needed. When S was finished, he handed the list back to E (who recorded the time taken by S), and then S immediately recalled the serial list just studied. Then the second through twelfth lists were gone through in the same way. For each Narrative S, a yoked Control S was run who received the 12 lists in the same order, each for a study-time equal to that taken by the Narrative S. The Control S was told simply to study and learn each serial list, and he also did an immediate recall of each list just after he had studied it. After the twelfth list had been studied and immediately recalled, S was asked to recall the first list again, then the second list, and all subsequent lists. The cue for recall of a list was the first word in that list; S was asked to recall the remaining nine words of that list in their correct order.

The Ss were 24 undergraduates fulfilling a service requirement for their introductory psychology course. Alternate Ss were assigned to be in the Narrative vs yoked Control condition. Each pair of Ss received the 12 lists in a different order within the day.

Results

The times taken by the Narrative Ss to construct their story varied from 40 sec to 199 sec with a grand mean of 104 sec. Fifty-seven per cent had times between 1 and 2 min. These times grew shorter over the first four lists, as though Ss were becoming more proficient at concocting their stories.

Neither group experienced any difficulty in the immediate recall test that followed study of a list. Median percentages recalled were 99.9% and 99.1% for the Narrative and Control Ss, respectively. However, the differential learning and/or forgetting for the Narrative Ss showed up strongly in their later recall, when S tried to recall all 12 lists. The median percentages of words recalled in their correct list and correct absolute position are shown in Figure 1 for the two groups for the 12 lists. There is a tremendous difference, with the Narrative Ss recalling six to seven times more than their yoked Controls. There was no overlap in recall scores of the two groups on any list; the average of the median scores was 93% for the Narrative Ss vs 13% for their yoked Controls.

FIGURE 1

Median percentages recalled over the 12 lists.

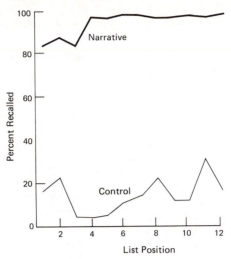

The picture is much the same if one scores recall leniently, counting a word correct regardless of the order or intended list in which it was recalled. For Control Ss the list words have simply become unavailable, whereas this has been prevented in some way by the narrative-story constructions.

There are small effects due to list order apparent in Figure 1, an improvement over early lists for Narrative Ss, and a slight serial-position curve for Control Ss. These are ancillary findings of no interest here.

We next examined the relationship between study-time on a list and later recall of that list. First, for each S, recall of the six lists with his longer study times was compared to recall of the six lists with his shorter study times. In this within-S comparison, there was no suggestion of a short vs long difference in recall for either the Narrative or Control Ss. This may have been because variation of an S's study times was relatively small. Second, over the 12 Ss by 12 lists in each condition, the 144 cases were divided at the median study time, and average recall scores computed for the shorter vs longer times. For the Narrative Ss, average recall for the lists with the shorter study times was 88% vs 92% for the lists with the longer study times. For the Control Ss, average recall was 12% for the shorter-time and 41% for the longer-time lists; these differ significantly, indicating that Control Ss yoked with fast Narrative Ss recalled less than those yoked with slow Narrative Ss.

These comparisons reveal that recall of Control Ss was affected by study time, while that of Narrative Ss was not. However, this effect of study time on Control Ss is still far from accounting for the main effect of the narrative elaboration. (Incidentally, Control Ss always felt that they had more than enough time to learn each list—until the final recall tests.)

Stories were taken from a few Narrative Ss after their final recall; a

TABLE 1

Sample Stories

A LUMBERJACK DARTed out of a forest, SKATEd around a HEDGE past a COLONY of DUCKs. He tripped on some FURNITURE, tearing his STOCKING while hastening toward the PILLOW where his MISTRESS lay.

A VEGETABLE can be a useful INSTRUMENT for a COLLEGE student. A carrot can be a NAIL for your FENCE or BASIN. But a MERCHANT of the QUEEN would SCALE that fence and feed the carrot to a GOAT.

One night at DINNER I had the NERVE to bring my TEACHER. There had been a FLOOD that day, and the rain BARREL was sure to RATTLE. There was, however, a VESSEL in the HARBOR carrying this ARTIST to my CASTLE.

---

sample of these are shown in Table 1 with the 10 critical words capitalized. These have a certain "stream of consciousness" sense and unity about them, and they are not bad solutions to the task of connecting 10 unrelated nouns in a specified order.

Discussion

We think the effect in this experiment is *probably* due to thematic organization. The person generates meaningful sentences to relate successive words, and he tries to relate successive sentences of his generated text around some central theme or action imagery. The sentences and themes from successive lists are different and probably are kept distinct from one another in memory. The first-word cue prompts recall of the theme, and from that the person appears to *reconstruct* the sentences and pull out the critical words. The reconstruction appears to be hierarchical, from theme to sentences to critical words. We would presume that this thematic organization affects learning and that it also reduces interference between the many lists S is learning. Further studies of this effect could yield more useful information by recording Ss' total verbal behavior ("thinking aloud") at study and at recall.

A remarkable aspect of the performance of Narrative Ss is that they rarely intruded nonlist words in their recall (less than .5 per S). One might first suppose that this discrimination between critical vs context words was based on form class, since all critical words were concrete nouns. But a glance at the sample stories in Table 1 shows (a) some context words are nouns, and (b) some critical words are used as verbs or adjectives in the stories. The basis for this high level discrimination between critical and context words added by S remains somewhat of a mystery.

References

Jensen, A. R., & Rowher, W. D., Jr. Verbal mediation in paired-associate and serial learning. *Journal of Verbal Learning & Verbal Behavior*, 1963, **1**, 346–352.

Young, M. N., & Gibson, W. B. *How to develop an exceptional memory*. Hollywood, California: Wilshire Book Co., 1962.

10/ **Memory for Meaning**

ABSTRACTION OF MEANING FROM TEXT

Suppose that you are told a story, or that you read a section of a textbook. As you read or listen to each part of the passage, the meaning of the passage begins to unwind. The process of comprehension was partially addressed in the section on "levels of processing." The first three papers in this section will deal with a related question: What is remembered from a prose passage? That is, after listening to or reading a passage, what memory representation does a learner have in his or her head?

In most cases adults tend to forget some parts of the passage, to remember other parts of the passage, and also to recall some ideas that are not part of the passage at all. One might summarize this result by stating that humans tend to remember the "gist" of the passage rather than recalling the sentences in verbatim form. At first glance, this memory storage process may seem quite inefficient: wouldn't we be better able to function if we had verbatim memory of everything we read or heard? The answer to this question lies partly in the fact that humans have only a limited capacity to handle information (see the section on "Multi-Stage Storage"); and because we can actively concentrate on only a few ideas at any one time, it may be more efficient, after all, to store the gist of information.

One challenge to psychologists is to better define what is meant by the gist of a given prose passage. The first three papers in this chapter are aimed at this question. The excerpt from Bartlett's famous book, *Remembering*, presents the first experiments in this area. This paper is included not for historical reasons only: Bartlett's work is often cited in current work and his ideas are widely recognized as useful constructs in this field. The other two papers may be seen as attempts to clarify and specify some of the comments made by Bartlett. The paper by Bransford and Franks presents updated evidence for the idea that humans remember the gist of stories rather than the verbatim sentences. And the paper by Kintsch provides a system for analyzing text into units (propositions) and for predicting which of these units will be best remembered.

SEMANTIC MEMORY

The remaining three papers in this chapter concern the process by which knowledge is *organized* in semantic memory. In this connection, we find that much of the research on human learning and memory has involved a study-test situation in which a subject learns something (by listening to a list of words or reading a passage, for instance) and then is tested on what has been presented. Another approach is to study the knowledge that a person brings to an experimental lab. This involves studying how information is organized and retrieved from semantic memory — a person's store of meaningful knowledge.

Certain intuitive ideas about semantic memory may be generated by trying to answer some factual questions; for example, "Who was McGovern's running mate in the 1968 American Presidential election?" To answer this question we may first think of Eagleton, then the 1000 percent backing given him by McGovern, and then the replacement of Eagleton by Shriver. In thinking of Shriver, one might not precisely recall his name, but may remember that he was in some way related to the Kennedy family. Another question might be "What was the name of the rock group that first recorded 'Not Fade Away'?" To answer this question, we may first think of the Rolling Stones, but then recall that the original group had a name associated with insects (like the Beatles, but *not* the Beatles). The answer, in this case, may be the Crickets!

The preceding examples suggest that answering a question is not always a matter of simply releasing information from semantic memory. One idea based on the above examples is that knowledge is organized (such as recalling Eagleton before Shriver); an additional idea is that knowledge may be stored on an abstract level (such as remembering insects before Crickets). Two basic types of models have been developed to describe how semantic knowledge is organized in humans: *network models* represent knowledge as a group of concepts linked by association whereas *feature models* represent knowledge as a group of concepts, each of which has a number of characteristics or features. Concepts that are very similar to one another (such as Beatles and Crickets) might be directly connected to one another in a network model, or might have many features in common within a set model.

The paper by Brown and McNeil (1966) investigates the *tip of the tongue phenomenon*—that is, the ability to recall abstract characteristics of a word before recalling the specific word. The last two papers, by Collins and Quillian (1969), and by Rips, Shoben, and Smith (1973), provide examples of the two major methods psychologists have devised for representing semantic knowledge. Collins and Quillian present a network model in which knowledge is represented as a hierarchy of concepts with relations among them, and Rips et al., present a set model in which knowledge is represented as a two-dimensional space characterized by similar and dissimilar features.

These last three papers, then, deal with *retrieval* of information from semantic memory; the three papers in the first part of this chapter focus on the process by which new information (such as a story) is *stored* in memory.

EXPERIMENTS ON REMEMBERING:
THE METHOD OF SERIAL REPRODUCTION

F. C. Bartlett

The first experiment in this chapter presents a well-known study by F. C. Bartlett (1932) who is recognized as the principal forerunner of modern cognitive psychology. Bartlett was concerned with the problems of learning and memory in a "real and meaningful" setting. Thus, instead of using nonsense syllables or word lists, as was the practice at his time, he dealt with actual stories or pictures. The main question that Bartlett asked was this: How is meaningful knowledge acquired, stored, and retrieved from memory?

In the typical experiment reproduced below, Bartlett used a native folk story called "The War of the Ghosts." Bartlett's subjects were several British college students, all of whom were unfamiliar with the various mystical aspects of native folk stories. The experimental procedure, called the *method of serial reproduction*, was similar to the child's game of "telephone." The first subject read the passage twice, waited several minutes, and then tried to reproduce the story. The reproduced version was then given to the second subject who repeated the entire process and passed his or her reproduction on to the third subject. In all, the "story" was passed on ten times.

The main results of this study consist of the ten reproductions of the story. Bartlett suggests that there is a systematic change in what is remembered from one reproduction to the next. Two processes that account for this change are what Bartlett calls *omission*—the process of leaving out minor details and all unfamiliar concepts—and *rationalization*—the process of making the story more compact and coherent by adding details.

What does Bartlett's work tell us about the nature of human learning and memory? Bartlett offers the idea of *schema*—an active organization of past reactions or of past experiences—and suggests that the acquisition of new knowledge involves relating new information to existing schemas. In the process of assimilating new information to existing schema, ideas that are not consistent with the schema may be lost, and some ideas that are consistent but were not part of the new information may be added. In short, Bartlett maintains that when humans are presented with meaningful information, there is an active *effort after meaning*—an attempt to see how this new information fits in with existing knowledge. This view of the learner as an active processor of information contrasts sharply with the empiricist idea that learning consists of passively registering one's experience. In this passage from Bartlett, we are introduced to the main evidence and concepts that some 40 years later have been established as part of modern cognitive psychology. However, as this paper demonstrates, the challenge for modern researchers is to clarify Bartlett's rather vague theory and to build a theory that has predictive power.

Introduction

The form which a rumour, or a story, or a decorative design, finally assumes within a given social group is the work of many different successive social reactions. Elements of culture, or cultural complexes, pass from person to person within a group, or from group to group, and, eventually reaching a thoroughly conventionalised form, may take an established place in the general mass of culture possessed by a specific group. Whether we deal with an institution, a mode of conduct, a story, or an art-form, the conventionalised product varies from group to group, so that it may come to be the very characteristic we use when we wish most sharply to differentiate one social group from another. In this way, cultural characters which have a common origin may come to have apparently the most diverse forms.

The experiments now to be described were designed to study the effects of the combination of changes brought about by many different individuals. The results produced are not entirely beyond the range of experimental research, as I shall show, and the main method which I have used is best called *The Method of Serial Reproduction.*

The Method Described, and the Plan of Treatment

In this method, A's reproduction is itself reproduced by B, whose version is subsequently dealt with by C, and so on. In this way chains of reproduction of folk-stories were obtained. The folk-stories were used because they are predominantly a type of material which passes very rapidly from one social group to another; because most subjects regard it as interesting in itself; because stories can easily be chosen which were fashioned in a social environment very different from that of any social group that is likely to yield subjects for a given experiment; and because, both as to form and as to content, they frequently contain characters which would normally be expected to undergo much change in the course of transmission.

I propose, in this chapter, to add very little to what has been said already concerning the factors affecting individual reproduction, but to concentrate upon a study of the main trends of change in series of reproductions obtained from a number of different subjects, and upon the principles which they illustrate.

Folk-Story Series

The original version of *The War of the Ghosts* is as follows:

One night two young men from Egulac went down to the river to hunt seals, and while they were there it became foggy and calm. Then they heard war-cries, and they thought: "Maybe this is a war-party." They escaped to the shore, and hid behind a log. Now canoes came up, and they heard the noise of paddles, and saw one canoe coming up to them. There were five men in the canoe, and they said:

"What do you think? We wish to take you along. We are going up the river to make war on the people."

One of the young men said: "I have no arrows."

"Arrows are in the canoe," they said.

"I will not go along. I might be killed. My relatives do not know where I have gone. But you," he said, turning to the other, "may go with them."

So one of the young men went, but the other returned home.

And the warriors went on up the river to a town on the other side of Kalama. The people came down to the water, and they began to fight, and many were killed. But presently the young man heard one of the warriors say: "Quick, let us go home: that Indian has been hit." Now he thought: "Oh, they are ghosts." He did not feel sick, but they said he had been shot.

So the canoes went back to Egulac, and the young man went ashore to his house, and made a fire. And he told everybody and said: "Behold I accompanied the ghosts, and we went to fight. Many of our fellows were killed, and many of those who attacked us were killed. They said I was hit, and I did not feel sick."

He told it all, and then he became quiet. When the sun rose he fell down. Something black came out of his mouth. His face became contorted. The people jumped up and cried.

He was dead.

The version of *The War of the Ghosts*, as reproduced by the tenth subject, is as follows:

Two Indians were out fishing for seals in the Bay of Manpapan, when along came five other Indians in a war-canoe. They were going fighting.

"Come with us," said the five to the two, "and fight."

"I cannot come," was the answer of the one, "for I have an old mother at home who is dependent upon me." The other also said he could not come, because he had no arms. "That is no difficulty," the others replied, "for we have plenty in the canoe with us"; so he got into the canoe and went with them.

In a fight soon afterwards this Indian received a mortal wound. Finding that his hour was come, he cried out that he was about to die. "Nonsense," said one of the others, "you will not die." But he did.

There we may leave this series. Short as it is, it has already achieved a fairly fixed form, though no doubt many minor changes might still be introduced, were the series continued. The transformation effected is already very considerable, and the story has become more coherent, as well as much shorter. No trace of an odd, or supernatural element is left: we have a perfectly straightforward story of a fight and a death. The ways in which all this change is achieved are: (i) by a series of omissions, (ii) by the provision of links between one part of the story and another, and of reasons for some of the occurrences; that is to say, by continued rationalisation; (iii) by the transformation of minor detail.

Omissions

All mention of ghosts disappeared in the very first reproduction of this series, and that in spite of the fact that special attention was called to the title. The same thing occurred at some stage in every series obtained with this story as a starting-point. This omission illustrates how any element of imported culture which finds very little background in the culture to which it comes must fail to be assimilated.

The disappearance of the ghosts carried with it other omissions. The details of the sudden and unexplained appearance of the warriors, near the beginning of the tale, were left out. The whole atmosphere was gradually transformed. No detail of omission, occurring in a consecutive series of material of this kind, produced by different individuals belonging to a homogeneous group, can be considered by itself. Each item in a story is set into relation with its general context. To the modern mind folk-lore material tends to appear inconsecutive, full of trivial detail loosely linked together. If it has been developed in an environment different from that of the group of observers, this impression is apt to be extremely strong; for in all popular stories, whether primitive or highly developed, much is left to be supplied by the reader or hearer, and links which are obvious to members of one group are not reacted to at all by members of another. Just as any complex structural material which is presented for perception is first apprehended by way of a 'general impression', so every piece of continuous verbal material tends to be so treated that all the details can be grouped about some central incident or incidents. The incidents selected vary from group to group in accordance with varying group interests or conventions.

Rationalisation

No omission has merely negative import. The story transmitted is treated as a whole, and the disappearance of any items means the gradual construction of a new whole which, within the groups concerned, has an appearance of being more closely organised. The tendency to make all detail fit together, so that a story marches to its end without turning off to particular, apparently disconnected and merely decorative material, is perhaps more strongly marked the higher the level of culture of the subjects concerned. At any rate, every series obtained from a folk-story as starting-point has speedily resulted in the fashioning of a more coherent, concise and undecorated tale, so long as it has been dealt with by normal members of an adult English community. This has been done by the provision of specific links between one part of a story and another, by the introduction of definite reasons, and by the actual transformation of out-of-the-way incidents. The process has been continued from reproduction to reproduction, but its general trend has remained constant.

An instance of the gradual transformation of an unusual incident also occurs over the entire series of reproductions. In the original version the death of the Indian is described thus:

"When the sun rose he fell down. Something black came out of his mouth. His face became contorted." In succession this became:

> When the sun rose he fell down. And he gave a cry, and as he opened his mouth a black thing rushed from it.
> When the sun rose he suddenly felt faint, and when he would have risen he fell down, and a black thing rushed out of his mouth.
> He felt no pain until sunrise the next day, when, on trying to rise, a great black thing flew out of his mouth.
> He lived that night, and the next day, but at sunset his soul fled black from his mouth.
> He lived through the night and the following day, but at sunset his soul fled black from his mouth.
> He lived during the night and the next day, but died at sunset, and his soul passed out from his mouth.
> Before the boat got clear of the conflict the Indian died, and his spirit fled.
> Before he could be carried back to the boat, his spirit had left this world.
> His spirit left the world.
> ("Nonsense", said one of the others, "you will not die.") But he did.

The changes come gradually, but the end is foreshadowed from the beginning. First the "something black" gains a kind of force or vivacity of its own: "it rushed out"; then, "it flew out". Then the activity receives explanation, for the black thing becomes the man's soul, and, by a common conventional phrase, it is said to have "passed out". Once the soul is introduced the mysterious blackness can be dropped, and this speedily occurs. Convention comes in again, and the phrase changes to "his spirit fled", and eventually to the commonplace and everyday: "his spirit left the world". Then this phrase also goes the way of the others and there is nothing left except the statement that the man died, as in the tenth version reported earlier. The initial elaboration, the subsequent simplification, and the final transformation are all built into a single serial change, the total effect of which is to make the whole incident ordinary and rational. But no one of the subjects worked with knowledge of the thing he was doing.

It is possibly significant that when the notion of a departing soul was definitely introduced the expression "black" disappeared. At the beginning of the series "black", as was shown by some of the comments, was apt to be regarded as symbolic. It carried its face significance of an object, a colour and a dreadful occurrence; but it also carried a vague and unformulated suggestion of "soul". When this was definitely named, the symbolic use dropped away.

As the record of the event became ripe for its final rationalisation, it is interesting that it should have undergone some elaboration. No sooner was the rationalisation effected, and the "something black" replaced by the explicit reference to soul, than all further processes were definitely in the direction of simplification. The conditions under which transmitted culture will tend to be elaborated or simplified are matters of very great interest, though many of them lie outside the range of experimental verification. But to some extent elaboration may be regarded as a stage in a process, the main end of which is rationalisation. Difficult or unfamiliar material is first elaborated by some admixture of more familiar elements. Then the familiar carries its own explanation with it, and the unfamiliar drops away, the whole becoming considerably simplified in the process.

Transformation of Detail

The immediate transformation of unfamiliar, or relatively unfamiliar, names into more familiar ones has already been discussed in connexion with the *Method of Repeated Reproduction*. Nothing more need be said about this at present, except that such transformations, readily achieved, are apt to be persistent and easily transmitted. Other series show this tendency more remarkably than the one just given, but here it is illustrated by the change of canoes into boats, and of paddling into rowing.

Order of Events

As this story passed from hand to hand it underwent one interesting change in the reported order of events which may perhaps be significant. Both of the excuses against going to the fight remained, but the second was put into the first place, and at the same time became more definite. Instead of "my relations do not know where I have gone", we get "I have an old mother at home who would grieve terribly if I did not return". These reproductions were all effected in the early days of the War, and this type of reason for shrinking from a fight was very effective in the kind of social group to which nearly all of my subjects belonged. We have here a part of a story which, owing in the main to the special circumstances of the time, produced a definitely emotional reaction. Perhaps that is a reason why this excuse should go up to a more prominent place in the narrative, and why it should also be elaborated. Here, however, confirmatory evidence is required.

THE ABSTRACTION
OF LINGUISTIC IDEAS

John D. Bransford and Jeffery J. Franks

In order to study "what is learned" from a passage, John D. Bransford and Jeffery J. Franks (1971) developed a set of English sentences with each sentence providing information about one of four different *idea sets*, or stories. Each idea set contained four main facts, and sentences about the idea set contained either one, two, three, or all four facts. Subjects listened to the sentences, presented in random order, and after each answered a simple question (to maintain attention). Then subjects were given a recognition test in which sentences were presented; for each sentence the subjects were asked to say "yes" or "no" depending on whether or not that sentence had been presented (verbatim) in the acquisition list. Subjects were also asked to rate, on a five-point scale, how confident they were of their recognition responses.

This same basic method was used in each experiment in the series described in this paper. In the first experiment, for example, only sentences containing one, two, or three facts about each idea set were presented during acquisition. The recognition test consisted of 24 sentences that were true based on the four idea sets but that had not actually been presented, as well as 4 sentences that had been presented. The second experiment was a replication of the first, except that here, several of the test sentences were *noncase*; that is, they had not been presented *and* they were not true based on the four idea sets.

What is learned in this case? One possibility is that when subjects are presented with simple sentences about the story such as "The ants were in the kitchen" (one fact), "The ants ate the sweet jelly" (two facts), and "The ants in the kitchen ate the jelly on the table" (three facts), they tend to integrate all of these into one single long idea-set: "The ants in the kitchen ate the sweet jelly that was on the table." If we conclude that subjects can integrate and construct the full story based on reading only parts of the story while forgetting the specific sentences that were read, then several "constructivist" predictions can be made. First, subjects should be no better at recognizing sentences that were actually presented during learning than at recognizing sentences that were not presented, as long as the sentences are consistent with the idea set. For example, "The sweet jelly was on the table" was not presented but it is true; thus, subjects should be just as likely to recognize this sentence as one that was actually presented (such as "The ants ate the sweet jelly."). Second, subjects should be most confident that they had seen the long idea set since that is actually all they remember.

An alternative to the constructivist theory is that subjects learn by adding the sentences to memory in verbatim form. This theory predicts that subjects should be better able to recognize sentences that were presented than to recognize those that were not.

The results of each study conducted by Bransford and Franks support the *constructivist theory*. The main results were as follows: (1) that subjects "recognized" sentences that were not presented and were just as likely to recognize a sentence that was actually presented as one that was not (as long as it was true), and (2) that subjects were most certain that they had seen the longer sentences, especially those sentences containing all four facts in a given story.

Bransford and Franks conclude that, in learning, subjects tend to integrate incoming information into four main stories. The particular sentences presented are not remembered verbatim; rather, the subject abstracts the facts for each of the four stories and remembers each as a coherent story.

In recent years many psycholinguistic studies dealing with the relation between language and memory have been conducted. Most of these have dealt with memory for sentences and have looked at the effect of various aspects of sentence structure on what is learned and stored in memory. Questions about the relation between syntactic structure and memory have received the most attention. Johnson (1965), for example, has demonstrated some effects of phrase structure on the recall of sentences. Savin and Perchonock (1965) suggest that increasing syntactic complexity produces increasing strain on short-term memory, and long-term memory studies like that of Mehler (1963) indicate a trend towards syntactic simplicity when sentences which have been stored for some time are recalled.

Other memory studies have stressed semantic rather than syntactic variables. Sachs (1967), for example, shows that information about the particular syntactic form of a sentence is quickly forgotten, while its semantic content is very well retained. The work by Kolers (1966) with bilinguals also demonstrates the primacy of semantic encodings, although in his study the effect is demonstrated at the level of individual words. Studies dealing with semantic variables have been much less frequent than those dealing with syntactic variables, presumably because linguistic theories provide a much better description of the syntactic than the semantic domain.

Irrespective of whether emphasis is placed on syntactic or semantic variables, all of the above studies have an important aspect in common. They all deal with memory for individual items. That is, they all study memory for individual sentences or individual words. The primary concern of the present paper is not with memory for individual words or sentences; rather it is with memory for wholistic, semantic ideas. Wholistic ideas need not be communicated by single sentences. They may result from the integration of information expressed by many different sentences experienced successively and often nonconsecutively in time. Emphasis on the acquisition and retention of wholistic ideas thus focuses on memory for sets of sentences expressing common semantic content. The purpose of the present paper is to discuss a methodology for studying the phenomenon of idea acquisition and to demonstrate the psychological reality of "inter-sententially defined" ideas.

THE EXPERIMENTS

The studies to be presented below were designed to communicate four different ideas to each subject, where each idea could be exhaustively characterized as those semantic relations contained in a single complex sentence (e.g., *The rock which rolled down the mountain crushed the tiny hut at the edge of the woods*). During an acquisition phase of the experiments, Ss were never presented with sentences expressing the complete complex ideas, however, but only with sentences encompassing various subsets of the four different semantic domains (*The rock crushed the tiny hut; the hut was at the edge of the woods, etc.*). Idea acquisition would be demonstrated to the extent that such an acquisition procedure resulted in Ss acquiring the complete ideas defined by the integration of the information contained in related sentences.

The experiments were designed to demonstrate the fact of idea acquisition and retention in as strong a manner as possible. Thus they sought to demonstrate that Ss not only could acquire the complete ideas from exposure only to partial ideas, but also that the acquisition of ideas is so natural and compelling that Ss would actually think they had heard sentences expressing the complete ideas during acquisition when in fact they had not.

In order to test the hypothesis of idea acquisition, a recognition test was administered immediately following the acquisition procedure. Ss were told that they would be read a set of sentences, all of which were very related to those just heard during acquisition. Their task was to decide which exact sentences they had heard during acquisition, which ones they had not, and how confident they felt about their answers. Recognition sentences included sentences actually heard during acquisition (OLD sentences), sentences not actually heard during acquisition but which were consonant with the general ideas expressed there (NEW sentences), and sentences neither heard during acquisition nor consonant with the ideas presumably acquired (NONCASE sentences).

To the extent that Ss acquired the complete ideas during acquisition, the following results were expected: First, Ss should show evidence of productivity. That is, they should think they recognize novel examples of the ideas acquired during acquisition in spite of the fact that they had not heard these sentences before. Some of these novel sentences contain combinations of relations never expressed by any single sentence presented during acquisition. It is especially important to see if Ss think they recognize these, since such recognition could not be accounted for by memory for any single previously experienced sentence. It is also important to see whether Ss can differentiate novel sentences from those actually heard during acquisition.

Assuming that Ss actually acquire the complete ideas, some additional results might be expected with respect to Ss' confidence ratings for having heard certain sentences. It seems reasonable to expect that these ratings will reflect the degree to which a sentence represents what was learned during acquisition. If Ss did indeed acquire the ideas, those complex sentences expressing the complete ideas might be expected to receive the highest confidence ratings. Confidence ratings might then decrease with the degree to which particular sentences fail to exhaust all the semantic relations characteristic of a complete idea. Of course, Ss should be confident that they have not heard NONCASE sentences, since these express meanings which differ from those presumably acquired.

An additional factor was incorporated into the acquisition procedure of the present experiments in order to rule out pure contiguity of sentences as an explanation of the results. Sentences related to each of the four ideas were presented randomly during acquisition, with the constraint that no sentences related to the same idea occurred consecutively on the acquisition list. Therefore, if evidence can be found that Ss acquired the complete ideas, they must have done this by integrating successive but nonconsecutive instances of the ideas. In addition, the acquisition procedure was in the form of a short-term memory task requiring Ss to remember a sentence long enough to answer a question about it after a 5-sec delay. Throughout acquisition, Ss were not told that they would be asked to perform on a later recognition task. If information from various nonconsecutive sentences is integrated, it will be done without explicit instructions telling Ss what to do.

Within the limits of the present experimental procedures, the strongest demonstration of idea acquisition and retention would be as follows: Ss would "recognize" novel examples of previously acquired ideas and would not be able to discriminate these novel sentences from ones previously heard. The only criterion affecting recognition confidence ratings for a given sentence would be the degree to which it exhausted all the relations of a complete idea as a whole.

EXPERIMENT I

Since the first two studies are closely related, we shall present the methodologies for both of them before discussing any results.

METHOD

Subjects

The Ss were 15 University of Minnesota undergraduates enrolled in introductory psychology courses.

Materials

Materials consisted of a set of English sentences constructed in the following manner: (1) Four complex sentences were constructed, each of which exhaustively represented the semantic information in one of the four ideas to be acquired. (2) Each complex sentence (complete idea) was constructed to represent the relations among four simple declarative sentences. These simple sentences were chosen intuitively without special regard for their theoretical status in existing linguistic theories. (3) Each of the four complex sentences was broken down into its four simple delcaratives. These simple sentences were then recombined in a variety of ways. Thus, the complete set of sentences used consisted of the following: (*a*) the four complex sentences (FOURS); (*b*) the four simple sentences of each of these complex sentences (ONES); (*c*) sentences constructed by combining (embedding) two simple sentences from a particular complex sentence (TWOS); and (*d*) sentences constructed by combining (embedding) three simple sentences from a particular complex sentence (THREES). The four complex sentences used were: Idea A——*The ants in the kitchen ate the sweet jelly which was on the table*; Idea B——*The warm breeze blowing from the sea stirred the heavy evening air*; Idea C——*The rock which rolled down the mountain crushed the tiny hut at the edge of the woods*; Idea D——*The old man resting on the couch read the story in the newspaper*.

An example of a complete set of sentences defining one particular idea is given in Table 1. The sets of sentences for the other three ideas were constructed in an analogous manner. Thus, the complete set of sentences for each idea contains one FOUR, three THREES, four TWOS, and four ONES.

Materials also included a set of cards, each of which contained four colors arranged in various orders. These were used in an intervening color-naming task.

Procedure

The Ss were divided into two groups for purposes of counterbalancing presentation order. There were eight Ss in Group I and seven in Group II. Each experimental session consisted of acquisition and recognition trials.

Acquisition. The Ss were told that their task would be to answer questions about sentences which would be read by the *E*. This acquisition procedure was as follows: (1) *E* read a sentence; (2) All Ss, in unison, named four colors in the order in which they appeared on the card held up by the *E*; (3) The *E* read an elliptical question concerning the sentence just read; (4) Ss wrote down the answer to the questions. This procedure continued for all the sentences on the acquisition list. The intervening task of color naming was imposed so that Ss would be required to hold each sentence in memory for a short time (color naming took about 4 sec).

Examples of possible elliptical questions (for the example sentence *The rock rolled down the mountain*) are as follows: *Did what?*, *What did?*, and *Where?*. However, only one question was asked for each sentence. Questions were chosen so that each constituent of each idea was questioned about as often as each other constituent.

The acquisition list consisted of 24 sentences, six from each of the four different idea sets. The acquisition sentences from each set consisted of two ONES, two TWOS, and two THREES. (For example, the acquisition sentences from Idea Set A can be found

TABLE 1

Sentences Comprising Idea-Set A

FOUR: The ants in the kitchen ate the sweet jelly which was on the table.
                (On Recognition Only)

THREES: The ants ate the sweet jelly which was on the table.
                (On Acquisition Only)
                The ants in the kitchen ate the jelly which was on the table.
                (On Acquisition Only)
                The ants in the kitchen ate the sweet jelly.
                (On Recognition Only)

TWOS: The ants in the kitchen ate the jelly.
                (On Acquisition Only)
                The ants ate the sweet jelly.
                (On Both Acquisition and Recognition)
                The sweet jelly was on the table.
                (On Recognition Only)
                The ants ate the jelly which was on the table.
                (On Recognition Only)

ONES: The ants were in the kitchen.
                (On Acquisition Only)
                The jelly was on the table.
                (On Acquisition Only)
                The jelly was sweet.
                (On Recognition Only)
                The ants ate the jelly.
                (On Recognition Only)

in Table 1.) Acquisition sentences were chosen so that, as a group, they exhausted the information characteristic of each idea.

The order of presentation of the 24 acquisition sentences was arranged so that in each successive sequence of four sentences there was one sentence from each of the four different idea sets. Sentences were randomized within each block of four sentences with the constraint that no two sentences from the same idea set occurred consecutively on the list. The ONES, TWOS, and THREES from each idea set were randomly distributed across the full acquisition list.

For Group I, acquisition sentences were presented in the order 1–24; for Group II the order was 24–1. Each group went through the acquisition list once.

During acquisition, Ss were not told that there would be a second part to the experiment (i.e., recognition).

Recognition. Following acquisition, Ss were given a 4–5 min. break. They were then told that the *E* was now going to read a new set of sentences, all of which were closely related to the set of sentences they had just heard. Their task was to indicate which of the sentences in the new set they had actually heard before and which ones they had not. In addition to making "yes" or "no" ratings (indicating whether or not they felt they had heard a particular sentence before), Ss were asked to indicate how confident they were about their answer. A 5-point confidence scale was provided for this purpose which ranged from "very low" to "very high" confidence.

The recognition list consisted of 28 sentences. All 28 sentences were from the original four idea sets. Twenty-four of these sentences were NEW sentences; that is, they had not been presented in acquisition. There were six of these sentences from each of the four idea sets. Each of these groups of six sentences contained two ONES, two TWOS, one THREE, and one FOUR (the only four). For example, those sentences marked Recognition in Table 1 are the sentences used in recognition for Idea Set A.

In addition to the 24 new sentences, four sentences from the acquisition list were included in recognition (OLD sentences). These include two ONES (*The rock rolled down the mountain* and *The breeze was blowing from the sea*), one TWO (*The ants ate the sweet jelly*), and one THREE (*The old man resting on the couch read the story*).

The order of presentation of the 28 sentences was similar to that of acquisition. Thus, each block of four sentences contained one sentence from each of the four different idea sets. The four OLD sentences were randomly assigned positions in this list. Again the list was constrained so that no two sentences from the same idea set were consecutive. ONES, TWOS, THREES, and FOURS were randomly distributed throughout the list.

Each group was given the recognition list twice with no break between the two presentations. For Group I, the order of presentation was 1– 28; 1– 28. For Group II, the order was 28– 1, 28– 1.

EXPERIMENT II

Experiment II is essentially a replication of Experiment I, except that this study contains certain NONCASE sentences, the importance of which will be discussed below.

METHOD

Subjects

The Ss were 16 University of Minnesota undergraduates enrolled in introductory psychology courses.

Materials

The construction of the sentences paralleled that of Experiment I. The four complex sentences or complete ideas (FOURS) used were: Idea E——*The scared cat running from the barking dog jumped on the table*; Idea F——*The old car pulling the trailer climbed the steep hill*; Idea G——*The tall tree in the front yard shaded the man who was smoking his pipe*; and Idea H——*The girl who lives next door broke the large window on the porch.*

The ONES, TWOS, and THREES were constructed as in Experiment I. In addition to all these sentences, six NONCASES were constructed. These contained information present in the four idea sets, but their composition violated relationships represented in the ideas to be learned. There were two types of violation: (1) One NONCASE had the same "units" as one of the FOURS, but the relations were changed (i.e., *The scared cat ran from the barking dog which jumped on the table*). (2) The other five NONCASES were constructed by combining information *across* rather than within idea sets, thus grossly changing the relationships involved. These NONCASES are as follows: *The old man who was smoking his pipe climbed the steep hill; The tall tree in the front yard shaded the old car; The barking dog jumped on the old car in the front yard; The scared cat which broke the window on the porch climbed the tree; The man who lives next door broke the large window on the porch.* Each NONCASE sentence represents four simple sentences, precisely the same number that are represented in the four complex FOURS.

Procedure

The procedure again included acquisition and recognition. Two groups were used. There were seven Ss in Group I and nine in Group II.

Acquisition. As in Experiment I, the acquisition list contained 24 sentences, six from each idea set. These were chosen, randomized, and presented exactly as in Experiment I (including the use of the intervening color-naming task).

Recognition. The recognition procedure paralleled that of Experiment I. The list consisted of 24 new sentences, six from each of the four idea sets. As in Experiment I, the list contained two ONES, two TWOS, one THREE, and one FOUR from each idea set. The order of presentation and randomization procedure paralleled Experiment I. One of the six NONCASES was presented within each block of four "clearcase" sentences (i.e., those that actually belong to one of the four idea sets). No sentences from acquisition appeared on recognition. Thus, there were a total of 30 sentences on the recognition list. Each group was presented with this list twice. The presentation order for Group I was 1– 15, 16– 30; 15– 1, 30– 16. For Group II, the order was 30– 16, 15– 1; 16– 30, 1– 15.

Results

Data were analyzed as follows: Ss' ratings were converted into numerical values. A "yes" response received a "plus"; a "no" response received a "minus." A "very high" confidence rating received a 5, a "high" confidence rating received a 4, and so on down to a 1 for "very low" confidence. Thus, a 10-point rating scale emerged ranging from plus 5 to minus 5 (excluding zero).

Ratings for each sentence by each S were summed algebraically for recognition trials I and II. The mean rating for each sentence per trial was then computed, as well as the mean rating per sentence summed over both trials I and II. All data are reported in terms of means (which, of course, must fall within the range of +5.0 to −5.0).

Figure 1 illustrates data which are representative of results from both experiments. This table contains recognition sentences presented for Idea Set A. The three numerical values above each sentence represent mean recognition ratings for (a) trials I and II, (b) trial I, and (c) trial II, respectively. Sentence number 4 is an OLD sentence; all others in Figure 1 are NEW.

The first important point about the data is that many NEW sentences (i.e., sentences not on acquisition) received positive recognition ratings, indicating that Ss actually thought they had heard these sentences during the acquisition task (e.g., see sentences 1, 2, and 5 in Figure 1). In both Experiments I and II, NEW FOURS, THREES, and TWOS generally received such positive ratings. ONES tended to vacillate between the low

FIGURE 1

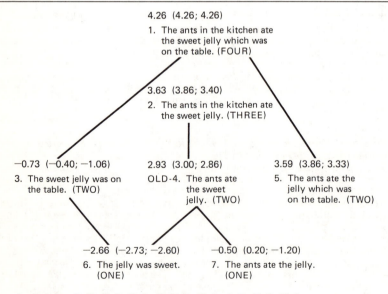

Predictions: 1>2>4>6; 1>3; 1>5>7; 2>7; 4>7; 3>6; 2>6

FIGURE 2

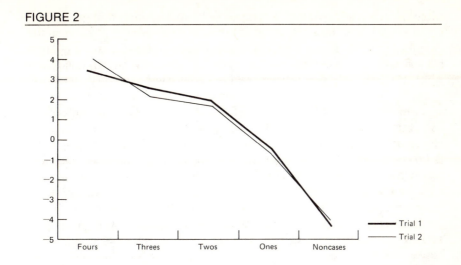

positive and negative range. All NEW FOURS and THREES received positive recognition ratings. This latter result is especially important, since those sentences contained combinations of relations which Ss had never experienced in any single acquisition sentence. It is especially impressive that Ss thought they recognized FOURS.

The second point to consider about the data concerns ratings for OLD sentences. In Experiment I, four OLD sentences were presented during recognition; an example is sentence 4 in Figure 1. Note that NEW sentences 1, 2, and 5 (in Figure 1) received higher recognition ratings than the OLD sentence. This result is typical of the other idea sets. Many NEW sentences received higher recognition ratings than OLD sentences Ss had actually heard before. In fact, 7 (of 24) NEWS received higher recognition ratings than the highest ranking OLD and 15 NEWS were higher than the lowest OLD. If Ss remembered those sentences heard during acquisition, OLD sentences should have received higher confidence ratings than all NEW sentences. Data clearly indicated, however, that OLD sentences did not receive the highest ratings on the recognition list. (Additional OLD–NEW data will be discussed in Experiment III below.)

The third point to consider about the data concerns the relationship between the number of semantic propositions comprising a sentence and recognition confidence ratings; that is, consider the relative recognition ratings for FOURS, THREES, TWOS, and ONES. Results of both experiments were very similar, and their combined averages are summarized in Figure 2 (the means are represented independently for trials I and II). Recognition ratings clearly ordered FOURS > THREES > TWOS > ONES, and the NONCASE sentences from Experiment II received the lowest ratings of all. It is possible to analyze the data in a much more sensitive manner than is represented by overall mean ratings, however. This more sensitive method is as follows.

Figure 1 illustrates a sample of the data from the two experiments. It shows a sentence-by-sentence analysis of the recognition ratings received by all sentences in Idea Set A. Such an analysis can be applied to all the data for both experiments. It allows one to look at the effects of the number of semantic propositions comprising a sentence under conditions where differences in semantic content are controlled.

The sentence-by-sentence analysis examines ordinal recognition ratings among various FOURS, THREES, TWOS, and ONES. The ordinal comparisons of interest are those among sentences within each idea set. Hence no comparisons are made between sentences from Idea Sets A and B (for example). In addition, valid comparisons can only be made between two sentences with equivalent qualitative content. That is, they must be identical except for the absence of one or more embedded semantic propositions. For example, a sentence like *The ants in the kitchen ate the sweet jelly* (Figure 1, sentence 2) can be compared with an identical sentence minus the phrase *in the kitchen* (Figure 1, sentence 4). It cannot, however, be compared with a sentence like *The ants ate the jelly which was on the table* (Figure 1, sentence 5) even though the first sentence is a THREE and the latter a TWO. The reason for this constraint is that the more complex sentence contains no phrase *which was on the table*, whereas the shorter sentence does (but is missing portions like *in the kitchen* as well). Hence the two sentences are not adequately equivalent as defined above. This a priori constraint on equivalence is very important for valid interpretation of the data. Thus, if the phrase *which was on the table* was not acceptable to Ss, the TWO sentence above might receive lower ratings than the THREE for reasons other than the fact that the two sentences differed in the degree to which they exhausted all the relations characteristic of the complete idea. The general formula for defining valid comparisons is as follows: a sentence X is predicted to receive a higher recognition rating than sentence Y if X contains all the basic propositions in Y plus one or more additional propositions (assuming, of course, that sentence X is not a NONCASE). The valid predictions among sentences in Idea Set A allowed by these constraints are presented immediately below Figure 1.

A set of predictions such as $a > b > c > d$ is considered to be transitive. Thus, the prediction includes comparisons between $a > c$, $a > d$, and $b > d$ as well. In Experiment I, 47 of 49 such ordinal predictions were in the predicted direction (for means summed over trials I and II). Experiment II yielded 39 out of 41. Table 2 summarizes the ordering results. Due to the lack of independence inherent in such transitivity predictions, plus the fact that the degree of interdependence differs for each idea set, there are no statistical tests applicable to the present results. Therefore, a Monte Carlo technique was used to analyze the data. The Monte Carlo program randomly assigned a set of ranks to all recognition sentences and checked to see how many of the appropriate predictions that FOUR > THREE > TWO > ONE came out by chance. This procedure was carried out 1000 times. The result was a frequency distribution specifying how many times the number of predictions confirmed by the data (or more) came out by chance. For both studies I and II, the probability values were $\ll .001$.

TABLE 2

Number of Ordering Predictions Confirmed

	Trials 1 and 2	Trial 1	Trial 2
Expt. 1	47 of 49	43 of 49	47 of 49
Expt. 2	39 of 41	35 of 41	39 of 41
Expt. 3	—	135 of 140 (GI)	—
		134 of 140 (GII)	

The final set of data to be considered are ratings for the NONCASES presented in Experiment II. These contained combinations of relations which were not consonant with any of the ideas presumably acquired during acquisition. Data indicated that Ss were quite confident that they had not heard these NONCASE sentences before as can be seen in Figure 2. Recognition ratings for the six NONCASES ranged from -2.37 to -4.87, and their overall mean was -4.19. With one exception, the distributions for individual NONCASE and CLEARCASE sentences were nonoverlapping (for means summed over trials I and II). The exception was that a ONE received a slightly lower recognition rating than the highest ranking NONCASE.

Throughout the present Results section the overall mean ratings for each sentence have been considered to be the most important data. Each sentence was presented twice during recognition in order to achieve a less noisy picture of the results. This procedure eliminated, to some extent, the effect of successive sentences upon one another, and it helped to control for momentary quirks in Ss' ratings. Most important, it allowed Ss to become better acquainted with the complex scaling procedures and makeup of the recognition list. When one examines the means for the two recognition trials computed separately, the same basic patterns of results nevertheless emerge. Product-moment correlation coefficients between mean values on trials I and II were .87 for Experiment I and .95 for Experiment II. In each study, the first trial means contained six reversals in ordinal predictions compared to two reversals when means were computed across both recognition trials (see Table 2). For each study the first trial results were still highly significant by the Monte Carlo test ($p < .001$). For the second trials in both studies, Table 2 shows that the means ordered just as well as the overall means (i.e., only two reversals per study). Evidently Ss were able to discriminate between having heard a sentence before during *recognition* and thinking they had heard it during acquisition, otherwise one might expect second trial ordering results to be worse than those of the first trial. For example, NONCASES might be expected to receive very high ratings on the second trial because Ss would actually have heard them before; similarly for ONES, TWOS, etc. In actuality, however, ratings for both trials were generally comparable. Average NONCASE values, for example, were -4.20 for trial I and -4.17 for trial II.

Discussion

Results of Experiments I and II are very congruent. Both show evidence of productivity, in that Ss thought they recognized many NEW sentences that were never actually presented during the acquisition task. In addition, recognition confidence ratings covaried with the number of semantic propositions comprising a sentence: for appropriate comparisons, FOURS > THREES > TWOS > ONES. NONCASE sentences received very low recognition ratings; Ss were quite confident that they had not heard them before.

GENERAL DISCUSSION

Data indicate that Ss acquired something more general or abstract than simply a list of those sentences experienced during acquisition. Ss integrated the information communicated by sets of individual sentences to construct wholistic semantic ideas. Memory was a function of those ideas acquired during acquisition. Ss thought that they "recognized" novel sentences (NEWS) consonant with the ideas abstracted but were quite confident that they had not heard NONCASE sentences that were not derivable from the ideas acquired. Ss were most confident of having heard those sentences expressing all the semantic information characteristic of the complete ideas acquired during acquisition; and for appropriate comparisons, confidence ratings ordered FOURS > THREES > TWOS > ONES. The fact that Ss "recognized" NEW THREES and FOURS was especially important, since these sentences contained combinations of semantic relations never expressed in any single acquisition sentence. The information encompassed by NOVEL THREES and FOURS could only have been acquired by integrating information across various acquisition sentences experienced nonconsecutively in time.

In general, Ss did not store representations of particular sentences. Individual sentences lost their unique status in memory in favor of a more wholistic representation of semantic events.

The results of these experiments suggest a strong, reliable phenomenon, and the experimental technique appears promising for studying the abstraction of linguistic ideas. The present paper merely scratches the surface of the problem of linguistic abstraction, however, and additional data are needed before more precise claims can be made about the phenomenon at hand. A very important problem, for example, concerns the question of *what is learned* in the above situations. How can one characterize the nature of the semantic ideas that are acquired? The fact that NONCASE sentences received highly negative recognition ratings indicates that the ideas Ss acquired encompassed a considerable degree of semantic precision. For example, Ss were not simply basing their recognition ratings on identities of individual words. However, there are still a number of alternate characterizations of what is learned that could account for the present results. The problem of precisely specifying what is learned is too complex to be handled in a short discussion section, however. A forthcoming paper will deal with this issue in detail.

Besides the problem of what is learned, many boundary conditions for the present phenomenon are still in question. For example, what effects will different types of acquisition instructions have on the results? In the present experiments we purposely used instructions encouraging semantic processing (as opposed to instructions emphasizing rote memory for individual items, for example), since we wanted to study memory as it is generally manifest in everyday life. In a recent Ph.D. thesis, Curnow (1969) has shown (among other things) the basic phenomenon to be replicable under a variety of different acquisition conditions. There are many different questions about the effect of instructions that Curnow did not have a chance to consider, however, hence additional research still needs to be done.

Other boundary conditions concern the composition of the acquisition list and its effects on whether Ss will actually think they have heard complex sentences. If all acquisition sentences were ONES, for example, one would not expect Ss to think they had heard sentences that were THREES and FOURS. It seems clear that any adequate account of the more general phenomenon of linguistic abstraction will have to postulate at least two relatively independent memory representations: (1) Ss will remember wholistic semantic structures, and (2) Ss will retain information about the general style in which the semantic information was originally expressed. An acquisition list composed entirely of ONES may be sufficient to allow Ss to integrate complex semantic structures, but memory for the general style of the acquisition sentences (i.e., that they were all extremely short and simple) would most likely cause Ss to reject recognition sentences that were THREES and FOURS (and maybe even TWOS). Experiments designed to separate memory for input style from memory for semantic structures are currently being conducted. A subsequent article will examine this research.

Although the experiments reported in this initial paper leave many questions unanswered, we are hopeful that the experimental techniques will allow investigation of the phenomenon of abstraction in considerable detail. Ultimately we hope to be able to characterize the semantic structures abstracted from exposure to connected discourse, and hence lend some precision to Bartlett's (1932) notions of abstract schemas as *what is learned*.

References

Bartlett, F. C. *Remembering*. Cambridge: Cambridge Univ. Press, 1932.
Curnow, P. F. Integration of linguistic materials. Unpublished Ph.D. Dissertation, University of Minnesota, 1969.

Johnson, N. F. The psychological reality of phrase-structure rules. *Journal of Verbal Learning and Verbal Behavior*, 1965, **4,** 469–475.

Kolers, P. A. Interlingual facilitation of short-term memory. *Journal of Verbal Learning and Verbal Behavior*, 1966, **5,** 314–319.

Mehler, J. Some effects of grammatical transformations on the recall of English sentences. *Journal of Verbal Learning and Verbal Behavior*, 1963, **2,** 346–351.

Sachs, J. D. S. Recognition memory for syntactic and semantic aspects of connected discourse. *Perception and Psychophysics*, 1967, **2,** 437–442.

Savin, H. B. & Perchonock, E. Grammatical structure and the immediate recall of English sentences. *Journal of Verbal Learning and Verbal Behavior*, 1965, **4,** 348–353.

MEMORY
FOR PROSE

Walter Kintsch

The third paper in this chapter, by Walter Kintsch (1975), presents an attempt to test a precise theory of learning from prose. The theory is based on the idea that a *text* is represented in memory as a hierarchical list of *propositions*. Each proposition contains a verb and one or more *arguments*. For example, "I love psychology" would be represented as "Love, Experiencer: I, Object: psychology," where "love" is the verb, and the arguments are "I" and "psychology." Under this system, a text can be rewritten as a *text base*—a hierarchy of propositions, similar to an outline, representing the meaning of a text. A more detailed summary of this theory is presented in Kintsch's book, *The Representation of Meaning in Memory* (1974).

As Bartlett had before, Kintsch examines "what is learned" from prose. However, Kintsch's work is an improvement over Bartlett's in the sense that Kintsch allows for testable predictions. One straightforward prediction of Kintsch's theory is that because propositions are the basic unit of memory, reading difficulty should depend on the number and complexity of propositions rather than on the number of words. To test this idea, subjects read several passages, each about a paragraph in length, and afterwards wrote down all they could recall. In Experiments 1 and 2, paragraphs were constructed in such a way that they each contained the same number of words but their propositions varied in complexity (that is, number of arguments). As predicted, reading time was faster and recall was more accurate for passages that contained less complex propositions. In addition, reading time was directly related to the number of propositions recalled: each proposition recalled added about 1 second for long passages and ½ second for short passages.

A second major prediction is that propositions at a high level of the hierarchy will be recalled more completely than those at a low level. In Experiments 1 and 2, subjects recalled about 80 percent of the high level propositions and less than 40 percent of the low level propositions. Unfortunately, as Kintsch points out, the "high" propositions often tend to be the first ones in the text; thus, the results may be accounted for by saying that subjects tend to remember the first few facts in a passage.

The two predictions of the "propositional" theory of Kintsch are both upheld in the results of this series of experiments. As Kintsch correctly acknowledges, his work tests only one aspect of Bartlett's original idea. This study deals only with predicting which parts of a passage will be recalled; it does not deal with inferences or the idea that humans add new ideas to the passage.

Studies of memory for prose require some means of dealing with the meaning of texts, apart from the actual words and sentences used to express this meaning. The psychologist must be able to score recall in terms of meaning, and he needs a description of the stimulus events—the texts to be remembered—in terms of their most relevant aspect: their semantic content.

The ability to represent the meaning of texts (recall protocols being one kind of text) is therefore a prerequisite for experimental work on prose memory. Usefulness in psychological research should be the criterion for any model formulated to represent meaning. Such a model need not be an original contribution to linguistics or logic, but it must be sufficiently sophisticated to deal explicitly with the traditional problems of semantic analysis such as quantification, modality, time, tense, and the inference rules involved in semantic memory.

Researchers have recently suggested several such representations of meaning, but I shall concentrate here only upon the one I have been working on (Kintsch, 1974). I shall outline very briefly the chief features of this proposed representation of meaning, without trying to either justify or explain it. Instead, I would like to show how this representation has been used in our laboratory as a tool for the investigation of prose memory.

The model under discussion represents the meaning of a *text* by *text bases* consisting of lists of *propositions*. Propositions are *n*-tuples of *word concepts*, formed according to a set of rules which are part of a person's *semantic memory*. In this context, semantic memory is synonymous with a person's "knowledge of the world." Let me explicate by means of the example presented in Table 1, which shows a brief text of 22 words and the eight-proposition text base from which this text is derived. The actual rules of derivation of texts from text bases do not concern us here and can be left to computational linguists. It is sufficient for us to agree that the text shown is, indeed, one way of expressing the corresponding text base (in general, there may be several paraphrases that express the same meaning equally well). For present purposes the main interest lies in analyzing the characteristics of text bases so that they can be used as independent variables in experiments on prose memory. Returning therefore to the eight propositions of Table 1, note first the proposition (FORM, TURBU-LENCE), which is a very simple verb frame consisting of the predicator *form* (usually expressed in English by means of the verb *form*) followed by one argument, the word concept *turbulence*. Like all word concepts, *turbulence* is defined in a person's lexicon, both by stating its relationship with other word concepts and by means of appropriate sensory imagery and motor programs. It is not known precisely how *turbulence* is defined, and surely this definition differs slightly from person to person, but the general principles are nevertheless clear: people define word concepts implicitly by the propositional contexts in which they appear.

TABLE 1

Sample Text Base and Text

Propositions	Connections and Levels
1 (FORM,TURBULENCE)	
2 (LOC:AT,1,EDGE)	
3 (PART OF, WING,EDGE)	
4 (GROW,TURBULENCE,STRENGTH)	
5 (LOC:OVER,4,SURFACE)	
6 (PART OF,WING,SURFACE)	
7 (CONTRIBUTE,TURBULENCE,LIFT,AIRCRAFT)	
8 (SUPERSONIC,AIRCRAFT)	

Text

Turbulence forms at the edge of a wing and grows in strength over its surface, contributing to the lift of a supersonic aircraft.

The second proposition in Table 1 (the numbers are merely for convenience of reference) has the predicator *location:at* and two arguments: one is simply a word concept, *edge*, the other is itself a proposition, namely Proposition 1. Instead of writing out this embedded proposition as (LOC:AT, (FORM,TURBULENCE),EDGE)—a very clumsy procedure for longer expressions, each proposition is written on a separate line and propositions are referred to by their corresponding line number. The third proposition relates the word concepts *edge* and *wing* by means of the predicator *part of*. In order to understand Proposition 4, consider the proposition frame of *grow* from the lexicon: *grow* is a frame with two slots, one to be filled by whatever is growing, the other to be filled by the dimension of growth; in the present case, *turbulence grows in strength*. Propositions 5 and 6 are a locative and a "part-of" proposition, respectively. The next proposition introduces a more complex frame, *contribute*, which has a slot for an animate or inanimate agent (here filled by *turbulence*), an object slot (*lift*), and a goal slot (*aircraft*), in addition to an instrument slot (left empty in Proposition 7). The final example of a proposition introduces an instance where the predicator is expressed as an adjective, *supersonic*.

The eight propositions in Table 1 form a connected list. They are connected by the repetition rule, which states that repeated arguments are identical. Thus, the *turbulence* that *grows* in Proposition 4 is the same *turbulence* as in Proposition 1. In longer texts, when identity of reference is not intended, this difference must be specially marked. A text base, then, by definition, consists of a list of connected propositions, with argument overlap providing the connections.

The repetition rule not only connects the propositions of a text base, it also serves to order them. This ordering is a partial one that permits us to define the *level* of a proposition in the text base. Given a set of propositions (such as the eight in Table 1) and the designation of one (or more) of that set as superordinate (Table 1 is about the *formation of turbulence*, hence Proposition 1 is the superordinate proposition), the repetition rule objectively orders all propositions of a set according to levels as shown in Table 1: Proposition 1, the designated superordinate, is connected to Propositions 4 and 7 via the repetition of the argument *turbulence*, and to Proposition 2, because the first proposition itself is repeated as an argument of the second proposition. Hence these three propositions form Level 2 of the text base. Three other propositions (3, 5, and 8) are connected to these level-2 propositions and therefore form the third level of propositions. Finally, Proposition 6 is a level-4 proposition, because its only connections are to level-3 propositions. We can thus distinguish four levels of propositions in the short text base of Table 1.

When someone writes a text he intends to communicate a message. We assume this message can be represented by a text base. Writing consists in expressing this text base in natural language. The reader uses this natural-language text as a set of cues for the construction of a new text base, which represents the information that he has obtained from the text. If the text is well written, and the reader is careful, the original text base in the writer's mind and the derived one in the reader's mind will correspond. But frequently there are discrepancies: the reader does not process all of the cues that are available to him and fails to construct some propositions, or he misconstructs others. He also may go beyond the text and use his inference capabilities to elaborate the text base. In fact, one of the most interesting and important unsolved problems in the study of text comprehension is how far this elaboration actually proceeds during comprehension. To remain with the example presented in Table 1, consider again the proposition (CONTRIBUTE,TURBULENCE,LIFT,AIRCRAFT). It is based upon the frame for the predicator *contribute*, which takes as argument an agent or event that contributes, something that is being contributed, someone or something to whom that is being contributed, and finally some action of the contributor that serves as the immediate cause in the process of contributing. In our example this latter instrument slot is vacant. It appears quite likely that some reader may fill it in by the following inference process: what is missing is some action of the contributor (*turbulence*, in our case); immediately preceding the "contribute" proposition some such actions are mentioned (*turbulence forms* and *grows*); under these circumstances it is reasonable to infer (and it happens to be correct, too) that the formation of turbulence causes the contribution. Formally, this may be represented either by a separate proposition (CAUSE,1,7), or by just filling in the instrument slot in Proposition 7: (CONTRIBUTE,TURBU-LENCE,LIFT,AIRCRAFT,1). Note that the writer easily could have provided an explicit cue for this proposition, for example, by a *thereby* after the comma in the sample sentence presented in Table 1.

Clearly, it is impossible to present the proposed theory for the representation of meaning in detail here. I have merely tried to introduce its main concepts and to give the reader enough of an idea about the proposal to enable him to understand the experimental work based upon that theory, which will be discussed below. But before turning to that work, I must point out explicitly one rather important feature of the theory. I do not propose to decompose lexically complex word concepts into their semantic elements. I hypothesize, and have tried to substantiate this hypothesis experimentally, that lexically complex word concepts are treated as unitary chunks in cognitive operations, except when a task specifically demands that they be decomposed. This hypothesis has important consequences for the way in which one conceives of propositions: what the model under discussion treats as a single proposition may, in other systems, be decomposed into several propositional elements. Consider, for one last time, the example (CONTRIBUTE,TURBULENCE,LIFT,AIR-CRAFT). I treat this quadruple as a propositional unit, unlike, for instance, Anderson and Bower (1973) who require all propositions to be binary, or Schank (1972) who would decompose a complex predicate like *contribute* into a set of semantic primitives in which *contribute* is described as "a

TRANS act where actor and originator are identical, performed jointly with other actors." I need to point this out specifically, because what one treats as a unit makes a great difference when it comes to counting propositions, as we shall do below.

Reproductive Memory as a Function of Text-Base Characteristics

In several studies conducted in our laboratory, we have investigated people's ability to comprehend a text and to recall it as a function of the properties of the underlying text base (Kintsch, 1974; Kintsch, Kozminsky, Streby, McKoon, and Keenan, 1975). The experimental procedure followed in these studies was quite simple: a subject read a text at his own rate and then attempted to recall it in writing, not necessarily verbatim. We obtained two dependent measures during the experiments: we recorded how long it took a subject to read a text, which indicated how easy or hard the text was for that subject, and we counted the number of text-base propositions the subject was able to reproduce in his recall protocol, which told us which portions of the text the subject had actually processed. There were of course other aspects of the subject's recall protocol, such as inferences, intrusions, and distortions, but we chose to neglect these for the moment in order to concentrate upon the subject's ability to reproduce the meaning of different types of texts.

The first text variable that we investigated is the most obvious one, namely, the number of propositions in the base structure of texts. In normal texts, the number of propositions in the base structure is, of course, correlated with the number of words in the text; however, it is possible to construct texts that contain an equal number of words but differ in the number of propositions forming the underlying base. One such set of sentences that Janice M. Keenan and I used consisted of 14–16-word sentences with 4 to 9 propositions in the sentence bases. The interesting result that we obtained with these sentences was that reading times increased regularly with an increase in the number of propositions in the sentence base, although the sentences did not differ in the number of words to be read. Thus, readers appear to be sensitive to the amount of information they have to process in a sentence, as measured by the propositional model.

We have since replicated this original result a number of times. The basic finding is illustrated in Figure 1 where we have plotted average reading times as a function of the number of propositions recalled. The subjects participating in the proposition-recall experiment read 70-word paragraphs, each based upon 25 propositions. The paragraphs were taken from articles in *Scientific American*, and they were much like the short paragraph on turbulence that I used as an example earlier. Figure 1 shows that the number of propositions a subject recalled right after reading a paragraph depended upon how long he had studied the text: for each additional proposition recalled an extra 1.26 seconds of reading time was required on the average. There is, of course, a great deal of variability around the regression line in Figure 1, but that merely demonstrates something that should be obvious anyway: even though the number of propositions in a text base partially determines the difficulty of the text (and hence reading times), it is surely not the only variable capable of producing such an effect. In fact, we have estimated that the number of propositions in the base accounts for about 25% of the variance of the reading times if the number of words in the text is controlled.

What are some of the other factors that affect the difficulty of a text? Dorothy Monk and I, as well as others (King and Greeno, 1974), have shown that even if the propositional base of a text remains the same, variations in the way the base is expressed syntactically can have strong effects upon reading times: a writer can say the same thing in either a straightforward or a very complicated manner. In both cases the meaning that is communicated to the reader is the same, that is, requires the reader to construct the same text base, but the reader will take longer to decode the complex message than the easy one.

Another factor that influences the difficulty of a passage is the mere length of the text. If one plots functions (like the one illustrated in Figure

FIGURE 1

Reading time as a function of the number of propositions recalled.

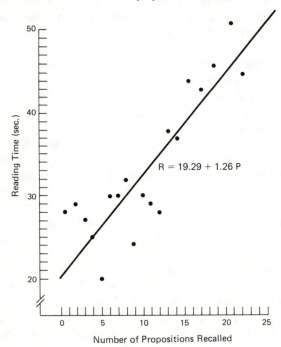

$R = 19.29 + 1.26 P$

Reading Time (sec.)

Number of Propositions Recalled

1) for texts of different lengths, the slope of these functions varies from less than 1 second for short sentences to over 4 seconds for very tough 60-word paragraphs (containing definitions of psychological terms). We have tried to find out why readers need only 1.26 seconds per proposition to recall *Scientific American* paragraphs, but more than three times that long to recall psychological definitions approximately equal in length to the magazine texts. In addition to the mere number of propositions in the base, we have been able to identify experimentally a property of text that is clearly related to text difficulty, namely, the number of different arguments that are employed in the text base. If we take another look at Table 1, we note that the eight text-base propositions employ seven different word concepts as their arguments: *turbulence, edge, strength, surface, wing, lift,* and *aircraft.* For comparison consider the following text: *Although it had been expected that Mercury would not show a magnetic field, satellites detected such a field around it.* It is about the same length as the text analyzed in Table 1 and its text base also contains eight propositions; but it employs only three different arguments: *mercury, field,* and *satellite.* We (Kintsch et al., 1975) compared texts like these, including longer ones, in our experiments and found that the number of different arguments in a text base affects processing difficulty quite strongly. Readers require considerably more time (around 12% in our studies) to read texts with many different arguments than texts with few different arguments, even if the texts are as comparable in all other respects as we can make them. However, people recall about the same amount of information from both kinds of text. If reading times are fixed, on the other hand, a difference in the amount of material recalled appears. Given a fixed time, readers can process more propositions from the few-different argument paragraphs than from the many-different argument paragraphs.

There are many other problems that can be studied with the tools we have developed. For instance, we can ask, given a particular text, what determines which propositions from that text will be recalled and which will be missed? A partial answer to that important question is that the level of a proposition in the text base significantly affects the probability that it will be processed and recalled. The concept of level was introduced above; it is objectively defined by the repetition rule, given a set of propositions and a superordinate, topical proposition to start with. Figure 2 shows some representative data from our experiments investigating the effect of level on recall. We again used the 70-word *Scientific American* paragraphs as texts. Our findings indicate that people recall superordinate, level-1 propositions 80% of the time after one reading, but the more subordinate the position of a proposition in the text hierarchy, the less likely it is to be recalled; the likelihood of recall decreases to about 30% for propositions on the most subordinate levels in these texts. Comparably large effects have been observed in all the studies we have conducted so far. The levels variable is of course correlated with a number of other possible confounding variables, but as far as we have been able to determine, it appears to be the basic determinant of recall.

What might the processing strategy of the reader be like to produce the strong levels effect shown in Figure 2? Remember how the repetition rule permits us to define levels: the repetition of arguments connects level-2 propositions to the topical, level-1 propositions; the third level of propositions in a text base consists of propositions connected via argument repetition to the level-2 propositions, and so on. Suppose that when a reader constructs a text base, he too is guided by argument repetitions. Assume that he first processes the most important superordinate propositions and then preferentially processes other propositions that are connected to the ones he has already processed. Figure 3 shows that this is indeed the case. The figure is based upon data (unpublished, collected by Gail McKoon at the University of Colorado Laboratory) from an experiment in which each of 30 subjects read four paragraphs (from the set already discussed) during each of five study/recall trials. For each trial we computed the probability that a proposition would be recalled (A) if its immediately superordinate proposition (to which it is connected via argument repetition) had been recalled or (B) if its immediately superordinate proposition had not been recalled. Clearly, readers are much more likely to process propositions they can connect to other propositions that have already been processed than to start with propositions they cannot yet connect to the growing network. The fact that the lower curve in Figure 3 increases over trials may mean either that readers do not always follow this strategy or that although

FIGURE 2

Recall probability of propositions as a function of their level in the text base hierarchy.

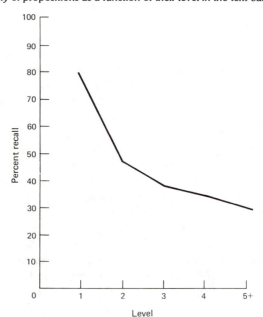

FIGURE 3

Recall probability of propositions as a function of their level in the text base: upper curve indicates recall probability for texts in which the superordinate proposition connected to the proposition in question has been recalled; lower curve indicates recall probability for texts in which the superordinate proposition has not been recalled.

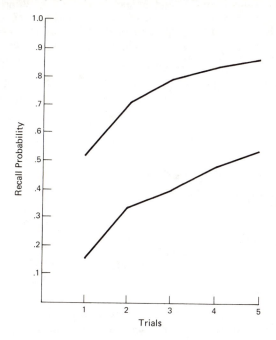

they use this strategy in general, the propositional network they construct from the text differs somewhat from the theoretical one we used to score the data.

References

Anderson, J. R. & Bower, G. H. *Human associative memory*, Washington, D. C.: Winston, 1973.

Baggett, P. Memory for explicit and implicit information in picture stories. *Journal of Verbal Learning and Verbal Behavior*, in press, 14.

Bartlett, F. C. *Remembering*. Cambridge, England: Cambridge University Press, 1932.

van Dijk, T. A. *Some aspects of text grammars*. The Hague: Mouton, 1972.

King, D. R. W. & Greeno, J. G. Invariance of inference times when information was presented in different linguistic formats. *Memory and Cognition*, 1974, **2**, 233–235.

Kintsch, W. *The representation of meaning in memory*. Hillsdale, N.J.: Erlbaum, 1974.

Kintsch, W. & van Dijk, T. A. Comment on se rappelle et on résume des histoires. *Langages*, 1975, **9**, 110–128.

Kintsch, W., Kozminsky, E., Streby, W. J., McKoon, G., & Kennan, J. M. Comprehension and recall of text as a function of content variables. *Journal of Verbal Learning and Verbal Behavior*, 1975, **14**, 196–214.

Minsky, M. A framework for representing knowledge. In P. H. Winston (Ed.), *The psychology of computer vision*. New York: McGraw-Hill, 1975.

Rumelhart, D. E. Notes on a schema for stories. In D. G. Bobrow and A. Collins (Eds.), *Representation and understanding*. New York: Academic Press, 1975.

Schank, R. C. Conceptual dependency: A theory of natural language understanding. *Cognitive Psychology*, 1972, **3**, 552–631.

Selz, O. *Zur Psychologie des produktiven Denkens*. Bonn: Cohen, 1922.

THE "TIP OF THE TONGUE" PHENOMENON

Roger Brown and David McNeill

Roger Brown and David McNeill (1966) define the *tip of the tongue (TOT) phenomenon* as a state in which a "person cannot recall a familiar word but can recall words of similar form and meaning." Although the TOT state may be a common experience in everyday life, the present selection provides a controlled laboratory study of the effect. The reason for interest in the TOT phenomenon is that it suggests that memory is organized and abstract; furthermore, a better understanding of this interesting effect can provide the framework for a theory of semantic memory.

In their study, Brown and McNeill read dictionary definitions of low frequency words, such as nepotism or sampan, to college students. For each word, the subject either knew it, did not know it, or was in a TOT state. In the experiment there were 233 positive cases of TOT; for each of these, subjects were asked to "guess" the number of syllables, the first letter, words with similar sounds, and words with similar meanings.

The results indicated that subjects in the TOT state—that is, subjects who could not initially name the target word but felt they were on the verge of naming it—knew about some of the letters in the word, the number of syllables, and the location of primary stress. Brown and

McNeill concluded that they had found laboratory evidence for *generic recall*, thus implying that semantic memory is like a giant dictionary with many inner associations between concepts and features.

William James wrote, in 1893: "Suppose we try to recall a forgotten name. The state of our consciousness is peculiar. There is a gap therein; but no mere gap. It is a gap that is intensely active. A sort of wraith of the name is in it, beckoning us in a given direction, making us at moments tingle with the sense of our closeness and then letting us sink back without the longed-for term. If wrong names are proposed to us, this singularly definite gap acts immediately so as to negate them. They do not fit into its mould. And the gap of one word does not feel like the gap of another, all empty of content as both might seem necessarily to be when described as gaps" (p. 251).

The "tip of the tongue" (TOT) state involves a failure to recall a word of which one has knowledge. The evidence of knowledge is either an eventually successful recall or else an act of recognition that occurs, without additional training, when recall has failed. The class of cases defined by the conjunction of knowledge and a failure of recall is a large one. The TOT state, which James described, seems to be a small subclass in which recall is felt to be imminent.

For several months we watched for TOT states in ourselves. Unable to recall the name of the street on which a relative lives, one of us thought of *Congress* and *Corinth* and *Concord* and then looked up the address and learned that it was *Cornish*. The words that had come to mind have certain properties in common with the word that had been sought (the "target word"): all four begin with *Co*; all are two-syllable words; all put the primary stress on the first syllable. After this experience we began putting direct questions to ourselves when we fell into the TOT state, questions as to the number of syllables in the target word, its initial letter, etc.

Woodworth (1934), before us, made a record of data for naturally occurring TOT states and Wenzl (1932, 1936) did the same for German words. Their results are similar to those we obtained and consistent with the following preliminary characterization. When complete recall of a word is not presently possible but is felt to be imminent, one can often correctly recall the general type of the word; *generic* recall may succeed when particular recall fails. There seem to be two common varieties of generic recall. (a) Sometimes a part of the target word is recalled, a letter or two, a syllable, or affix. Partial recall is necessarily also *generic* since the class of words defined by the possession of any *part* of the target word will include words other than the target. (b) Sometimes the abstract form of the target is recalled, perhaps the fact that it was a two-syllable sequence with the primary stress on the first syllable. The whole word is represented in *abstract form recall* but not on the letter-by-letter level that constitutes its identity. The recall of an abstract form is also necessarily *generic*, since any such form defines a class of words extending beyond the target.

Wenzl and Woodworth had worked with small collections of data for naturally occurring TOT states. These data were, for the most part, provided by the investigators; were collected in an unsystematic fashion; and were analyzed in an impressionistic nonquantitative way. It seemed to us that such data left the facts of generic recall in doubt. An occasional correspondence between a retrieved word and a target word with respect to number of syllables, stress pattern or initial letter is, after all, to be expected by chance. Several months of "self-observation and asking-our-friends" yielded fewer than a dozen good cases and we realized that an improved method of data collection was essential.

We thought it might pay to "prospect" for TOT states by reading to S definitions of uncommon English words and asking him to supply the words. The procedure was given a preliminary test with nine Ss who were individually interviewed for 2 hrs each.[1] In 57 instances an S was, in fact, "seized" by a TOT state. The signs of it were unmistakable; he would appear to be in mild torment, something like the brink of a sneeze, and if he found the word his relief was considerable. While searching for the target S told us all the words that came to his mind. He volunteered the information that some of them resembled the target in sound but not in meaning; others he was sure were similar in meaning but not in sound. The E intruded on S's agony with two questions: (a) How many syllables has the target word? (b) What is its first letter? Answers to the first question were correct in 47% of all cases and answers to the second question were correct in 51% of the cases. These outcomes encouraged us to believe that generic recall was real and to devise a group procedure that would further speed up the rate of data collection.

METHOD

Subjects

Fifty-six Harvard and Radcliffe undergraduates participated in one of three evening sessions; each session was 2 hrs long. The Ss were volunteers from a large General Education Course and were paid for their time.

Word List. The list consisted of 49 words which, according to the Thorndike-Lorge *Word Book* (1952) occur at least once per four million words but not so often as once per one million words. The level is suggested by these examples: *apse, nepotism, cloaca, ambergris,* and *sampan.* We thought the words used were likely to be in the passive or recognition vocabularies of our Ss but not in their active recall vocabularies. There were 6 words of 1 syllable; 19 of 2 syllables; 20 of 3 syllables; 4 of 4 syllables. For each word we used a definition from *The American College Dictionary* (Barnhart, 1948) edited so as to contain no words that closely resembled the one being defined.

Response Sheet. The response sheet was laid off in vertical columns headed as follows:

Intended word (+ One I was thinking of).
            (– Not).
Number of syllables (1–5).
Initial letter.

---

[1] We wish to thank Mr. Charles Hollen for doing the pretest interviews.

Words of similar sound. (1. Closest in sound)
                               (2. Middle   )
                               (3. Farthest in sound)
Words of similar meaning.
Word you had in mind if not intended word.

Procedure

We instructed Ss to the following effect.

In this experiment we are concerned with that state of mind in which a person is unable to think of a word that he is certain he knows, the state of mind in which a word seems to be on the tip of one's tongue. Our technique for precipitating such states is, in general, to read definitions of uncommon words and ask the subject to recall the word.

(1) We will first read the definition of a low-frequency word.

(2) If you should happen to know the word at once, or think you do, or, if you should simply not know it, then there is nothing further for you to do at the moment. Just wait.

(3) If you are unable to think of the word but feel sure that you know it and that it is on the verge of coming back to you then you are in a TOT state and should begin at once to fill in the columns of the response sheet.

(4) After reading each definition we will ask whether anyone is in the TOT state. Anyone who is in that state should raise his hand. The rest of us will then wait until those in the TOT state have written on the answer sheet all the information they are able to provide.

(5) When everyone who has been in the TOT state has signalled us to proceed, we will read the target word. At this time, everyone is to write the word in the leftmost column of the response sheet. Those of you who have known the word since first its definition was read are asked not to write it until this point. Those of you who simply did not know the word or who had thought of a different word will write now the word we read. For those of you who have been in the TOT state two eventualities are possible. The word read may strike you as definitely the word you have been seeking. In that case please write '+' after the word, as the instructions at the head of the column direct. The other possibility is that you will not be sure whether the word read is the one you have been seeking or, indeed, you may be sure that it is not. In this case you are asked to write the sign '−' after the word. Sometimes when the word read out is not the one you have been seeking your actual target may come to mind. In this case, in addition to the minus sign in the leftmost column, please write the actual target word in the rightmost column.

(6) Now we come to the column entries themselves. The first two entries, the guess as to the number of syllables and the initial letter, are required. The remaining entries should be filled out if possible. When you are in a TOT state, words that are related to the target word do almost always come to mind. List them as they come, but separate words which you think resemble the target in sound from words which you think resemble the target in meaning.

(7) When you have finished all your entries, but before you signal us to read the intended target word, look again at the words you have listed as 'Words of similar sound.' If possible, rank these, as the instructions at the head of the column direct, in terms of the degree of their seeming resemblance to the target. This must be done without knowledge of what the target actually is.

(8) The search procedure of a person in the TOT state will sometimes serve to retrieve the missing word before he has finished filling in the columns and before we read out the word. When this happens please mark the place where it happens with the words "Got it" and *do not provide any more data.*

Results

Classes of Data

There were 360 instances, across all words and all Ss, in which a TOT state was signalled. Of this total, 233 were positive TOTs. A positive TOT is one for which the target word is known and, consequently, one for which the data obtained can be scored as accurate or inaccurate. In those cases where the target was not the word intended but some other word which S finally recalled and wrote in the rightmost column his data were checked against that word, his effective target. A negative TOT is one for which the S judged the word read out not to have been his target and, in addition, one in which S proved unable to recall his own functional target.

The data provided by S while he searched for the target word are of two kinds: explicit guesses as to the number of syllables in the target and the initial letter of the target; words that came to mind while he searched for the target. The words that came to mind were classified by S into 224 words similar in sound to the target (hereafter called "SS" words) and 95 words similar in meaning to the target (hereafter called "SM" words). The S's information about the number of syllables in, and the initial letter of the target may be inferred from correspondences between the target and his SS words as well as directly discovered from his explicit guesses. For his knowledge of the stress pattern of the target and of letters in the target, other than the initial letter, we must rely on the SS words alone since explicit guesses were not required.

To convey a sense of the SS and SM words we offer the following examples. When the target was *sampan* the SS words (not all of them real words) included: *Saipan, Siam, Cheyenne, sarong, sanching,* and *sympoon.* The SM words were: *barge, houseboat,* and *junk.* When the target was *caduceus* the SS words included: *Casadesus, Aeschelus, cephalus,* and *leucosis.* The SM words were: *fasces, Hippocrates, lictor,* and *snake.* The spelling in all cases is S's own.

We will, in this report, use the SM words to provide baseline data against which to evaluate the accuracy of the explicit guesses and of the SS words. The SM words are words produced under the spell of the positive TOT state but judged by S to resemble the target in meaning rather than sound. We are quite sure that the SM words are somewhat more like the target than would be a collection of words produced by Ss with no knowledge of the target. However, the SM words make a better comparative baseline than any other data we collected.

Number of Syllables

As the main item of evidence that S in a TOT state can recall with significant success the number of syllables in a target word he has not yet found we offer Table 1. The entries on the diagonal are instances in which guesses were correct. The order of the means of the explicit guesses is the same as the order of the actual numbers of syllables in the target words. The rank order correlation between the two is 1.0 and such a correlation is significant with a $p < .001$ (one-tailed) even when only five items are correlated. The modes of the guesses correspond exactly with the actual numbers of syllables, for the values one through three; for words of four and five syllables the modes continue to be three.

TABLE 1

Actual Numbers of Syllables and Guessed Numbers for all TOTs in the Main Experiment

		Guessed numbers						
		1	2	3	4	5	No guess	Mode	Mean
Actual numbers	1	9	7	1	0	0	0	1	1.53
	2	2	55	22	2	1	5	2	2.33
	3	3	19	61	10	1	5	3	2.86
	4	0	2	12	6	2	3	3	3.36
	5	0	0	3	0	1	1	3	3.50

Initial Letter

Over all positive TOTs, the initial letter of the word S was seeking was correctly guessed 57% of the time. The pretest result was 51% correct. The results from the main experiment were analyzed with each word counting just once by entering a word's score as "correct" whenever the most common guess or the only guess was in fact correct; 62% of words were, by this reckoning, correctly guessed. The SS words had initial letters matching the initial letters of the target words in 49% of all cases. We do not know the chance level of success for this performance but with 26 letters and many words that began with uncommon letters the level must be low. Probably the results for the SM words are better than chance and yet the outcome for these words was only 8% matches.

Syllabic Stress

We did not ask S to guess the stress pattern of the target word but the SS words provide relevant data. The test was limited to the syllabic location of the primary or heaviest stress for which *The American College Dictionary* was our authority. The number of SS words that could be used was limited by three considerations. (a) Words of one syllable had to be excluded because there was no possibility of variation. (b) Stress locations could only be matched if the SS word had the same number of syllables as the target, and so only such matching words could be used. (c) Invented words and foreign words could not be used because they do not appear in the dictionary. Only 49 SS words remained.

As it happened all of the target words involved (whatever their length) placed the primary stress on either the first or the second syllable. It was possible, therefore, to make a 2 × 2 table for the 49 pairs of target and SS words which would reveal the correspondences and noncorrespondences. As can be seen in Table 2, the SS words tended to stress the same syllable as the target words. The χ^2 for this table is 10.96 and that value is significant with $p < .001$. However, the data do not meet the independence requirement, so we cannot be sure that the matching tendency is significant. There were not enough data to permit any other analyses, and so we are left suspecting that S in a TOT state has knowledge of the stress pattern of the target, but we are not sure of it.

Letters in Various Positions

We did not require explicit guesses for letters in positions other than the first, but the SS words provide relevant data. The test was limited to the following positions: first, second, third, third-last, second-last, and last. A target word must have at least six letters in order to provide data on the six positions; it might have any number of letters larger than six and still provide data for the six (relatively defined) positions. Accordingly we included the data for all target words having six or more letters.

Figure 1 displays the percentages of letters in each of six positions of SS words which matched the letters in the same positions of the corresponding targets. For comparison purposes these data are also provided for SM words. The SS curve is at all points above the SM curve; the two are closest together at the third-last position. The values for the last three positions of the SS curve quite closely match the values for the first three positions. The values for the last three positions of the SM curve, on the other hand, are well above the values for the first three positions. Consequently the *relative* superiority of the SS curve is greater in the first three positions.

The letter-position data were also analyzed in such a way as to count each target word just once, assigning each position in the target a single score representing the proportion of matches across all Ss for that position in that word. The order of the SS and SM points is preserved in this finer analysis. We did Sign Tests comparing the SS and SM values for each of the six positions. As Figure 1 would suggest the SS values for the first three positions all exceeded the SM values with p's less than .01 (one-tailed). The SS values for the final two positions exceeded the SM values with p's less than .05 (one-tailed). The SS values for the third-last position were greater than the SM values but not significantly so.

TABLE 2

Syllables Receiving Primary Stress in Target Words and SS Words

		Target words	
		1st syllable	2nd syllable
SS Words	1st syllable	25	6
	2nd syllable	6	12

FIGURE 1

Percentages of letter matches between target words and SS words for six serial positions.

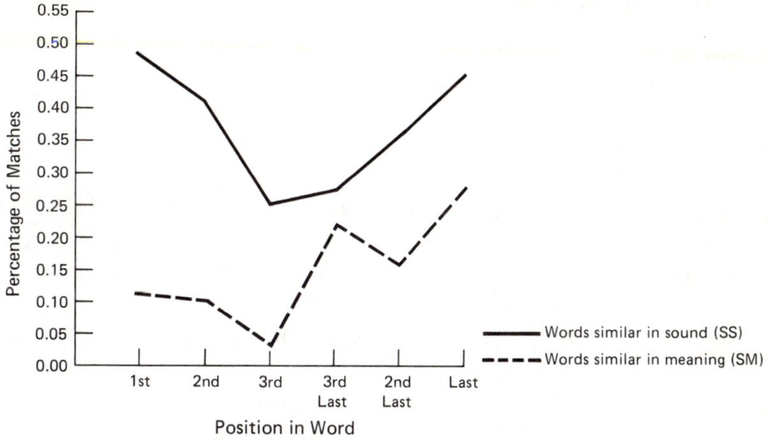

Conclusions

When complete recall of a word has not occurred but is felt to be imminent there is likely to be accurate generic recall. Generic recall of the *abstract form* variety is evidenced by S's knowledge of the number of syllables in the target and of the location of the primary stress. Generic recall of the *partial* variety is evidenced by S's knowledge of letters in the target word. This knowledge shows a bowed serial-position effect since it is better for the ends of a word than for the middle and somewhat better for beginning positions than for final positions. The accuracy of generic recall is greater when S is near the target (complete recall is imminent) than when S is far from the target. A person experiencing generic recall is able to judge the relative similarity to the target of words that occur to him and these judgments are based on the features of words that figure in partial and abstract form recall.

A Model of the Process

Let us suppose (with Katz and Fodor, 1963, and many others) that our long-term memory for words and definitions is organized into the functional equivalent of a dictionary. In real dictionaries, those that are books, entries are ordered alphabetically and bound in place. Such an arrangement is too simple and too inflexible to serve as a model for a mental dictionary. We will suppose that words are entered on keysort cards instead of pages and that the cards are punched for various features of the words entered. With real cards, paper ones, it is possible to retrieve from the total deck any subset punched for a common feature by putting a metal rod through the proper hole. We will suppose that there is in the mind some speedier equivalent of this retrieval technique.

The Reason for Generic Recall

In adult minds words are stored in both visual and auditory terms and between the two there are complicated rules of translation. Generic recall involves letters (or phonemes), affixes, syllables, and stress location. In this section we will discuss only letters (legible forms) and will attempt to explain a single effect—the serial position effect in the recall of letters. It is not clear how far the explanation can be extended.

Feigenbaum (1963) has written a computer program (EPAM) which simulates the selective-attention aspect of verbal learning as well as many other aspects. " . . . EPAM has a *noticing order for letters of syllables*, which prescribes at any moment a letter-scanning sequence for the matching process. Because it is observed that subjects generally consider end letters before middle letters, the noticing order is initialized as follows: first letter, third letter, second letter" (p. 304). We believe that the differential recall of letters in various positions, revealed in Figure 1 of this paper, is to be explained by the operation in the perception of real words of a rule very much like Feigenbaum's.

References

Barnhart, C. L. (Ed.) *The American college dictionary.* New York: Harper, 1948.

Broadbent, D. E. *Perception and communication.* New York: Macmillan, 1958.

Bruner, J. S. & O'Dowd, D. A note on the informativeness of words. *Language and Speech*, 1958, **1**, 98–101.

Feigenbaum, E. A. The simulation of verbal learning behavior. In E. A. Feigenbaum and J. Feldman (Eds.) *Computers and thought.* New York: McGraw-Hill, 1963. Pp. 297–309.

Hockett, C. F. *A course in modern linguistics.* New York: Macmillan, 1958.

James, W. *The principles of psychology*, Vol. I. New York: Holt, 1893.

Jensen, A. R. Spelling errors and the serial-position effect. *J. educ. Psychol.*, 1962, **53**, 105–109.

Katz, J. J. & Fodor, J. A. The structure of a semantic theory. *Language*, 1963, **39**, 170–210.

Miller, G. A. & Friedman, Elizabeth A. The reconstruction of mutilated English texts. *Inform. Control*, 1957, **1**, 38–55.

Thorndike, E. L. & Lorge, I. *The teacher's word book of 30,000 words.* New York: Columbia Univer., 1952.

Underwood, B. J. Stimulus selection in verbal learning. In C. N. Cofer and B. S. Musgrave (Eds.) *Verbal behavior and learning: problems and processes.* New York: McGraw-Hill, 1963. Pp. 33–48.

Wenzl, A. Empirische und theoretische Beiträge zur Erinnerungsarbeit bei erschwerter Wortfindung. *Arch. ges. Psychol.*, 1932, **85**, 181–218.

Wenzl, A. Empirische und theoretische Beiträge zur Erinnerungsarbeit bei erschwerter Wortfindung. *Arch. ges. Psychol.*, 1936, **97,** 294–318.

Woodworth, R. S. *Psychology.* (3rd ed.). New York: Holt, 1934.

Woodworth, R. S. & Schlosberg, H. *Experimental psychology.* (Rev. ed.). New York: Holt, 1954.

RETRIEVAL TIME
FROM SEMANTIC MEMORY

Allan M. Collins and M. Ross Quillian

Allan M. Collins and M. Ross Quillian (1969) provide one of the earliest and best known systems for representing semantic knowledge. Their system is a network model consisting of categories (such as animals, birds, canaries), properties (such as "has wings," "is yellow"), and pointers (links between canary and bird, or between bird and "has wings"). The structure of knowledge is hierarchical in this system, with pointers going from subsets to supersets (such as from canary to bird, and from bird to animal). In addition, properties are stored at the highest possible level; for example, since all birds have wings, that property is stored at the generic (bird) level rather than at the species (canary) level.

Collins and Quillian make certain assumptions about the retrieval process for questions such as "Is a canary a bird?" First, it takes time to move up a level in the hierarchy of knowledge or to determine the property for a category. Second, the time it takes to move up two levels is additive when one level must be reached before the other. Third, the time to move up a level or to find a property of a category is always the same, regardless of the actual level of the category. These assumptions allow Collins and Quillian to make some predictions, the primary one being that time to answer questions should depend on the number of levels in the hierarchy involved. Questions involving one level ("Is a canary yellow?") should take less time than those involving two levels ("Does a canary have wings?") and those with three levels ("Does a canary have skin?") should take the longest.

To test these predictions, subjects were presented with sentences on a screen, one every four seconds. For each sentence the subject was asked to press one button if the statement was true and the other button if it was false. A computer recorded the response times. The results clearly indicated that increasing the number of levels in the sentence increased response time, with each additional level adding about one-tenth of a second.

These preliminary results are consistent with the idea that semantic memory is simply a hierarchy of concepts with features associated with each concept. However, subsequent work in this area has raised certain questions about Collins and Quillian's original model. A discussion of this model and ways of refining it have been offered in a recent paper by Collins and Loftus (1975).

Quillian (1967, 1969) has proposed a model for storing semantic information in a computer memory. In this model each word has stored with it a configuration of pointers to other words in the memory; this configuration represents the word's meaning. Figure 1 illustrates the organization of such a memory structure. If what is stored with canary is "a yellow bird that can sing" then there is a pointer to bird, which is the category name or *superset* of canary, and pointers to two *properties*, that a canary is yellow and that it can sing. Information true of birds in general (such as that they can fly, and that they have wings and feathers) need not be stored with the memory node for each separate kind of bird. Instead, the fact that a canary can fly can be inferred by retrieving that a canary is a bird and that birds can fly. Since an ostrich cannot fly, we assume this information is stored as a property with the node for ostrich, just as is done in a dictionary, to preclude the inference that an ostrich can fly. By organizing the memory in this way, the amount of space needed for storage is minimized.

If we take this as a model for the structure of human memory, it can lead to testable predictions about retrieving information. Suppose a person has only the information shown in Figure 1 stored on each of the nodes. Then to decide "A canary can sing," the person need only start at the node canary and retrieve the properties stored there to find the statement is true. But, to decide that "A canary can fly," the person must move up one level to bird before he can retrieve the property about flying. Therefore, the person should require more *time* to decide that "A canary can fly" than he does to decide that "A canary can sing." Similarly, the person should require still longer to decide that "A canary has skin," since this fact is stored with his node for animal, which is yet another step removed from canary. More directly, sentences which themselves assert something about a node's supersets, such as "A canary is a bird," or "A canary is an animal," should also require decision times that vary directly

FIGURE 1

Illustration of the hypothetical memory structure for a 3-level hierarchy.

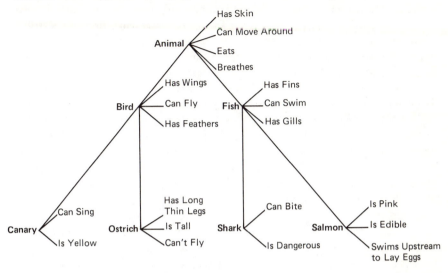

with the number of levels separating the memory nodes they talk about.

A number of assumptions about the retrieval process must be made before predictions such as those above can be stated explicitly. First, we need to assume that both retrieving a property from a node and moving up a level in a hierarchy take a person time. Second, we shall assume that the times for these two processes are additive, whenever one step is dependent on completion of another step. This assumption is equivalent to Donders' assumption of additivity (Smith, 1968) for the following two cases: (a) When moving up a level is followed by moving up another level, and (b) when moving up a level is followed by retrieving a property at the higher level. Third, we assume that the time to retrieve a property from a node is independent of the level of the node, although different properties may take different times to retrieve from the same node. It also seems reasonable to assume that searching properties at a node and moving up to the next level occur in a parallel rather than a serial manner, and hence are not additive. However, this assumption is not essential, and our reasons for preferring it are made clear in the Discussion section.

We have labeled sentences that state property relations P sentences, and those that state superset relations S sentences. To these labels numbers are appended. These indicate the number of levels the model predicts it would be necessary to move through to decide the sentence is true. Thus, "A canary can sing" would be a P0 sentence, "A canary can fly" would be a P1 sentence, and "A canary has skin" would be a P2 sentence. Similarly, "A canary is a canary" would be an S0 sentence, "A canary is a bird" would be an S1 sentence, and "A canary is an animal" would be an S2 sentence.

It follows from the assumptions above that the time differences predicted for P0, P1, and P2 sentences are entirely a result of moving from one level in the hierarchy to the next. Thus, the increase in time from S0 to S1 should be the same as from P0 to P1 since both increases are a result of moving from level 0 to level 1. Likewise, the time increase from S1 to S2 should equal the time increase from P1 to P2. In fact, if we assume that the time to move from one level to the next is not dependent on which levels are involved, all the time increases (from P0 to P1, P1 to P2, S0 to S1, and S1 to S2) should be equal.

Recently, reaction time (RT) has been used as a measure of the time it takes people to retrieve information from memory. By constructing a large number of true sentences of the six types discussed and interspersing these with equal numbers of false sentences, we can measure the reaction time for Ss to decide which sentences are true and which are false. Thus, this method can be used to test the prediction we have derived from the model and our assumptions about the retrieval process.

A caution is in order here: Dictionary definitions are not very orderly and we doubt that human memory, which is far richer, is even as orderly as a dictionary. One difficulty is that hierarchies are not always clearly ordered, as exemplified by dog, mammal, and animal. Subjects tend to categorize a dog as an animal, even though a stricter classification would interpose the category mammal between the two. A second difficulty is that people surely store certain properties at more than one level in the hierarchy. For example, having leaves is a general property of trees, but many people must have information stored about the maple leaf directly with maple, because of the distinctiveness of its leaf. In selecting examples, such hierarchies and instances were avoided. However, there will always be Ss for whom extensive familiarity will lead to the storing of many more properties (and sometimes supersets) than we have assumed. By averaging over different examples and different subjects, the effect of such individual idiosyncrasies of memory can be minimized.

METHOD

Three experiments were run, with eight Ss used in each experiment. The Ss were all employees of Bolt Beranek and Newman, Inc. who served voluntarily and had no knowledge of the nature of the experiment. Because of a faulty electrical connection, only three Ss gave usable data in Expt. 3. The same general method was used for all three experiments, except in the way the false sentences were constructed.

Apparatus. The sentences were displayed one at a time on the cathode ray tube (CRT) of a DEC PDP-1 computer. The timing and recording of responses were under program control.[1] Each sentence was centered vertically on one line. The length of line varied from 10 to 34 characters (approximately 4–11° visual angle). The S sat directly in front of the CRT with his two index fingers resting on the two response buttons. These each required a displacement of ¼ in to trigger a microswitch.

---

[1] The authors thank Ray Nickerson for the use of his program and his help in modifying it to run on BBN's PDP-1.

Procedure. The sentences were grouped in runs of 32 or 48, with a rest period of approximately 1 min between runs. Each sentence appeared on the CRT for 2 sec, and was followed by a blank screen for 2 sec before the next sentence. The *S* was instructed to press one button if the sentence was generally true and the other button if it was generally false, and he was told to do so as accurately and as quickly as possible. The *S* could respond anytime with the 4 sec between sentences, but his response did not alter the timing of the sentences. Each *S* was given a practice run of 32 sentences similarly constructed.

Sentences. There were two kinds of semantic hierarchies used in constructing sentences for the experiments, 2-level and 3-level. In Figure 1, a 2-level hierarchy might include bird, canary, and ostrich and their properties, whereas the whole diagram represents a 3-level hierarchy. A 2-level hierarchy included true P0, P1, S0 and S1 sentences; a 3-level hierarchy included true P2 and S2 sentences as well. Examples of sentence sets with 2-level and 3-level hierarchies are given in Table 1.[2] As illustrated in Table 1, equal numbers of true and false sentences were always present (but in random sequence) in the sentences an *S* read. Among both true and false sentences, there are the two general kinds: Property relations (P) and superset relations (S).

In Expt 1, each *S* read 128 two-level sentences followed by 96 three-level sentences. In Expt 2 each *S* read 128 two-level sentences, but different sentences from those used in Expt 1. In Expt 3, a different group of *S*s read the same 96 three-level sentences used in Expt 1. Each run consisted of sentences from only four subject-matter hierarchies.

To generate the sentences we first picked a hierarchical group with a large set of what we shall call *instances* at the lowest level. For example, baseball, badminton, etc. are instances of the superset games. Different instances were used in each sentence because repetition of a word is known to have substantial effects in reducing RT (Smith, 1967). In constructing S1 and S2 sentences, the choice of the category name or superset was in most cases obvious, though in a case such as the above 2-level example, sport might have been used as the superset rather than game. To assess how well our choices corresponded with the way most people categorize, two individuals who did not serve in any of the three experiments were asked to generate a category name for each S1 and S2 sentence we used, e.g., "tennis is ———." These two individuals generated the category names we used in about ¾ of their choices, and only in one case, "wine is a drink" instead of "liquid", was their choice clearly not synonymous.

In generating sentences that specified properties, only the verbs "is," "has," and "can" were used, where "is" was always followed by an adjective, "has" by a noun, and "can" by a verb. To produce the P0 sentence one of the instances such as baseball was chosen that had a property (in this case innings) which was clearly identifiable with the instance and not the superset. To generate a P1 or P2 sentence, we took a salient property of the superset that could be expressed with the restriction to "is," "has," or "can." In the first example of Table 1, rules were felt to be a very salient property of games. Then an instance was chosen, in this case badminton, to which the P1 property seemed not particularly associated. Our assumption was that, if the model is correct, a typical *S* would decide whether badminton has rules or not by the path, badminton is a game and games have rules.

In Expt 1, false sentences were divided equally between supersets and properties. No systematic basis was used for constructing false sentences beyond an attempt to produce sentences that were not unreasonable or semantically anomalous, and that were always untrue rather than usually untrue. In Expt 2, additional restrictions were placed on the false sentences. The properties of the false P0 sentences were chosen so as to contradict a property of the instance itself. In example 3 of Table 1, "Coca-cola is blue" contradicts a property of Coca-cola, that it is brown or caramel-colored. In contrast, the properties of false P1 sentences were chosen so as to contradict a property of the superset. In the same example, alcoholic was chosen, because it is a contradiction of a property of soft drinks in general. The relation of elements in the false S0 and S1 sentences can be illustrated by reference to Figure 1. The false S0 sentences were generated by stating that one instance of a category was equivalent to another, such as "A canary is an

---

[2] To obtain the entire set of true sentences for Expt 1 order NAPS Document NAPS-00265 from ASIS National Auxiliary Publications Service, % CCM Information Sciences, Inc., 22 West 34th Street, New York, New York 10001; remitting $1.00 for microfiche or $3.00 for photocopies.

ostrich." The false S1 sentence was constructed by choosing a category one level up from the instance, but in a different branch of the structure, such as "A canary is a fish."

The sequence of sentences the S saw was randomly ordered, except for the restriction to four hierarchies in each run. The runs were counterbalanced over Ss with respect to the different sentence types, and each button was assigned true for half the Ss, and false for the other half.

Results and Discussion

In analyzing the data from the three experiments, we have used the mean RT for each S's correct responses only. Error rates were on the average about 8% and tended to increase where RT increased.

Deciding a Sentence is True

The data from all three experiments have been averaged in Figure 2. To evaluate the differences shown there for true sentences, two separate analyses of variance were performed: One for the 2-level runs and one for the 3-level runs. For the 2-level data the difference between P sentences and S sentences was significant, $F(1, 60) = 19.73, p < .01$, the difference between levels was significant, $F(1, 60) = 7.74, p < .01$, but the interaction was not quite significant, $F(1, 60) = 2.06$. For the 3-level data, the difference between P and S sentences was significant, $F(1, 60) = 27.02$,

TABLE 1

Illustrative Sets of Stimulus Sentences

Sentence type	True sentences	Sentence type [a]	False sentences
Expt 1, 2-level			
P0	Baseball has innings	P	Checkers has pawns
P1	Badminton has rules	P	Ping pong has baskets
S0	Chess is chess	S	Hockey is a race
S1	Tennis is a game	S	Football is a lottery
Expt 1, 3-level			
P0	An oak has acorns	P	A hemlock has buckeyes
P1	A spruce has branches	P	A poplar has thorns
P2	A birch has seeds	P	A dogwood is lazy
S0	A maple is a maple	S	A pine is barley
S1	A cedar is a tree	S	A juniper is grain
S2	An elm is a plant	S	A willow is grass
Expt 2, 2-level			
P0	Seven-up is colorless	P0	Coca-cola is blue
P1	Ginger ale is carbonated	P1	Lemonade is alcoholic
S0	Pepsi-cola is Pepsi-cola	S0	Bitter lemon is orangeade
S1	Root beer is a soft drink	S1	Club soda is wine

[a] There were no distinctions as to level made for false sentences in Expt 1.

FIGURE 2

Average reaction times for different types of sentences in three experiments.

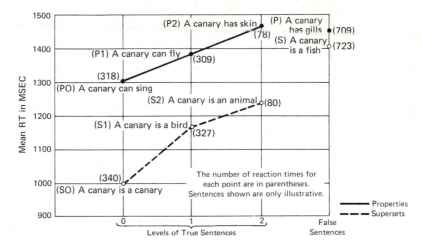

Mean RT in MSEC

- (P2) A canary has skin (78)
- (P) A canary has gills (709)
- (S) A canary is a fish (723)
- (P1) A canary can fly (309)
- (318)
- (P0) A canary can sing
- (S2) A canary is an animal (80)
- (S1) A canary is a bird (327)
- (340)
- (S0) A canary is a canary

The number of reaction times for each point are in parentheses. Sentences shown are only illustrative.

——— Properties
– – – Supersets

Levels of True Sentences — False Sentences

$p < .01$, the difference between levels was significant, $F (2, 60) = 5.68$, $p < .01$, and the interaction was not significant, $F < 1$.

Our prediction was that the RT curves for P0, P1, and P2 sentences and for S0, S1, and S2 sentences should be two parallel straight lines. The results are certainly compatible with this prediction, except for the S0 point, which is somewhat out of line. It was anticipated that presenting the entire sentence on the CRT at one time would permit the Ss to answer the S0 sentences, e.g., "A maple is a maple," by pattern matching. That they did so was substantiated by spontaneous reports from several Ss that on the S0 sentences they often did not even think what the sentence said. Overall, the underlying model is supported by these data.

It can also be concluded, if one accepts the model and disregards the S0 point as distorted by pattern matching, that the time to move from a node to its superset is on the order of 75 msec, this figure being the average RT increase from P0 to P1, P1 to P2, and S1 to S2. The differences between S1 and P1 and between S2 and P2, which average to about 225 msec, represent the time it takes to retrieve a property from the node at the level where we assume it is stored.

We have assumed that retrieval of properties at a node and moving up to the superset of the node are parallel processes, but this was not a necessary assumption. In actual fact the computer realization of the model completes the search for properties at a node *before* moving up one level to its superset. If the property search is assumed to be complete before moving up to the next level, then the 75 msec would have to be divided into two processes: (a) The time spent searching for properties, and (b) the time to move up to the superset. If such an assumption is made, then there is no clear prediction as to whether the increases for P sentences should parallel the increases for S sentences. If, given an S-type sentence, the S could dispense with process (a) above, then the slope of the curve for S sentences would be less than for P sentences; if he could not, then the prediction of two parallel lines would still hold. However, the fact that the time attributable to retrieving a property from a node is much longer than the time to move from one node to the next suggests that the processing is in fact parallel. It is unlikely that a search of all the properties at a node could be completed before moving up to the next level in less than 75 msec, *if* it takes some 225 msec actually to retrieve a property when it is found at a node. This might be reasonable if most of the 225 msec was spent in verification or some additional process necessary when the search at a node is successful, but attributing most of the 225 msec to such a process involves the unlikely assumption that this process takes much longer for P sentences than for S sentences. If it were the same for both sentence types, then it would not contribute to the difference (the 225 msec) between their RTs.

Since any other systematic differences between sentence types might affect RTs, we did three further checks. We computed the average number of letters for each sentence type and also weighted averages of the word-frequencies based on the Thorndike-Lorge (1944) general count. Then we asked four Ss to rate how important each property was for the relevant instance or superset, e.g., how important it is for birds that they can fly. In general, we found no effects that could account for the differences in Figure 2 on the basis of sentence lengths, frequency counts, or subject ratings of importance. The only exception to this is that the higher frequency of superset words such as bird and animal in the predicates of S1 and S2 sentences may have lowered the averages for S1 and S2 sentences relative to those for P sentences.

Deciding a Sentence is False

There are a number of conceivable strategies or processes by which a person might decide a sentence is false. All of these involve a search of memory; they fall into two classes on the basis of how the search is assumed to terminate.

The Contradiction Hypothesis.   Under this hypothesis, false responses involve finding a contradiction between information stored in memory and what the statement says. For example, if the sentence is "Coca-cola is blue," the S searches memory until he finds a property of Coca-cola (that it is brown or caramel colored) which contradicts the sentence.

The Contradiction Hypothesis was tested by the construction of false sentences for Expt 2. We predicted that the RT increase from P0 to P1 found for true sentences might also be found for false sentences. The difference found was in the right direction, but it was negligibly small (7 msec). Similarly, it was thought that if Ss search for a contradiction, false S0 sentences should produce faster times than the false S1 sentences since there is one less link in the path between the two nodes for an S0 sentence. (This can be seen by comparing the path in Figure 1 between canary and ostrich as in S0 sentences to the path between canary and fish as in S1 sentences.) The difference turned out to be in the opposite direction by 59 msec on the average, $t(7) = 2.30$, $p < .1$. If anything, one should conclude from the false S0 and S1 sentences in Expt 2 that the closer two nodes are in memory, the longer it takes to decide that they are not related in a stated manner.

The Unsuccessful Search Hypothesis. This is a generalization of what Sternberg (1966) calls the "self-terminating search," one of the two models he considered with regard to his RT studies of short-term memory search. Under this hypothesis an S would search for information to decide that a given sentence is true, and, when the search fails, as determined by some criterion, he would respond false. One possible variation, suggested by the longer RTs for false responses, would be that Ss search memory for a fixed period of time, responding true at any time information is found that confirms the statement is true, and responding false if nothing is found by the end of the time period. Such a hypothesis should lead to smaller standard deviations for false sentences than for true sentences, but the opposite was found for Expt 2, where it could be checked most easily.

The Search and Destroy Hypothesis. We developed another variation of the Unsuccessful Search Hypothesis after the Contradiction Hypothesis proved unsatisfactory and Ss had been interrogated as to what they thought they were doing on false sentences. Under this hypothesis we assume the S tries to find paths through his memory which connect the subject and predicate of the sentence (e.g., the path "canary →bird→animal→has skin" connects the two parts of "A canary has skin"). Whenever he finds such a path he must check to see if it agrees with what is stated in the sentence. When the S has checked to a certain number of levels or "depth" (Quillian, 1967), all connections found having been rejected, the S will then respond false. Under this hypothesis, the times for false sentences will be longer, in general, and highly variable depending upon how many connective paths the S has to check out before rejecting the statement. For instance, assuming people know Coca-cola comes in green bottles, a statement such as "Coca-cola is blue" would on the average take less time than "Coca-cola is green." This is because the S would have to spend time checking whether or not the above path between Coca-cola and green (i.e., that its bottles are green) corresponds to the relation stated in the sentence.

This hypothesis would explain the longer times in Expt 2 for sentences such as "A canary is an ostrich" as compared with "A canary is a fish" in terms of the greater number of connections between canary and ostrich that presumably would have to be checked out. This difference in the number of connections would derive from the greater number of properties that are common to two nodes close together in the network, such as canary and ostrich, than are common to nodes further apar and at different levels, such as canary and fish.

Finding contradictions can be included in this hypothesis, as is illustrated with "Gin is wet." Here the S might make a connection between gin and wet through the path "gin is dry and dry is the opposite of wet." Seeing the contradiction, he rejects this as a basis for responding true, but continues to search for an acceptable path. In this example, if he searches deep enough, he will find the path "gin is liquor, and liquor is liquid, and liquid is wet" which is, in fact, what the sentence requires. The point we want to emphasize here is that even though a contradiction can be used to reject a path, it cannot be used to reject the truth of a statement.

There are certainly other possible hypotheses, and it is possible that a combination of this hypothesis with the Contradiction Hypothesis may be necessary to explain false judgments. Needless to say, the process by which a person decides that a statement is false does not seem to be very simple.

Conclusion

In a computer system designed for the storage of semantic information, it is more economical to store generalized information with superset nodes, rather than with all the individual nodes to which such a generalization might apply. But such a storage system incurs the cost of additional processing time in retrieving information. When the implications of such a model were tested for human Ss using well-ordered hierarchies that are part of the common culture, there was substantial agreement between the predictions and the data.

There is no clear picture that emerges as to how people decide a statement is false. Our current hypothesis, that people must spend time checking out any interpretations that are possible (see the discussion of the Search and Destroy Hypothesis), should be testable, but even corroborative evidence would not clear up many of the questions about such decisions.

The model also makes predictions for other RT tasks utilizing such hierarchies. For instance, if Ss are given the task of deciding what common category two instances belong to, then RT should reflect the number of supersets the S must move through to make the decision. (Consider fish and bird, vs. shark and bird, vs. shark and canary; see Figure 1). Such RT differences should parallel those in our data. Furthermore, if utilizing a particular path in retrieval increases its accessibility temporarily, then we would expect prior exposure to "A canary is a bird" to have more effect in reducing RT to "A canary can fly" than to "A canary can sing." There are many similar experiments which would serve to pin down more precisely the structure and processing of human semantic memory.

References

Quillian, M. R. Word concepts: A theory and simulation of some basic semantic capabilities. *Behavioral Sci.*, 1967, **12**, 410–430.
Quillian, M. R. The Teachable Language Comprehender: A simulation program and theory of language. *Communications Assn. Comp. Mach.*, 1969.

Smith, E. E. Effects of familiarity on stimulus recognition and categorization. *J. exp. Psychol.*, 1967, **74,** 324–332.

Smith, E. E. Choice reaction time: An analysis of the major theoretical positions. *Psychol. Bull.*, 1968, **69,** 77–110.

Sternberg, S. High-speed scanning in human memory. *Science*, 1966, **153,** 652–654.

Thorndike, E. L. and Lorge, I. *The teacher's word book of 30,000 words.* New York: Columbia Univ. Press, 1944.

SEMANTIC DISTANCE
AND THE VERIFICATION OF SEMANTIC RELATIONS

Lance J. Rips, Edward Shoben, and Edward E. Smith

An alternative to the network models of semantic memory is highlighted in the following selection by Lance J. Rips, Edward J. Shoben, and Edward E. Smith (1973). In this study, subjects answered a series of questions of the form "An S is a P" by pressing a true or false button as soon as the sentence appeared on a screen. For example, the S term could be a bird name such as bluejay or chicken or robin, whereas the P term could be a superset such as bird or a superset of the superset such as animal. Other items required subjects to judge whether or not certain animals such as sheep or cat or lion were members of a superset (mammal) or members of a second level superset (animal).

According to Collins and Quillian's model, the response time (RT) should be longer when the P term is animal than when it is a lower level such as bird or mammal. However, whereas this prediction was true for birds ("A robin is a bird" required less time than "A robin is an animal"), the reverse trend occurred for mammals ("A rabbit is a mammal" required *more* time than "A rabbit is an animal"). These results cast serious doubts on Collins and Quillian's idea that questions crossing three levels (rabbit to mammal to animal) should take more time than questions crossing just two levels (rabbit to mammal).

Rips, et al., suggested that subjects' responses depend not on some a priori logical hierarchy, but rather on how similar the two words are in the subject's own memory. Concepts that have many features in common should be very similar and are thus stored close to one another in memory, whereas concepts that share few features would be stored far apart. Apparently, most college students in the Rips study felt that rabbit had more in common with animal than with mammal. In order to test this idea, Rips asked a second group of subjects to *rate* pairs of words on the basis of how related the words were. Subjects rated all possible pairs of twelve types of birds and all possible pairs of twelve types of mammals, as well as the relatedness between each type of bird with the category "bird" and with the category "animal," and the relatedness between each type of mammal and the category "mammal" and with the category "animal." Using a scaling technique, these ratings were then converted into a two dimensional space such that the distance between each pair of terms corresponded to the average relatedness rating. The distance between each pair of concepts represented how many features they have in common. A third experiment was conducted to test the prediction that RT would be faster for shorter distances, and positive results were obtained: semantic distance (the distance between pairs) was, in fact, determined to be a good predictor of response time.

These results seem to cast some doubts on the network model proposed by Collins and Quillian, while at the same time providing better support for a semantic distance representation of semantic knowledge. In fact, the work of Collins and Quillian and of Rips, et al. provides examples that clarify Brown and McNeill's TOT phenomena by proposing specific, concrete models of the means by which semantic memory is organized. And finally, Collins and Loftus (1975) have since been able to incorporate many of the refinements suggested by Rips, et al., into a network model.

Current interest in how semantic relations are represented in memory has led to the use of tasks in which a pair of nouns is presented and the subject is required to make a rapid semantic decision about them. In one such task (Collins & Quillian, 1969), the subject verifies statements of the form "An S is a P" (such as, A robin is a bird), where S and P, the two nouns of interest, serve as subject and predicate noun, respectively. In this kind of paradigm it is possible to compare sentences that use the same subject noun but different predicate nouns, P_i and P_j, where P_i is a subset of P_j (for example, A robin is a bird vs A robin is an animal). The finding resulting from such a comparison is that the statement involving the subset predicate (bird) is verified faster than that containing the superset predicate (*animal*). This finding has played a pivotal role in the development of semantic memory models and it is worthwhile to consider its implications in depth.

Semantic Distance

We shall refer to the above finding as the subset effect, but, as we shall try to make clear, it may be more generally described as a semantic distance effect. By this we mean that when the subset was used as the predicate noun, the memorial representations of the subject and predicate nouns (*robin* and *bird*) were closer together in some underlying semantic structure than when the superset was used as the predicate noun. Using this terminology, the subset effect merely indicates that the time to confirm a semantic relation between two nouns increases with the semantic distance between them.

The benefit of describing the subset effect in terms of semantic distance is that it relates this effect to results obtained in other paradigms. Thus, Schaeffer and Wallace (1969) presented to a subject a pair of nouns and required him to decide whether both nouns were living things, while Meyer and Schvanaveldt (1971) presented a pair of letter strings and required him to determine whether both strings were words. Despite the fact that the former study necessitated a semantic judgment while the latter involved only a word–nonword decision, both studies found that the subject's positive response was faster when the nouns were highly related to one another (*lion* and *elephant*) than when they were not (*lion* and *daisy*). Again, the finding of interest may be described as showing that verification time increases with semantic distance. Indeed, this description covers numerous other findings on verification time (Collins & Quillian, 1970a; Meyer, 1970), and may be one of the most important generalizations to emerge from semantic memory studies.

Semantic Distance and Semantic Memory Models

One purpose of the present paper is to explicate the notion of semantic distance. In terms of current theory, there are two types of explanations to be considered, and they are derived from two types of semantic memory models—network models (Anderson, 1972; Collins & Quillian, 1969, 1970a, 1970b; Rumelhart, Lindsay, & Norman, 1972) and set-theoretic models (Meyer, 1970; Schaeffer & Wallace, 1970). Network models assume that words, or their counterparts, exist as independent units in semantic memory, connected in a network by labeled relations. For example, in Rumelhart *et al.* (1972), a proposition such as *A robin is a bird* is represented as two nodes, corresponding to *robin* and *bird*, and a relation between them, the *isa* relation. Higher-order superordinates, like *animal*, may be connected directly to *robin* by other *isa* relations, or indirectly through the intermediate node *bird*. In set models, concepts such as *robin*, *bird*, and *animal* are represented by a set of elements where these elements might be exemplars, attributes, subsets, or supersets of the concept (Meyer, 1970).

A second distinction that can be made between some of the models concerns the hypothesized locus of semantic distance effects, and this is of direct concern to the present paper. Collins and Quillian's (1969; 1970a) network model places semantic distance effects at a retrieval stage, while the set model of Schaeffer and Wallace (1970) attributes such effects to a subsequent comparison process. To see how this can be so, consider a network model and our sample statements *A robin is a bird* and *A robin is an animal*. If the connection between *robin* and *animal* is indirect (*robin* is connected to *animal* via the intermediate node *bird*) verification of the latter statement involves retrieval of two relations, while verification of the former involves retrieval of only one relation. If verification time increases with the number of relations that must be retrieved, then the former sentence would be verified faster than the latter one. Thus, this type of network model explains the subset effect via intermediate nodes, which can also be invoked to explain other semantic distance effects.

To illustrate how a set comparison model might explain semantic distance, suppose that the elements of such sets are exemplars. Then verification of *A robin is a bird* occurs when a comparison process indicates that each robin-exemplar matches some bird-exemplar. Similarly, verification of the statement *A robin is an animal* requires that each robin-exemplar match some animal-exemplar. Since there are more animal-exemplars than bird-exemplars, then, given specific assumptions about the comparison process, more comparisons would have to be made to verify the robin–animal relation. If verification time increases with the number of comparisons, the subset effect is predicted. Note that the critical component in this explanation is what Meyer (1970) has termed the category difference—the number of exemplars contained in the two concepts that are not shared by the concepts, that is, the amount of non-overlap between the concepts. Thus the notion of category difference accomplishes much of the theoretical work done by intermediate nodes in the Collins and Quillian (1969, 1970a) model, and we would argue that both concepts tap what we have called semantic distance.

The basic differences among these models, then, concern the nature of the underlying structural representation (networks vs sets) and where in the processing sequence certain effects can be placed (retrieval vs comparison). While these differences are important, we are, for now, primarily concerned with a major communality among these models. Specifically, the network and set models that have thus far been proposed tend to be constructed so that memory structure mirrors logical structure, and logically valid relations can be read directly from the structure of stored semantic information, that is, logical relations can be determined by checking either internode relations or category overlap. While any viable model of semantic memory must have some means of verifying logical relations, there are now indications that such verification is not accomplished by a direct reading of the memory structure. For one thing, these network and set models, without additional assumptions, do not predict any variations in the semantic distance between an instance and a category for the different instances of that category (since, for example, set-theoretically, all instances are equally good members of the category). Yet, definite inequalities in instance–category distance seem to exist at the psychological level. For example, Wilkins (1971) measured the conjoint frequency of instance–category pairs of the same category, where conjoint frequency is defined as the frequency with which an instance is given as an exemplar of a category in some previously obtained norms, and found that instance–category pairs of high conjoint frequency (for example, *robin-bird*) were responded to faster than comparable pairs of low conjoint frequency (*goose-bird*). Assuming that conjoint frequency may be equated with semantic distance, these results indicate that even with regard to the instances of a single category, verification time increases with semantic distance, where the latter cannot be derived from a logical structure. Also, Meyer (1970) has examined five different single-stage set models in which verification is determined by checking category overlap, and has shown that these models cannot explain differences in verification times that are obtained when the sizes of subset and superset categories are varied.

Overview of the Present Experiments

The above arguments suggest that many semantic distance effects cannot be readily explained by models in which memory structure mirrors logical structure. It remains to be determined what changes in semantic memory models would make them consistent with semantic distance effects, but to do this requires more information about the nature of semantic distance. Our approach to this problem is to measure semantic distance independently of verification times and then determine the extent to which semantic distance influences the verification of instance–category and interinstance relations in several tasks before relating it to the relevant models. In doing so we will study multiple instances of just a few categories rather than a few instances of many categories, since we are particularly interested in documenting within-category distance effects.

The specific purposes of the present experiments are as follows: Experiment I establishes categories in which either all (or almost all) instances show either the subset effect, or the reverse effect. The latter finding calls into question the predictive validity of current assumptions regarding intermediate nodes and category differences, since such assumptions would have to be substantially modified to account for this finding. Experiment II obtains ratings of semantic distances for many of the statements used in Experiment I, and demonstrates that these ratings can predict the previously obtained verification time differences. This establishes the predictive validity of the present approach to semantic distance, but tells us little about the psychological core of rated semantic distance.

TABLE 1

Classification of Type of Sentences Used in Experiment I

True sentences (72)
  Level 1 (36)
    An S_B is a bird (12)   An S_M is a mammal (12)   An S_C is a car (12)
  Level 2 (36)
    An S_B is an animal (12)   An S_M is an animal (12)   An S_C is a vehicle (12)
False sentences (64)
    An S_B is a mammal (8)   An S_M is a bird (8)   An S_C is a bird (4)
    An S_B is a car (6)   An S_M is a car (6)   An S_C is a mammal (4)
    An S_B is a vehicle (6)   An S_M is a vehicle (6)   An S_C is an animal (16)

Experiment I

METHOD

Materials. The items included 75 true and 67 false sentences, and all were of the form "An S is a P." The predicate nouns were the category names, *car, vehicle, bird, mammal,* and *animal,* while every subject noun was an instance of one of these categories. A classification of the sentences is given in Table 1. Here S_B is a type of bird, S_M a type of mammal, and S_C a type of car, while the numbers in parentheses indicate the number of different statements of the type shown. For example, for true sentences of the form "An S_B is a Bird," twelve different instances of the bird category were used. Level is used to refer to the inclusiveness of the predicate nouns in a classification of subsets and supersets; thus Level 1 sentences have the predicate nouns *bird, mammal,* or *car* while Level 2 sentences have *animal* or *vehicle* as predicate nouns. In addition to the sentences schematized in Table 1, there were three other true items (*A bird is an animal, A mammal is an animal,* and *A car is a vehicle,*) as well as three other false items (*A bird is a vehicle, A mammal is a vehicle,* and *A car is an animal*). All in all, there were 53 per cent true and 47 per cent false statements in a total of 142. Excluding the six additional sentences listed above, the words *bird, mammal, car,* and *vehicle* appeared equally often in true and false statements.

In choosing the instances, S_B S_M, and S_C, it was desirable that each instance be familiar to all subjects. To insure this, 19 students from an Introductory Psychology class were asked to list as many names of birds as they could within a 5-minute period, and the 12 most frequently listed items were used as S_B instances in the experiment. The 12 mammal instances used were taken from Henley (1969), who had used a procedure identical to that just described to select her items. Finally, the 12 car instances used were selected informally by choosing the most common makes from several different varieties — luxury, compact, and so on. (As will soon become clear, the car instances were less crucial than the animal instances to the present experiments.) The instances from all three categories are listed in the first column of Table 2. Each sentence was typed, in capital letters, on a 4 × 6 inch white card.

Procedure. The subject's task was to decide whether each sentence presented was true or false, and to indicate his decision by pressing either a True or a False button. For half the subjects the True button was on the right and the False button on the left, while the remaining subjects had the reverse assignment. All subjects were instructed to respond as quickly as possible without making errors.

Two random presentation orders of the 142 test sentences were used, with half the subjects receiving each order. The sequence of events on each trial was: (*a*) The onset of a warning light signaled that a test item would be presented in 2 seconds. (*b*) A sentence was presented in an exposure device that consisted of a half-silvered mirror illuminated from behind, and a Standard Electric Timer was started. (*c*) The subject's response terminated the sentence presentation and stopped the clock. (*d*) During the 7-second intertrial interval, the experimenter informed the subject if he had made an error. Preceding

TABLE 2

Subject Nouns (Instances) and Mean Reaction Times (in msec) for True Sentences in Experiment I

Subject noun	Level 1 predicate noun	Level 2 predicate noun	Difference (Level 2 – Level 1)
	Bird	Animal	
Bluejay	1364	1455	91
Cardinal	1383	1584	201
Chicken	1362	1463	101
Duck	1280	1339	59
Eagle	1309	1360	51
Goose	1350	1417	67
Hawk	1239	1726	487
Parakeet	1210	1398	188
Parrot	1284	1342	58
Pigeon	1214	1481	267
Robin	1346	1424	78
Sparrow	1339	1477	138
Category mean	*1307*	*1456*	*149*
	Mammal	Animal	
Bear	1318	1258	−60
Cat	1355	1278	−77
Cow	1258	1322	64
Deer	1342	1305	−37
Dog	1466	1279	−187
Goat	1442	1315	−127
Horse	1356	1296	−60
Lion	1318	1244	−74
Mouse	1440	1288	−152
Pig	1476	1268	−208
Rabbit	1418	1290	−128
Sheep	1266	1250	−16
Category mean	*1371*	*1283*	*−88*
	Car	Vehicle	
Cadillac	1303	1490	187
Continental	1362	1553	191
Corvette	1292	1446	154
Dodge	1208	1278	70
Edsel	1232	1445	213
Model T	1215	1522	307
Porsche	1348	1395	47
Rolls	1160	1286	126
Studebaker	1318	1405	87
Toyota	1320	1136	−184
Triumph	1256	1227	−29
Volkswagen	1202	1380	178
Category mean	*1268*	*1380*	*112*

the test trials were 12 practice trials, in which the subject and predicate nouns were drawn from categories other than those used on the test trials.

    Subjects.   The subjects were 12 Stanford University undergraduates, six male and six female, who were paid for their participation.

Results

The overall error rate was 4 per cent and the results of major interest were the reaction times, RTs, for correct True responses. The second and third columns of Table 2 present mean True RT as a function of the level of the predicate noun, while the final column indicates whether the subset effect obtained (Level 2 RT greater than Level 1 RT) for each instance. It should be noted that three True statements are not represented in the table, namely *A bird (mammal) is an animal* and *A car is a vehicle.* Since subjects did not expect to see words frequently used as predicate nouns in the subject position, the RTs for these statements were extremely long and consequently they have been excluded from the analysis.

    Table 2 shows that for the birds and cars categories, the subset effect obtains for all but two instances. On the other hand, all but one of the mammal instances show the opposite effect! Within each category the difference due to levels is significant by a sign test; $p < .01$ in all cases. An analysis of variance was also performed on the logarithmic transformation of all the mean True RTs (logarithmic transforms being used to eliminate the correlation between mean and variance), with the exception of the RTs to statements involving *hawk* and *Triumph* since these statements contained some ambiguity (that is, a Hawk is a type of car and a Triumph may be considered to be a motorcycle rather than a car). This analysis indicated that there was no effect due to categories [$F(2, 30) = 2.02, p > .10$]; that there was an overall levels effect, as Level 1 nouns were responded to faster than Level 2 nouns [$F(1, 30) = 12.08, p < .01$]; and that the interaction between categories and levels was significant [$F(2,30) = 9.15, p < .01$], which reflects the fact that the subset effect obtained for birds and vehicles but the reverse was true for mammals.

    The finding of a reverse subset effect is quite similar to results reported by Collins and Quillian (1970b; 1971) in two recent experiments. In their first study they found that a subject could decide whether or not instances were animals as quickly as he could make comparable decisions for birds; that is, there was no subset effect. But different instances were confounded with different categories. In Collins and Quillian's second study, which was brought to our attention after the completion of the present experiment, *mammal* was used as one of the target categories, and, like the present experiment, a reverse subset effect obtained for this category. This effect, taken at face value, is evidence that memory structure does not mirror logical structure. Further evidence for this point is given by the result that, within both the birds and mammals category, there are significant RT differences among the various instance-superordinate statements: for the bird instances, $\chi_r^2(10) = 51.4, p < .01$, and for the mammal instances, $\chi_r^2 (10) = 45.2, p < .01$. That is, contrary to a set-theoretic perspective, not all instances were equally good members of a category.

There are, however, three potential problems with drawing strong conclusions from the reverse subset effect. The first difficulty is that the effect may really be due to frequency (Freedman & Loftus, 1971). That is, statements containing *mammal* may have been responded to slower than statements containing *animal* because the former word is far less frequent than the latter. But two findings argue against this frequency argument: (a) The word *bird* is also less frequent than *animal*, yet statements involving *bird* were verified faster than those including *animal*; and (b) For statements dealing with birds and mammals, there was no correlation between a statement's True RT and the sum of the frequencies (Kucera & Francis, 1967) of the two nouns in that statement [$r(42) = .09, p > .10$]. (Statements dealing with vehicles were excluded from this computation since most of our instances had no entries in the frequency norms.) The second problem with making inferences from the reverse subset effect is that this effect may be a rare one, perhaps unique to mammals and not generalizable to other categories. But recent data by Loftus and Scheff (1971) indicate that this phenomenon is, in fact, quite widespread. Loftus and Scheff obtained norms by instructing subjects to list three superordinates for each of 50 instances. Considering only the two most frequently named superordinates for each instance, the logically immediate superordinate was actually given less frequently than the higher-level superordinate in 23 cases. Further, Loftus (in press) has shown that these norms predict RTs in a verification task somewhat similar to our own. The final problem in interpreting the reverse subset effect concerns the linguistic status of the word *animal*. Specifically, this word may be used in two senses, a general one in which it is the direct superordinate of the categories mammals and birds, and a more restricted sense in which it may be roughly synonymous to mammals (Deese, 1965) or perhaps even a subset of mammals. Again, one may take this observation to question the generality of the present results, but once more there is independent evidence that this phenomenon is widespread. For example, Clark (in press) has provided an extensive analysis of spatial adjectives that can be used in either a general (unmarked) or a restricted (marked) sense. Further, Lehrer (1969, 1970) has discussed marked and unmarked meanings of certain classes of nouns and verbs. In particular, Lehrer (1970) points out that the noun *fish* has an unmarked sense, corresponding to "water animal" and a marked sense, corresponding to the biological class "Pisces." *Bird* can also be given a double interpretation, though this is more difficult in the case of *mammal*. Thus, it is doubtful that the reverse subset effect is due to the use of words with two interpretations (see also later discussion in this paper).

Finally, some comment should be made about False RTs for statements involving bird and mammal instances. Recall that the False items (in Table 1) were constructed so that the subject and predicate nouns were either both from the animal domain (*A robin is a mammal* or *A bear is a bird*), or from different domains (*A robin is a car* or *A bear is a car*). The basic finding of interest was that False RT was shorter when the nouns were from different domains (1308 msec) than when they were both from the animal domain (1582 msec) [$F(1, 24) = 23.50, p < .01$]. Moreover, this effect was greater for items that contained bird instances than for those containing mammal instances [$F(1, 24) = 8.17, p < .01$]. This interaction was almost entirely due to the fact that False RT was far longer for statements pairing a bird instance with the word *mammal* (1762 msec) than for statements that combined a mammal with the word *bird* (1401 msec); also, the error rate for the bird instance-mammal statements, 25 per cent, was more than an order of magnitude greater than the average error rate for the other types of statements, approximately 1.5 per cent. The implications of these results are as follows: (*a*) The basic finding indicates that False RT is shorter for unrelated than for related noun pairs; this result, which has been obtained by several other investigators (Collins & Quillian, 1970a; Schaeffer & Wallace, 1970), may be construed as a semantic distance effect for False RT, where False RT tends to decrease with increasing distance. (*b*) The fact that this effect was greater when the word *mammal* was involved again attests to the difficulty subjects have in verifying relations about this concept.

Experiment II

The purpose of Experiment II was to obtain semantic distance ratings of the subject–predicate noun pairs used in Experiment I. These ratings were then used to account for the True RTs of Experiment I and were also subjected to a multidimensional scaling analysis.

METHOD

Materials and procedure. There were two conditions, corresponding to whether subjects rated the semantic distance of mainly bird instances, the Birds condition, or of mainly mammal instances, the Mammals condition. In both conditions the subject was given a 16 page booklet, each page containing a standard word and a group of comparison words, and was instructed to indicate the degree of relatedness, on a 4-point scale, between the standard word and each comparison word.

Consider first the Birds condition. In the first 12 pages of the booklet each of the bird instances used in Experiment I appeared as a standard word, while the comparison words on each page were the 11 remaining bird instances. The order of these 12 pages was randomized anew for each subject. The data from these pages yield a full matrix of rated semantic distances for birds that can be used as an intact proximity matrix for purposes of multidimensional scaling. In the last four pages of the booklet the words *bird, mammal,* and *animal* appeared as standard words, *animal* appearing on two different pages. The comparison words for each of these four pages included the appropriate group of bird or mammal instances, that is, the 12 bird instances were the comparison words for *bird*, the mammal instances were the comparison words for *mammal*, and the bird and mammal instances each served as comparison words for *animal*. Also, when *bird* or *mammal* was the standard word, *animal* appeared as a comparison word; when *animal* was the standard, *bird* or *mammal* was contained in the comparison set. The ratings from these last four pages yield sets of rated semantic distances for instance–category statements — one for bird instances rated with respect to *bird* and *animal* and one for mammal instances rated with respect to *mammal* and *animal*. These ratings can be related to the True RTs obtained in Experiment I.

The booklet for the Mammals condition was similar to that described above, except that in the first 12 pages each of the mammal names was used as a standard word and the comparison words were the remaining mammals. The last four pages of the booklet were identical to the last four pages of the booklet in the Birds condition.

Subjects. The subjects were 24 Stanford University undergraduates, 15 males and nine females. Twelve served in the Birds condition and 12 in the Mammals condition.

Results and Discussion

Analysis of instance–category ratings. The ratings from the last four pages of the booklets in the Birds and Mammals conditions were combined to obtain the final ratings of semantic distances for instance–category pairs. As expected, these ratings closely paralleled the True RT results of Experiment I. That is, for all bird instances, except *chicken, duck,* and *goose*, the rated semantic distance between it and *bird* was less than that between the instance and *animal*; for every mammal instance, however, the rating between it and *mammal* was greater than that between the instance and *animal*. Thus the rating data show the same interaction as the True RT data of Experiment I (see Table 2). In order to assess quantitatively this parallelism between the ratings and the RTs, a correlation was computed between the transformed True RT and the rating for each statement represented in Table 2 that contains a bird or mammal instance. The resulting correlation was $r(42) = -.63, p < .01$. (The correlation was negative because high relatedness ratings were associated with the higher number on the 4-point scale.) When this correlation was computed separately for birds and mammals, the results were $r(20) = -.73, p < .01$, and $r(20) = -.52, p < .05$, respectively.

These results show that rated semantic distance can account for differences in verification times in cases where derivations based on notions of intermediate nodes and category distance either make no predictions (that is, within-category differences) or make faulty predictions (such as, mammals). This suggests that in those cases where these notions led to correct predictions (for example, birds), the results were really due to a confounding with rated semantic distance. If this suggestion is correct, one would expect that if differences in rated instance–category distance were removed, then the subset effect found with birds (and the reverse effect obtained with mammals) would disappear. Accordingly, all of the True RTs to bird and mammal statements that had been analyzed in Experiment I were reanalyzed by a new analysis of variance. In this analysis, rated distance functioned as a covarying factor. There were no significant effects: for the categories effect, $F(1, 19) < 1$; for the levels effect, $F(1, 19) < 1$; and for the interaction between categories and levels, $F(1, 19) = 3.63, p > .05$. Thus, the previously obtained subset effect with birds resulted only from variations in rated semantic distance.

General Discussion

A recapitulation of the major results seems in order. Experiment I used a true–false RT task and indicated that, even within the limited domain of animal terms, the subset effect occurred for one category, birds, but not for the other, mammals. Experiment II obtained ratings of semantic distance and revealed that the previously obtained subset effect only occurred when the rated semantic distance between the instance and its immediate superordinate was less than that between the instance and its higher level superordinate. This suggests that the subset effect was mediated by variations in rated distance. Moreover, even within a single category there was a correlation between True RT and rated distance.

The basic problem is: How should information about semantic distance be represented in semantic memory? It is possible to build semantic distance into network models in an ad hoc manner. Thus, we might revive Collins and Quillian's (1969) intermediate-node construct, but this time base it on a posteriori measures of semantic distance rather than a priori calculations. As one example, the rated semantic distance between *chicken* and *bird* was greater than that between *robin* and *bird*; this could be interpreted as indicating that there are more intermediate nodes between *chicken* and *bird* (such as, the node for *fowl*) than between *robin* and *bird*, which would explain why True RT was longer to the former pair than to the latter. Thus, in general, the semantic distance between an instance and a category reflects the number of intermediate nodes involved, and the latter determines verification time. A similar interpretation may be given to the finding that for most birds the distance between an instance and *bird* was less than that between the instance and *animal*. This simply means that *bird* typically functioned as an intermediate node between each bird instance and *animal*, as Collins and Quillian (1969) originally intended. Another finding was that for mammals, the distance between an instance and *mammal* was greater than that between the instance and *animal*. This would be taken to indicate that *animal* is actually an intermediate node between each mammal instance and *mammal*; but this interpretation raises a problem, for if it were valid, then people should erroneously verify *All animals are mammals* as a true statement, a possibility that seems most implausible. One can try to circumvent this problem by referring to our earlier argument that *animal* has two senses, one of which can function as an intermediate node between each mammal instance and *mammal* and a more general sense that can disconfirm *All animals are mammals*. But then there is need to further specify a decision rule that enables the subject to select the correct sense of *animal,* so that he may disconfirm the above statement but confirm *All mammals are animals*, and it is not at all clear how this can be done.

The revised intermediate-node hypothesis is more a description of the data than an explanation of it. This is also true of a second way of representing semantic distance in a network model, which is to assume that all pairs of memory nodes are linked by a single relation or path (see Smith *et al.*, 1972) and the length of a path represents both the internode semantic distance and the time needed to retrieve one node from the other. (Thus, length of a path may be thought of as an inverse measure of the strength of the relation depicted by the path.) This accounts for the correlation between distance and verification time, as well as many of our other findings, by fiat. It is worth noting, however, that this type of explanation differs from the intermediate-node hypothesis in that the present proposal assumes that distance (in the sense of length of a direct path) is the primary theoretical variable, while the earlier hypothesis assumes that distance is a derivative of a more fundamental variable (number of intermediate nodes).

Finally, some mention should be made of how an intermediate-node or direct-path model could accommodate our finding in Experiment I that False RT was faster for unrelated than related noun pairs. One possibility, in part based on Meyer's (1970) work, involves the assumption that there is a processing stage, prior to the one we have been considering, that determines the semantic distance between the noun pair. If this distance is greater than some criterion, then a False response is triggered without further processing, while if this distance is less than the criterion then the relevant relations must be retrieved by the processes we have considered thus far. Other related possibilities for explaining semantic distance effects on False RT in the context of a network model are discussed by Collins and Quillian (1970a).

Set-Comparison Models and the Present Results

In a set-comparison model each item is represented as a set of elements. Before endeavoring to represent distance information in this type of model some consideration must be given to the nature of the elements. Here we will concern ourselves only with the possibility that these elements are attribute-values or features, as this will permit us to explain both our analogy and RT results with the same theoretical mechanisms. In this case the distance between an instance and its category may be represented by the degree of feature overlap between the two. However, a problem still remains in specifying those features that function in a determination of degree of overlap. If these features are limited to those necessary for defining category membership, then all instances would be equally distant from the category, a possibility the present results argue strongly against. On the other hand, letting the functional features include all possible features of the item also runs into difficulties. Specifically, both *chicken* and *bird* share the features of being warm blooded and egglaying, as well as the features of being less than 20 feet tall, not horses, and examples used in this article; but surely the latter features should count less than the former in determining the distance of *chicken* from *bird*. Clearly, the set of functional features must lie between these two extremes; that is, the functional features must include those that strictly define the category membership plus some others that characterize most instances of the category, for example, a determinate size or degree of predacity.

Given this definition of functional features (that is, defining and characteristic features), a modification of the Meyer (1970) or Schaeffer and Wallace (1970) set-comparison models can now be shown to be consistent with the present study. We depart from these set models in assuming that all features can be treated as continuous variables like size (though we recognize that size and predacity probably take on more values than many other features, like animateness). We posit a two-stage comparison process, in which the first stage determines the degree to which all functional features are shared by an instance and a category. In the second stage, the defining features are discriminated from the characteristic ones, and a second comparison is made on the basis of the defining features alone. It is important to note that a second stage is often needed because the first stage merely determines overall similarity of functional features and does *not* yield information about which *specific* features (that is, defining or characteristic) are in fact similar.

A critical assumption in the present model is that in verification tasks, the second stage may be abbreviated or omitted entirely if first-stage processing indicates either a very high or very low degree of similarity of functional features. This assumption permits fast confirmations (or disconfirmations) of instance–category relations where first stage processing yields high (or low) similarity and consequently little or no second stage processing is required.

With semantic distance represented as the degree of similarity determined by first-stage processing, this model can easily handle the obtained findings for True RT. The subjects' distance ratings are based on the outcome of the first stage; and the correlation between distance and True RT follows from the assumptions that distance reflects functional feature similarity, which in turn governs the duration of second-stage processing and hence RT. The subset effect for birds means that there was greater similarity between the functional features of a bird instance and *bird* than between that instance and *animal*. Similarly, the reverse subset effect for mammals can be explained in terms of greater similarity between the functional features of a mammal instance and *animal* than between that instance and *mammal*. This, in turn, may be due to the subject having imperfect knowledge about the defining features of *mammal*, which means that some of these features cannot contribute to the overall similarity judgment in first-stage processing. Thus, we can account for our semantic distance findings mainly in terms of first-stage processing, for it is at this stage that memory structure deviates from logical structure. The use of derived distance and multidimensional information found in the analogy solutions is also easily reconcilable with this model. To solve each analogy the subject need merely determine the differences between the characteristic features of the first two terms and then select that alternative that differs from the third term in the same way. This model also leads to a natural explanation of why False RT was faster for unrelated than related noun pairs in Experiment I. Unrelated noun pairs would be more likely to yield a low degree of functional feature similarity in the first stage, and this will lead to abbreviated second-stage processing.

All in all, this feature comparison model seems more promising than the network models with regard to offering a feasible explanation of results such as the present ones. It is important to note that this model assumes that determinate values for size and predacity can be assigned to the superordinate terms *birds, mammal*, and *animal*. This conforms with our intuition that these category names describe some of their subsets better than others (see Heider, in press). For example, *robin* seems to be a better or more representative instance of birds than is *duck*. This notion appears to have broad implications. Thus, Bierwisch (1971) notes that sentences (a)–(c) are paraphrases:

(a) Those animals are big.
(b) Those animals are big for animals.
(c) Those animals are bigger than average animals.

This implies that sentences like (a), which employ relative adjectives (for example, *big, tall, high, long*), contain implicit comparisons to the average or most representative members of the class to which the subject noun belongs. The comparative construction in (c) is then close to the interpretation underlying (a) and (b). Furthermore, Lakoff (in press) points out that certain "hedges" (such as, the term *technically*) can be used acceptably only with instances of particular degrees of representativeness. For this reason, (d) is acceptable while (e) is not.

(d) A duck is technically a bird.
(e) A robin is technically a bird.

According to Lakoff, different hedges (as, *technically, strictly speaking, loosely speaking*) pick out different components of the category meaning an instance must possess, or not possess, if the hedge is to apply correctly. Lakoff represents these meaning components as dimensions in a vector space. These dimensions include both definitional properties as well as properties (like size) that are usual characteristics of the category. Like the comparison model suggested above, Lakoff's suggestion is consistent with the results of the present experiments. Lastly, Kahneman and Tversky (1972) have shown that in estimating the probability of an uncertain event, subjects tend to rely on how representative the event happens to be, where a representative event is defined, in part, as one that is similar in essential properties to its parent population. All in all, representativeness appears to be an important construct, and Experiments I and III, like the experiment of Heider (in press), demonstrate the importance of representativeness for sentence verification and word classification tasks.

References

Anderson, J. R. Fran. A simulation model of free-recall. In G. H. Bower (Ed.), *The psychology of learning and motivation*, Vol. 5. New York: Academic Press, 1972.

Battig, W. F., & Montague, W. E. Category norms for verbal items in 56 categories: A replication and extension of the Connecticut Category Norms. *Journal of Experimental Psychology Monograph*, 1969, **80** (3, Pt. 2).

Bierwisch, M. On classifying semantic features. In D. D. Steinberg & L. A. Jakobovits (Eds.), *Semantics: An introductory reader in philosophy, linguistics, and psychology*. Cambridge: University Press, 1971.

Carroll, J. D. & Chang, J. J. Analysis of individual differences in multidimensional scaling via an *n*-way generalization of "Eckart–Young" decomposition. *Psychometrika*, 1970, **36**, 283–319.

Clark, H. H. On the meaning and use of prepositions. *Journal of Verbal Learning and Verbal Behavior*, 1968, **7**, 421–431.

Clark, H. H. Semantics and comprehension. In T. A. Sebeok (Ed.), *Current trends in linguistics*, Vol. 12. The Hague: Mouton, in press.

Collins, A. M. & Quillian, M. R. Retrieval time from semantic memory. *Journal of Verbal Learning and Verbal Behavior*, 1969, **8**, 241–248.

Collins, A. M. & Quillian, M. R. Experiments on semantic memory and language comprehension. In L. W. Gregg (Ed.), *Cognition in leaning and memory*. New York: Wiley, 1970. (a)

Collins, A. M. & Quillian, M. R. Does category size affect categorization time? *Journal of Verbal Learning and Verbal Behavior*, 1970, **9**, 432–438. (b)

Collins, A. M. & Quillian, M. R. Categories and subcategories in semantic memory. Paper presented at the annual meeting of Psychonomic Society, St. Louis, MO, 1971.

Deese, J. *The structure of associations in language and thought*. Baltimore, MD: Johns Hopkins Press, 1965.

Fillenbaum, S. & Rapaport, A. *Structures in the subjective lexicon*. New York: Academic Press, 1971.

Freedman, J. L. & Loftus, E. F. Retrieval of words from long-term memory. *Journal of Verbal Learning and Verbal Behavior*, 1971, **10**, 107–115.

Heider. E. R. On the internal structure of perceptual and semantic categories. In T. M. Moore (Ed.), *Cognitive development and acquisition of language*. New York: Academic Press, in press.

Henley, N. M. A psychological study of the semantics of animal terms. *Journal of Verbal Learning and Verbal Behavior*, 1969, **8**, 176–184.

Kahneman, D. & Tversky, A. Subjective probability: A judgment of representativeness. *Cognitive Psychology*, 1972, **3**, 430–454.

Kučera, H., & Francis, W. N. *Computational analysis of present-day American English*, Providence, RI: Brown University Press, 1967.

Lakoff, G. Hedges: A study in meaning criteria and the logic of fuzzy concepts. *Papers from the Eighth Regional Meeting, Chicago Linguistics Society*, Chicago: University of Chicago Linguistics Department, in press.

Lehrer, A. Semantic cuisine. *Journal of Linguistics*, 1969, **5**, 38–56.

Lehrer, A. Interdeterminancy in semantic description. *Glossa*, 1970, **4**, 87–110.

Loftus, E. F. Category dominance, instance dominance, and categorization time. *Journal of Experimental Psychology*, in press.

Loftus, E. F., & Scheff, R. W. Categorization norms for 50 representative instances. *Journal of Experimental Psychology*, 1971, **91**, 355–364.

Luce, R. D. *Individual choice behavior*. New York: Wiley, 1959.

McNemar, Q. *Psychological statistics*. New York: Wiley, 1962.

Meyer, D. E. On the representation and retrieval of stored semantic information. *Cognitive Psychology*, 1970, **1,** 242–300.

Meyer, D. E. & Schvaneveldt, R. W. Facilitation in recognizing pairs of words. *Journal of Experimental Psychology*, 1971, **90,** 227–234.

Rumelhart, D. E. & Abrahamson, A. A. Toward a theory of analogical reasoning. Center for Human Information Processing, Technical Report No. 18, University of California at San Diego, 1971.

Rumelhart, D. E., Lindsay, P. H., & Norman, D. A. A process model for long-term memory. In E. Tulving & W. Donaldson (Eds.), *Organization and Memory*, New York: Academic Press, 1972.

Schaeffer, B. & Wallace, R. Semantic similarity and the comparison of word meanings. *Journal of Experimental Psychology*, 1969, **82,** 343–346.

Schaeffer, B. & Wallace, R. The comparison of word meanings. *Journal of Experimental Psychology*, 1970, **86,** 144–152.

Smith, E. E., Haviland, S. E., Buckley, P. B., & Sack, M. Retrieval of artificial facts from long-term memory. *Journal of Verbal Learning and Verbal Behavior*, 1972, **11,** 583–593.

Snedecor, G. W. & Cochran, W. G. *Statistical methods*. Ames: Iowa State University Press, 1967.

Wilkins, A. T. Conjoint frequency, category size, and categorization time. *Journal of Verbal Learning and Verbal Behavior.*, 1971, **10,** 382–385.

11/ Memory Processes: Stage Analysis of Intellectual Tasks

The following answers were given by student A in the arithmetic lesson:

$$\begin{array}{cccc} 12 & 26 & 42 & 56 \\ -\ 3 & -13 & -25 & -17 \\ \hline 11 & 23 & 23 & 31 \end{array}$$

Another student, B, gave the following answers to the same lesson:

$$\begin{array}{cccc} 12 & 36 & 42 & 56 \\ -\ 3 & -13 & -25 & -17 \\ \hline 11 & 23 & 117 & 319 \end{array}$$

Finally, a third student, C, gave the following answers:

$$\begin{array}{cccc} 12 & 36 & 42 & 56 \\ -\ 3 & -13 & -25 & -17 \\ \hline 11 & 23 & 27 & 49 \end{array}$$

One way of analyzing the performance of these students is to say that each missed three problems out of four. However, this "behavioral" description fails to convey what the students actually "know" about subtraction. If you carefully examine the pattern of errors for each student, you may notice that a given student behaves consistently. For example, what do you think student A will answer for $62 - 26 =$ ___? (44). What will student B or C answer? More powerful predictions about the students' performances and more information about "what" they have learned is available if one applies a *cognitive* description of the chain of mental steps followed by each student.

In the previous section we examined the way in which semantic information, such as knowledge about the characteristics of birds or about a written passage, is stored in memory. The present section deals with algorithmic knowledge—knowledge about procedures—and how it is stored in memory and used to answer questions. The basic method of building cognitive stage models is to analyze an intellectual task into its parts, and then to represent the task as a series of stages. Each stage may involve a decision, such as "Is the top number in the column larger than the bottom number?" or a procedure to perform, such as "Subtract the bottom number in the column from the top number in the column."

This section provides an introduction to stage models by Miller, Galanter, and Pribram (1960), and two applications—one showing how performance on addition problems can be analyzed into a stage model (Parkman and Groen, 1972) and one showing how logical reasoning can be analyzed into a stage model (Potts, 1972).

Stage analysis is used because it allows researchers to more precisely describe "what is going on inside the subject's head." Like models of semantic memory, stage models allow for detailed predictions concerning human performance on intellectual tasks. Also, they allow for alternative theories to be tested against one another.

THE UNIT
OF ANALYSIS

George A. Miller, Eugene Galanter, and Karl H. Pribram

The first paper in this chapter is excerpted from a classic book by Miller, Galanter, and Pribram, entitled *Plans and the Structure of Behavior* (1960). In the text reproduced below, the authors argue for the use of stage models to represent what a person knows about an intellectual skill. This influential book by Miller, et al., is often credited as re-establishing interest in stage models in modern cognitive psychology.

First, Miller, et al., suggest that the traditional behaviorist concept of *reflex arc*—the idea that a given stimulus will evoke a given response—is too limited to be useful as the *unit of analysis* of behavior. They maintain, instead, that the basic unit of behavior must involve a *recursive feedback loop*—the idea that a person tests the environment, then performs a behavior based on that test, then tests again to see if the environment is now in the desired state, and stops only when this is found to be the case. Next, Miller offers the TOTE unit as the basic unit of behavior. This representation contains two main stages, a *test* and an *operate* phase, whereby a person tests the environment and performs the operation only if there is an incongruity between the observed state of the world and the desired state. And finally, Miller shows how complex skills may be represented as a series of TOTE units.

The importance of this paper rests in the idea that intellectual skills may be represented in more detail, such as in flow charts, than is achieved by the traditional S–R theories. Although new models of representation have evolved since the introduction of the TOTE, all still share the idea of representing skills as a series of stages.

The elementary unit that modern, experimental psychologists generally select for their analysis of behavior is the *reflex*. "The isolation of a reflex," B. F. Skinner tells us, "is the demonstration of a predictable uniformity in behavior. In some form or other it is an inevitable part of any science of

Adapted from PLANS AND THE STRUCTURE OF BEHAVIOR by George A. Miller, Eugene Galanter and Karl H. Pribram. Copyright © 1960 by Holt, Rinehart and Winston, Inc. Reprinted by permission of Holt, Rinehart and Winston.

behavior. . . . A reflex is not, of course, a theory. It is a fact. It is an analytical unit, which makes the investigation of behavior possible."

There is some reason to think that the reflex unit has been vastly overrated and that a good many psychologists would like to get out from under it if they could. The reflex arc may have been helpful in getting psychology started along scientific paths, but the suspicion has been growing in recent years that the reflex idea is too simple, the element too elementary.

The neural mechanism involved in reflex action cannot be diagrammed as a simple reflex arc or even as a chain of stimulus-response connections. A much more complex kind of monitoring, or testing, is involved in reflex action than the classical reflex arc makes any provision for. The only conditions imposed upon the stimulus by the classical chain of elements are the criteria implicit in the thresholds of each element; if the distal stimulus is strong enough to surmount the thresholds all along the arc, then the response must occur. In a sense, the threshold is a kind of test, too, a condition that must be met, but it is a test of strength only. And it must have encouraged psychologists to believe that the only meaningful measurement of a reflex was its strength (probability, magnitude, or latency).

The threshold, however, is only one of many different ways that the input can be tested. Moreover, the response of the effector depends upon the outcome of the test and is most conveniently conceived as an effort to modify the outcome of the test. The action is initiated by an "incongruity" between the state of the organism and the state that is being tested for, and the action persists until the incongruity (i.e., the proximal stimulus) is removed. The general pattern of reflex action, therefore, is to test the input energies against some criteria established in the organism, to respond if the result of the test is to show an incongruity, and to continue to respond until the incongruity vanishes, at which time the reflex is terminated. Thus, there is "feedback" from the result of the action to the testing phase, and we are confronted by a recursive loop. The simplest kind of diagram to represent this conception of reflex action—an alternative to the classical reflex arc—would have to look something like Figure 1.

Obviously, the reflex is not the unit we should use as the element of behavior: the unit should be the feedback loop itself. If we think of the Test-Operate-Test-Exit unit—for convenience, we shall call it a TOTE unit—as we do of the reflex arc, in purely anatomical terms, it may de-

FIGURE 1

The TOTE unit

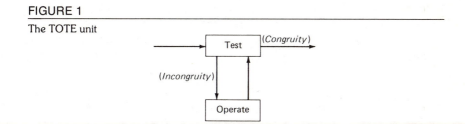

FIGURE 2

Hammering as a hierarchy

scribe reflexes, but little else. That is to say, the reflex should be recognized as only one of many possible actualizations of a TOTE pattern. The next task is to generalize the TOTE unit so that it will be useful in a majority—hopefully, in all—of the behavioral descriptions we shall need to make.

We should note well the construction of a "two-phase" TOTE unit out of two simpler TOTE units. Consider hammering a nail as an example. As a Plan, of course, hammering has two phases, lifting the hammer and then striking the nail. We could represent it by a tree, or hierarchy, as in Figure 2. If we ask about details, however, the representation of hammering in Figure 2 as a simple list containing two items is certainly too sketchy. It does not tell us, for one thing, how long to go on hammering. What is the "stop rule"? For this, we must indicate the test phase, as in Figure 3. The diagram in Figure 3 should indicate that when control is transferred to the TOTE unit that we are calling "hammering," the hammering continues until the head of the nail is flush with the surface of the work. When the test indicates that the nail is driven in, control is transferred elsewhere. Now, however, we seem to have lost the hierarchical structure. The hierarchy is recovered when we look at the box labeled "hammer," for there we find two TOTE units, each with its own test, as indicated in Figure 4. When the pair of TOTE units combined in Figure 4 are put inside the operational phase in Figure 3, the result is the hierarchical Plan for hammering nails that is shown in Figure 5.

If this description of hammering is correct, we should expect the sequence of events to run off in this order: Test nail. (Head sticks up.) Test hammer. (Hammer is down.) Lift hammer. Test hammer. (Hammer is up.) Test hammer. (Hammer is up.) Strike nail. Test hammer. (Hammer is down.) Test nail. (Head sticks up.) Test hammer. And so on, until the test of the nail reveals that its head is flush with the surface of the work, at

FIGURE 3

Hammering as a TOTE UNIT

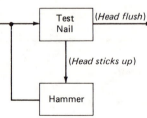

FIGURE 4

Dashed line indicates how two simple TOTE units are connected to form the operational phase of the more complicated TOTE unit in Figure 3.

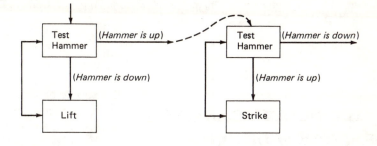

which point control can be transferred elsewhere. Thus the compound of TOTE units unravels itself simply enough into a coordinated sequence of tests and actions, although the underlying structure that organizes and co-ordinates the behavior is itself hierarchical, not sequential.

It may seem slightly absurd to analyze the motions involved in hammering a nail in this explicit way, but it is better to amuse a reader than to confuse him. It is merely an illustration of how several simple TOTE units, each with its own test-operate-test loop, can be embedded in the operational phase of a larger unit with its particular test-operate-test loop. Without such an explicit illustration it might not have been immediately obvious how these circles within circles could yield hierarchical trees.

More complicated Plans—Woodworth refers to them as "polyphase motor units"—can be similarly described as TOTE units built up of sub-plans that are themselves TOTE units. A bird will take off, make a few wing strokes, glide, brake with its wings, thrust its feet forward, and land on the limb. The whole action is initiated as a unit, is controlled by a single Plan, yet is composed of several phases, each involving its own Plan, which may in turn be comprised of subplans, etc.

FIGURE 5

The hierarchical Plan for hammering nails

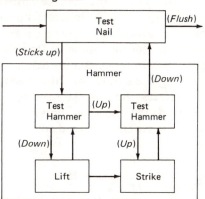

Reference

Skinner, B. F. *The Behavior of Organisms.* New York: Appleton-Century-Crofts, 1938, p. 9.

A CHRONOMETRIC ANALYSIS
OF SIMPLE ADDITION

Guy J. Groen and John M. Parkman

The following paper examines the use of stage models to represent and test children's knowledge about the addition algorithm. Guy J. Groen and John M. Parkman (1972) examine five different algorithms, all of which are capable of generating the correct answer for simple one-digit addition problems of the form, $m + n =$ ____. The general procedure for all five models is quite simple: first a counter is set to some number, then it is incremented by ones until some condition is reached, and finally, the answer is given.

In a problem like $2 + 6 =$ ____, model 1 requires that the counter is first set to zero; then it is incremented by ones for m (2) times and then for n (6) times, or 8 times in all. Thus, time to respond should depend on how high the answer is: larger answers (such as 9) require more time than smaller answers (such as 2). Model 2 requires the subject to set the counter to m (2) and then increment it n (6) times. Here, problems with larger values of n should take longer when the value m is irrelevant. Model 3 is the reverse of model 2; in this case, larger values of m should result in longer solution times when the value of n is irrelevant. Model 4 requires that the subject set the counter to the smaller of the two addends (in this case 2 is smaller) and then increment the counter based on the larger number (in this case, 6 times). Thus, response time should increase for larger "large" numbers. Model 5 requires that the subject set the counter to the larger of the two addends (6) and then increment the counter (twice, in this case) so that response time depends on the value of the smaller of the two addends.

In order to test these five models, Groen and Parkman asked a group of first graders to solve simple addition problems. All 55 single-digit problems of the form $m + n =$ _____ were given to all subjects and the time to respond for each problem was recorded. Subjects saw the problems on a screen and responded by pressing one of ten buttons labeled 0 through 9. The response times for the largest percentage of children in the group most closely matched the predictions of the fifth model. For problems in which the smaller addend was 1, response time was fastest (as in $2 + 1$, $3 + 1$, $4 + 1$, and so on); more time was required when the smaller addend was 2 (as in $2 + 2$, $2 + 3$, $2 + 4$, and so on); response times were longer when the smaller addend was 3 (as in $3 + 3$); and the longest response times occurred when the smaller addend was 4 (as in $4 + 5$). However, the performance of some children fit the predictions of one of the other models more closely. In other words, although most students seemed to use the fifth model, there were nevertheless consistent individual differences.

These results are noteworthy because they suggest that the same behavior can be supported by different solution algorithms. The results further provide an important demonstration of the way in which stage models can be used to test theories of "what is in the learner's memory." There are, of course, other analyses of arithmetic tasks that use similar methods (see Resnick, 1976).

In recent years, it has become common to make a distinction between two kinds of processes in long-term memory: reproductive processes, which are concerned with the retrieval of stored facts, and reconstructive processes, which are concerned with the generation of facts on the basis of stored rules. A principal reason for the emergence of these reconstructive theories is the fact that reproductive theories do not appear to provide a satisfactory explanation of the kind of everyday remembering studied, for example, by Bartlett (1932). Another is that constructive processes appear to play an important role in perception and language. Yet another is the implicit role of constructive processes in Piagetian theory. Unfortunately, most accounts of reconstructive processes have been somewhat metaphorical in their nature and have lacked the explicitness of current models of semantic memory based primarily on reproductive notions. A possible reason for this lack of explicitness, which is shared by many reproductive theories, has been suggested by Reitman (1970) who points out that most memory theories have been concerned with defining global functions rather than specific processes. Since memory may actually consist of a large number of heterogeneous processes, it may be more profitable to investigate the processes applicable to a highly limited task domain. The purpose of this paper is to examine the processes being used in one such limited task domain: the addition of two integers.

The addition of two single-digit numbers can be viewed as either a reproductive or a reconstructive process. Most frequently, it is viewed as the former, consisting of the retrieval of a stored number fact which has been previously learned as part of the addition table. Indeed, this assumption, which goes back at least as far as Thorndike (1922), forms one of the chief bases for the way arithmetic is taught, a child's ability to add two digits being viewed as evidence that he has memorized an association between the two digits and their sum. Although this assumption has never been examined empirically, there are commonsense grounds for rendering such a reproductive process plausible. For example, considerable time is devoted in elementary school to making children memorize the addition table, by means of such techniques as flash cards. Moreover, no effort is usually made to teach any specific algorithmic rule, such as is later taught in connection with the addition of two-digit numbers.

On the other hand, it is clear that addition is closely associated with some kind of counting process. Although a counting algorithm is almost never specifically taught,[1] addition is usually introduced by demonstrating, in some way, its relationship to counting. Also, children (and some adults) frequently add by overtly "counting on their fingers," despite the fact that behavior of this kind tends to be severely discouraged in the elementary school. In fact, many children actually learn to add by counting before they ever reach the elementary school. Clearly, adding by counting involves the application of a learned rule rather than the retrieval of a number fact. It is a reconstructive process.

There are two advantages to beginning an analysis of the processes used by individuals in solving simple addition problems with a consideration of possible counting models. The first is that given the current state of our knowledge of semantic memory, the possible range of counting models is considerably narrower than the possible range of memory models. The second is that it is a relatively simple matter to construct counting models that will predict systematic differences in reaction times to different problems. This is important because reaction time is the simplest dependent measure to use with problems of this type. Solutions to such problems are usually generated so rapidly that problem-solving protocols yield little insight into the process. Similarly, errors are infrequent enough, except with very young children, that adequate error analysis is not feasible.

A classical technique for inferring, from reaction time data, the nature of the processes involved in performing a simple task is the method of chronometric analysis, first proposed by Donders and more recently reformulated by Sternberg (1969a). Although this technique lapsed into disuse for many years, it has recently received a number of applications to the analysis of processes in pattern recognition (Posner, 1969), memory search (Sternberg, 1969b), and elementary deductive reasoning (Chase & Clark, 1971). It essentially consists of a set of techniques for partitioning reaction times into additive components. The simplest case occurs when a process

---

[1]An exception is the educational television program "Sesame Street."

can be decomposed into a number of identical steps. If this is the case, then it can easily be shown that under suitable statistical assumptions, the reaction time will be a linear function of the number of steps required to perform the task. The memory search processes considered by Sternberg are of this type, as are the counting models considered in the present paper.

Five Counting Models

For problems of the form $m + n$, where m and n are nonnegative integers, and the sum is less than or equal to 9, it is possible to distinguish between five different counting procedures that might be used to solve the problem. In order to distinguish between these procedures, it is convenient to consider a counter on which two operations are possible. One operation is setting the counter to a specified value. It is assumed that this automatically erases the previous value of the counter. The other operation is incrementing the value of the counter by one. The addition operation is performed by setting the counter to an appropriate number and then successively incrementing it by one a suitable number of times. This process is illustrated in Figure 1.

Using this counter, an addition problem can be solved in the following ways:

1. The counter is set to zero; both m and n are added in by increments of one.
2. The counter is set to m (the leftmost number); n (the rightmost number) is then added by increments of one.
3. The counter is set to n (the rightmost number); m (the leftmost number) is then added by increments of one.
4. The counter is set to the minimum of m and n. The maximum of m and n is then added by increments of one.
5. The counter is set to the maximum of m and n. The minimum of m and n is then added by increments of one.

In order to derive predictions from these five models, it is necessary to make two assumptions regarding the time required to perform the set-

FIGURE 1

A device which sets a counter to a and adds x to a by increments of one.

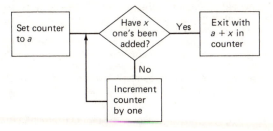

ting and incrementing operations: (*a*) The time required to set the counter is assumed to be a random variable *A* that is independent of the value to which the counter is set. (*b*) The time required to increment the counter by one is assumed to be a random variable *B* that is independent of the number of times the counter is incremented. Suppose that the counter is set to a certain value and then incremented *x* times by one. Then the total time *T* taken by the counter to perform these operations is given by the equation:

$$T = A + Bx \qquad [1]$$

If the counter is being used to solve an addition problem then, corresponding to the five models defined above, *x* is determined as follows:

Model 1. $x = m + n$
Model 2. $x = n$
Model 3. $x = m$
Model 4. $x = \max(m, n)$
Model 5. $x = \min(m, n)$

An Experimental Test of the Five Models[2]

This experiment was designed to evaluate the five counting models in a more adequate fashion. In particular, a wider range of problems was used. It also seemed desirable to provide a means of deciding whether or not subjects were using different processes. As a result, the experiment was designed so that each subject's data could be analyzed separately.

METHOD

The subjects consisted of 37 children (15 males and 22 females) in the first grade of an elementary school in a predominantly upper-middle-class community in the San Francisco Bay area. Their average age was 6 years 10 months, and their average Binet IQ was 125. The experiment was conducted toward the end of the school year, and all the subjects had been taught addition. Enquiries of the teachers revealed that none of the counting algorithms had been specifically taught.

The materials used as stimuli consisted of all 55 problems with a sum less than or equal to 9. The problems were presented as row-addition problems of the form $m + n$ =____, the subject's task being to find the missing number. Six different random presentation sequences, each containing exactly the same set of 55 problems, were prepared. The random ordering was constrained in such a way that the following sequences did not appear: two problems with the same answer; $m + n$ followed by $m + k$; $m + n$ followed by $k + n$.

The subject saw each problem projected onto a screen by means of a Carousel Projector. He had in front of him a response panel with a row of 10 buttons marked 0 through 9, and made his response by pressing one of these buttons. He was allowed as long as necessary to make the response, and there was an interval of 2½ seconds between the subject's response and the presentation of the next problem. During this interval, the correct answer was displayed on the screen. Both the slide projector and the response panel were connected to a Beckman timer, which measured the response latency to an accuracy of 5 milliseconds.

---

[2] A more extended account of this experiment is given by Groen (1967).

TABLE 1

Reaction Times of Children to Addition Problems

Min (m, n)	Number of observations	Reaction times		
		Predicted	Observed	Ties
0	10	3.26	3.23	2.98
1	7	3.97	4.05	2.67
2	2	4.68	4.52	3.70

The experiment was performed in a soundproof trailer located on the premises of the school. Subjects went from their classes to the experiment in the course of a normal school day. Each subject was run in sessions lasting at most 15 minutes each on five successive days.

The first day began with a preliminary task, in which the subject was successively shown the numbers from 0 to 9 in random order. His instructions were to press the button that was the same as the number he saw on the screen. After having completed this preliminary task, the subject was told that he would be shown some slides on which there were two numbers, and that he was to "press down on the button that is the same as the answer you get when you add the two numbers together." The main sequence of 55 addition problems was then presented. During the course of the experiment, the experimenter sat behind the subject, so that he could not be seen unless the subject deliberately turned around. If the subject seemed at all uncertain of what to do, he was told to punch the button that was the same as the missing number.

The procedure during subsequent sessions was almost identical to that on the first day, the subject being required to perform both the preliminary task and the main task. The only differences were that the instructions were omitted and a different sequence of problems was used on each day, according to a suitably counterbalanced design.

Results

The first day of the experiment was viewed as a training day, the function of which was to familiarize the subjects with the task. The evaluation of the models was based on the mean latency of a correct response, computed over the last four days for each subject and each problem. Hence, each data point was a mean based ideally on four observations. In computing these means, two types of observations were omitted: incorrect responses and outliers with excessively long response latencies. As far as the outliers were concerned, the cutoff point was set at 10 seconds. All responses with a latency greater than this value were omitted from the analysis. The average rate of outliers was under 1%. Only 12 subjects had any outliers at all, and only 2 had more than three outliers. The overall error rate was also low. No subject had an error rate of more than 10%, the mean being 3%. Twenty-seven subjects had an error rate of less than 5%. The problems with the highest error rates were 2 + 5, 5 + 2, 2 + 6, and 5 + 3. These four problems all had 13 errors out of a possible 148, an error rate of slightly under 9%.

The models were evaluated by fitting five regression lines, one for each model, to the mean success latencies of each subject over the last four days. In this way, five values of F, the standard statistic for the significance of the slope parameter b, were obtained for each subject. In order to decide which of the five models provided the most adequate account of the data, two criteria were used: The first criterion was which model maximized F. This criterion was used to select the best model for a given subject. The second criterion was whether F ($df = 1/53$) was significant at the .01 level. This criterion was used to reject subjects whose maximal F might reflect random error rather than the fit of any model.

The outcome of applying this analysis to the data of each subject was that an individual's data were either accounted for most adequately by Model 5 or they were not adequately accounted for by any of five models. Twenty out of the 37 subjects received significant maximum Fs on Model 5. All but one of the remaining subjects failed to receive a significant F on any of the five models.

It seemed possible that the superiority of Model 5 over Model 1 might have been due to a statistical artifact, since the independent variable had a range of 5 values for this model, whereas it had a range of 10 values for Model 1. In order to check this possibility the entire analysis was repeated using a subset of 18 problems selected in such a way that Model 1 placed six of them at each of the points $x = 7, x = 8, x = 9$, while Model 5 placed six at each of the points $x = 1, x = 2, x = 3$. The results of this analysis were almost identical to the preceding one, except for a tendency for the values of F to be lower.

For subjects whose data were best accounted for by Model 5, the value of the intercept parameter a ranged from 1.87 seconds to 4.65 seconds, while the slope parameter b ranged from .12 second to .73 second. In order to obtain an overall estimate of these parameters, the mean success latencies, averaged over the 19 subjects best fitted by Model 5, were computed for each problem. A regression line was then fitted for each model. Not surprisingly, Model 5 gave by far the best fit ($F = 70.8$ vs. $F = 10.6$ for Model 1). The intercept parameter was estimated to be 2.53 seconds while the slope was .34 second. These estimates are sufficiently close to those obtained by Suppes and Groen (1967) to indicate the results of the two experiments are actually reflecting the same process. The estimate of the slope is also close to the estimate of the speed of silent counting (Beckwith & Restle, 1966; Landauer, 1962), which adds a considerable amount of plausibility to the notion that subjects are, indeed, using an actual counting process as defined by Model 5.

References

Bartlett, F. *Remembering*. London: Cambridge University Press, 1932.

Beckwith, M., & Restle, F. Process of enumeration. *Psychological Review*, 1966, **73**, 437–444.

Chase, W. G. & Clark, H. H. Semantics in the perception of verticality. *British Journal of Psychology*, 1971, **62**, 311–326.

Groen, G. J. *An investigation of some counting algorithms for simple addition problems.* (Tech. Rep. No. 118) Stanford, Calif.: Stanford University Institute for Mathematical Studies in the Social Sciences, 1967.

Hoving, K. L., Morin, R. E., & Konick, D. Recognition reaction time and size of the memory set: A developmental study. *Psychonomic Science*, 1970, 21, 248–249.

Landauer, T. K. Rate of implicit speech. *Perceptual and Motor Skills, 1962,* **15,** 646.

Posner, M. Abstraction and the process of recognition. In G. Bower (Ed.), *The psychology of learning and motivation.* Vol. 3. New York: Academic Press, 1969.

Reitman, W. What does it take to remember? In D. Norman (Ed.), *Models of human memory.* New York: Academic Press, 1970.

Restle, F. Speed of adding and comparing numbers. *Journal of Experimental Psychology*, 1970, **83,** 274–278.

Thomas, H. B. G. Communication theory and the constellation hypothesis of calculation. *Quarterly Journal of Experimental Psychology*, 1963, **15,** 173–191.

Thorndike, E. L. *The psychology of arithmetic.* New York: Macmillan, 1922.

INFORMATION PROCESSING STRATEGIES
USED IN THE ENCODING OF LINEAR ORDERING

George R. Potts

The following paper by George R. Potts (1972) concerns the way in which humans store and use logical premises. In this study, subjects read a passage that describes a linear ordering such as "The bear was smarter than the hawk. The hawk was smarter than the wolf. The wolf was smarter than the deer." These three premises can be used to form the four-term linear ordering of the form $A>B>C>D$ (bear > hawk > wolf > deer). The adjacent pairs in the ordering ($A>B$, $B>C$, $C>D$) were explicitly stated in the passage whereas the remote pairs ($B>D$, $A>C$, $A>D$) were explicitly stated for some subjects but not for others. Then, all of the subjects took a test consisting of all twelve possible pairings of the terms in the form, "____ is smarter than ____", in which the blanks contained two of the categories bear, hawk, wolf, deer. Half of the items were true (such as $A>B$) and half were false (such as $D>A$); of these, half presented adjacent pairs and half presented remote pairs of terms. Subjects saw the questions on a screen and responded by pressing one of two buttons.

How does a subject store and use the presented information? A simple *copy theory* states that subjects merely store the presented premises: when a question is presented they find the appropriate premise or, if needed, they combine several premises to produce an inference. This theory predicts that subjects who are presented only with adjacent pairs should perform faster and more accurately on questions involving adjacent pairs rather than remote pairs.

An alternative theory, suggested by the work of Bransford and Franks, is that subjects integrate the presented information at the time of encoding to form a unified cognitive structure. In this case, "what is learned" could be the linear ordering, A B C D. When an item is presented, the subjects are required to perform an *end-anchoring* procedure in which "decisions" are made about each hierarchal element in the series. Some items (such as A>D, A>C, A>B) involve only one decision, whereas others such as (B>C, C>B) require up to five decisions. In general, this alternate model predicts that performance should be better on remote items than on adjacents, regardless of whether remote items are presented.

The results clearly indicate that subjects make fewer errors and generate faster response times for remote pairs than for adjacent pairs. This *distance effect* is more consistent with the end anchoring model than with the copy theory. Subsequent work by Potts and others (Shultz and Potts, 1974; Mayer, 1977; Moyer, 1977) has provided alternative models and refinements of this original study.

The classical empiricist argument that memory consists of no more than a set of slightly faded copies of sensory impressions linked together by associations has fallen into disfavor among many contemporary psychologists. Cognitive psychologists have been more receptive to Bartlett's (1932) notion that memories are the result of an active constructive process which subjects perform on the input information, and that the final encoded version of this information may bear little resemblance to the material as it was actually presented. According to Bartlett, incoming information is incorporated into "active, organized settings" called schemata. When asked a question about the presented material, subjects must use these active schemata to reconstruct the required information. In Bartlett's words, "the organism would say, if it were able to express itself: 'This and this and this must have occurred, in order that my present state should be what it is' " (p. 202). Unfortunately, Bartlett's conceptualization of the nature of these schemata was, at best, sketchy; and, to date, attempts to clarify the notion have met with only limited success.

One such attempt was the proposal (e.g., Miller, 1962; Mehler, 1963) that subjects transform each incoming sentence into its linguistic deep structure or sentence kernel (Chomsky, 1957, 1965), and then store that kernel along with a list of the transformations which would be necessary to regenerate the original sentence from the stored kernel. Mehler (1963) referred to this coding strategy as a schema-plus-correction strategy, with the stored kernel corresponding to the schema and the list of transformations comprising a set of corrections to that basic schema. A large number of studies have been reported which seem to support this linguistic theory of individual sentence memory (e.g., Mehler, 1963; Mehler & Miller, 1964; Gough, 1965; Savin & Perchonock, 1965; Sachs, 1967).

It has recently become clear, however, that subjects' information processing strategies extend far beyond merely altering the form of each input sentence and then storing that altered form. Subjects trying to encode meaningful verbal material, it seems, do not store individual sentences at all. This was demonstrated clearly in two series of experiments by Bransford and Franks (1971) and Bransford, Barclay, and Franks (1972). During the acquisition phase of these experiments, subjects were presented with a series of sentences, being told to read each for comprehension. After the whole set of acquisition sentences had been presented, subjects were shown another series of sentences, some of which were identical to one of the sentences presented during acquisition, and some of which were not. Their task was to determine whether each test sentence was or was not word-for-word identical to any of the acquisition sentences. It was found that if a test sentence contradicted any information which had been presented during acquisition, subjects were very accurate in recognizing that the sentence had not been presented. As long as the test sentence was not inconsistent with any of the acquisition sentences, however, subjects were unable to make the desired discrimination. Specifically, subjects were unable to distinguish between information which had actually been presented and information which they, themselves, had deduced from their knowledge of the presented information.

On the basis of this evidence, it was concluded that subjects do not encode individual sentences at all, neither verbatim nor in terms of their linquistic deep structure representations. Instead, subjects integrate the information presented in related sentences into complex, wholistic ideas. These ideas are then incorporated into subjects' existing cognitive structures or, as Barlett (1932) called them, schemata. Unfortunately, though these studies do indicate that incoming sentences are not encoded in terms of their linguistic deep structure, they still do not explain how the incoming information is encoded. In the words of Bransford and Franks (1971), "a very important problem . . . concerns the question of *what is learned* in the above situations. How can one characterize the nature of the semantic ideas that are acquired?" (p. 349).

What coding strategy could account for the fact that subjects can accurately recount the meaning of a sentence but are unable to distinguish between information which had actually been presented and information which they, themselves, had deduced? One reasonable coding strategy that could account for this result was suggested by Kintsch (1972, p. 274), who noted that it would be very efficient for subjects to delete from memory any information which was redundant in the sense that it could be deduced from other information stored in memory. In what follows, this will be referred to as a *deletion theory*. This would be an efficient coding strategy for it would allow subjects to reduce their memory load without any corresponding loss of information; subjects could deduce any of the deleted material whenever they needed it. Using this coding strategy, however, subjects would not be able to determine if a particular piece of redundant information had actually been presented or not, for the redundant information would not be present in memory in either case.

A second alternative is that subjects make inferences while studying and that these inferences are stored along with the information which was actually presented. Since this would imply that redundant information is stored regardless of whether it was actually presented or not, such a theory could also account for subjects' inability to determine whether a particular piece of redundant information had actually been presented. This theory, which is the antithesis of the deletion theory, will be referred to as an *addition theory*.

The present experiment was designed to test these two alternatives and to compare them to a simple *copy theory*, which argues that subjects attempt to store the material verbatim.

It was decided that transitive relations or linear orderings of the form A>B>C>D would be employed. In all of what follows, the letters, A, B, C, and D will be used to represent the first, second, third, and fourth terms in this ordering, respectively. Linear orderings were chosen for the present study because this type of material enables one to clearly identify redundant information. Specifically, a four-term series A>B>C>D, can be broken into six pairs of terms, three of which are absolutely essential to the establishment of the ordering, and three of which are redundant in the sense that they can be deduced from some subset of the necessary pairs. The three necessary pairs, A>B, B>C, and C>D, will be referred to as *adjacent pairs* since each consists of a pair of terms which are adjacent to one another in the ordering. The three redundant pairs, A>C, A>D, and B>D, will be referred to as *remote pairs* since each consists of two terms which are separated by at least one other term in the ordering. A second reason for employing linear orderings was the similarity of these orderings to the material employed by Bransford *et al.* (1972). It was hoped that the conclusions drawn on the basis of the present experiment would generalize to this earlier work.

Each subject in the present experiment was given three study and three test trials on each of two four-term series. For one of these relations, only the three adjacent pairs were presented; for the other, all six pairs were presented. Subjects were tested for their knowledge of all six pairs in both conditions, measures being taken of both proportion correct and reaction time.

If subjects store exactly what is presented, then when the remote pairs are not presented, performance on these pairs would have to be poorer than performance on the adjacent pairs. Proportion correct would have to be lower because, in order to be correct on the remote pairs, subjects would have to deduce them from the adjacent pairs at the time of test and, thus, could not be correct on the remote pairs unless they remembered the adjacent ones. Since deducing the remote pairs is known to take time (Huttenlocher, 1968; Clark, 1969), reaction time to these pairs would have to be longer than reaction time to the adjacent pairs. Furthermore, performance on the remote pairs would have to be better when these pairs were actually presented than when they were not, since in the former case subjects would actually store the remote pairs and therefore would not need to deduce them at the time of test.

When the remote pairs are not presented, the deletion theory is identical to the copy theory in terms of the predictions it makes regarding what information will be stored. Since there is no redundant information in the presented material, subjects must store exactly what is presented. Thus, in this case, the predictions of the deletion theory are the same as the predictions of the copy theory; performance should be better on the adjacent pairs than on the remote pairs. Since the deletion theory argues that subjects delete from memory any remote pairs which are presented, however, this theory would predict that performance on the remote pairs should not depend on whether those pairs had actually been presented or not.

On the other hand, if subjects deduce the remote pairs while studying and then store these remote pairs along with the information which was actually presented, then proportion correct should be higher on the remote pairs than on the adjacent pairs. This is because subjects can be correct on an adjacent pair only if they remember that pair, but can be correct on a remote pair either if they remember that pair or if they remember some subset of the other pairs sufficient to deduce that pair at the time of test. Though proportion correct would be higher on the remote pairs, however, reaction time would still be longer since reaction time to those remote pairs which had to be deduced would serve to raise the overall reaction time to the remote pairs.

METHOD

Subjects

Subjects were 255 Indiana University undergraduates who participated to fulfill a course requirement. Each participated in one 30-minute session.

Apparatus

The experiment was conducted in the Mathematical Psychology Laboratory at Indiana University. The experimental room was divided into four individual booths, separated by plywood partitions. Each booth contained a solid-state Sony TV receiver and a response box. Mounted on each response box were two microswitch buttons, one marked TRUE and the other marked FALSE. In the first and third booths, the left button was marked TRUE and the right FALSE; in the second and fourth booths, the order was reversed. Subjects responded by pushing one of these buttons, and both the responses and their latencies were recorded automatically by an IBM 1800 computer.

The stimuli which subjects responded to were listed on a computer printout for presentation. A closed-circuit TV camera was used to project an image of a single line of this printout onto the four individual monitors. A modified IBM paper puller advanced the printout between presentations. All timing was controlled by the same computer that recorded the responses.

Procedure

Subjects were tested in squads of four or less. Prior to the beginning of the main session, subjects were given a brief practice paragraph to learn, followed by a set of four test sentences to answer. This training sequence was designed to enable subjects to become more familiar with the kind of material they would be expected to learn. Following this training sequence, the experimenter read the instructions and then gave each subject a paragraph to study for 1.5 minutes. Subjects were provided with paper and pencil which they could use to take notes while studying. It was made clear that this was optional, however, and that they did not have to take notes if they did not want to. It was also made clear to the subjects that they would not have either the paragraph or their notes in front of them while they were being tested.

After this study period, the experimenter collected the paragraphs and note sheets, left the experimental room, and initiated the first sequence of test sentences. This study–test alternation was repeated for a total of three trials.

Each test sequence consisted of a set of sentences, presented one at a time, on the TV monitors. Each sentence remained on the screen for 6 seconds. A 1-second pause, during which time the screen was blank, was inserted between successive sentences. Though the same set of test sentences was used for each test sequence throughout the experiment, the order of presentation of these sentences was randomly permuted both for each test sequence within a session and for each session.

Subjects were instructed to respond "true" or "false" to each sentence; "true" if the sentence was consistent with the information presented in the paragraph, "false" if it was not. The importance of fast, though accurate responding was stressed. To make fast responding possible, subjects were instructed to hold the response boxes in both hands, with their left thumb over the left button and their right thumb over the right button.

Materials and Design

The paragraph learned by subjects in the present experiment was concerned with contests between a bear, a hawk, a wolf, and a deer for dominion over a forest; and between a fish, a frog, a clam, and a duck for dominion over a pond. The paragraph ordered the forest animals linearly on the criterion of intelligence; it ordered the pond animals linearly on the criterion of friendliness. A sample paragraph is presented in Table 1.

For one of the two relations (the "smarter than" relation in Table 1), the ordering was established by presenting only the three adjacent pairs in the relation (A>B, B>C, and C>D). This presentation condition will be referred to as the "not presented" (NP) condition to indicate that the remote pairs (A>C, B>D, and A>D) were not presented. For the other relation (the "friendlier than" relation in Table 1), the ordering was established by presenting all six pairs in the relation, both the three adjacent and the three remote ones. This presentation condition will be referred to as the "presented" (P) condition. The specific presentation condition (NP or P) used in presenting each of the critical relations was

TABLE 1

Sample Paragraph Presented to Subjects in Group 2

In a small forest just south of nowhere, a deer, a bear, a wolf, and a hawk were battling for dominion over the land. It boiled down to a battle of wits, so intelligence was the crucial factor. The bear was smarter than the hawk, the hawk was smarter than the wolf, and the wolf was smarter than the deer. On a small pond in the middle of the same forest, another contest for dominion was being waged. The contenders were a frog, a clam, a duck, and a fish. In this case, however, the battle was to be decided by an election, and friendliness was the crucial factor. The fish was friendlier than the frog, the frog was friendlier than the clam, and the clam was friendlier than the duck. In addition, the fish was friendlier than the clam, the frog was friendlier than the duck, and the fish was friendlier than the duck. In the end, each of the battles was decided in its own way and tranquility returned to the area.

counter-balanced. Approximately half the subjects were presented only the adjacent pairs in the intelligence relations and all the pairs in the friendliness relation. The remainder were presented only the adjacent pairs in the friendliness relation and all the pairs in the intelligence relation.

Subjects were divided into two groups according to the order in which the pairs comprising each of the two relations were presented in the paragraph. For subjects in group 1 (n = 127), the order in which the pairs were presented bore no simple relation to the actual ordering of the terms. For this group, the adjacent pairs in the NP condition were presented in the order C>D, A>B, B>C. Group 2 (n = 128) differed from group 1 in that the pairs were presented in an order which did reflect the actual ordering of the terms. For this group, the adjacent pairs in the NP condition were presented in the simple chained order A>B, B>C, C>D.

A set of 24 test sentences was used to test subjects' knowledge regarding the information contained in the paragraphs. Half the sentences were true, half were false. Of the 12 true sentences, six were statements of the six pairs presented in the P condition, three were statements of the three adjacent pairs presented in the NP condition, and three were statements of the three remote pairs in the NP condition. Though these last three sentences were true statements which could be deduced from the three adjacent pairs in the NP condition, they represented information which was never explicitly stated in the paragraphs. Each of the 12 false sentences corresponded to one of the true sentences but had the order of the terms reversed. Thus, for each true test sentence, "X is smarter (friendlier) than Y," there was a corresponding false test sentence "Y is smarter (friendlier) than X."

Results

Except where explicitly noted, the performance measures presented here were averaged over the true and false test sentences corresponding to each pair. Statistical analyses were performed using two-tailed sign tests for matched samples (Siegel, 1956). For each subject, the appropriate linear combination of his scores on the various test questions was calculated and the sign of the resultant was recorded. In all cases, the number of nonzero scores was sufficiently large to enable the use of a normal approximation, so the results are stated in terms of z scores.

Proportion Correct Data

Table 2 presents the mean proportions correct, averaged over trials and groups, on the adjacent pairs and on the remote pairs as a function of condition. As can be seen, performance on the remote pairs was superior

TABLE 2

Proportion Correct on the Adjacent and Remote Pairs in Each Presentation Condition

Type of pair tested	Presentation condition	
	Remote pairs not presented	Remote pairs presented
Adjacent	.775	.782
Remote	.792	.849

TABLE 3

Proportion Correct on the Adjacent and Remote Pairs in Each Presentation Condition of a Replication Study Using More Difficult Material

	Presentation condition	
Type of pair tested	Remote pairs not presented	Remote pairs presented
Adjacent	.606	.633
Remote	.676	.726

to performance on the adjacent pairs, even in the NP condition where these remote pairs had never been presented. This difference between proportion correct on the adjacent and remote pairs was highly significant in both the NP and P conditions [$z = 3.49, p < .001$, and $z = 7.68, p < .001$, respectively]. It should be noted that this superiority on the remote pairs was observed in both groups and thus did not depend on the order of presentation of the pairs in the paragraph.

Proportion correct on the remote pairs was significantly better when these pairs were actually presented than when they were not [$z = 3.58, p < .001$]; but proportion correct on the adjacent pairs, which were always presented, did not differ significantly as a function of condition [$z = 1.22, p = .22$].

Overall proportions correct on the 24 test sentences for groups 1 and 2 were .747 and .851, respectively. This difference, tested by means of a t test for independent samples, was highly significant [$t(253) = 6.86, p < .001$]. Thus, not surprisingly, performance was improved by presenting the pairs in an order which reflected the structure inherent in the actual linear ordering of the terms.

At this point, it should be noted that overall performance in the present study was quite high. This was essential if a meaningful analysis of the reaction time scores were to be performed. One might expect that with more difficult material, subjects would find it considerably harder to deduce the remote pairs, and that the observed superiority on these pairs might then disappear. This appears not to be the case.

One hundred and fifty-three subjects were tested in a replication of the present study. The same design and similar materials were employed (for details, see Experiment I in Potts, 1971). The paragraph to be learned contained considerably more information, however; and, consequently, overall performance was considerably lower. The resulting proportions correct in this study are presented in Table 3. It can be seen that, far from being diminished, the superiority of the remote pairs was even more pronounced in the replication. The difference between the adjacent and remote pairs was again highly significant in both the NP and P conditions [$z = 4.54, p < .001$, and $z = 6.03, p < .001$, respectively].

Reaction Time Data

In what follows, only the latencies for correct answers will be given. Reaction time to the remote pairs was shorter than reaction time to the adjacent pairs, even when the remote pairs were never presented. This difference between reaction time to the adjacent and remote pairs was significant in both the NP and P conditions [$z = 6.64, p < .001$, and $z = 8.02, p < .001$, respectively]. The effect of conditions was much smaller, though reaction time to the remote pairs was slightly shorter when those pairs were actually presented than when they were not [$z = 2.13, p = .03$]. Reaction time to the adjacent pairs did not differ significantly as a function of condition [$z = 1.63, p = .10$].

These effects are illustrated clearly in Figure 1, which shows the improvement in reaction time over trials for the adjacent and remote pairs in each condition. The data for groups 1 and 2 are presented separately. The superiority of the remote pairs is clearly demonstrated on all trials, for both

FIGURE 1

Change in reaction time over trials for the adjacent and remote pairs as a function of whether the remote pairs were presented (P) or not presented (NP). The data for groups 1 and 2 are shown separately.

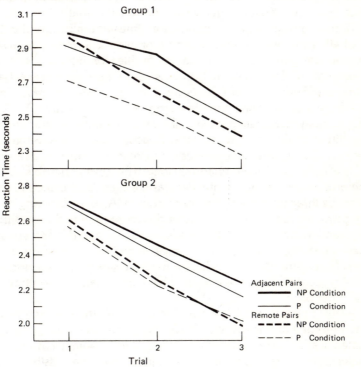

FIGURE 2

Mean reaction time to the six pairs as a function of whether the remote pairs were presented (P) or not presented (NP), and whether the test sentence was true or false.

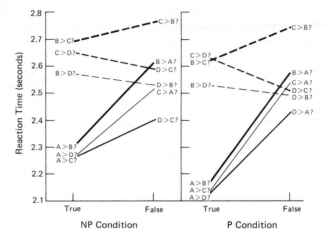

conditions, and in both groups. It is also clear that, for subjects in group 2, actually presenting the remote pairs had virtually no effect on reaction times to those pairs. Thus, the slight beneficial effect of actually presenting the remote pairs can be attributed entirely to subjects in group 1, and even in that group the difference decreases after the first trial.

Figure 2 presents the mean reaction times as a function of condition and whether the test sentence was true or false. The scores are averaged over trials and groups. It is clear that the profiles for the two conditions are almost identical. This is definitely not the case for the comparison between the true and false sentences, however. For true sentences, reaction times to the three pairs containing the first term, A, in the ordering (A>B, A>C, A>D) were approximately equal, all being considerably shorter than reaction times to the other three pairs. Reaction time to the remaining remote pair, B>D, was next shortest; and reaction times to the adjacent pairs B>C and C>D were uniformly long. The most noticeable difference in the profiles for the false sentences was the dramatic increase in reaction time to the three pairs containing the first term, A, in the ordering. Of these three pairs, reaction time was shorter the more remote the pair. Interestingly, reaction times to the false sentences, D>C? and D>B? were actually somewhat shorter than reaction times to the corresponding true sentences, C>D? and B>D? Finally, for the false sentences, reaction time to the test sentence C>B? was considerably longer than reaction time to any of the other pairs.

At this point, it should be noted that, though the proportions correct in the present experiment were quite high, they were not perfect. Since the latencies for correct answers were found to be somewhat shorter than the latencies for wrong answers, one cannot ignore the possibility that the observed differences in latencies might reflect only a difference in proportions correct. First, it should be noted that this seems unlikely in the present experiment, for the speed of responding to the individual pairs did not correspond at all closely to the error profiles on the individual pairs. Still acknowledging the possibility of bias, however, the trial-3 reaction time scores of the 44 subjects who got all 24 test sentences correct on that trial were examined. It is reasonable that subjects performing this well should have very few, if any, answers correct by guessing. Even when the remote pairs had never been presented, 38 of the 44 subjects had shorter reaction times to those remote pairs than to the adjacent pairs. Only five subjects exhibited the opposite effect, with one tied score. This difference was, of course, highly significant [$z = 4.88$, $p < .001$]. Thus, the trial-3 reaction time scores of these high-performing subjects replicated the results obtained from all the subjects.

As a final check for bias, a revised latency score was examined. This revised latency score was designed to give a measure of mean latency for those cases where subjects were responding on the basis of a knowledge of the correct answer. It was arrived at by employing an adaptation of Yellott's (1971, p. 167, Equation 24) correction for fast guesses in a reaction time task. The proportion of errors was used as an estimate of the proportion of correct guesses, and the reaction time to the incorrect answers was used as an estimate of the reaction time on the correct guesses. The conclusions to be drawn from this revised latency score were completely consistent with the conclusions drawn from the unrevised latency scores. This fact, in itself, provides further support for the contention that the latency scores provide a measure of performance which is distinct from the proportion correct data. Since the results using the three latency scores were consistent, only one of the scores, the average latency for correct items, was presented.

Note-taking Data

Upon examination of the note sheets, it became immediately apparent that, in taking notes, a large proportion of the subjects had written down the two complete linear relationships which had been presented in the paragraph. Subjects did this by placing the animals, from smartest or friendliest to least smart or friendly, either one above another with the smartest or friendliest on top, or one next to another with the smartest or friendliest on the left. For the purposes of the following analyses, subjects were scored according to whether they ever, on any trial, took notes; and whether they ever arrived at the correct ordering. Classification of the note sheets was performed by a laboratory secretary who was completely unfamiliar with the design of the experiment.

A comparison of the note-taking performance in the NP and P conditions was accomplished by examining the proportion of subjects who, having taken notes on either relation, wrote down the complete linear ordering on any of the three trials. These proportions for the NP and P conditions were .723 and .736, respectively. The difference did not approach significance, $z < 1$. Thus, condition does not appear to have affected note-taking performance.

The differences in note-taking performance between groups 1 and 2 were large and highly reliable, however. The proportion of subjects in group 1 who took notes on at least one of the relations was .937. For group 2, the proportion was only .789. The difference in these proportions, tested by means of a chi-square test (Siegel, 1956), was highly significant, $[\chi^2 (1) = 11.78, p < .001]$. Of those subjects who took notes, however, averaging over condition, the proportion who at some time wrote down the correct ordering in groups 1 and 2 were .655 and .812, respectively. This difference was also highly significant $[\chi^2 (1) = 6.74, p < .01]$. Thus, it is clear that fewer subjects took notes when the order of presentation of the pairs reflected the actual ordering of the terms in the relation (group 2) than when it did not (group 1). Among those who did take notes, however, subjects were far more likely to arrive at the correct ordering when the order in which the pairs had been presented did reflect the ordering of the terms in the relation.

Discussion

Proportion Correct Data

Proportion correct on the remote pairs was found to be higher than proportion correct on the adjacent pairs, even when the remote pairs were never presented. This result is in direct contradiction to any theory which proposes that subjects use the adjacent pairs to deduce the remote pairs at the time of test. All such theories require that, in order to establish the truth or falsity of a test sentence referring to a remote pair, subjects would have to know all the adjacent pairs necessary to deduce that remote pair. Clearly, if this were the case, then performance on any remote pair could, at very best, be no better than performance on the worst adjacent pair necessary to deduce it.

Thus, neither a copy theory nor a deletion theory is acceptable in light of the present data, for both propose that when the remote pairs are not presented, subjects store only the adjacent pairs which were actually presented and deduce the remote pairs at the time of test. The deletion theory goes even a step further, proposing that when the remote pairs are presented, subjects delete them since they represent redundant information which can be regenerated whenever necessary

It should be noted that, as far as the present experiment is concerned, the predictions of a simple copy theory are identical to the predictions of any linguistic model which argues that subjects store the linguistic deep structures of the input sentences. This is true because the linguistic surface structure of the material employed in the present experiment was so similar to the corresponding deep structure (all pairs were of the form "A is better than B") that storing the deep structure would consist basically of storing the actual pairs as they were presented. Thus, in rejecting a copy theory, the linguistic model must also be rejected.

On the basis of the present results, then, it is clear that subjects memorize neither exactly what was presented nor the linguistic deep structure of the sentences which were presented, but instead integrate the information prior to the test, drawing conclusions from this information at that time. These inferences, furthermore, do not serve merely to enable subjects to delete redundant information in the presented material; the inferences are stored in memory along with the information that was actually presented.

The simplest model of this type is the addition theory which proposes that subjects deduce the remote pairs while studying the material, and then store these remote pairs along with the adjacent pairs. Such a theory could account for the fact that proportion correct was higher on the remote pairs than on the adjacent pairs for, according to this theory, a subject would be correct on an adjacent pair if and only if he remembered that pair. A subject could be correct on a remote pair, however, either if he remembered that pair itself or if he remembered a set of other pairs sufficient to deduce it.

Reaction Time Data

Though the addition theory can account for the proportion correct results of the present experiment, it can not account for the reaction time results. According to this addition theory, some of the correct responses on a particular remote pair result from subjects having remembered that pair, others result from subjects having remembered some subset of the other five pairs which enabled them to deduce that remote pair at the time of the test. Reaction time on the former responses should be equal to reaction time to the adjacent pairs; reaction time on the latter responses would have to be longer than reaction time to the adjacent pairs. Clearly, then, this theory could not account for the present finding that, regardless of whether the remote pairs were actually presented or not, overall reaction time to these remote pairs was shorter than overall reaction time to the adjacent pairs.

One modified version of the addition theory needs to be examined more closely. The shorter reaction time to the remote pairs could be accounted for by such a theory if one were willing to assume that subjects not only generated and stored all six pairs, but also ordered these pairs in memory in certain ways. If one assumed, for example, that the pairs were stored in such a way that the remote pairs were examined first, then one could explain the shorter reaction time to those pairs. Figure 2 reveals that the reaction time results are not that simple; it is not merely the case that reaction time is shorter the more remote the pair. Whatever the reaction time profile, however, this modified addition theory could account for that profile since the theory puts no restrictions on the order in which the pairs can be arranged in memory. Thus, one only needs to postulate that the pair with the shortest reaction time is stored in the first memory slot (and is therefore retrieved first), and so on. Such a theory is, of course, more complex than the simple addition theory described above since it argues that subjects impose a structure on the six pairs. It is also somewhat unsatisfying since the account of the reaction time profiles is entirely arbitrary. Unsatisfying as the theory may be, however, it is necessary to provide more than six data points before the theory can be challenged empirically.

These extra data points can be provided by examining reaction times to true and false sentences separately, as was done in Figure 2. While the model can account for any reaction time profile for the six pairs, it would have to predict that the profile for the false sentences should be approximately the same as the profile for the true sentences. This prediction becomes clear when one notes that, to answer a test question, subjects would first have to retrieve the relevant pair (the pair having the same two terms as the test sentence) from memory. This is true regardless of whether the test sentence is true or false. Thus, though the average time required to answer a false sentence might be longer than the average time required to answer a true sentence, the relative ease or difficulty of the six pairs should be the same regardless of whether the test sentence was true or false. As was observed in discussing Figure 2, this was clearly not the case in the present experiment.

It should be noted that these reaction time results contradict not only the copy, deletion, and addition theories, but also any of the class of theories which would propose that subjects learned the linear orderings by storing some subset of the pairs which comprised that ordering. According to any such theory, subjects could still be correct on a particular remote pair in only one of two ways; by remembering the pair itself, or by remembering a set of other pairs sufficient to deduce that remote pair at the time of test. Any such theory, then, would have to share with the addition theory the inability to account for the fact that reaction time on the remote pairs is shorter than reaction time on the adjacent pairs.

Thus, it appears that in trying to learn the transitive relations in the present experiments, subjects did not store the actual pairs at all. Instead, in the process of actively manipulating the presented material, they must have changed its form altogether. On the basis of subjects' note-taking data, it is clear that a large number of subjects used the pairs that were presented to arrange or order the terms serially, placing the four terms one next to each other from top to bottom or from left to right. Having worked to establish this sequential arrangement, it is reasonable that the modified form in which subjects stored the information is this sequential arrangement, that is, the actual ordering of the four terms itself.

This suggestion is consistent with the observed effects of the order of presentation of the pairs of terms. Several studies have reported that varying the order of presentation of the adjacent pairs comprising a linear ordering drastically affects the ease with which subjects are able to establish that ordering (Hunter, 1957; DeSoto, London, & Handel, 1965; Huttenlocher, 1968; Handel, DeSoto, & London, 1968). The note-taking results of the present experiment are consistent with this conclusion in that, of those subjects who took notes, the proportion who got the correct ordering was substantially higher in group 2 where the pairs had been presented in an order which reflected the actual ordering of the terms in the series. The fact that a larger proportion of subjects took notes in group 1 could be taken as an indication that subjects in that group felt more of a need to take notes since the establishment of the ordering was more difficult due to the haphazard order in which the pairs were presented. It follows that the improvement in proportion correct observed in going from group 1 to group 2 may have been due directly to the ease with which the linear ordering was established by subjects in group 2.

Other researchers have also noted the tendency for subjects to order terms linearly even when not specifically required to do so (DeSoto, 1960, 1961; DeSoto & Bosley, 1962; Kuethe, 1962; Henley, Horsfall, & De-Soto, 1969). In light of his results, DeSoto concluded that the linear ordering acts as a powerful schema in directing the analysis and encoding of certain types of information. The results of the present experiments would certainly appear to support this contention. Many questions still remain, however, regarding the actual form of this stored serial arrangement.

Associative Chaining Hypotheses

The most prominent theory regarding the process involved in learning a serial list is the associative chaining hypothesis (consult Young, 1968). This theory can be eliminated immediately on the basis of the present results. The predictions of a theory which argues that subjects deduce the remote pairs by establishing a chain of associations between various adjacent terms are the same as the predictions of the deletion theory. Neither theory can account for the superior performance on the remote pairs that was observed in the present experiment. The addition of a remote association assumption does not help, for the resulting theory makes the same predictions as the addition theory. Though both theories can account for the higher proportion correct on the remote pairs, neither can account for the fact that reaction times to these remote pairs are shorter.

Rating Scale Hypothesis

A more viable alternative is a rating scale theory which argues that subjects learned the orderings in the present experiments by placing the four terms on imaginary scales of "smartness" and "friendliness." On such a scale, quantitative differences in smartness or friendliness between two animals are represented by spacial distances between those terms on the scale; and the farther apart on the scale two terms are, the higher the proportion correct on the pair comprised of those terms. This theory could easily explain the higher proportion correct on the remote pairs, since the terms comprising these remote pairs would have to be placed farther apart on the scale than the terms of the adjacent pairs necessary to deduce them. While this model, as it stands, makes no predictions regarding the reaction time data, it could be modified to account for this data by the addition of various decision criteria. It is questionable, however, whether any such model could account for the obtained difference in reaction time profiles for true and false sentences, or for the fact that the observed reaction times were not a simple decreasing function of remoteness.

End-Term Anchoring

It has been proposed by several researchers (Wishner, Shipley, & Hurvich, 1957; Feigenbaum & Simon, 1962; DeSoto & Bosley, 1962; DeSoto *et al.*, 1965; Handel *et al.*, 1968) that serial lists are learned from the end points inward and that the first and last terms in the list share a special status in serving as "anchors" for the other terms in the list. If one accepts that subjects learn the endpoints first, and are therefore more confident of the position of these terms in the list, then one can account for a large portion of the reaction time data presented in Figure 2.

To account for this data, one needs only to argue that subjects examine each of the terms in the test sentence successively, checking if each is an end term, A or D. If it is, subjects can respond immediately without processing the rest of the ordering. For the four-term series employed in the present experiments, the only term not containing such an end term is the pair B>C; so, as was observed, reaction time to the two test questions (B>C? and C>B?) relating to that pair should be noticeably long. A flow chart presenting one such processing strategy in detail is shown in Figure 3. According to this strategy, a subject first examines the first term in the test sentence and asks himself if it is the first term (A) in the ordering. If it is, he can respond immediately, indicating that the sentence is true. Thus, reaction time to the true test sentences A>B?, A>C?, and A>D? should be uniformly short, as was observed. If the first term in the test sentence is not the first term in the ordering, the subject then asks if the first term in the test sentence is the last term (D) in the ordering. If it is, the subject can again respond immediately, indicating that the test sentence is false. Thus, reaction time to the false sentences, D>A?, D>B?, and D>C?, should be uniformly short, though longer than reaction time to the test sentences A>B?, A>C?, and A>D? At this point, the model's predictions deviate from the obtained results in that reaction time to the test sentence D>A? was found to be shorter than reaction time to the test sentences D>B? or D>C? One explanation for this discrepancy is that the reaction time data from the present experiments is based on group averages, and thus the profiles represent composite profiles rather than the profile for any one given subject. It may be that not all subjects employ the same strategy for answering the questions.

Assume for the moment that all subjects employ the first decision

FIGURE 3

Flow diagram depicting a possible strategy for answering test questions.

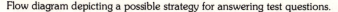

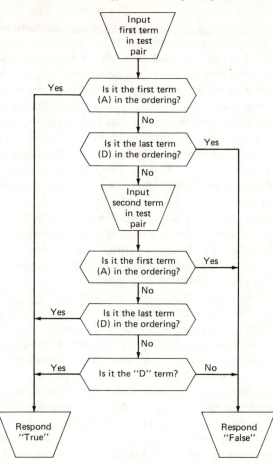

criterion as it was described above. This seems a reasonable assumption given the extremely short reaction times to the test sentences A>B?, A>C?, and A>D? Having failed to meet that criterion, however, assume that, instead of staying with the first term in the test sentence, some subjects go immediately to the second term and, as the second decision point, ask themselves if that second term in the test question is the first term in the ordering. These subjects will be able to correctly respond "false" to the test sentences D>A?, C>A?, and B>A? at the second decision stage. Assuming that half the subjects proceed according to the first strategy and half proceed according to the second, it follows that all subjects can answer the test sentence D>A? in the second processing stage. A given subject can answer only two of the four question, C>A?, B>A?, D>B?, D>C?, in the second stage, however; the other two cannot be answered until some later stage. Thus, as was observed, the composite (averaged over subjects) reaction time should be shorter on the test sentence D>A? than on any of the other four test sentences.

Of course, this is a highly speculative account. The theory can easily account for the superior performance on the remote pairs which was observed in the present experiments, but it has an interesting characteristic in that it argues that this high performance on the remote pairs is related only indirectly to the remoteness of the pair. According to this theory, performance is better on the remote pairs because the remote pairs are more likely to contain one of the end terms. Specifically, with a four-term series, all three remote pairs contain at least one end term; and one pair, A>D, contains both. It would prove informative to replicate the present experiment using an ordering which consisted of more than four terms, so that at least one remote pair would contain no end term. Also, enough data should be collected from each subject to enable one to examine the reaction time profiles of individual subjects.

The present experiment was designed to determine the strategies subjects employ when trying to learn meaningful verbal material. The material to be learned consisted of linear orderings presented in paragraph form. Performance, both proportions correct and reaction times, was better on redundant information, which could be deduced, than it was on information which was necessary to establish the ordering. Surprisingly, this was the case even when the redundant material was never presented. This result was shown to be inconsistent with a number of possible theories regarding how subjects encoded the information. It should be noted that, though highly reliable in the present experiment, this result is not obtained by all researchers. Specifically, Frase (1970) has examined the learning of set-theoretic relations and has found that proportion correct on the deducible information is noticeably poorer than performance on the necessary information. Frase's experiments differed from the present experiments in several procedural points, however, as well as in the type of information employed. Examples of such possibly important procedural differences are the type of test employed, the retention interval, and the presence or absence of irrelevant information in the paragraph. Further experiments are necessary to determine the exact reasons for the differing results. Such experiments should go far towards clarifying the strategies employed by subjects attempting to remember meaningful verbal material.

References

Bartlett, F. C. *Remembering.* Cambridge: Cambridge University Press, 1932.

Bransford, J. D. & Franks, J. J. The abstraction of linguistic ideas. *Cognitive Psychology*, 1971, **2**, 331–350.

Bransford, J. D., Barclay, J. R., & Franks, J. J. Sentence memory: A constructive versus interpretive approach. *Cognitive Psychology*, 1972, **3**, 193–209.

Chomsky, N. *Syntactic structures.* The Hague: Mouton, 1957.

Chomsky, N. *Aspects of the theory of syntax.* Cambridge: M.I.T. Press, 1965.

Clark, H. H. Linguistic processes in deductive reasoning. *Psychological Review,* 1969, **76,** 387–404.

DeSoto, C. B. Learning a social structure. *Journal of Abnormal and Social Psychology,* 1960, **60,** 417–421.

DeSoto, C. B. The predilection for single orderings. *Journal of Abnormal and Social Psychology,* 1961, **62,** 16–23.

DeSoto, C. B. & Bosley, J. J. The cognitive structure of a social structure. *Journal of Abnormal and Social Psychology,* 1962, **64,** 303–307.

DeSoto, C. B., London, M., & Handel, S. Social reasoning and spatial paralogic. *Journal of Personality and Social Psychology,* 1965, **2,** 513–521.

Feigenbaum, E. A., & Simon, H. A. A theory of the serial position effect. *British Journal of Psychology,* 1962, **53,** 307–320.

Frase, L. T. Influence of sentence order and amount of higher level text processing upon reproductive and productive memory. *American Educational Research Journal,* 1970, **7,** 307–319.

Gough, P. B. Grammatical transformations and speed of understanding. *Journal of Verbal Learning and Verbal Behavior,* 1965, **4,** 107–111.

Handel, S., DeSoto, C. B., & London, M. Reasoning and spatial representations. *Journal of Verbal Learning and Verbal Behavior,* 1968, **7,** 351–357.

Henley, N. M., Horsfall, R. R., & DeSoto, C. B. Goodness of figure and social structure. *Psychological Review,* 1969, **76,** 194–204.

Hunter, I. M. L. The solving of three-term series problems. *British Journal of Psychology,* 1957, **48,** 286–298.

Huttenlocher, J. Constructing spatial images: A strategy in reasoning. *Psychological Review,* 1968, **75,** 550–560.

Kintsch, W. Notes on the structure of semantic memory. In E. Tulving and W. Donaldson (Eds.) *Organization of memory.* New York: Academic Press, 1972. Pp. 247–308.

Kuethe, J. L. Social schemas. *Journal of Abnormal and Social Psychology,* 1962, **64,** 31–38.

Mehler, J. Some effects of grammatical transformations on the recall of English sentences. *Journal of Verbal Learning and Verbal Behavior,* 1963, **2,** 346–351.

Mehler, J. & Miller, G. A. Retroactive interference in the recall of simple sentences. *British Journal of Psychology,* 1964, **55,** 295–301.

Miller, G. A. Some psychological studies of grammar. *American Psychologist,* 1962, **17,** 748–762.

Potts, G. R. A cognitive approach to the encoding of meaningful verbal material. *Indiana Mathematical Psychology Report Series,* Report No. 71–7, 1971.

Sachs, J. S. Recognition memory for syntactic and semantic aspects of connected discourse. *Perception and Psychophysics,* 1967, **2,** 437–442.

Savin, H. B. & Perchonock, E. Grammatical structure and the immediate recall of English sentences. *Journal of Verbal Learning and Verbal Behavior.* 1965, **4,** 348–353.

Siegel, S. *Nonparametric statistics for the behavioral sciences.* New York: McGraw-Hill, 1956.

Wishner, J., Shipley, T. E., & Hurvich, M. S. The serial–position curve as a function of organization. *American Journal of Psychology,* 1957, **70,** 258–262.

Yellott, J. I., Jr. Correction for fast guessing and the speed–accuracy tradeoff in choice reaction time. *Journal of Mathematical Psychology,* 1971, **8,** 159–199.

Young, R. K. Serial learning. In T. R. Dixon and D. L. Horton (Eds.), *Verbal behavior and general behavior theory.* Englewood Cliffs, N. J.: Prentice-Hall. 1968.

12/ Concept Learning

A young boy sits at his window, watching the sidewalk in front of his house. First, a poodle walks along, to which he says "dog," and his mother responds by saying, "That's right!" Then a collie wanders by; the little boy shouts, "dog," and receives another, "That's right!" Finally, a third furry creature races by and the boy screams, "dog"; but this time his mother says, "No, Bill. That was a cat."

This is an example of concept learning—learning to make a common response to a certain set of different stimuli. Unfortunately, Bill's concept for dog was a little too general. A concept learning situation such as this can be taken into the lab for further study; in fact, the concept learning paradigm has been used in hundreds of experiments because concept learning appears to be a fundamental type of human learning (see Neimark and Santa's chapter in the 1975 *Annual Review of Psychology*).

One major question raised by psychologists concerns the process by which subjects induce the solution rule in concept learning tasks; for example, does learning occur gradually or is learning an all-or-none process? The gradual-learning theory is based on the idea that people gradually build stronger and stronger responses for the stimuli in a situation involving increased practice. The all-or-none theory is based on the idea that people pick a hypothesis (such as furry–dog), keep it if it works, and pick a new one if it does not. Traditionally, these theories have been part of what is called *continuity* (gradual-learning) vs. *noncontinuity* (all-or-none) controversy.

The papers presented in this section each provide information on the learning theories that attempt to best describe the process by which humans induce rules. The first paper, by Bower and Trabasso (1963), provides a direct test of the continuity and noncontinuity theories using a standard concept learning situation; the study by the Kendlers (1962) provides evidence on developmental changes in children's learning strategies; and the paper by Restle and Brown investigates the two aforementioned theories using a rule-learning task that is somewhat different from "standard" concept learning paradigms.

REVERSALS PRIOR TO SOLUTION
IN CONCEPT IDENTIFICATION

Gordon Bower and Thomas Trabasso

Gordon Bower and Thomas Trabasso (1963) devised an experiment that directly tests the continuity and noncontinuity theories of concept learning for humans. In a typical study, subjects viewed letter patterns (such as VFYQ) and responded by choosing one of two categories to which the pattern belonged; then, the experimenter gave the correct answer based on a simple classification rule. One such solution rule might be, "If there is a V in the first space, the pattern is in one category, but if there is a W in that space the pattern is in the other category." Some subjects (Control Group) were given answers based on the same rule for the entire experiment. Other subjects (Reversal Group) were given answers based on one rule for the first five trials; but as soon as a subject made an error, the rule was reversed and this alternate rule was used for the rest of the experiment. Finally, subjects in a third group (Non-reversal Group) were given answers based on one rule for the first five trials; but as soon as a subject made an error, a *new* rule was used (based on another feature of the pattern) for the rest of the experiment.

If learning involves a gradual strengthening of stimulus–response associations, as proposed by the continuity theory, then the Control Group should perform better than the others. That is, this theory assumes that the Reversal and Non-reversal Groups spend the early stages of the experiment building associations that would not help in learning the ultimate rule, whereas the Control Group spends these early stages building up associations that are needed for learning.

If, however, learning involves an all-or-none testing of hypotheses, as proposed by noncontinuity theory, then all groups should learn at equal rates. That is, regardless of the group designation, a subject must return to the original starting position and choose a hypothesis all over again when an error is made.

When Spence (1945) performed a similar experiment with rats, the results clearly favored the continuity theory; however, the work of Bower and Trabasso, some twenty years later, clearly favored the noncontinuity theory for concept learning in humans. That is, in the present experiment, there were no differences in learning errors between the groups. Thus, the Bower and Trabasso experiment can be considered one of the landmark studies aimed at determining the process by which humans learn concepts. More recent evidence for the *hypothesis testing* theory of concept learning has been summarized by Levine in *A Cognitive Theory of Learning: Research on Hypothesis Testing* (1975).

In the typical two-category concept identification experiment S is shown a series of complex patterns which vary in several, binary attributes. As each pattern is presented. S attempts to anticipate the correct classification; following his response, he is informed of the correct response. The patterns are divided into two mutually exclusive classes, R_1 and R_2. If, say, color (red or blue) is the relevant attribute, then red objects might be assigned to Response Class R_1 and blue objects to Class R_2. We will refer to this rule as a particular S-R assignment.

In recent studies (Bower & Trabasso, 1963a; Trabasso, 1963) of this situation with college students, Ss appeared to learn suddenly. Backward learning curves were horizontal at the chance level of 50% correct classifications over all trials until S's last error before solving. The performance of an S might be characterized by saying that on any given trial he is either in the presolution state or in the solution state, with corresponding probabilities of .50 or 1.00 of correctly classifying the stimuli. According to this two-state description of the performance, learning would be identified as a discrete, one-trial transition from the initial, presolution state into the terminal, solution state.

The theories of cue-selection learning proposed by Restle (1962) and Bower and Trabasso (1963a) imply this two-state description of individual performance. These theories assume that S is selectively attending to or sampling cues from the stimulus display and that he is testing hypotheses regarding the relevance of these cues to the correct solution. If S's response is correct, it is supposed that he continues to use the same hypothesis; if his response is incorrect, he resamples at random from the set of possible hypotheses. Assume further that the proportion of correct hypotheses is c whereas the remaining proportion 1 − c is irrelevant hypotheses which lead to correct and incorrect responses half the time. By these assumptions, the probability that S solves the problem after any given error is a fixed constant, c. This elementary theory has been used successfully in predicting quantitative details of several sets of data (Bower & Trabasso, 1963a).

The present studies investigate whether S acquires partial knowledge about the solution to the problem. The all-or-nothing theory supposes that he does not. Specifically, it says that when S makes an error, he has not yet learned anything of relevance regarding the correct concept. Three experiments were performed to provide tests of this assumption; the first two are described now.

Experiments I and II

Experiments I and II are identical in design; Exp. II was a replication of Exp. I with an easier problem and different stimulus materials. The design resembles that used in several animal experiments conducted on the continuity-noncontinuity issue in discrimination learning theory (e.g., Krechesvky, 1938; McCulloch & Pratt, 1934). Control Ss in Group C learned a problem with the same S-R assignments throughout (Cue A-R_1, Cue B-R_2). Two other groups worked on different S-R assignments initially and then were transferred to the assignments of the control group. This transfer occurred immediately after S made an error following a critical trial of the initial series. Group R, a reversal group, was trained initially with the opposite assignments, A-R_2 and B-R_1. Group NR, a nonreversal-shift group, was trained initially with Cues A and B present but irrelevant while another set of cues was relevant (C-R_1, D-R_2).

The question of interest is whether the initial wrong-way training retards performance of Ss in Groups R and NR who are shifted to the final, transfer problem before solving their initial problem. If Ss partially learn responses to the initially relevant cues before the shift, then such partial learning should induce negative transfer on the final problem. However, if S's error initiating the shift indicates that nothing of importance has yet been learned, then the performance on the final problem should be the same for the three groups, independent of the initial S-R assignments.

METHOD

Experimental design—A schematic outline of the design is presented in Table 1. Only two of the several stimulus attributes are represented in the left columns of Table 1. The rows give the combinations of stimulus values in the patterns and the correct responses to each pattern are listed under each condition. The Control and Reversal groups had Cues A and B relevant but they had opposite response assignments during initial training (10 trials in Exp. I and 5 trials in Exp. II). The Nonreversal group had one of the other dimensions (Cues C and D) relevant during initial training.

TABLE 1

Design for Exp. I and II

Patterns		Response Assignments			
		Initial Trials			Final Problem
Dimension 1	Dimension 2	Control	Reversal	Nonreversal	
A	C	R_1	R_2	R_1	R_1
A	D	R_1	R_2	R_2	R_1
B	C	R_2	R_1	R_1	R_2
B	D	R_2	R_1	R_2	R_2

The Ss who made an error on Trial 10 in Exp. I or Trial 5 in Exp. II or soon thereafter were immediately shifted to the final problem listed in the right hand column of Table 1. We wished to compare on this final problem only those Ss who had not yet learned their initial problem by Trial 10 (or 5 in Exp. II). Consequently, if an S in any group began a criterion run of 16 consecutive correct responses on or before the critical trial (10 or 5), he was not shifted but was, as a result, excluded from the critical comparison between those Ss who did get put onto the final problem. According to the theory, these latter Ss were equalized at the start of the final problem since each S made an error before the shift was effected.

Procedure. — The same instructions were read to all Ss. The S was to classify a set of patterns into two classes. In Exp. I, the classificatory responses were MIB and CEJ; in Exp. II, the numerals 1 and 2. The S was told that the patterns could be classified by a simple principle.

Patterns were presented one at a time on a card holder. The S paced his verbal responses and E then stated the correct classification. The S was allowed 4 sec. to view the pattern after reinforcement. A different order was presented each S by shuffling the cards before the session. Cards were reshuffled at the end of every 64 trials if S had not yet reached the learning criterion of 16 successive correct responses.

Stimulus materials. — For Exp. I, patterns were constructed by sampling a single letter from each of four pairs of letters, (V or W), (F or G), (X or Y), (Q or R). Thus, VFYQ was a pattern, WVXR was not. The four letters were printed in a diamond shape on a 3 × 5 in. card. The letters appeared fixed in the order given above, but their locations at the four diamond corners rotated randomly from trial to trial. Location was an irrelevant cue. For Groups C and R, the letter pair (V, W) was relevant; the classification depended on which one of the letters was present on the card. One of the other letter pairs was selected randomly to be initially relevant for each S in Group NR, whereas (V, W) was irrelevant. The final problem was with (V, W) as the relevant cues with response assignments V-MIB and W-CEJ.

For Exp. II, the stimuli were geometric figures drawn in crayon pencil from templates on white 3 × 5 in. file cards. There were six binary dimensions: color (red or blue); size (large or small); shape (square or hexagon); number (three or four figures); position (figures arranged along right or left diagonal); and colored area within each figure (upper-right and lower-left or upper-left and lower-right quadrants). There was one relevant dimension and five irrelevant dimensions for each group. Color was relevant for Groups C and R. One of the other five dimensions was randomly selected and made relevant during initial training for each S in Group NR.

Subjects. — For Exp. I, the Ss were 65 students in the introductory psychology course at Stanford University. Eleven Ss began a criterion run on or before Trial 10; there were 4, 3, and 4 Ss in Groups C, R, and NR, respectively. These Ss do not enter into the comparison on the final problem since they were not transferred. Setting aside these Ss, 18 Ss (13 males and 5 females) remained in each group.

For Exp. II, the Ss were 46 students in the introductory psychology course at Stanford University. Since the problem was easier, a larger proportion of Ss was expected to solve within a few trials. Hence, fewer initial training trials (five) were used so that the majority of Ss would not have to be set aside. Sixteen Ss, 5 in Group C, 4 in Group R, and 7 in Group NR, began a criterion run on or before Trial 5. These Ss were excluded from comparisons on the final problem. There remained 10 Ss (6 males and 4 females) in each group for comparison on the final problem.

Results

In Exp. I, one S in Group C and one in Group NR failed to reach criterion within 140 trials on the final problem; all other Ss solved within 140 trials. In Exp. II, all Ss solved the final problem. Comparisons among groups on final-problem performance refer to trials following the error trial that initiated the shift to the final problem for a given S. Average errors and trial of last error are shown in Table 2 for the three conditions in both experiments.

The group differences on mean errors and mean trial of last error on the final problem were negligible in both experiments. The learning-parameter estimates (reciprocal of mean errors) are shown in Table 2; a likelihood ratio test for equality of c's was nonsignificant in both experiments. Further, a likelihood ratio test that each S's learning parameter, c_i, was equal to a common c was tested for all 65 Ss in Exp. I and for all 45 Ss in Exp. II. In each case, the null hypothesis could not be rejected—for Exp. I, $\chi^2 (64) = 53.3, p > .05$; for Exp. II, $\chi^2 (45) = 42.4, p > .05$ (Bower & Trabasso, 1963b). Thus, the data were consistent with the hypothesis of a common c for Ss in each experiment; the differences among Ss' error scores could be attributed to the variability inherent in the theoretical process.

The lack of group differences indicates that performance on the final problem was unrelated to the response assignments reinforced during the initial series. Correspondingly, there was no evidence for partial learning of the relevant cues or partial elimination of irrelevant cues (cf. Group NR). Effectively, we may rely upon a single error by S to indicate that he is "naive" about the correct solution. An error in this situation has the properties of an uncertain recurrent event (Restle, 1962); when S commits an error, we may, so to speak, reset him back to the starting point from which he began working on the problem. It should be noted that the null effects of reversal and nonreversal shifts before solution differ from the effects of such shifts after initial solution has occurred (Kendler & Kendler, 1962). What differs in the two cases is that after solution, S has a strong bias to attend to the formerly relevant cue, whereas before solution he is sampling cues at random to test (Kendler, Glucksberg, & Keston, 1961).

A criticism that might be made is that the theory asserts the null hypothesis, and what has been shown is that our experiments had inade-

TABLE 2

Mean Errors and Trial of Last Error, SDs, and c Estimates for the Final Problem

Group	N	c	Mean Errors	SD	Mean Trial of Last Error	SD
		Exp. I				
Control	18	.052	19.11	19.01	38.33	32.50
Reversal	18	.052	19.11	16.42	39.56	32.27
Nonreversal	18	.055	18.28	19.28	36.94	38.23
		Exp. II				
Control	10	.078	12.90	8.42	28.60	20.82
Reversal	10	.067	14.90	9.77	29.00	19.71
Nonreversal	10	.071	14.00	14.15	26.90	26.45

quate power to reject the null hypothesis. The methodological status of such matters has been discussed elsewhere (Binder, 1963; Grant, 1962). Our opinion is that if the partial learning is of such small magnitude that it does not appear with a combined total of 28 Ss in each condition, then indeed it may be considered a negligible effect.

Discussion

The Reversal and Control conditions in Exp. I and II resemble the standard ones used with this design on the continuity-noncontinuity issue. Judging from the review by Blum and Blum (1949), nearly all of the previous studies involved rats learning simultaneous discriminations with a small number of cues. On balance, that evidence favored a continuity position supplemented by constructs such as receptor orienting acts (e.g., Ehrenfreund, 1948). Whether such results should have a crucial bearing on a situational theory of adult human concept identification is a moot question. Writing for the continuity position, Spence (1940) pointed out early that the results from the animal studies may not be directly relevant to adult human learning mediated by complex symbolic mechanisms. Such mechanisms evidently are used by adults in solving concept problems, and current theorizing emphasizes such mechanisms (e.g., Bower & Trabasso, 1963a; Hunt, 1962; Kendler & Kendler, 1962; Underwood & Richardson, 1956). Our working hypothesis is that the extent to which an S's discrimination learning fits the all-or-none as opposed to the incremental description depends on the extent to which symbolic mediating responses are available to S.

It would appear that one reason why the all-or-nothing model predicts accurately in these experiments is that the conditions promote "focus sampling" (Bruner, Goodnow & Austin, 1956) because the memory load on S is otherwise overwhelming. The random-cue selection postulate implies that S's selection following an error of a new focus sample of cues to test is not affected by the past history of response assignments for the various cues. Such random selection of a sample focus is reasonable only if S's memory of specific past information is in some way impoverished. The experimental conditions presumably responsible for such poor memory include (a) the complexity of the stimuli, here 5 or 6 bits plus the 1-bit response, (b) the relatively rapid rate of presentation of this information (average time viewing each card was approximately 6 sec.), and (c) S has a specific set to identify the relevant cue, not to memorize and later recall the information he is seeing. In other experiments by us, direct tests of recall of specific information under these conditions showed the memory for six-card series to be very poor. Judging from the limited capacity of Ss for quickly processing and storing such large amounts of information, it is not surprising to find that they resort to focus sampling of specific cues to test.

The present results extend previous findings (Trabasso, 1963) that single-cue concept problems can be characterized as a one-step learning process. However, it is clear that not all varieties of concept learning can be so simply described. Our aim was to explore initially the most elementary form of concept learning, in a situation similar to a conventional discrimination learning procedure. Obviously, the simple all-or-nothing model must be elaborated and extended before it will account for learning of compounds of simpler concepts (e.g., conjunctions or disjunctions of several cues). Such extensions are currently under investigation.

References

Blum, R. A. & Blum, J. S. Factual issues in the "continuity controversy." *Psychol. Rev.*, 1949, **56,** 33–50.

Binder, A. Further considerations on testing the null hypothesis and the strategy and tactics of investigating theoretical models. *Psychol. Rev.*, 1963, **70,** 107–115.

Bower, G. H. & Trabasso, T. R. Concept identification. In R. C. Atkinson (Ed.), *Studies in mathematical psychology.* Stanford: Stanford Univer. Press, 1963, in press.

Bruner, J. S., Goodnow, J. J., & Austin, A. *A study of thinking.* Wiley: New York, 1956.

Ehrenfreund, D. An experimental test of the continuity theory of discrimination learning with pattern vision. *J. comp. physiol. Psychol.*, 1948, **41,** 408–422.

Grant, D. A. Testing the null hypothesis and the strategy and tactics of investigating theoretical models. *Psychol. Rev.*, 1962, **69,** 54–61.

Hayes, K. J. The backward curve: A method for the study of learning. *Psychol. Rev.*, 1953, **60,** 269–275.

Hunt, E. B. *Concept learning.* New York: Wiley, 1962.

Kendler, H. H., Glucksberg, S., & Keston, R. Perception and mediation in concept learning. *J. exp. Psychol.*, 1961, **61,** 1–16.

Kendler, H. H. & Kendler, T. S. Vertical and horizontal processes in problem solving. *Psychol. Rev.*, 1962, **69,** 1–16.

Krechevsky, I. A study of the continuity of the problem-solving process. *Psychol. Rev.*, 1938, **45,** 107–133.

McCulloch, T. L., & Pratt, J. G. A study of the pre-solution period in weight discrimination by white rats. *Psychol. Rev.*, 1934, **18,** 271–290.

Restle, F. The selection of strategies in cue learning. *Psychol. Rev., 1962,* **69,** 329–343.

Spence, K. W. Continuous versus noncontinuous interpretations of discrimination learning. *Psychol. Rev.*, 1940, **54,** 223–229.

Trabasso, T. R. Stimulus emphasis and all-or-none learning in concept identification *J. exp. Psychol.*, 1963, **65,** 398–406.

Trabasso, T. R. & Bower, G. H. Component learning in the four-category problem. *J. math. Psychol.*, in press.

Underwood, B. J. & Richardson, J. Verbal concept learning as a function of instructions and dominance level. *J. exp. Psychol.*, 1956, **51,** 229–238.

MEDIATED RESPONSES
TO SIZE AND BRIGHTNESS
AS A FUNCTION OF AGE

Tracy S. Kendler, Howard H. Kendler,
and Beulah Learnard

Tracy S. Kendler, Howard H. Kendler, and Beulah Learnard (1962)
provide further information concerning the way in which humans
learn concepts, focusing in particular on developmental changes in the
learning process. Their two major paradigms are the *mandatory shift*
paradigm and the *optional shift* paradigm (Kendler and Kendler, 1977).
In the first case, subjects participate in two discrimination tasks. In
task 1, pairs of objects are presented and the subject must choose
between them, with immediate feedback. The stimuli, for example,
could be a white circle, a black circle, a white triangle, and a black
triangle. For discrimination 1, a rule could be "black wins and white
loses." After the subjects have reached criterion on the initial task, a
second discrimination task is presented (although the subjects are not
told that there has been any shift). Half of the subjects are given a
reversal shift in which the same dimension (such as "color") is relevant but the values are reversed (such as "white wins"); the remaining
subjects are given a nonreversal, or extradimensional, shift in which a
new dimension (such as shape) is relevant, with a value such as "triangle wins." Research on rats indicates that nonreversal shifts are
generally easier to learn, but Kendler and Kendler (1977) found that
these results are not obtained for humans; as age increases, the relative ease of reversal over nonreversal shifts increases as well.

The optional shift paradigm uses the same initial discrimination
procedure; however, the second discrimination task is ambiguous,
such as in the presentation of a black circle and white triangle, where
white triangle wins. This is ambiguous because the subject who learns
to answer correctly for this pair may interpret it either as a reversal
shift ("white is now the winner") or as a nonreversal shift ("triangle is
now the winner"). To test the validity of these interpretations, a third
discrimination task is given, such as black triangle and white circle,
and *any* response is reinforced. If the subject interpreted the shift as a
reversal, then the white circle would be chosen; but if the subject in-

terpreted the shift as a nonreversal, then the black triangle would be chosen. The results for this method are similar to those obtained for the mandatory shift; rats prefer nonreversals but children show a preference for reversal shifts as they get older.

According to the authors, there are two major theories of learning for these tasks. The *single association theory* postulates that subjects form four separate S−R associations during the initial discrimination (for example, black circle is yes, white triangle is no, black triangle is yes, white circle is no). A reversal shift requires changing all four of these links, but a nonreversal requires changing only two. Thus, it appears that rats and very young children are most likely to use the single association learning process—a process essentially similar to that proposed by the continuity theory. Older children, however, appear to use the mediation model, which postulates that subjects go through two stages in learning: first they determine which dimension (such as shape or color) is critical and then they determine which value of the dimension goes with which response. In this case, the nonreversal shift requires relearning both stages, whereas the reversal shift requires only changing one stage (the second stage); thus, a reversal shift should be easier.

The results suggest that the mediation model is consistent with the idea that a simple continuity theory is not adequate for explaining adult conceptual learning. A summary of these results is published in *Psychological Review*, under the title "Vertical and Horizontal Processes in Problem Solving" (1962). The selection printed below provides a test of the mediation and single-association theories using the optional shift paradigm. The results indicate that preference for a reversal shift increases with age, and, therefore, that the tendency to use mediational strategies is related to age.

For those who investigate higher mental processes within the domain of S−R psychology, the concept of the mediating response is of singular importance (Cofer and Foley, 1942; Hull, 1930; Miller and Dollard, 1941; Osgood, 1957). It is usually treated as a response which intercedes between the external stimulus and the overt response to provide stimulation that influences the course of overt behavior. Since this response is, ordinarily, more often implicit than explicit, its investigation poses problems. One method of dealing with such problems is to develop techniques that make the mediating responses overt, as in the measurement of movements of the tongue during the solution of problems in arithmetic (Sokolov, 1959). Another method, exemplified by the present study, is to infer the process from overt behavior as manifested under a prescribed set of conditions. In this latter method, the mediated response has the status of an hypothetical construct which may or may not be ultimately measurable, but which justifies its use by its theoretical and heuristic function (Kendler, 1961).

The general technique used in this investigation is based on procedures developed by Buss (1953) and Kendler and D'Amato (1955). It consists essentially of studying mediation by means of the transfer demonstrated from an initial to a subsequent discrimination. The initial discrimination presents stimuli that differ simultaneously on two dimensions, but only one of the dimensions is relevant. After criterion is reached, another discrimination is presented that utilizes the same or similar stimuli but requires a shift in response. One type of shift, called a reversal-shift, requires S to continue to respond to the previously relevant dimension but in an opposite way. In another type of shift, called a non-reversal shift, S is required to respond to the previously irrelevant dimension. For example, if S is initially trained on stimuli that differ in brightness (black vs. white) and size (large vs. small) by being rewarded for responses to black, regardless of size, a reversal-shift would consist of learning to respond to white and a non-reversal shift would consist of learning to respond to small. Comparison between these two types of shifts is of particular interest because theories based on single-unit and on mediated S–R connections yield opposed predictions about their relative efficiency. A single-unit theory that assumes a direct association between the external stimulus and the overt response would predict reversal-shift to be more difficult than non-reversal shift. This is because reversal-shift requires the replacement of a response that has previously been consistently reinforced with a response that has previously been consistently extinguished. In a non-reversal shift, previous training has reinforced responses to the newly positive and newly negative stimuli equally often. Strengthening one of these associations does not require as much extinction of its competitor as in a reversal-shift and should therefore be acquired more easily. Kelleher confirmed the prediction that, for rats, reversal-shift was more difficult than non-reversal shift (1956).

A theory that includes a mediating link (or links) between the external stimulus and the overt response leads to a different prediction. The mediating link is conceived of as a perceptual or verbal response, often covert, to the relevant dimension which produces cues that determine the overt response. In a reversal-shift, the initial dimension maintains its relevance; hence, so does the mediated response. Only the overt response needs to be changed, and since the experimental situation provides only one alternative overt response, this change presents no great difficulty. In a non-reversal shift, the previously acquired mediation is no longer relevant, consequently both the mediating and the overt response must be replaced, making this a more difficult task than a reversal-shift. Experiments by Buss (1953), Kendler and D'Amato (1955), and Harrow and Friedman (1958), using a more complex variation of the technique of reversal and non-reversal shift with college students as Ss, confirmed the prediction of the mediational analysis. Unlike rats, college students acquire a reversal-shift more easily than a non-reversal shift.

This discontinuity between rats and adult humans led to two investigations with young children to determine whether their behavior, in this type of situation, was more consistent with the single-unit or mediational formulation. The results suggested that children between 3 and 4 yr. of age respond predominantly in the single-unit manner (Kendler, Kendler, and Wells, 1960), and that children between 5 and 7 yr. of age divide about evenly with half mediating and half not (Kendler and Kendler, 1959). These data imply a developmental process in which very young children's behavior is governed by a relatively primitive single-unit S–R process, with increasing maturity leading to increases in the proportion of children who mediate. The purpose of the present investigation was to provide a direct test of this implication. Previous procedures were modified to allow each S to choose whether they would behave mediationally or not. This was done by presenting a shift that could be accomplished on either a reversal or non-reversal basis. Since the choice was left with the Ss, each one could be identified as a mediator or non-mediator, depending on whether he chose a reversal or a non-reversal shift. Buss used such a procedure on college students and found that 72% chose a reversal-shift (1956). The present study applied this method to children at five chronological age levels; namely 3, 4, 6, 8 and 10 yr. of age, to determine whether there is an increase in the proportion of children who mediate and, if so, to study the course of this increase.

METHOD

Subjects.

The Ss were 171 children of both sexes drawn from schools in the metropolitan area of New York, ranging in age from 3 to 10 yr. Of these, 19 were eliminated; 8 because their estimated *IQ* was below 80, 8 because of the rough matching in *IQ*, and 3 because they did not learn the initial discrimination within 130 trials. The 3 non-learners were all in the 3- and 4-yr. old groups.

The 152 Ss who met the requirements of the experiment were distributed as shown in Table I. The Ss were run in two replications, each with a different *E*.[1] The replications were identical with reference to procedure and experimental conditions, similar with reference to population sampled, and, except for the youngest group, equal in number. In the 3-yr. group, one replication consisted of 16 Ss and the other of 8.

Apparatus.

The discriminative apparatus used was 17 in. high, 10 in. wide and 4 in. deep. Paired windows, manipulanda, and slots for delivery of the reward were arranged symmetrically on the frontal surface. The windows, through which the discriminanda were exposed, were 3 × 3 in. The manipulanda were round steel-rods, ⅜ in. in diameter and 4¼ in. in exposed length, long enough slightly to overlap the stimulus-cards. S manipulated the rods by pushing them toward the discriminanda, an operation accompanied by a loud mechanical click. The base of each rod was attached to a concealed arm of an electronically controlled marble-magazine, which when activated delivers marbles to the openings beneath the manipulanda.

The discriminanda consisted of four mid-gray pasteboard-cards on which squares that differ in size and brightness were mounted. Two of the squares were black and two were white. Two were small (1 sq. in.) and two were large (3 sq. in). The four discriminanda were so paired as to vary simultaneously in two dimensions. Thus small black (SB) was always paired with large white (LW) and large black (LB) with small white (SW). The

[1] Beulah Learnard was *E* in one replication and Helen S. Pollack in the other.

TABLE I

Number, Age and Estimated *IQ* of *Ss* in Each Group

Age in months			
mean	range	N	Mean estimated *IQ*
43.3	37 – 47	24	120.2
54.3	49 – 59	32	112.0
77.3	73 – 82	32	112.2
101.7	96 – 109	32	113.8
127.0	121 – 134	32	113.6

cards were inserted by hand into a grooved container behind the windows. A red plastic screen could be slid into place to cover the windows and conceal *E*'s manipulations from *S*.

Procedure.

The *Ss* were run individually in a room in which *E* and *S* were alone. The procedure was begun with the administration of selected sub-tests from the Stanford-Binet and the Wechsler Intelligence Scale for Children (*WISC*) in order to provide a quick, albeit rough, basis for equating the *IQs* of the various age-groups in the experiment. First the vocabulary sub-test of the WISC was given. If a child attained the minimal score (equivalent to an *MA* of 58 mo.) or more, that ended the *IQ*-test. Children who did not attain this level were presented with the following items from the Stanford-Binet test: picture vocabulary, comprehension- and definition-items for years II, II-6, III, III-6, IV, IV-6, and V until a basal level was established. In all cases, tests were administered and scored in accordance with the scale from which they were drawn.

Following the *IQ*-test, *S* was seated comfortably in front of the apparatus and *E* read the following instructions.

This is a game in which you will try to win as many marbles as you can. Here are some marbles for you to start with. [*E* handed five marbles to *S*.] Put them in the holes in this board. [In front of *S* was a grooved board to hold the marbles he won.]

Now (name of child), [*E* dropped screen] look at these two pictures. The way we play this game is that there will always be one picture in each of these little windows. One picture is a winning picture and the other picture is a losing picture. This is how you find out which picture is a winner. Look at these two sticks. Each stick points to one of the pictures like this. When we start the game you will press the stick that points to the picture that you think is the winner. If you are right, a marble will drop out of one of these little holes and you may put it with the rest of the marbles you have. If you are wrong, no marble will drop out. Instead, you will give one of your marbles back to me. Each time I drop this screen, you will have *one* turn to press. On each of these turns, one of the pictures is a winner and the other picture is a loser. Sometimes the winner will be in this window and sometimes the winner will be in that window. If you try, you can win a marble every time you choose. Remember, each time I drop this screen you will have only one turn to choose.

Ready? Then we'll start. Now press one of the sticks and see if it points to the winning picture. [After the first correct choice, *E* said]: That was the winning picture. Every time you win a marble, pick it up and put it with the rest of your marbles. [*E* pointed to a grooved marble board. At this point, *E* explained that at the end of the game *S* would be allowed to keep one of the marbles but the rest had to be returned so that *E* could play the game with the rest of the children. After the first incorrect choice, *E* said]: That was the losing picture. So you'll have to give back one of your marbles. [After every tenth trial, *E* said]: Don't forget to look at the pictures. Remember, if you try, you can win a marble every time you choose.

Three series of trials were presented with no noticeable break in the procedure between them. Series I provided training in an initial discrimination; Series II, training in a second discrimination; and Series III, the test-trials.

In Series I, both pairs of stimuli were presented alternately in a prearranged irregular sequence so designed that (1) each pair appeared equally often but no more than twice in succession; and (2) the correct stimulus appeared equally often on the right and the

FIGURE 1

Illustration of One of the Arrangements of Stimuli and Reinforcement Used in the Experiment

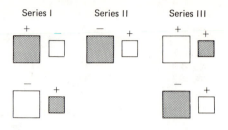

left but no more than twice in succession in either position. The actual sequence presented to each S depended, however, to some extent on his performance. Because children, especially the younger ones, are prone to form position-habits early in learning that can considerably prolong the acquisition of a discrimination, each pair was presented in the same position as many times as it was necessary before the child chose the correct stimulus. After a correct response, the next pair in the prearranged sequence described above was presented. This procedure reduced the intermittent reinforcement that could otherwise sustain a position-habit for a long time.

During this series, a response to one member of each pair was always correct and, consequently, rewarded with a marble. If the response was to the negative member of the pair, S was obliged to return a marble to E. The positive stimuli shared one aspect of the stimulus and differed on the other. Figure 1 presents an illustration of one of the arrangements of the stimuli and reinforcements presented in each series, which will be used as an example throughout. In the illustration both positive members are black and size is irrelevant. S was run in this series until a criterion of 9 out of 10 consecutive correct responses was reached. Each aspect of the stimulus, i.e. B (black), W (white), S (small), and L (large) was the positive stimulus for one quarter of the Ss, as arranged by random assignment.

After criterion was reached in Series I, Series II was presented. During this series only one pair of stimuli was presented. For half of the Ss it was one of the pairs, for the other half it was the remaining pair. For all Ss the previously negative stimulus became positive and the previously positive stimulus became negative. In this series, the stimuli differed on two dimensions and there was no second pair to make one dimension more relevant than the other. In the illustration provided, the positive stimulus is both small and white. S could learn by responding to the size, to the brightness, or to both. The third series was designed to ascertain the basis on which S learned Series II.

After criterion (9 out of 10 consecutive correct responses) was reached on Series II, Series III began. Here, as in Series I, both pairs of stimuli were presented alternately, except that this time any response was rewarded to the pair of stimuli that had not appeared in Series II. Responses to this test-pair served to determine the basis of response in Series II, since these discriminanda separated the critical aspects of the stimuli that were previously merged, and the procedure required a choice of one. In the illustration provided, if S responded in Series II to the whiteness of the positive member, he could be expected to choose LW in Series III. If he were responding to size, he could be expected to choose SB. If he had been responding to both size and brightness, he would distribute his choices between the members of the pair.

The presentation of the other stimulus-pair was interlaced with the test-pair. It retained the pattern of reward and was designed to help keep S responding on the same basis as in Series II. Each pair was presented 10 times in the same alternating sequence as in Series I.

At the completion of Series III, the Ss were shown the pair from Series II once again and asked some questions designed to provide information about the verbal processes associated with this task. The first question was, "Which one was the winner?" If the child made no relevant verbal response, or if he merely pointed, he was asked, "What does it look like?" If there was still no relevant verbal comment, he was asked, "How do you know?"

After the end of the session, *S* was pledged to keep secret the nature of the 'game' until everyone in his school had had a turn.

Classification.

S's choices on the test-pair during Series III provided the basis for classification into one of the following three categories: reversal, non-reversal, and inconsistent.

(1) *Reversal.* If, on the test-pair, *S* made eight or more responses to the stimulus that had been incorrect in Series I, he was classified as a reverser. For example, if, as in Fig. 1, B was positive in Series I and *S* chose LW consistently in the test-series, it would indicate that Series II had been learned by shifting from B to W, or in other words, by making a reversal-shift.

(2) *Non-reversal.* If, on the test-pair, *S* made eight or more responses to the stimulus that had been irrelevant in Series I, he was classified as a non-reverser. In our example, this *S* would choose the SB in the test-series, thereby indicating that although Series I was acquired by responding to brightness, Series II had been acquired by responding primarily to the size of the positive stimulus. This learning is based on a shift to the previously irrelevant dimension and has in previous research been called a non-reversal shift.

(3) *Inconsistent.* Another possibility is that *S*'s choices in Series III may be inconsistent, *i.e.* neither stimulus of the test-pair may be chosen more than seven times. This behavior would indicate that by the end of Series II. *S* was responding equally, or almost so, to the size and brightness of the positive stimulus.

Results and Discussion

The main concern of this research was with the changes in the proportion of children who used a mediating response as a function of chronological age. Whether a child mediated was inferred from choice-behavior in Series III, and so the analysis of results begins there. The experimental design included two replications with two different *E*s in order to assess the stability of the results. Therefore, a preliminary series of χ^2-tests were made comparing the results of the two replications for each age-level to determine whether the replications required separate treatment or whether they could be treated as though drawn from the same population. None of the χ^2-tests approached statistical significance at the 5% level; consequently the two replications were combined for all the ensuing analyses.

Figure 2 presents the major results of the experiment, *i.e.* the percentage of children in each category of choice plotted as a function of age. To develop fully the implications of these results, each category will be given separate consideration.

For reasons previously presented, reversers are considered to have made mediated responses. These are the children who, when faced with a shift, continue to respond to the same dimension in a reverse manner, *e.g.* shift from black to white. The expectation about this category, based on previous results and theoretical considerations, was that it would lie below 50% between the ages of three and four (Kendler, Kendler, and Wells, 1960), rise to about 50% between five and seven (Kendler and Kendler, 1959), and then continue to increase with increasing age until some relatively high asymptote is reached (Buss, 1956). The results were that 37.5% of the 3-yr. olds mediated, and this proportion increased to 50% at 4 yr., remained level at 6, and then rose gradually to 62.5% at age

FIGURE 2

Percentage of Children at Each Age-Level Responding in Each Category

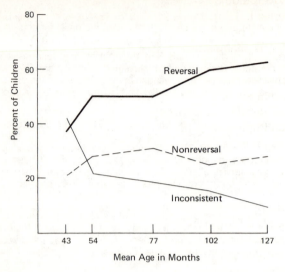

10 yr. A test of the significance of differences between 3- and 10-yr. olds, based on an estimate of the 'true' proportion drawn from the total group, yielded a one-tail $p = 0.03$. Although the curve appears to be approaching a rather low asymptote, these results confirm the general developmental implications of previous studies and also show an almost surprising measure of agreement where specific comparisons are possible.

On the basis of the following brief rationale, derived from Spence's single-unit theory of discrimination-learning (Spence 1936; 1952), the non-mediators were expected to be distributed between the non-reversal and inconsistent categories. In this framework, each discriminandum is viewed as a complex consisting of two stimulus-components, each of which can acquire its own excitatory tendency as a function of the pattern of reinforcement. Thus at the end of Series I, the excitatory tendency of the positive component of the relevant dimension (e.g. B, as in Figure 1) should be relatively high, since responses to it have always been reinforced. The excitatory tendency of the negative component of the relevant dimension (W) should be relatively low, since responses to it have never been reinforced.[2] The excitatory tendencies of the two components of the irrelevant dimension (L and S), which have been reinforced roughly half of the time, should be of a magnitude somewhere between those of B and W. At the outset of Series II, the child should continue to respond to the stimulus-compound that was previously correct (LB) until the tendencies previously built up become sufficiently weakened through non-reinforcement to permit responses to the other stimulus-compound (SW), which

[2] It is assumed, for the present, that the removal of a positive reinforcer for an incorrect response does not alter the gross relationships between reinforcement and extinction postulated here.

are immediately reinforced. Each component of the newly positive stimulus-compound should have different excitatory strengths as a result of the training in Series I. Thus, the response to W should be weaker than the response to S. If a non-mediating child reaches criterion during the time this differential is maintained and is then required, as in Series III, to choose between W and S, he should choose S predominantly. This response would place him in the non-reversing category.

But the analysis of single-unit behavior is not yet complete. If, as is assumed here, there is no selective process operating in non-mediators, then all stimuli impinging on the child at the time of reinforced response should acquire an increase in excitatory strength for that response. Consequently responses to SW should lead to increases in the strength of both stimulus-components. As the strength of S approaches its asymptote, the difference between the strengths of S and W should gradually diminish and finally disappear. If a child has sufficient trials before criterion is reached in Series II for the strengths of S and W to approach equality, he should choose one stimulus as often as the other in Series III. He would be classified as inconsistent. Let it be noted as an aside to be taken up presently that this analysis implies that Series II should be learned more slowly by inconsistent than by non-reversing children. Consideration of the mechanism of acquired distinctiveness of stimuli would lead to the expectation that mediators, *i.e.*, reversers, would learn Series II more rapidly than either of the two non-mediating groups (Cantor, 1955; Norcross and Spiker, 1958).

As a corollary to the rise in the percentage of mediators with age, there should, of course, be a decrease in the percentage of non-mediators. There seemed, at the outset of the research, no reason why the decrease should not occur for both non-mediating categories. Figure 2 shows, however, that while there was a sharp and statistically significant drop for the inconsistent category ($p = 0.001$), there was no drop for the non-reversals, a result that bears explanation.

Despite the failure of the non-reversal category to reveal any decreasing trend, it seems reasonable to conclude that, in general, the results of Figure 2 bear out the implication that there is a transition in the course of human development from unmediated, single-unit S–R behavior to mediated behavior, at least with reference to the acquisition of the concepts of size and brightness. They suggest further that the proportion of children who have made this transition increases in a gradual and lawful manner.

Summary

The study was undertaken to test the implications of previous research to the effect that children below 5 or 6 yr. of age tend to behave predominantly on a single-unit S–R basis and that with increasing chronological age an increasing proportion of children behave in a mediated manner. Children at 5 age-levels; namely 3, 4, 6, 8, and 10 yr., were presented with an initial discriminative task of concept-formation that included a relevant and an irrelevant stimulus-dimension. After criterion they were presented with a shift in which the same stimuli were employed but the pattern of reinforcement was reversed. The shift could be accomplished by responding to the previously relevant dimension in an opposite manner (a reversal-shift); by responding to the previously irrelevant dimension (a non-reversal shift); or by responding to both stimulus-aspects indiscriminately (an inconsistent shift). The choice of which shift he made lay with S. On the basis of a theoretical analysis, reversal-shift was taken to be indicative of a mediating process intervening between the external stimuli and the overt response. The results confirmed the prediction that the proportion of children who respond with a reversal-shift i.e. mediate, would increase with age. Both the non-reversal and the inconsistent shifts were presumed to be indicative of a more primitive single-unit S–R process. Both of these types of shift were expected to decrease with age. The prediction was verified for the inconsistent shifts but not for the non-reversal shifts.

References

Buss, A.H. Rigidity as a function of reversal and nonreversal shifts in the learning of successive discriminations. *J. Exp. Psychol.*, 1953, **45,** 75–81.

Buss, A.H. Reversal and nonreversal shifts in concept formation with partial reinforcement eliminated. *J. Exp. Psychol.*, 1956, **52,** 162–166.

Cantor, G.N. The effects of three types of pretraining on discrimination learning in preschool children. *J. Exp. Psychol.*, 1955, **49,** 339–342.

Cofer, C.N. & Foley, J.P. Mediated generalization and the interpretation of Verbal behavior: I. Prolegomena. *Psychological Review*, 1942, **49,** 513–540.

Harrow, M. & Friedman, G.B. Comparing reversal and nonreversal shifts in concept Formation with partial reinforcement controlled. *J. Exp. Psychol.*, 1958, **55,** 592–597.

Hull, C.L. Knowledge and purpose of habit mechanisms. *Psychological Review*, 1930, **37,** 511–525.

Kelleher, R.T. Discrimination learning as a function of reversal and nonreversal shifts. *J. Exp. Psychol.*, 1956, **51,** 379–384.

Kendler, H.H. Problems of problem-solving research, in *Current Trends in Psychological Theory: A Bicentennial Program*, 1961.

Kendler, H.H. & D'Amato, M.F. A comparison of reversal shifts and nonreversal shifts in human concept formation behavior. *J. Exp. Psychol.*, 1955, **49,** 165–174.

Kendler, T.S. & Kendler, H.H. Reversal and nonreversal shifts in kindergarten children. *J. Exp. Psychol.*, 1959, **58,** 56–60.

Kendler, T.S., Kendler, H.H., & Wells, D. Reversal and nonreversal shifts in nursery school children. *J. Comp. Physiol. Psychol.*, 1960, **53,** 83–87.

Miller, N.E. & Dollard, J. *Social Learning and Imitation*, 1941, pp. 69–90.

Norcross, K.J. & Spiker, C.C. Effects of mediated associations on transfer in paired-associate learning. *J. Exp. Psychol.*, 1958, **55,** 129–134.

Osgood, C.E. A behavioristic analysis of perception and language in cognitive phenomena, in *Contemporary Approaches to Cognition*, 1957, pp. 75–118.

Solokov, reported by A. Mintz. Further developments in psychology in the U.S.S.R., *American Review of Psychology*, 1959, **10,** 464.

Spence, K.W. The nature of discrimination learning in animals. *Psychological Review*, 1936, **43,** 417–449.

Spence, K.W. The nature of response in discrimination learning. *Psychological Review*, 1952, **59,** 89–93.

SERIAL PATTERN LEARNING

Frank Restle and Eric R. Brown

Frank Restle and Eric R. Brown (1970) investigated several theories concerning the way in which subjects learn to form serial patterns of behavior. In their study, Restle and Brown asked subjects to face a panel of six light bulbs each equipped with a press-button underneath. As soon as one of the six lights came on, the subjects had three seconds to press the button under the next light they thought would come on. Then another light would come on, the subjects would have to guess which would be next, and so on. For example, the pattern **6542344543** might be repeated, without a break, for 20 trials. Thus, the subject would have to anticipate the next light 200 times.

What theories can account for the ability of subjects to learn the correct "guesses" in this task? Brown and Restle suggest several theories based on the gradual formation of S−R bonds. For example, the *simple associative chain theory* postulates that subjects learn to associate each stimulus with the stimulus that comes next to it in the pattern. This theory predicts that many errors should occur at points where differential use of two S−R associations occur with the same stimulus (that is, locations 1, 4, 6, 7, 8, and 10 for the above example, in which positions 1 and 6 are most difficult because both are preceded by a position 3 light coming on). A related idea is the *compound stimulus theory* which states that subjects form a chain (as in the above theory), but the stimulus in the S−R pair may be more than one simple stimulus. For example, in order to answer correctly at positions 4 and 10, the subject is required to remember *three* previous lights (that is, 654 before 2, and 454 before 3). Thus, these two positions should receive the most errors.

As an alternative to chaining theories, Restle and Brown suggest the *continuation of runs theory*, which postulates that subjects induce rules based on simple runs such that errors should occur where new runs begin (that is, at locations 1, 4, 7, and 9). An analysis of the pattern of errors in this learning task indicated that most errors did in fact occur at positions predicted by the continuation of runs theory rather than by the other theories.

This experiment, like those of Bower and Trabasso, and Kendler et al., suggests that subjects do not learn by forming simple S–R associations; rather, subjects seem to generate "rules," and errors result from systematically misapplying these rules. In a recent book entitled *Learning: Animal Behavior and Human Cognition*, Restle (1975) has related this line of research to such diverse topics as learning to play music, simple motor performance, and linguistic grammar.

Recent studies of serial list learning have asked whether items in the list are chained each to the next or whether each item is associated with its serial position in the list. The chain hypothesis says that each item is a response to the previous item and a stimulus for the next and that learning is the acquisition of such interitem associations. The position hypothesis supposes that the serial position of an item is the stimulus for that item and that learning is the acquisition of position-item associations. Both approaches have received some recent experimental support (Brown & Rubin, 1967; Crowder, 1968; Jensen & Rohwer, 1965; Saufley, 1967; Slamecka, 1967; Winnick & Dornbush, 1968; Young, Hakes, & Hicks, 1967).

Lashley (1951) put forward the idea that the serial organization of behavior, particularly language, cannot be explained by associative chains and involves more complex, hierarchically (or syntactically) organized control systems. This position has been strengthened by recent developments in psycholinguistics (Chomsky, 1959; Chomsky, 1965; Fodor, 1966; McNeill 1966; Miller & Chomsky, 1963).

The question regarding chains vs. serial position cues is a question of the nature of the stimulus element of an S–R association, whereas the questions raised by Lashley (1951) and the psycholinguists ask whether any associative model, no matter how S and R are defined, can explain serial learning. The aim of the present study was to determine if serial pattern learning involves the acquisition of nonassociative cognitive structures. To this end, several S–R interpretations of serial learning were evaluated with respect to an experimental task in which Ss learned periodic sequences of (nonlinguistic) events. Particular attention was paid to the associative chain and serial position theories of serial learning (Jensen & Rohwer, 1965; Saufley, 1967; Young, 1962).

METHOD

The Ss in each of eight groups learned a repeating sequence of events by the method of anticipation. The events were six lights arranged in a row on a panel. The responses were six buttons, one beneath each event light.

Each of the eight groups learned a different sequence. The eight sequences were derived from two distinct patterns, each pattern having four different forms: (a) an *initial* form which used Events 1–5, i.e., the leftmost five of the six events; (b) a *transposed* form obtained by shifting the initial form one event to the right; (c) an *inverted* form obtained by replacing Event N of the initial form with Event 6–N; and (d) an *inverted and transposed* form obtained by replacing Event N of the initial form with Event 7–N.

Each group of Ss learned only one of the four forms (initial, transposed, inverted, inverted and transposed) of one of the two patterns. The dependent variables were the number of errors made at each location (serial position) of the pattern and the frequency of particular errors.

Subjects.

The Ss were 225 undergraduate students from introductory lecture and laboratory classes in psychology at Indiana University. Their participation in the experiment was in partial fulfillment of a course requirement. The Ss were tested in squads of four (or fewer), and all Ss in a given squad were tested on the same sequence. The assignment of squads to the eight groups (sequences) was unsystematic, although not truly random.

Apparatus and materials.

The experiment was conducted in a dimly lit, 12 × 14 ft. room. Each S was visually isolated from his neighbors by black, plywood partitions. In front of each S was a slanting panel equipped with an amber ready light centered at its top, six red push buttons arranged in a row, and a small white event light above each button. The ready light and event lights were controlled from an adjoining room by an IBM 1800 process-control computer, and responses were sensed and recorded by that same device.

The eight sequences, four forms of each pattern, and the number of Ss tested on each sequence are shown in Table 1.[1] The two patterns were chosen so that no run of events, e.g., 3–4–5, would terminate at an end event light (1 or 6) in any of their forms. Notice that both initial forms use Events 1–5 and that both patterns are 10 events in length.

TABLE 1

Initial Form and Variations of Each Pattern

Sequence	Location									
	1	2	3	4	5	6	7	8	9	10
Pattern 1 (N = 110)										
Initial form (n = 26)	1	2	3	5	4	3	3	2	3	4
Transposed form (n = 28)	2	3	4	6	5	4	4	3	4	5
Inverted form (n = 27)	5	4	3	1	2	3	3	4	3	2
Transposed and inverted form (n = 29)	6	5	4	2	3	4	4	5	4	3
Pattern 2 (N = 115)										
Initial form (n = 32)	1	2	3	4	2	3	2	5	4	3
Transposed form (n = 25)	2	3	4	5	3	4	3	6	5	4
Inverted form (n = 26)	5	4	3	2	4	3	4	1	2	3
Transposed and inverted form (n = 32)	6	5	4	3	5	4	5	2	3	4

Note.—The numbers 1–6 in table body refer to the event lights from left to right across S's' panel.

---

[1] In actuality, 237 Ss were tested. However, any S was discarded who (a) consistently followed the events instead of predicting them or (b) made 10% or more omissions. The enforcement of these criteria resulted in the discarding of 12 Ss. Eight Ss were discarded from the Pattern 1 groups: two from the initial form, one from the transposed form, four from the inverted form, and one from the inverted and transposed form. Four Ss were discarded from the Pattern 2 groups, two from the initial form and two from the inverted form.

Procedure.

The Ss were instructed to perform by anticipation and to make their predictions quickly. They were told that the event lights would come on in a repeating pattern, but were given no information about the pattern's characteristics.

Each squad of Ss served in a single experimental session during which one of the four forms of Pattern 1 or Pattern 2 was repeated 20 times with no break between successive repetitions of the pattern (trials). A binary version of this kind of experiment has been described as a "circular maze for humans" (Restle, 1967).

At each presentation the ready light was lit, and S had 3 sec. to respond. At the end of the 3-sec. response interval, the correct event light was lit for 1 sec. Then, after a 1-sec. delay, the ready light was again lit, and the apparatus was ready for the next anticipation. Since the procedure was completely automatic, E was present in the testing room only at the start of each session to give instructions.

Results

The eight sequences were learned by most Ss and were equal in overall difficulty. There were easy and hard locations in each pattern, and the two patterns produced quite different detailed performance. The more specific results are taken up as they bear on available hypotheses regarding serial learning.

Associative chain hypothesis.   If serial pattern learning were the formation of associations between one event and the next, then Ss could not master any "branching" sequence that contained the same event followed by two different events, for this would require the differential use of two S–R associations with the same stimulus. Branches occur at Locations 1, 4, 6, 7, 8, and 10 of Pattern 1 and at Locations 1, 3, 4, 5, 6, 7, 8, and 10 of Pattern 2. All eight sequences were well learned. For all sequences, performance on Trials 8–20 was better than 75% correct at every location and above 90% at most locations. This level of performance is impossible without differentiation of the branches in the sequences.

FIGURE 1

Mean errors at each location (serial position) for each form of Pattern 1.

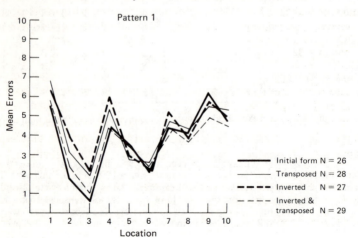

FIGURE 2

Mean errors at each location (serial position) for each form of Pattern 2.

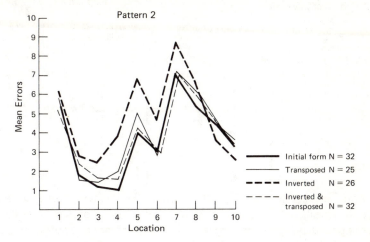

Pattern 2

Initial form N = 32
Transposed N = 25
Inverted   N = 26
Inverted &
transposed N = 32

Serial position hypothesis. If serial pattern learning is the association of events with their serial positions in the pattern, then S could learn branching sequences. As stimuli, the serial positions should be comparable, and the 10 locations of each pattern should be equally difficult or else display some version of a serial position effect.

Figures 1 and 2 show the mean errors made at each location for the four forms of Patterns 1 and 2, respectively. The four forms of Pattern 1 have error profiles which are quite jagged and similar in shape. The Pattern 2 profiles are likewise similar and jagged, but differ markedly in shape from those of Pattern 1. A profile analysis verified that the (pooled) error profiles for Patterns 1 and 2 are significantly nonparallel, $F(9,215) = 22.7$, $p < .001$. The hypothesis of a flat profile was rejected at the .001 level for the Pattern 1 profile, $F(9,98) = 30.8$, and the Pattern 2 profile, $F(9,103) = 28.3$. Since the profiles are jagged and quite different in shape for the two patterns, learning must depend on more than just the serial positions of the events, and mastery of the sequences is not attributable to S's use of serial positions as cues.

Compound stimulus hypothesis. The facts (a) that these branching sequences were learned and (b) that the error profiles were jagged and of different shape for the two patterns indicate that both conventional S–R interpretations, the associative chain hypothesis and the serial position hypothesis, are inadequate explanations of serial pattern learning. However, these facts might be explained by the idea that Ss learn S–R associations in which the stimulus is not one but several adjacent past events. In the sequences used, the correct response at some locations can be learned merely on the basis of one preceding event; other locations require two previous events, and still others require three. In Figure 3A are shown the locations of Pattern 1 (its four forms) with each location classified according to the number of previous events required to specify

FIGURE 3

Mean errors at each location plotted as a function of the number of previous events required to specify next event.

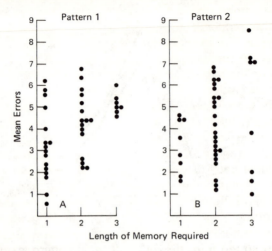

the next event and the mean errors at that location. Figure 3B shows the corresponding results for Pattern 2. Since each point in these figures is the mean performance of a whole group of Ss at a given location, it appears that the relationship of mean errors to length of memory required, though positive, is very weak and leaves much to be explained.

Transfer of training hypothesis. Another simple explanation of the results might be to suppose that Ss bring past experience to bear on the experimental task by importing familiar sequences of digits or positions, e.g., 1-2-3. However, as shown in Figures 1 and 2, the four forms of a pattern yield similar profiles, although they involve different events and different subsequences. The Ss may have encoded the events as digits, but they did not simply bring specific sequences of numbers into the problem as expectations. Also, it is unlikely that specific motor sequences from some preexperimental situation, e.g., playing the piano, transferred to the present task, again, because the four forms of a pattern produced very similar error profiles.

The four forms of a pattern are similar, not only in terms of their error profiles, but also with respect to more detailed performance. Suppose that Response N is the most frequent error made at a given location in the pattern's initial form. Then, $N + 1$ would be the corresponding error in the transposed form, $6 - N$ in the inverted form, and $7 - N$ in the transposed and inverted form. To a remarkable degree, the most common error at a given location of one form corresponded to the most common error at that same location of the other forms. At Location 4 of Pattern 1, e.g., the most frequent error was "4" in the initial form, "5" in the transposed form, "2" in the inverted form, and "3" in the transposed and inverted form. In fact, at 7 of the 10 locations of Pattern 1 and at 9 of the 10 locations of Pattern 2, there was perfect correspondence of the most frequent error in all four forms of the pattern.

Continuation of runs hypothesis. This correspondence of dominant errors among the four forms of a pattern requires an explanation in terms of those properties which are invariant with respect to transposition and inversion. For example, the subsequences 1-2-3, 3-4-5, and 4-3-2 are all "runs." A run can be defined as any subsequence in which the same interval (in the musical sense of a *length* of transition) occurs two or more times in succession.

At four locations in each pattern, it is possible to err by the continuation of a run. In Pattern 1 these locations are 1, 4, 7, and 9. The run continuation error was most frequent at all of these locations and occurred, on the average, 2.92, 3.61, 2.60, and 2.87 times. No other single error in the entire pattern occurred more than a mean of 1.88 times. In Pattern 2, run continuation errors are possible at Locations 1, 5, 7, and 8. At the first three of these locations, the run continuation error was most frequent, occurring a mean of 3.32, 2.56, and 3.86 times, whereas at locations where run continuation errors were not possible, the most frequent errors occurred from .69 to 1.56 times. These findings isolate the run continuation error as a major factor contributing to the structure of the data in the present experiment.

One explanation of the run continuation error might be that Ss enter the experiment with a learned tendency to continue runs. An alternative hypothesis is that Ss rapidly develop a general description of the sequences properties and tend to continue runs because run subsequences occur in the two patterns. Pattern 1 can be organized into three run subsequences of three in length and one additional event. This organization is 1-2-3 5-4-3 3 2-3-4 in the initial form of Pattern 1. A natural organization of Pattern 2 is into two run subsequences and one short trill or alternating subsequence, 1-2-3-4 2-3-2 5-4-3 in its initial form.

Location 8 in Pattern 2 provides a test of the two interpretations. Since the previous three events were 2-3-2 (or a transformation thereof), S can err by continuing a run (3-2-1) and by continuing a trill (2-3-2-3). The most frequent error is, in fact, the trill continuation error "3", which occurs a mean of 3.44 times. In contrast to the other locations in Pattern 2 at which run continuation errors could occur, the run error at Location 8 was relatively infrequent, occurring a mean of only 1.06 times. Thus, it appears that Ss do not bring to the task a fixed tendency to continue runs.

However, if the tendency to extend a run is, in fact, adopted during training, it is adopted quickly. The Ss having Pattern 2 begin training with the events 1-2-3-4 (or a transformation thereof). The next event cannot realistically be predicted, for clearly the sequence has not yet begun to repeat. Nevertheless, at this point the next anticipatory response is "5," the run continuation error, with probability .80. This very early overextension of a run indicates that Ss are organizing their experience into more general cognitive structures from the very beginning of training.

Discussion

The results of the present experiment indicate that the following S-R interpretations of serial pattern learning are inadequate: (a) simple associative chain, (b) serial position as a cue, (c) sequences of events as stimuli, (d) transfer of training of specific event sequences, and (e) a fixed tendency to continue runs. Instead, Ss detect abstract properties of the sequence, such as the existence of runs and trills, that can be represented as systems of rules. These rules are then applied by Ss to generate anticipation responses.

Serial pattern learning is a function of the sequence, and, as the present study shows, of its more abstract properties. Although performance depended on the pattern, it did not depend strongly on the particular lights used or on the particular intervals in the sense that inverting and/or transposing the pattern did not markedly change performance.

Logically, one cannot conclude from the present study that the patterns of response observed in serial pattern learning should also appear in serial verbal learning. In conventional serial learning tasks the elements of the list are, by design, disjoint and the fixed order of presentation is randomly determined. In contrast, the task of serial pattern learning studied in the present experiment involved elements that were spatially related to each other and arranged to form "patterns."

What *is* implied by the results of the present study is that the conventional theories of serial verbal learning are inadequate to account for serial learning *in general* since they do not deal with S's ability to generate abstract and flexible rules to guide his performance. The notions of "run" and "trill" used by Ss in serial pattern learning are simple but abstract ideas and do not depend on particular events or particular intervals. Within a run the same interval is repeated, and within a trill there is alternation between two events. Thus, runs and trills are subunits that can be generated using simple abstract properties, and it may be logical rather than accidental that serial learning in the present experiment involved these subunits.

It should be emphasized that no explanation has been given for the fact that Ss mastered the sequences with as few as 1–7 errors per location in 20 trials. Obviously, an S who has constructed run and trill subsequences must also learn to terminate these subunits at the correct point and to link them together. However, additional experiments need to be done before a complete account can be given of how Ss form and integrate subunits and then generate repeating sequences.

References

Brown, S. C. & Rubin, E. D. Cue utilization in serial learning. *Journal of Experimental Psychology*, 1967, **74,** 550–555.

Chomsky, N. A review of Skinner's *Verbal behavior. Language*, 1959, **35,** 26–58.

Chomsky, N. *Aspects of the theory of syntax.* Cambridge, Mass.: M.I.T. Press, 1965.

Crowder, R. G. Evidence for the chaining hypothesis of serial verbal learning. *Journal of Experimental Psychology,* 1968, **76,** 497–500.

Fodor, J. A. How to learn to talk: Some simple ways. In F. Smith & G. A. Miller (Eds.), *The genesis of language.* Cambridge, Mass.: M.I.T. Press, 1966.

Jensen, A. R. & Rohwer, W. D., Jr. What is learned in serial learning? *Journal of Verbal Learning and Verbal Behavior,* 1965, **4,** 62–72.

Lashley, K. S. The problem of serial order in behavior. In L. A. Jeffress (Ed.), *Cerebral mechanisms in behavior.* New York: Wiley, 1951.

McNeill, D. Developmental psycholinguistics. In F. Smith & G. A. Miller (Eds.), *The genesis of language.* Cambridge, Mass.: M.I.T. Press, 1966.

Miller, G. A. & Chomsky, N. Finitary models of language users. In R. D. Luce, R. Bush & E. Galanter (Eds.), *Handbook of mathematical psychology.* Vol. 2. New York: Wiley, 1963.

Restle, F. Analysis of a circular maze for humans: An application of mathematical models to the analysis of experimental data. In, *Les modèles et la formalisation du comportement.* Paris: Centre National de la Recherche Scientifique, 1967.

Saufley, W. H., Jr. An analysis of cues in serial learning. *Journal of Experimental Psychology,* 1967, **74,** 414–419.

Slamecka, N. J. Serial learning and order information. *Journal of Experimental Psychology,* 1967, **74,** 62–66.

Winnick, W. A. & Dornbush, R. L. Ordinal position in serial learning. *Journal of Experimental Psychology,* 1968, **78,** 536–538.

Young, R. K. Tests of three hypotheses about the effective stimulus in serial learning. *Journal of Experimental Psychology,* 1962, **63,** 307–313.

Young, R. K., Hakes, D. T., & Hicks, R. Ordinal position number as a cue in serial learning. *Journal of Experimental Psychology,* 1967, **73,** 427–438.

Bibliography

Baddeley, A. D. *The psychology of memory.* New York: Basic Books, 1976.

Collins, A. M. & Loftus, E. A spreading-activation theory of semantic processing. *Psychological Review*, 1975, *82*, 407 –28.

Craik, F. I. M. & Watkins, M. J. The role of rehearsal in short-term memory. *Journal of Verbal Learning and Verbal Behavior*, 1973, *12*, 599 –607.

Kendler, H. H. & Kendler, T. S. From discrimination learning to cognitive development: A neobehaviorist odyssey. In W. K. Estes (Ed.) *Handbook of Learning and Cognitive Processes* (Vol. 1), Hillsdale, N. J.: Erlbaum, 1975.

Kendler, H. H. & Kendler, T. S. Vertical and horizontal processes in problem solving. *Psychological Review*, 1962, *69*, 1 –16.

Kintsch, W. *The representation of meaning in memory.* Hillsdale, N. J.: Erlbaum, 1974.

Levine, M. A. *A cognitive theory of learning: Research on hypothesis testing.* Hillsdale, N. J.: Erlbaum, 1975.

Mayer, R. E. Qualitatively different storage and processing strategies due to meaningfulness of premises in linear reasoning. *Journal of Experimental Psychology: Human Learning and Memory*, 1977, *4*, 5 –18.

Morris, C. D., Bransford, J. D., & Franks, J. J. Levels of processing versus transfer appropriate processing. *Journal of Verbal Learning and Verbal Behavior*, 1977, *16*, 519 –33.

Moyer, R. S. Comparing objects in memory: Evidence suggesting an internal psychophysics. *Perception and Psychophysics*, 1973, *13*, 180–84.

Neimark, E. D. & Santa, J. L. Thinking and concept attainment. In *Annual Review of Psychology* (Vol. 26). Palo Alto, California: *Annual Review*, 1975, 173 – 205.

Resnick, L. Task analysis in instructional design: Some cases from mathematics. In D. Klahr (Ed.), *Cognition and Instruction.* Hillsdale, N. J.: Erlbaum, 1976.

Restle, F. *Learning: Animal behavior and human cognition.* New York: McGraw-Hill, 1975.

Scholz, K. W. & Potts, G. R. Cognitive processing of linear orderings. *Journal of Experimental Psychology*, 1974, *102*, 323 –26.

Spence, K. W. An experimental test of the continuity and non-continuity theories of discrimination learning. *Journal of Experimental Psychology*, 1945, *35*, 253 –66.

Stein, B. S. The effects of cue-target uniqueness on cued recall performance. *Memory and Cognition*, 1977, *5*, 319 –22.

Wickens, D. D. Encoding categories of words: An empirical approach to meaning. *Psychological Review*, 1970, 77, 1 –15.